Yuto Tsukuda

Good luck, first-years!
You can do it!

Shun Saeki

Look at them, all sound
asleep! Lately, I've been
having trouble staying
asleep, so on my days off,
I make sure to get as much
quality sleep as possible!

About the authors

Yuto Tsukuda won the 34th Jump Juniketsu Newcomers' Manga Award
for his one-shot story *Kiba ni Naru*. He made his *Weekly Shonen Jump*
debut in 2010 with the series *Shonen Shikku*. His follow-up series, *Food
Wars!: Shokugeki no Soma*, is his first English-language release.

Shun Saeki made his *Jump NEXT!* debut in 2011 with the one-shot story
Kimi to Watashi no Renai Soudan. *Food Wars!: Shokugeki no Soma* is his
first *Shonen Jump* series.

Food Wars!
SHOKUGEKI NO SOMA

Volume 29
Shonen Jump Advanced Manga Edition
Story by Yuto Tsukuda, Art by Shun Saeki
Contributor Yuki Morisaki

Translation: Adrienne Beck
Touch-Up Art & Lettering: James Gaubatz, Mara Coman
Design: Alice Lewis
Editor: Jennifer LeBlanc

SHOKUGEKI NO SOMA © 2012 by Yuto Tsukuda, Shun Saeki
All rights reserved.
First published in Japan in 2012 by SHUEISHA Inc., Tokyo.
English translation rights arranged by SHUEISHA Inc.

The stories, characters and incidents mentioned in this publication
are entirely fictional.

Printed in the U.S.A.

Published by VIZ Media, LLC
P.O. Box 77010
San Francisco, CA 94107

10 9 8 7 6 5 4 3 2 1
First printing, April 2019

viz.com   shonenjump.com

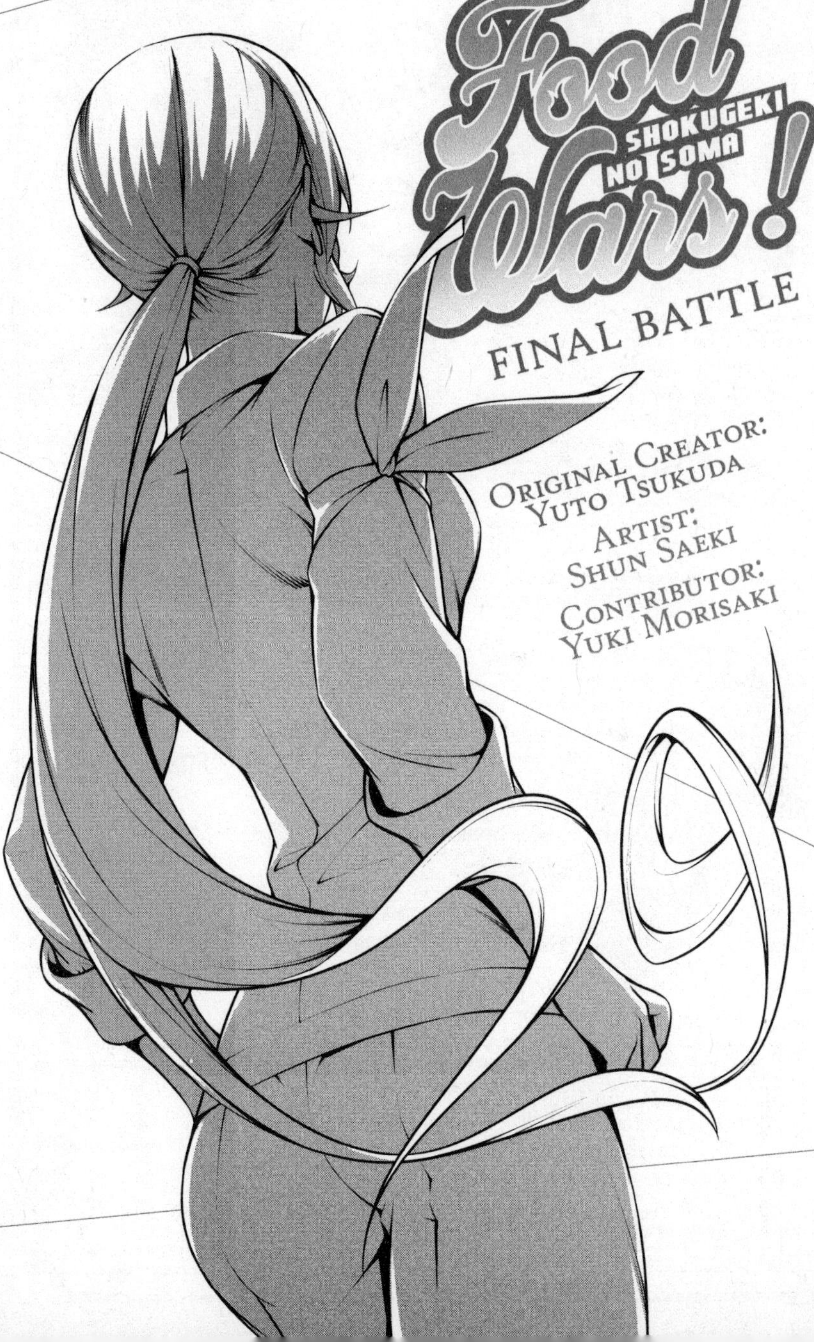

Food Wars! Shokugeki no Soma

FINAL BATTLE

Original Creator:
Yuto Tsukuda
Artist:
Shun Saeki
Contributor:
Yuki Morisaki

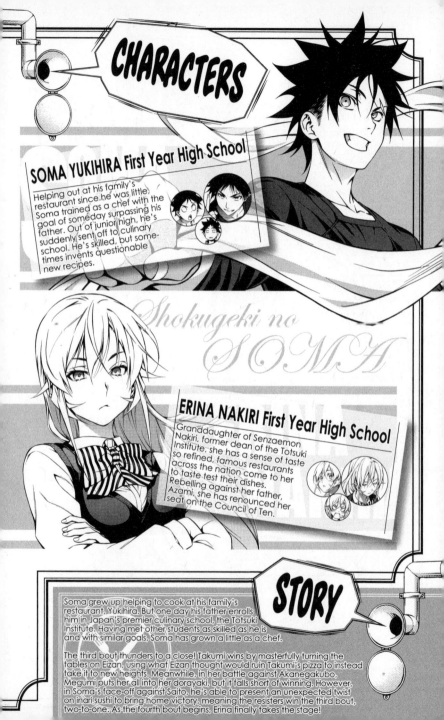

CHARACTERS

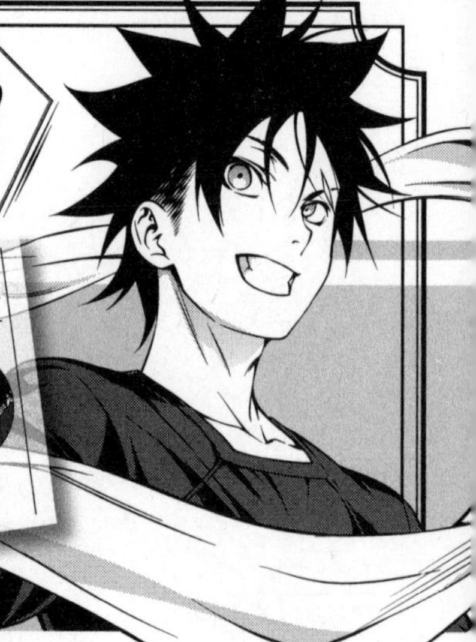

SOMA YUKIHIRA First Year High School

Helping out at his family's restaurant since he was little, Soma trained as a chef with the goal of someday surpassing his father. Out of junior high, he's suddenly sent off to culinary school. He's skilled, but sometimes invents questionable new recipes.

Shokugeki no SOMA

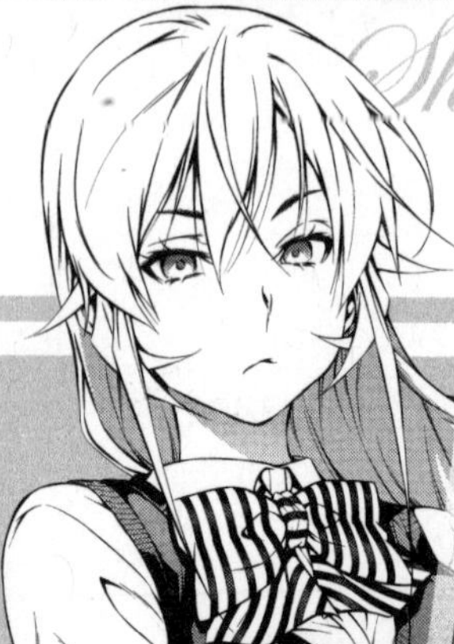

ERINA NAKIRI First Year High School

Granddaughter of Senzaemon Nakiri, former dean of the Totsuki Institute, she has a sense of taste so refined, famous restaurants across the nation come to her to taste test their dishes. Rebelling against her father, Azami, she has renounced her seat on the Council of Ten.

STORY

Soma grew up helping to cook at his family's restaurant, Yukihira. But one day his father enrolls him in Japan's premier culinary school, the Totsuki Institute. Having met other students as skilled as he is and with similar goals, Soma has grown a little as a chef.

The third bout thunders to a close! Takumi wins by masterfully turning the tables on Eizan, using what Eizan thought would ruin Takumi's pizza to instead take it to new heights. Meanwhile, in her battle against Akanegakubo, Megumi puts her all into her dorayaki, but it falls short of winning. However, in Soma's face-off against Saito, he's able to present an unexpected twist on inari sushi to bring home victory, meaning the resisters win the third bout, two-to-one. As the fourth bout begins, Erina finally takes the stage!

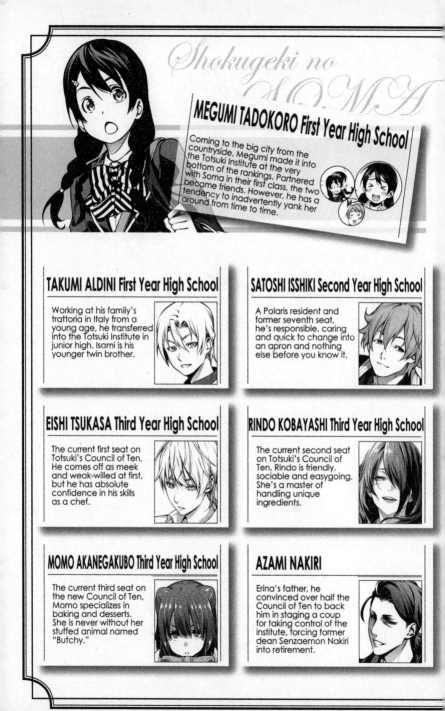

Shokugeki no SOMA

MEGUMI TADOKORO First Year High School

Coming to the big city from the countryside, Megumi made it into the Totsuki Institute at the very bottom of the rankings. Partnered with Soma in their first class, the two became friends. However, he has a tendency to inadvertently yank her around from time to time.

TAKUMI ALDINI First Year High School

Working at his family's trattoria in Italy from a young age, he transferred into the Totsuki Institute in junior high. Isami is his younger twin brother.

SATOSHI ISSHIKI Second Year High School

A Polaris resident and former seventh seat, he's responsible, caring and quick to change into an apron and nothing else before you know it.

EISHI TSUKASA Third Year High School

The current first seat on Totsuki's Council of Ten. He comes off as meek and weak-willed at first, but he has absolute confidence in his skills as a chef.

RINDO KOBAYASHI Third Year High School

The current second seat on Totsuki's Council of Ten, Rindo is friendly, sociable and easygoing. She's a master of handling unique ingredients.

MOMO AKANEGAKUBO Third Year High School

The current third seat on the new Council of Ten, Momo specializes in baking and desserts. She is never without her stuffed animal named "Butchy."

AZAMI NAKIRI

Erina's father, he convinced over half the Council of Ten to back him in staging a coup for taking control of the institute, forcing former dean Senzaemon Nakiri into retirement.

Food Wars! SHOKUGEKI NO SOMA

29

Table of Contents

245. An Expert on Cute 7

246. The Queen of Cute 27

247. Ice Queen 47

248. What the Average Feel 67

249. Watching from Beside You 87

250. The Man Named Eishi Tsukasa 107

251. Uninvited Guests 127

252. Final Battle 147

253. True Gourmet 167

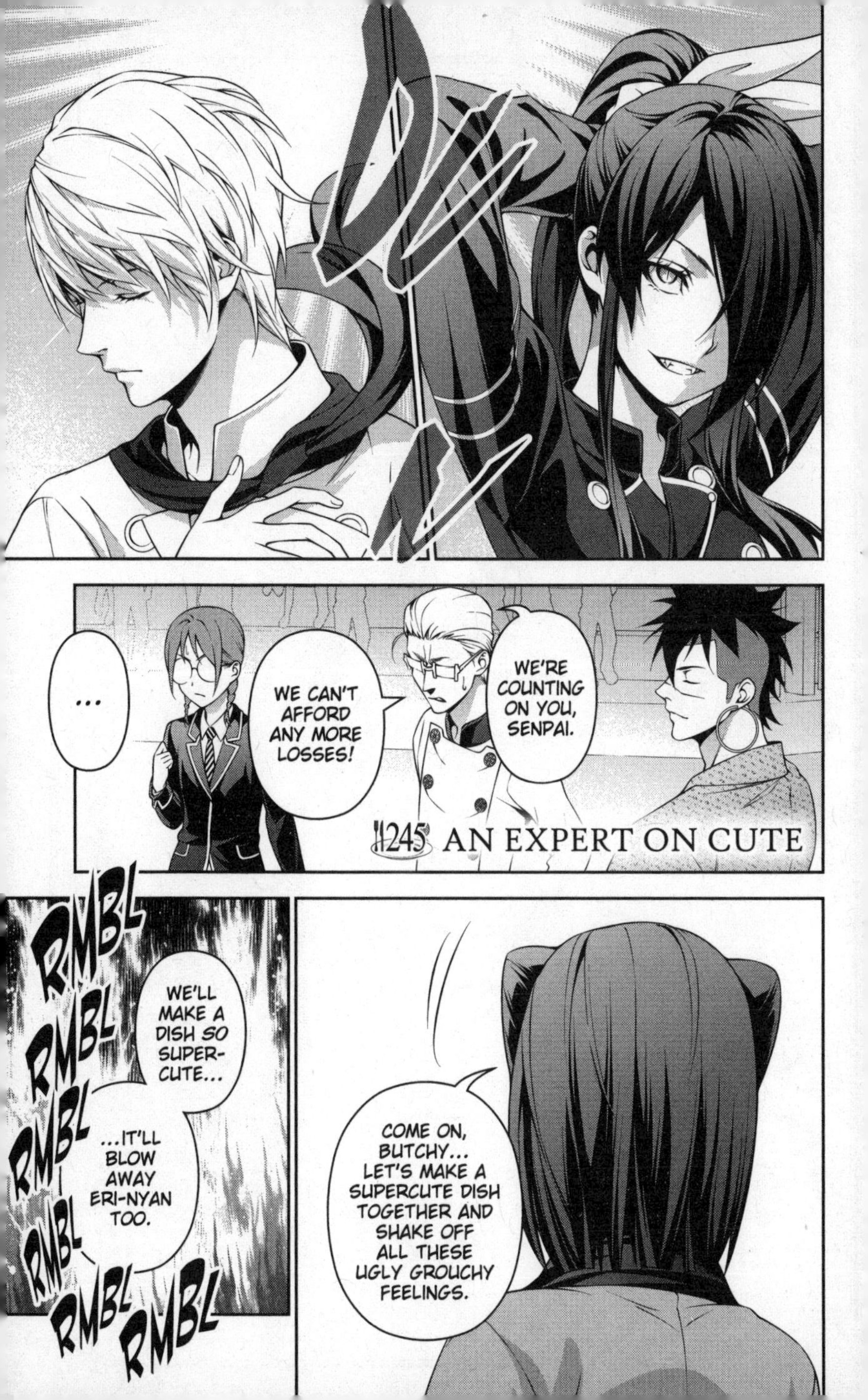
WE'RE COUNTING ON YOU, SENPAI.
WE CAN'T AFFORD ANY MORE LOSSES!
...
245 AN EXPERT ON CUTE
COME ON, BUTCHY... LET'S MAKE A SUPERCUTE DISH TOGETHER AND SHAKE OFF ALL THESE UGLY GROUCHY FEELINGS.
WE'LL MAKE A DISH SO SUPER-CUTE...
...IT'LL BLOW AWAY ERI-NYAN TOO.
RMBL RMBL RMBL RMBL RMBL RMBL RMBL RMBL

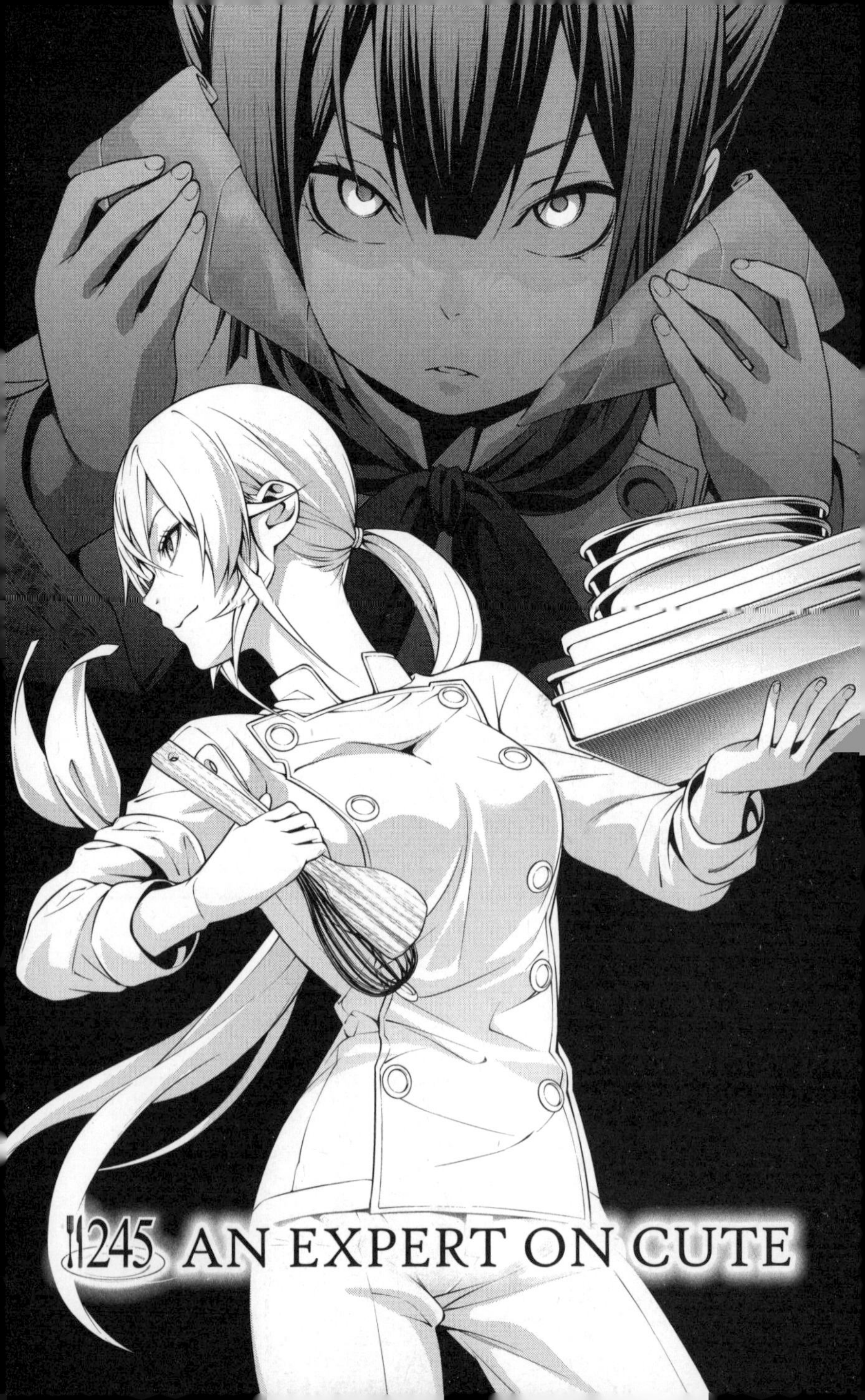
245 AN EXPERT ON CUTE

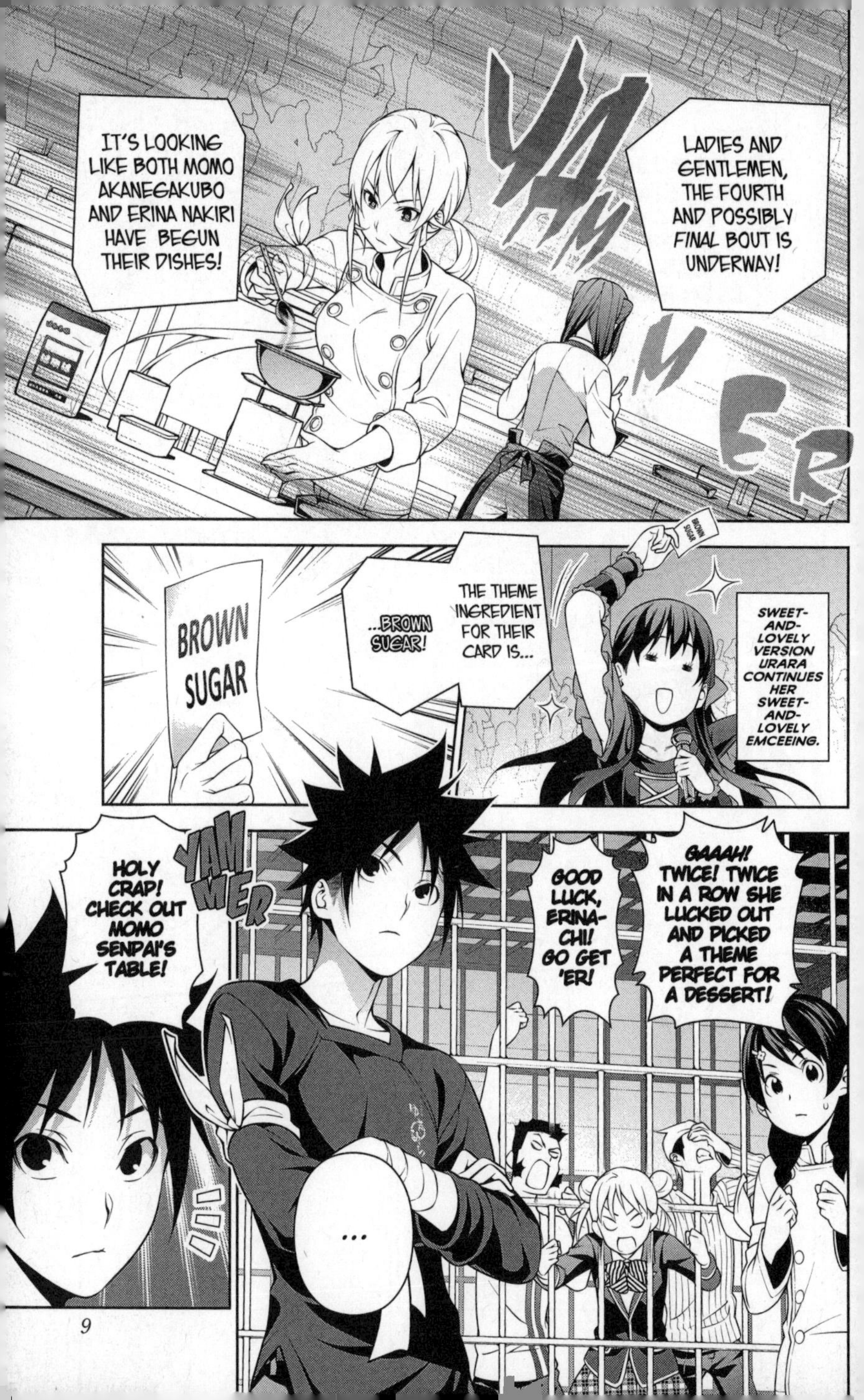
LADIES AND GENTLEMEN, THE FOURTH AND POSSIBLY *FINAL* BOUT IS UNDERWAY!
YAMMER
IT'S LOOKING LIKE BOTH MOMO AKANEGAKUBO AND ERINA NAKIRI HAVE BEGUN THEIR DISHES!
BROWN SUGAR
SWEET-AND-LOVELY VERSION URARA CONTINUES HER SWEET-AND-LOVELY EMCEEING.
THE THEME INGREDIENT FOR THEIR CARD IS...
...BROWN SUGAR!
BROWN SUGAR
GAAAH! TWICE! TWICE IN A ROW SHE LUCKED OUT AND PICKED A THEME PERFECT FOR A DESSERT!
GOOD LUCK, ERINA-CHI! GO GET 'ER!
YAMMER
HOLY CRAP! CHECK OUT MOMO SENPAI'S TABLE!
...

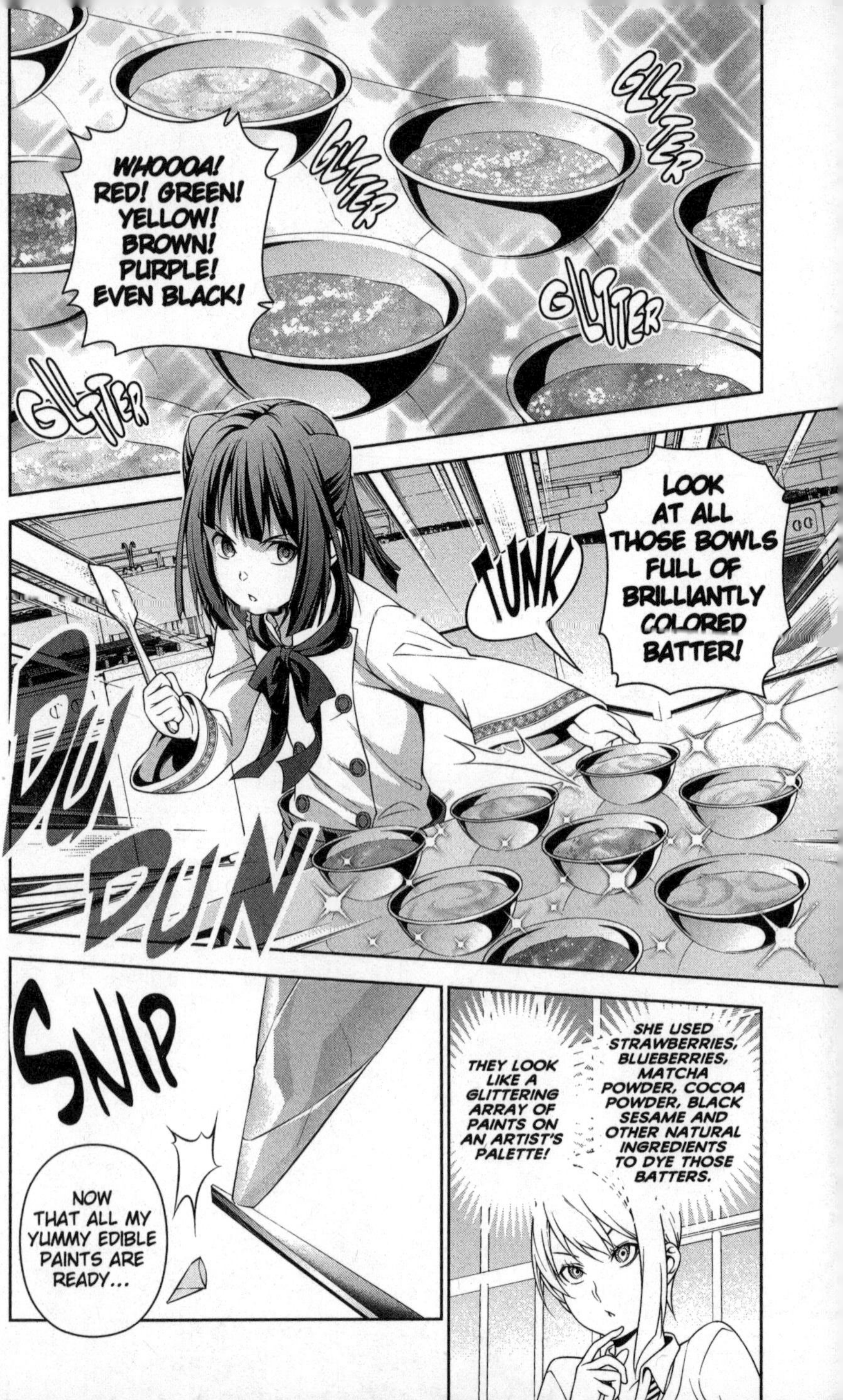
GLITTER
GLITTER
WHOOOA! RED! GREEN! YELLOW! BROWN! PURPLE! EVEN BLACK!
GLITTER
GLITTER
LOOK AT ALL THOSE BOWLS FULL OF BRILLIANTLY COLORED BATTER!
TUNK
DUN DUN
SHE USED STRAWBERRIES, BLUEBERRIES, MATCHA POWDER, COCOA POWDER, BLACK SESAME AND OTHER NATURAL INGREDIENTS TO DYE THOSE BATTERS.
THEY LOOK LIKE A GLITTERING ARRAY OF PAINTS ON AN ARTIST'S PALETTE!
SNIP
NOW THAT ALL MY YUMMY EDIBLE PAINTS ARE READY...

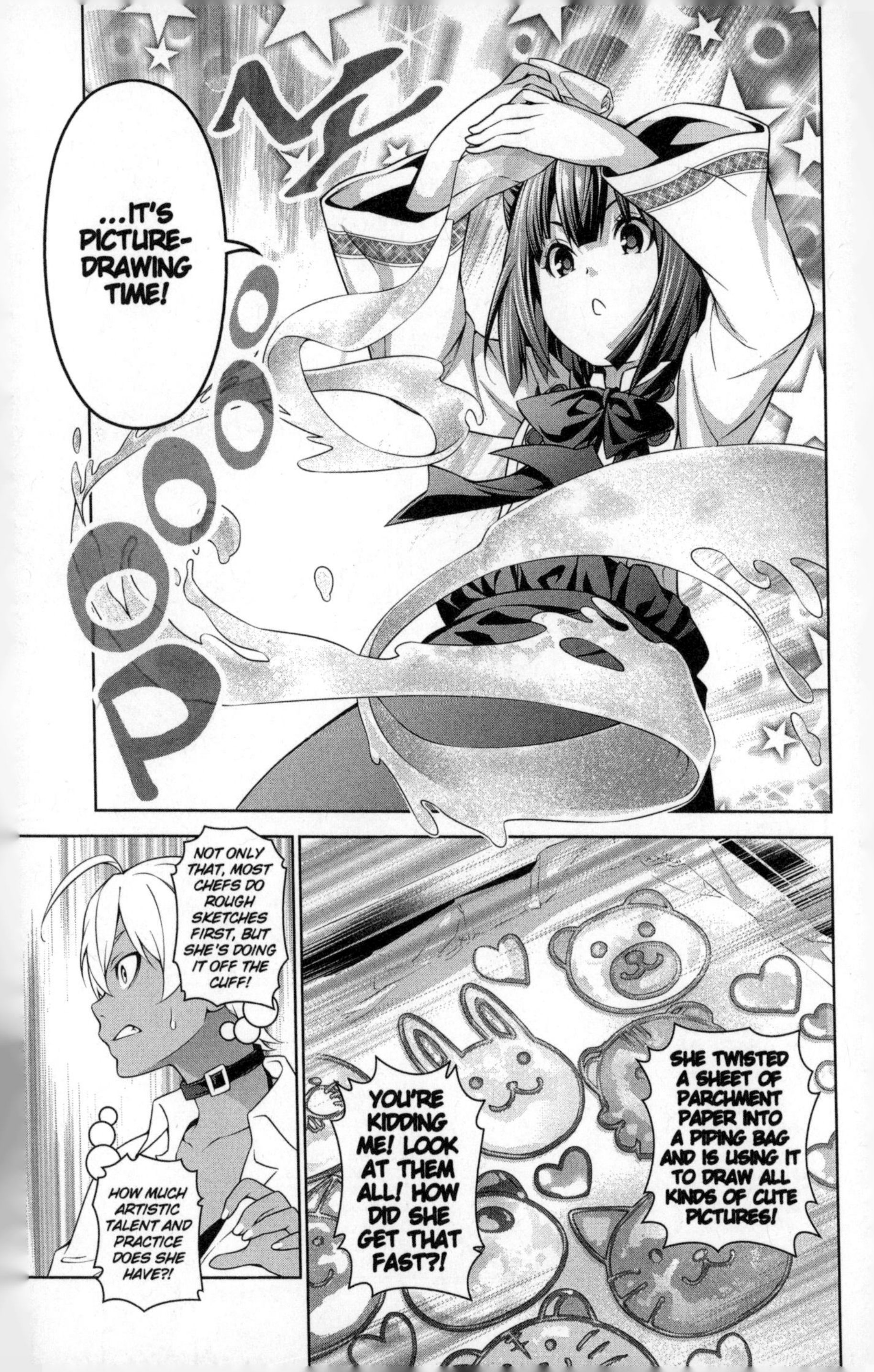
...IT'S PICTURE-DRAWING TIME!
SHE TWISTED A SHEET OF PARCHMENT PAPER INTO A PIPING BAG AND IS USING IT TO DRAW ALL KINDS OF CUTE PICTURES!
YOU'RE KIDDING ME! LOOK AT THEM ALL! HOW DID SHE GET THAT FAST?!
NOT ONLY THAT, MOST CHEFS DO ROUGH SKETCHES FIRST, BUT SHE'S DOING IT OFF THE CUFF!
HOW MUCH ARTISTIC TALENT AND PRACTICE DOES SHE HAVE?!

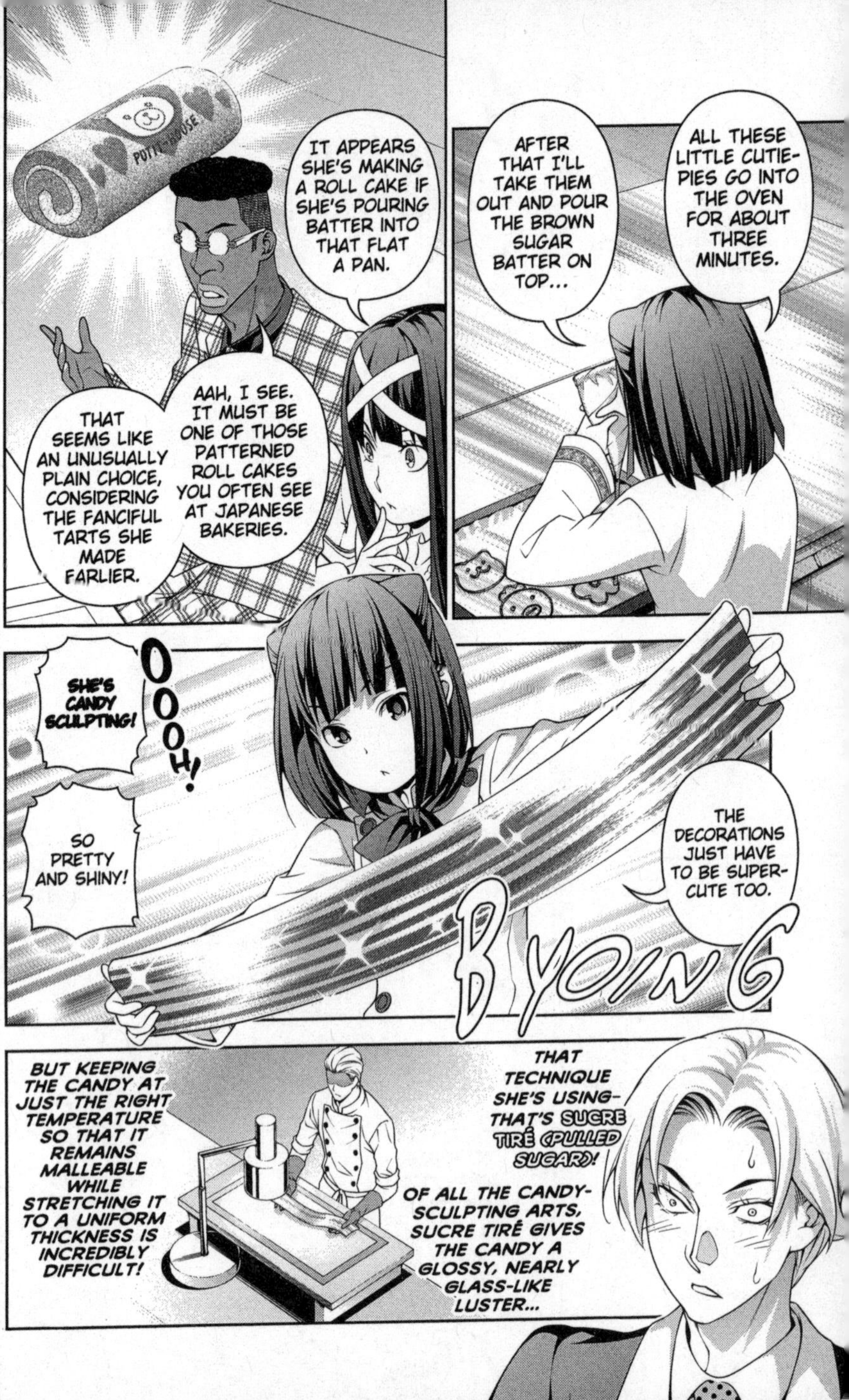
ALL THESE LITTLE CUTIE-PIES GO INTO THE OVEN FOR ABOUT THREE MINUTES.
AFTER THAT I'LL TAKE THEM OUT AND POUR THE BROWN SUGAR BATTER ON TOP...
IT APPEARS SHE'S MAKING A ROLL CAKE IF SHE'S POURING BATTER INTO THAT FLAT A PAN.
AAH, I SEE. IT MUST BE ONE OF THOSE PATTERNED ROLL CAKES YOU OFTEN SEE AT JAPANESE BAKERIES.
THAT SEEMS LIKE AN UNUSUALLY PLAIN CHOICE, CONSIDERING THE FANCIFUL TARTS SHE MADE EARLIER.
THE DECORATIONS JUST HAVE TO BE SUPER-CUTE TOO.
BYOING
OOOOH!
SHE'S CANDY SCULPTING!
SO PRETTY AND SHINY!
THAT TECHNIQUE SHE'S USING—THAT'S SUCRE TIRÉ (PULLED SUGAR)!
OF ALL THE CANDY-SCULPTING ARTS, SUCRE TIRÉ GIVES THE CANDY A GLOSSY, NEARLY GLASS-LIKE LUSTER...
BUT KEEPING THE CANDY AT JUST THE RIGHT TEMPERATURE SO THAT IT REMAINS MALLEABLE WHILE STRETCHING IT TO A UNIFORM THICKNESS IS INCREDIBLY DIFFICULT!

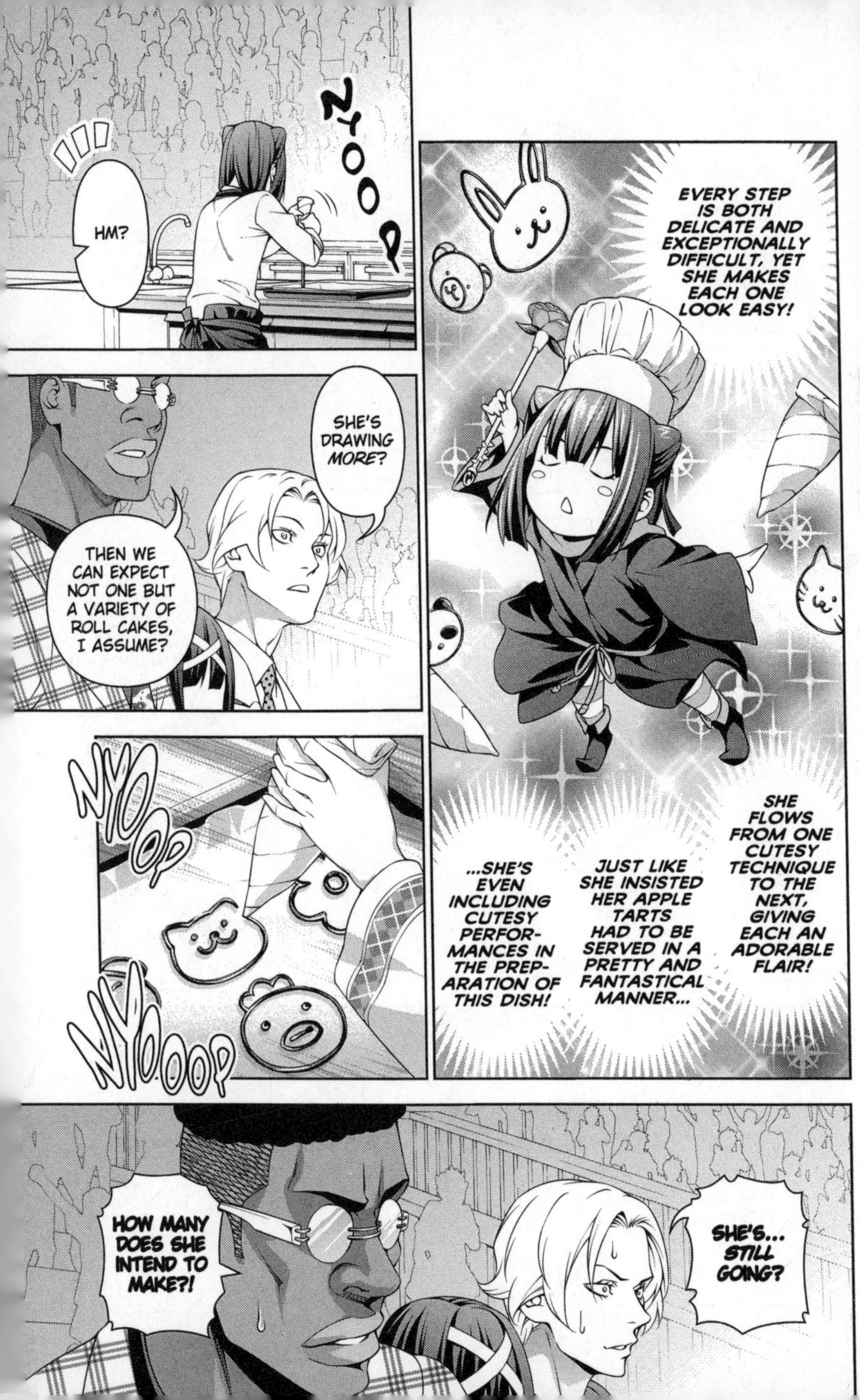
EVERY STEP IS BOTH DELICATE AND EXCEPTIONALLY DIFFICULT, YET SHE MAKES EACH ONE LOOK EASY!
SHE FLOWS FROM ONE CUTESY TECHNIQUE TO THE NEXT, GIVING EACH AN ADORABLE FLAIR!
JUST LIKE SHE INSISTED HER APPLE TARTS HAD TO BE SERVED IN A PRETTY AND FANTASTICAL MANNER...
...SHE'S EVEN INCLUDING CUTESY PERFOR-MANCES IN THE PREP-ARATION OF THIS DISH!
NYOOP
HM?
SHE'S DRAWING MORE?
THEN WE CAN EXPECT NOT ONE BUT A VARIETY OF ROLL CAKES, I ASSUME?
NYOOP
NYOOOP
SHE'S... STILL GOING?
HOW MANY DOES SHE INTEND TO MAKE?!

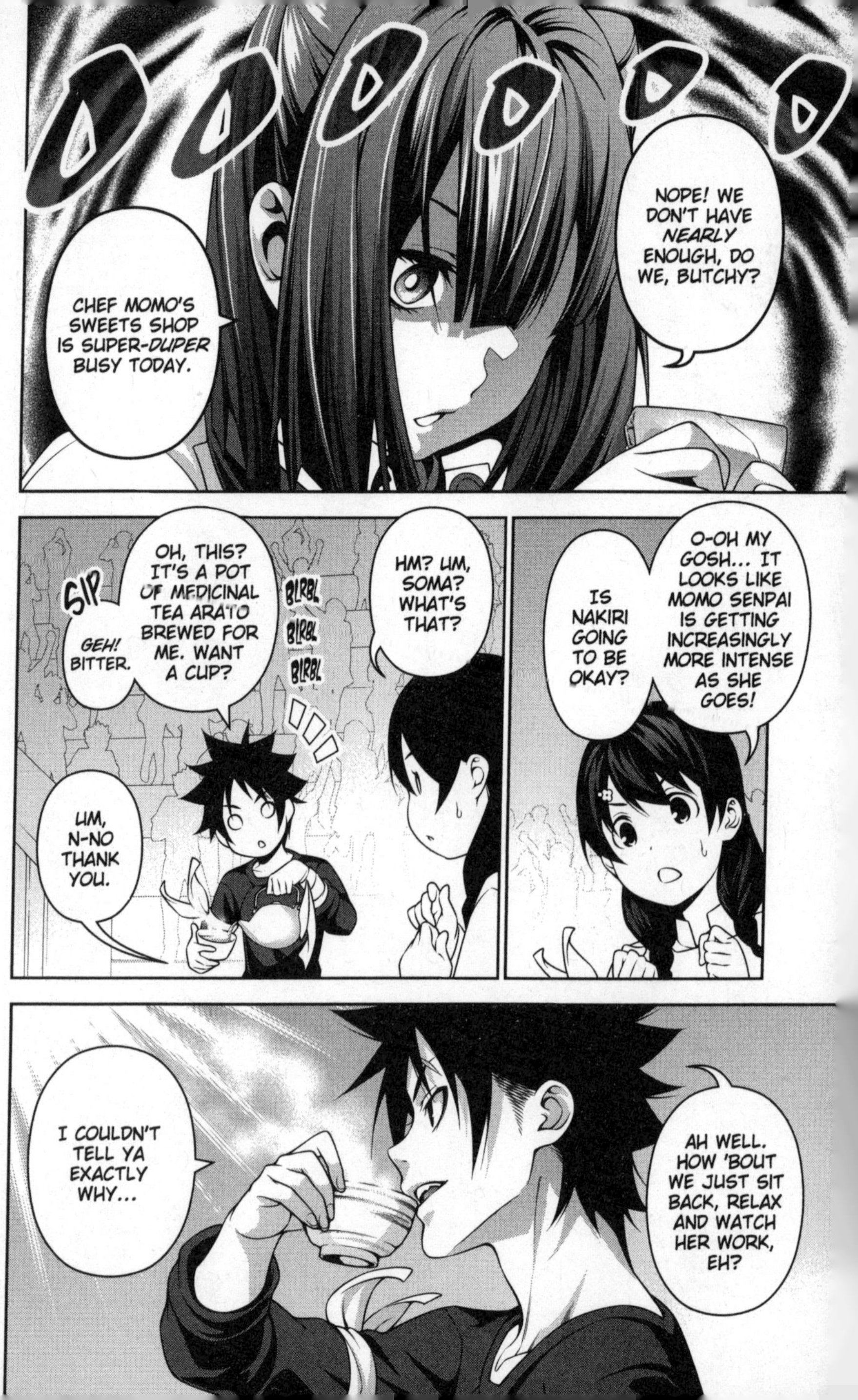
NOPE! WE DON'T HAVE *NEARLY* ENOUGH, DO WE, BUTCHY?
CHEF MOMO'S SWEETS SHOP IS SUPER-*DUPER* BUSY TODAY.
O-OH MY GOSH... IT LOOKS LIKE MOMO SENPAI IS GETTING INCREASINGLY MORE INTENSE AS SHE GOES!
IS NAKIRI GOING TO BE OKAY?
HM? UM, SOMA? WHAT'S THAT?
BLRBL
BLRBL
BLRBL
OH, THIS? IT'S A POT OF MEDICINAL TEA ARATO BREWED FOR ME. WANT A CUP?
SIP
GEH! BITTER.
UM, N-NO THANK YOU.
AH WELL. HOW 'BOUT WE JUST SIT BACK, RELAX AND WATCH HER WORK, EH?
I COULDN'T TELL YA EXACTLY WHY...

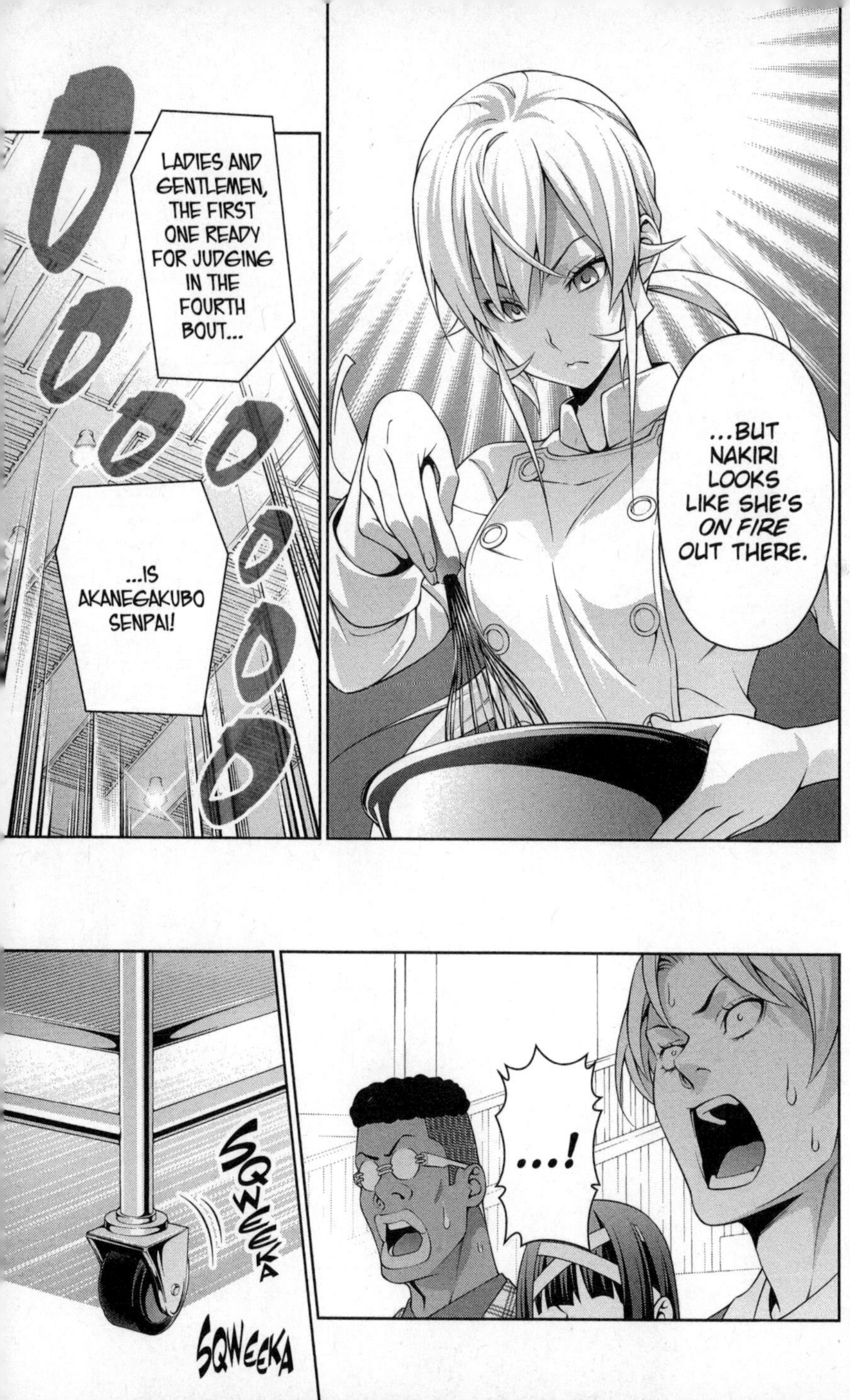
...BUT NAKIRI LOOKS LIKE SHE'S *ON FIRE* OUT THERE.
LADIES AND GENTLEMEN, THE FIRST ONE READY FOR JUDGING IN THE FOURTH BOUT...
...IS AKANEGAKUBO SENPAI!
...!
SQWEEKA
SQWEEKA

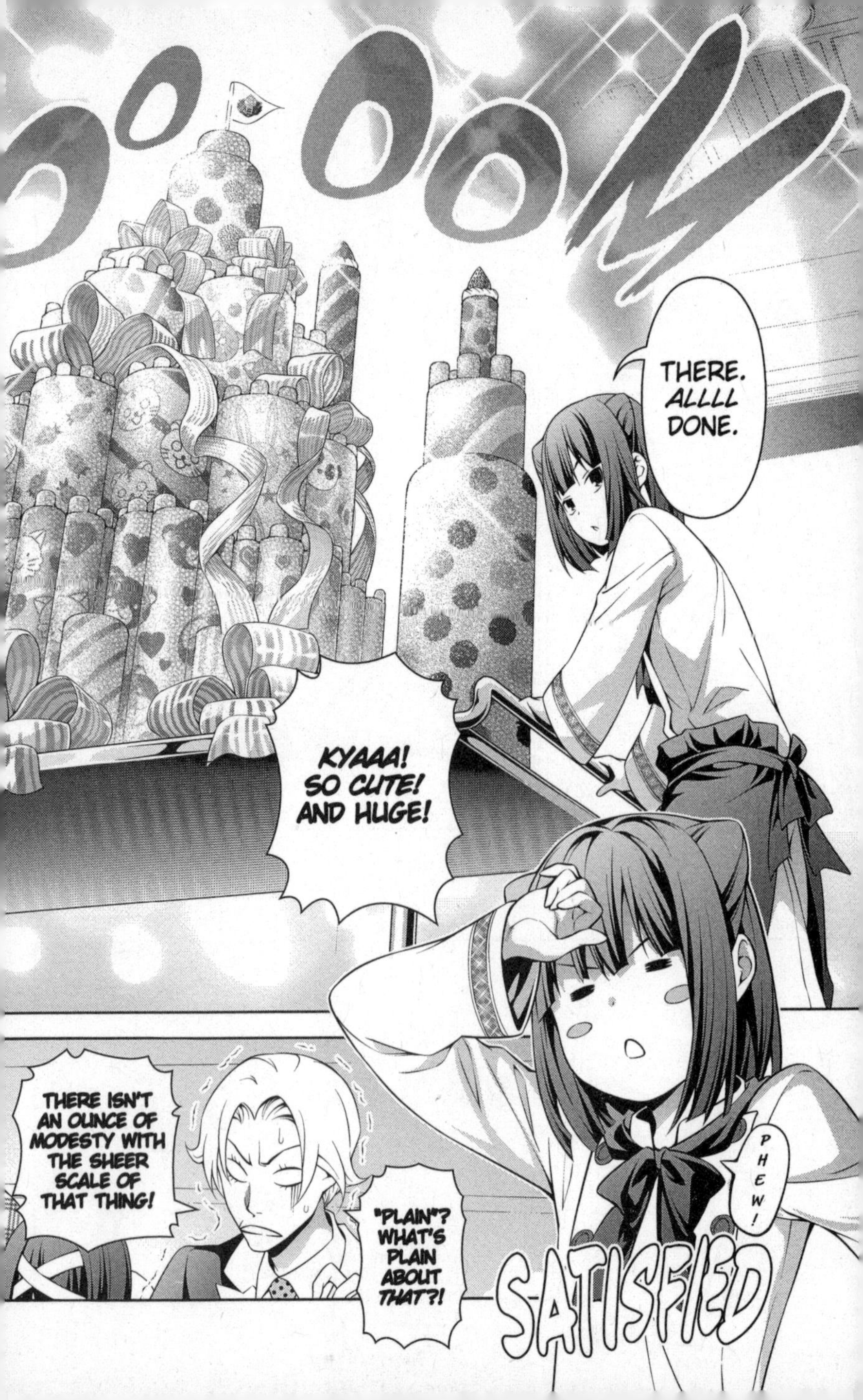
THERE. ALLLL DONE.
KYAAA! SO CUTE! AND HUGE!
PHEW!
SATISFIED
"PLAIN"? WHAT'S PLAIN ABOUT THAT?!
THERE ISN'T AN OUNCE OF MODESTY WITH THE SHEER SCALE OF THAT THING!

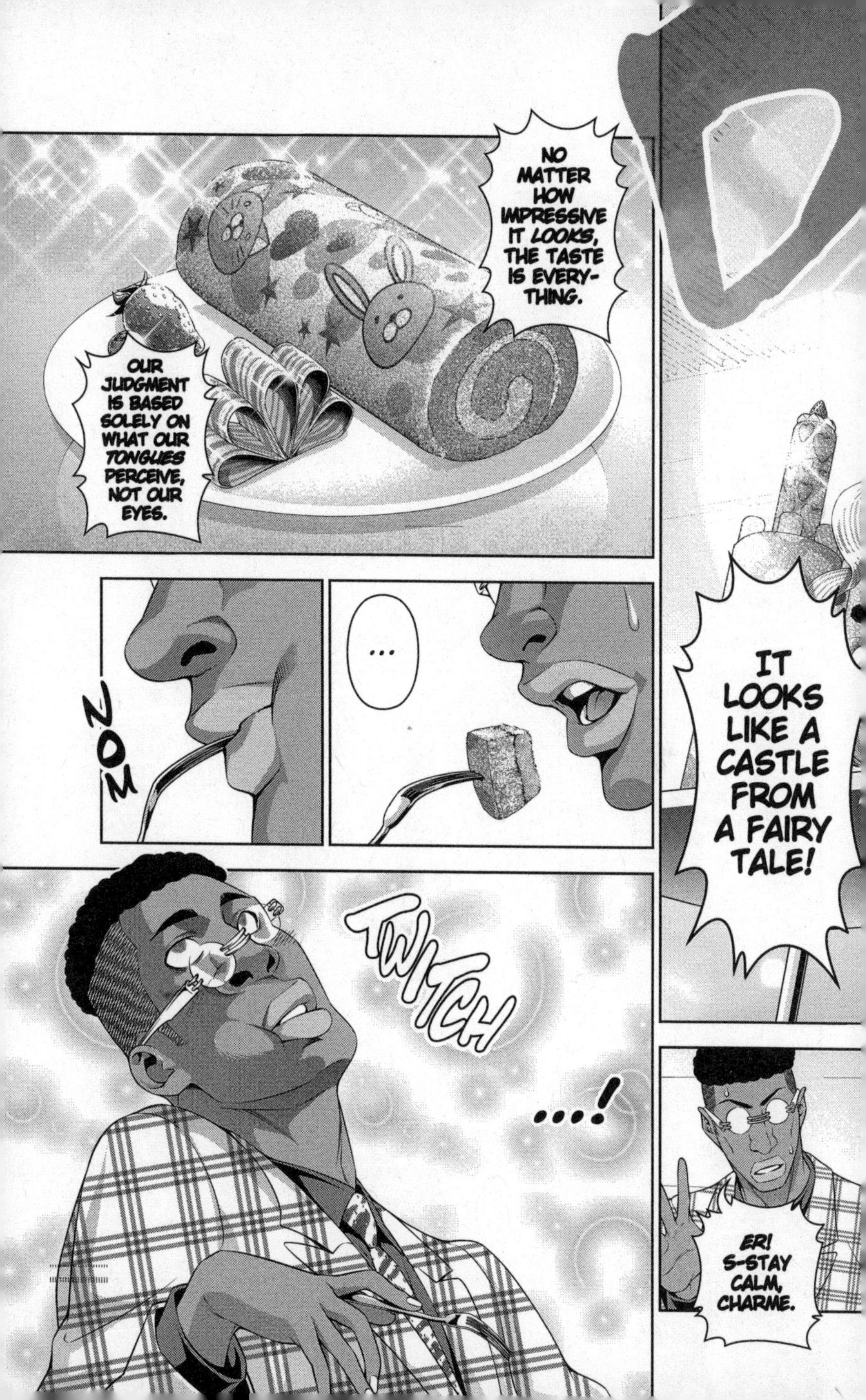
IT LOOKS LIKE A CASTLE FROM A FAIRY TALE!
NO MATTER HOW IMPRESSIVE IT *LOOKS*, THE TASTE IS EVERY-THING.
OUR JUDGMENT IS BASED SOLELY ON WHAT OUR *TONGUES* PERCEIVE, NOT OUR EYES.
...
NOM
ER! S-STAY CALM, CHARME.
TWITCH
...!

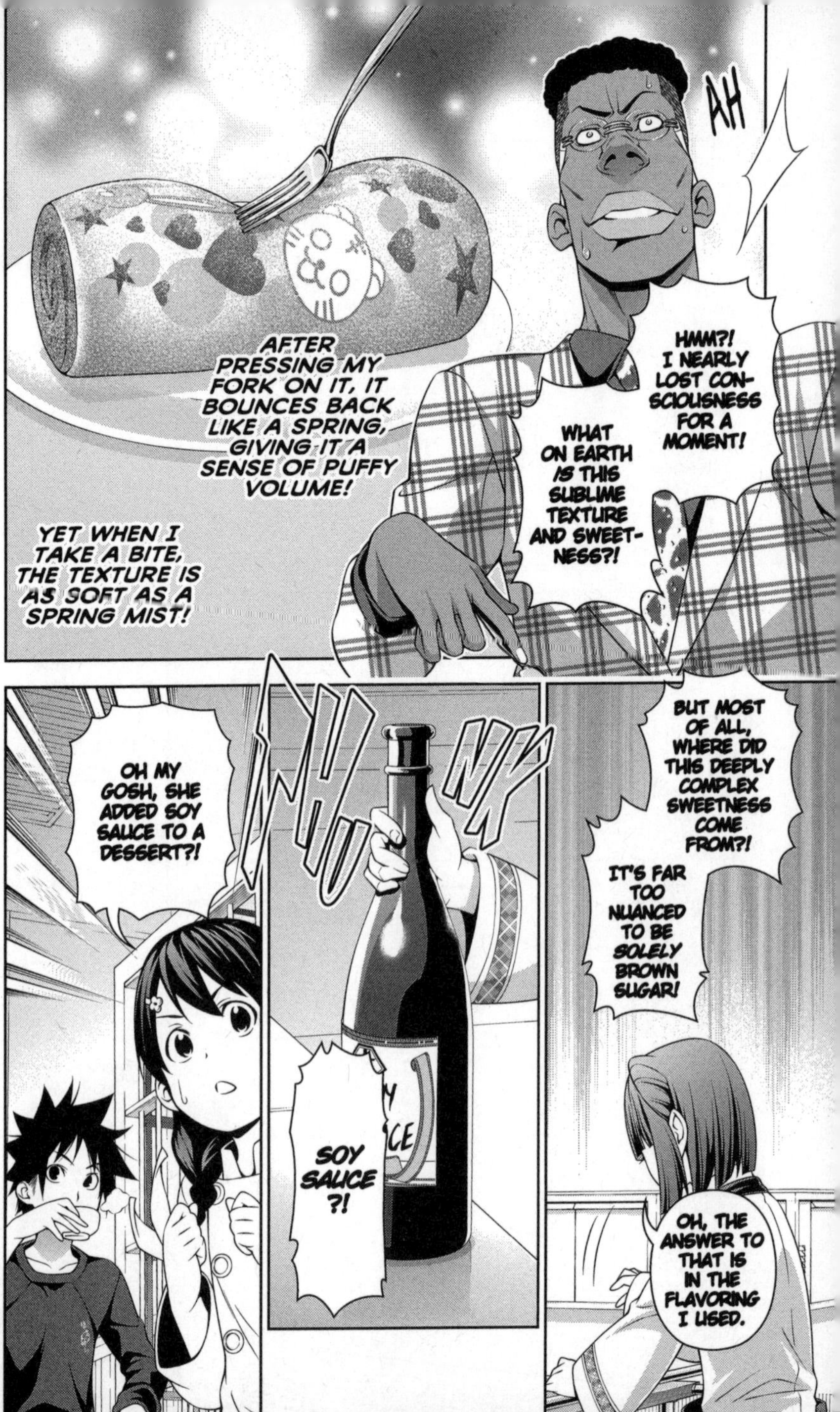
AH
HMM?! I NEARLY LOST CON-SCIOUSNESS FOR A MOMENT!
WHAT ON EARTH IS THIS SUBLIME TEXTURE AND SWEET-NESS?!
AFTER PRESSING MY FORK ON IT, IT BOUNCES BACK LIKE A SPRING, GIVING IT A SENSE OF PUFFY VOLUME!
YET WHEN I TAKE A BITE, THE TEXTURE IS AS SOFT AS A SPRING MIST!
BUT MOST OF ALL, WHERE DID THIS DEEPLY COMPLEX SWEETNESS COME FROM?!
IT'S FAR TOO NUANCED TO BE SOLELY BROWN SUGAR!
OH, THE ANSWER TO THAT IS IN THE FLAVORING I USED.
SOY SAUCE ?!
OH MY GOSH, SHE ADDED SOY SAUCE TO A DESSERT?!

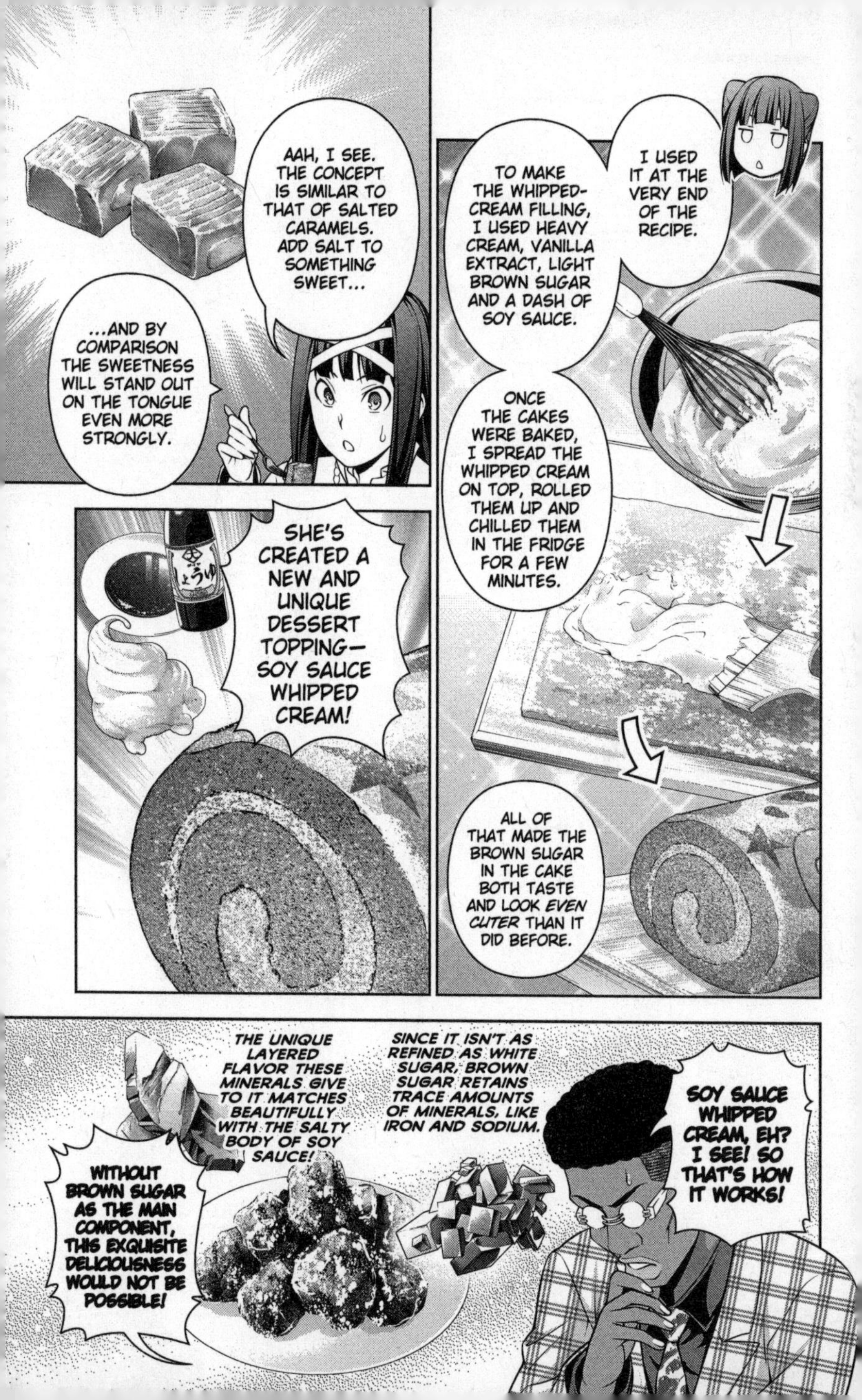
I USED IT AT THE VERY END OF THE RECIPE.
TO MAKE THE WHIPPED-CREAM FILLING, I USED HEAVY CREAM, VANILLA EXTRACT, LIGHT BROWN SUGAR AND A DASH OF SOY SAUCE.
ONCE THE CAKES WERE BAKED, I SPREAD THE WHIPPED CREAM ON TOP, ROLLED THEM UP AND CHILLED THEM IN THE FRIDGE FOR A FEW MINUTES.
ALL OF THAT MADE THE BROWN SUGAR IN THE CAKE BOTH TASTE AND LOOK *EVEN CUTER* THAN IT DID BEFORE.
AAH, I SEE. THE CONCEPT IS SIMILAR TO THAT OF SALTED CARAMELS. ADD SALT TO SOMETHING SWEET...
...AND BY COMPARISON THE SWEETNESS WILL STAND OUT ON THE TONGUE EVEN MORE STRONGLY.
しょうゆ
SHE'S CREATED A NEW AND UNIQUE DESSERT TOPPING—SOY SAUCE WHIPPED CREAM!
SOY SAUCE WHIPPED CREAM, EH? I SEE! SO THAT'S HOW IT WORKS!
SINCE IT ISN'T AS REFINED AS WHITE SUGAR, BROWN SUGAR RETAINS TRACE AMOUNTS OF MINERALS, LIKE IRON AND SODIUM.
THE UNIQUE LAYERED FLAVOR THESE MINERALS GIVE TO IT MATCHES BEAUTIFULLY WITH THE SALTY BODY OF SOY SAUCE!
WITHOUT BROWN SUGAR AS THE MAIN COMPONENT, THIS EXQUISITE DELICIOUSNESS WOULD NOT BE POSSIBLE!

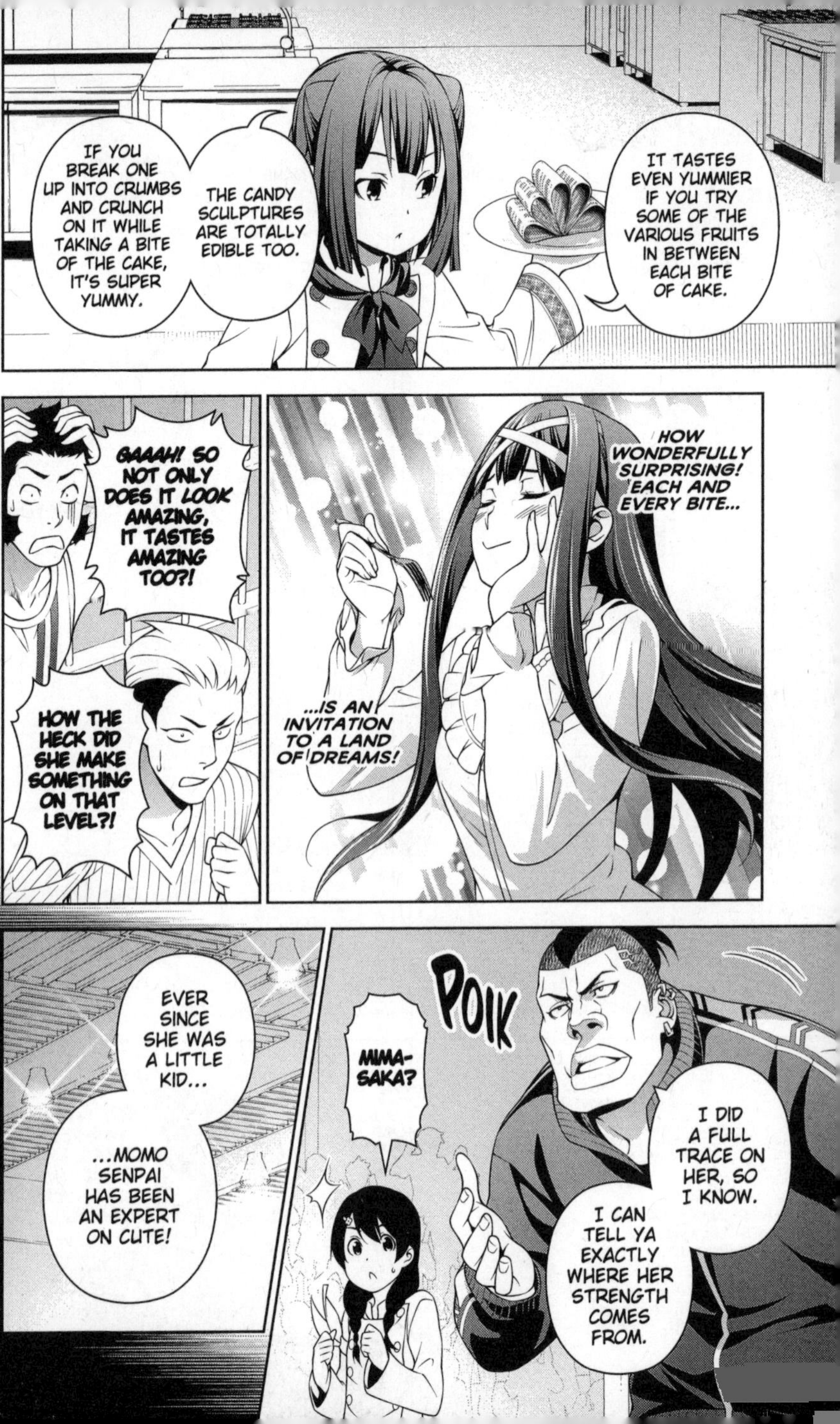
IT TASTES EVEN YUMMIER IF YOU TRY SOME OF THE VARIOUS FRUITS IN BETWEEN EACH BITE OF CAKE.
THE CANDY SCULPTURES ARE TOTALLY EDIBLE TOO.
IF YOU BREAK ONE UP INTO CRUMBS AND CRUNCH ON IT WHILE TAKING A BITE OF THE CAKE, IT'S SUPER YUMMY.
HOW WONDERFULLY SURPRISING! EACH AND EVERY BITE...
...IS AN INVITATION TO A LAND OF DREAMS!
GAAAH! SO NOT ONLY DOES IT LOOK AMAZING, IT TASTES AMAZING TOO?!
HOW THE HECK DID SHE MAKE SOMETHING ON THAT LEVEL?!
POIK
MIMA-SAKA?
I DID A FULL TRACE ON HER, SO I KNOW.
I CAN TELL YA EXACTLY WHERE HER STRENGTH COMES FROM.
EVER SINCE SHE WAS A LITTLE KID...
...MOMO SENPAI HAS BEEN AN EXPERT ON CUTE!

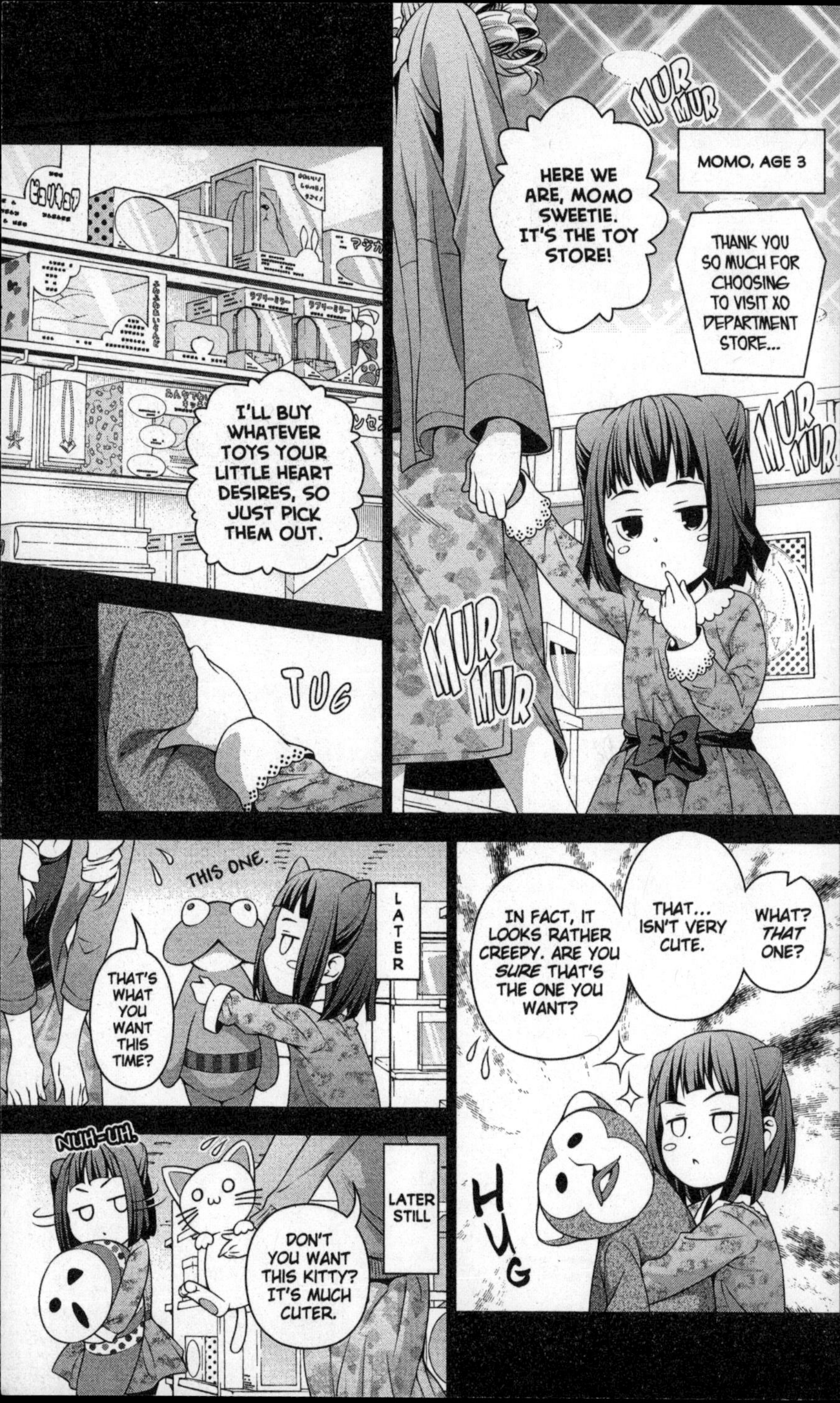
MUR MUR
MOMO, AGE 3
THANK YOU SO MUCH FOR CHOOSING TO VISIT XO DEPARTMENT STORE...
HERE WE ARE, MOMO SWEETIE. IT'S THE TOY STORE!
MUR MUR
MUR MUR
I'LL BUY WHATEVER TOYS YOUR LITTLE HEART DESIRES, SO JUST PICK THEM OUT.
TUG
WHAT? *THAT* ONE?
THAT... ISN'T VERY CUTE.
IN FACT, IT LOOKS RATHER CREEPY. ARE YOU *SURE* THAT'S THE ONE YOU WANT?
HUG
LATER
THIS ONE.
THAT'S WHAT YOU WANT THIS TIME?
LATER STILL
DON'T YOU WANT THIS KITTY? IT'S MUCH CUTER.
NUH-UH.

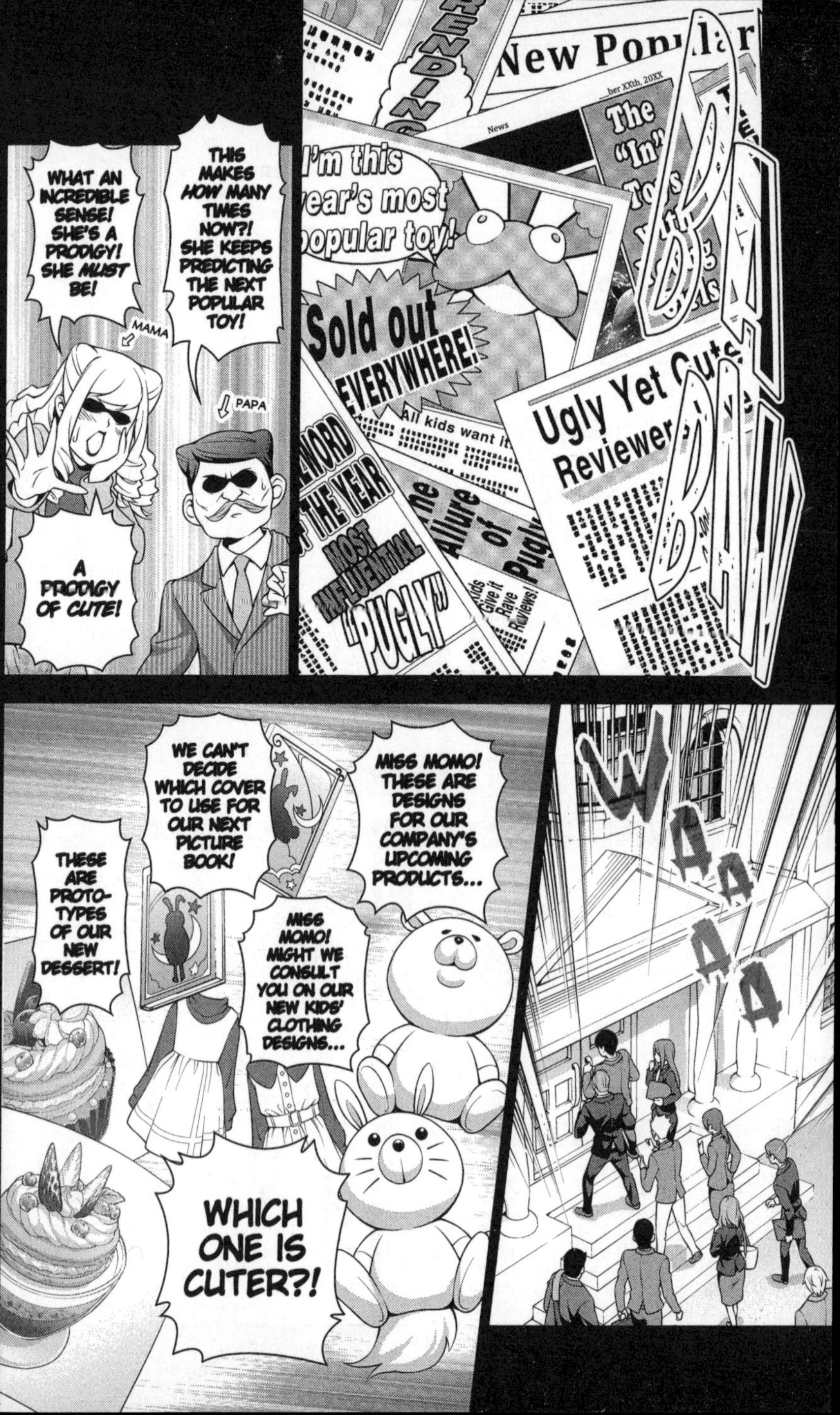
TRENDING
New Popular
ber XXth, 20XX
News
The "In" Toys
I'm this year's most popular toy!
Sold out EVERYWHERE!
All kids want it
WORD OF THE YEAR
MOST INFLUENTIAL "PUGLY"
The Allure of Pugly
Kids Give it Rave Reviews!
Ugly Yet Cute
Reviewers
THIS MAKES HOW MANY TIMES NOW?! SHE KEEPS PREDICTING THE NEXT POPULAR TOY!
PAPA
WHAT AN INCREDIBLE SENSE! SHE'S A PRODIGY! SHE MUST BE!
MAMA
A PRODIGY OF CUTE!
WAAAA
MISS MOMO! THESE ARE DESIGNS FOR OUR COMPANY'S UPCOMING PRODUCTS...
WE CAN'T DECIDE WHICH COVER TO USE FOR OUR NEXT PICTURE BOOK!
THESE ARE PROTO-TYPES OF OUR NEW DESSERT!
MISS MOMO! MIGHT WE CONSULT YOU ON OUR NEW KIDS' CLOTHING DESIGNS...
WHICH ONE IS CUTER?!

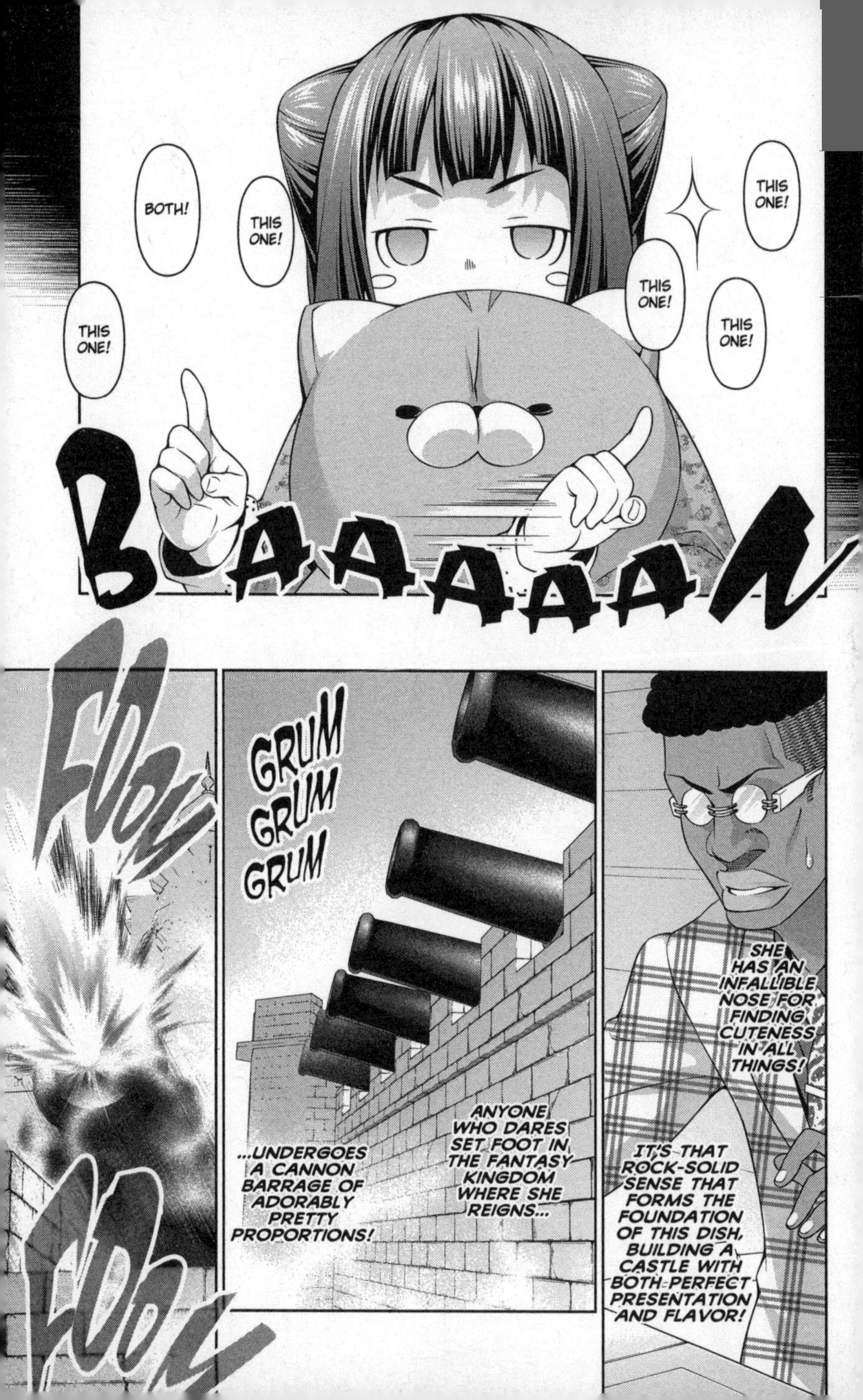
THIS ONE!
THIS ONE!
THIS ONE!
THIS ONE!
BOTH!
THIS ONE!
BAAAAAN
SHE HAS AN INFALLIBLE NOSE FOR FINDING CUTENESS IN ALL THINGS!
IT'S THAT ROCK-SOLID SENSE THAT FORMS THE FOUNDATION OF THIS DISH, BUILDING A CASTLE WITH BOTH PERFECT PRESENTATION AND FLAVOR!
GRUM GRUM GRUM
ANYONE WHO DARES SET FOOT IN THE FANTASY KINGDOM WHERE SHE REIGNS...
...UNDERGOES A CANNON BARRAGE OF ADORABLY PRETTY PROPORTIONS!

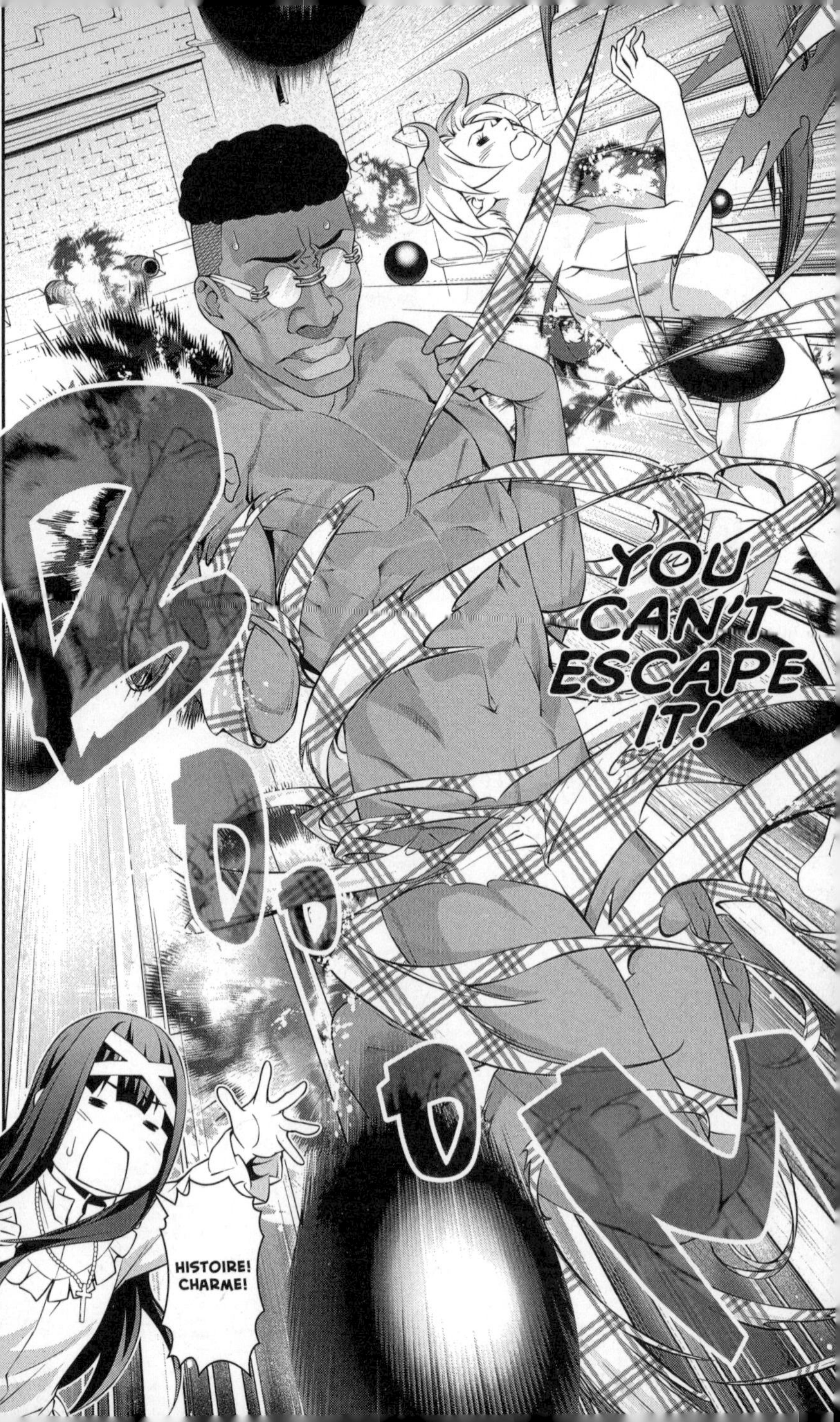
YOU CAN'T ESCAPE IT!
HISTOIRE! CHARME!

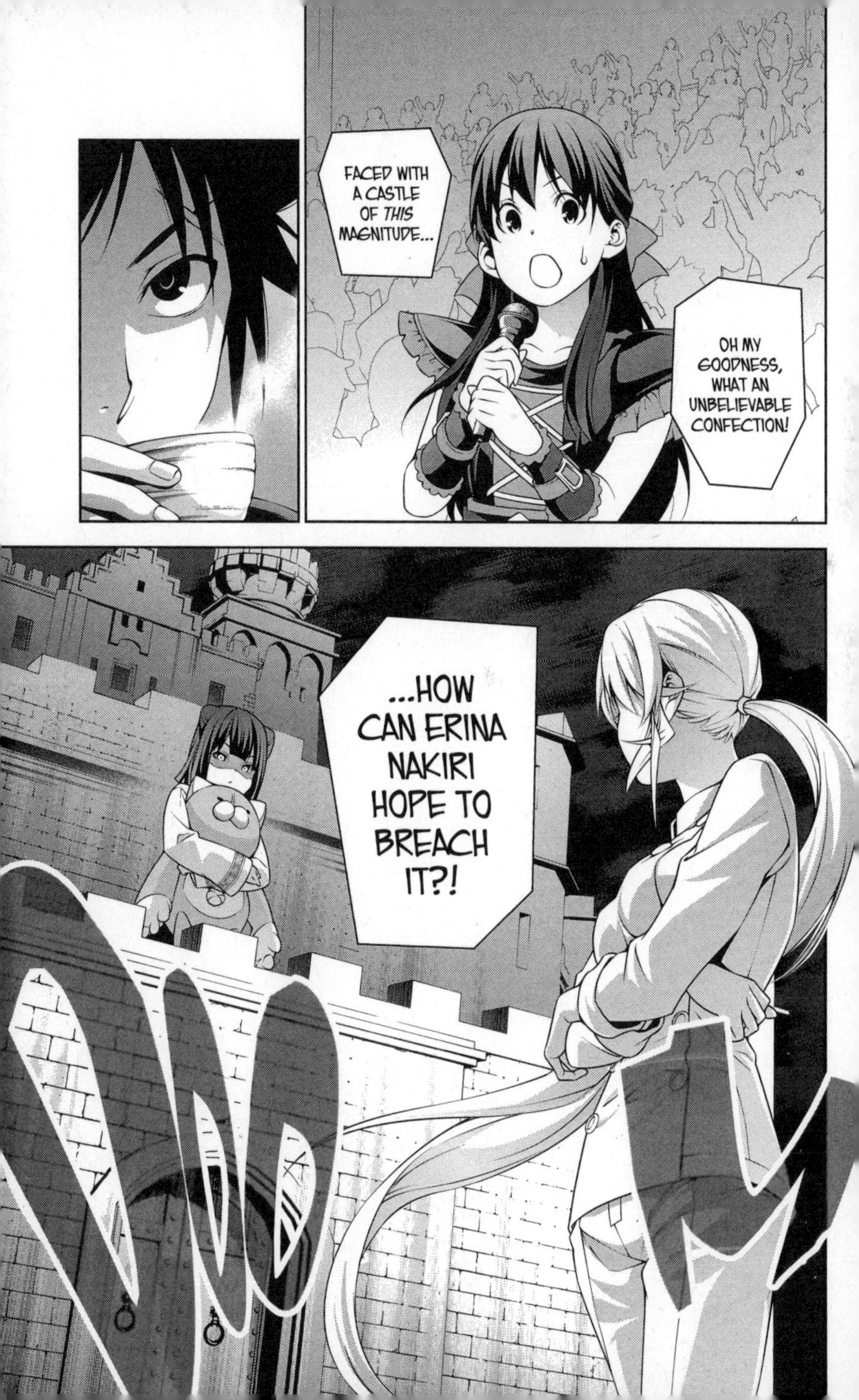
OH MY GOODNESS, WHAT AN UNBELIEVABLE CONFECTION!
FACED WITH A CASTLE OF *THIS* MAGNITUDE...
...HOW CAN ERINA NAKIRI HOPE TO BREACH IT?!

GLARE

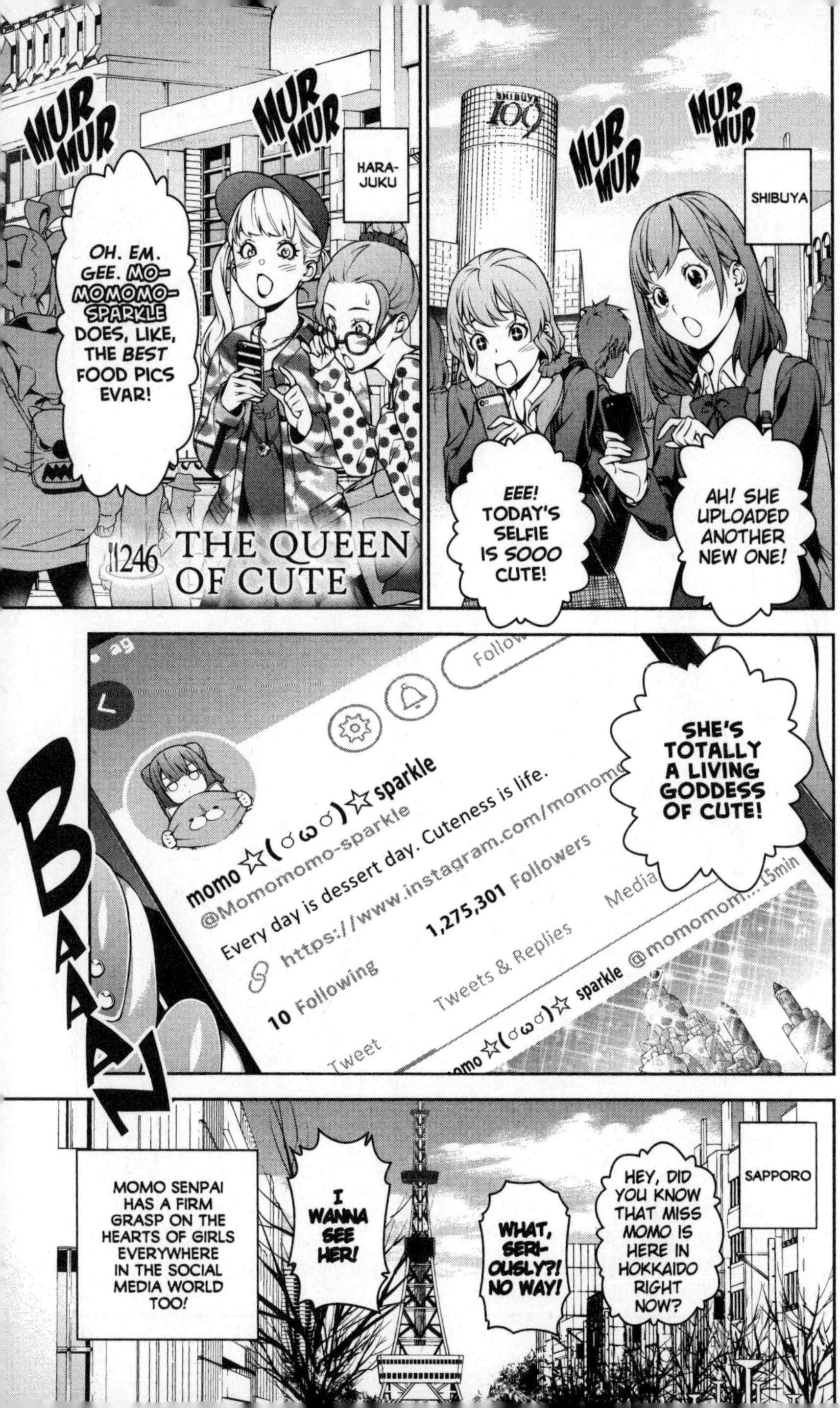
MUR MUR
SHIBUYA
MUR MUR
SHIBUYA 109
AH! SHE UPLOADED ANOTHER NEW ONE!
EEE! TODAY'S SELFIE IS SOOO CUTE!
HARA-JUKU
MUR MUR
MUR MUR
OH. EM. GEE. MOMOMOMO-SPARKLE DOES, LIKE, THE BEST FOOD PICS EVAR!
1246 THE QUEEN OF CUTE
SHE'S TOTALLY A LIVING GODDESS OF CUTE!
Follow
momo☆(σωσ)☆sparkle
@Momomomo-sparkle
Every day is dessert day. Cuteness is life.
https://www.instagram.com/momom
10 Following
1,275,301 Followers
Tweet
Tweets & Replies
Media
momo☆(σωσ)☆ sparkle @momomom... 15min
BAAAN
SAPPORO
HEY, DID YOU KNOW THAT MISS MOMO IS HERE IN HOKKAIDO RIGHT NOW?
WHAT, SERI-OUSLY?! NO WAY!
I WANNA SEE HER!
MOMO SENPAI HAS A FIRM GRASP ON THE HEARTS OF GIRLS EVERYWHERE IN THE SOCIAL MEDIA WORLD TOO!

246 THE QUEEN OF CUTE

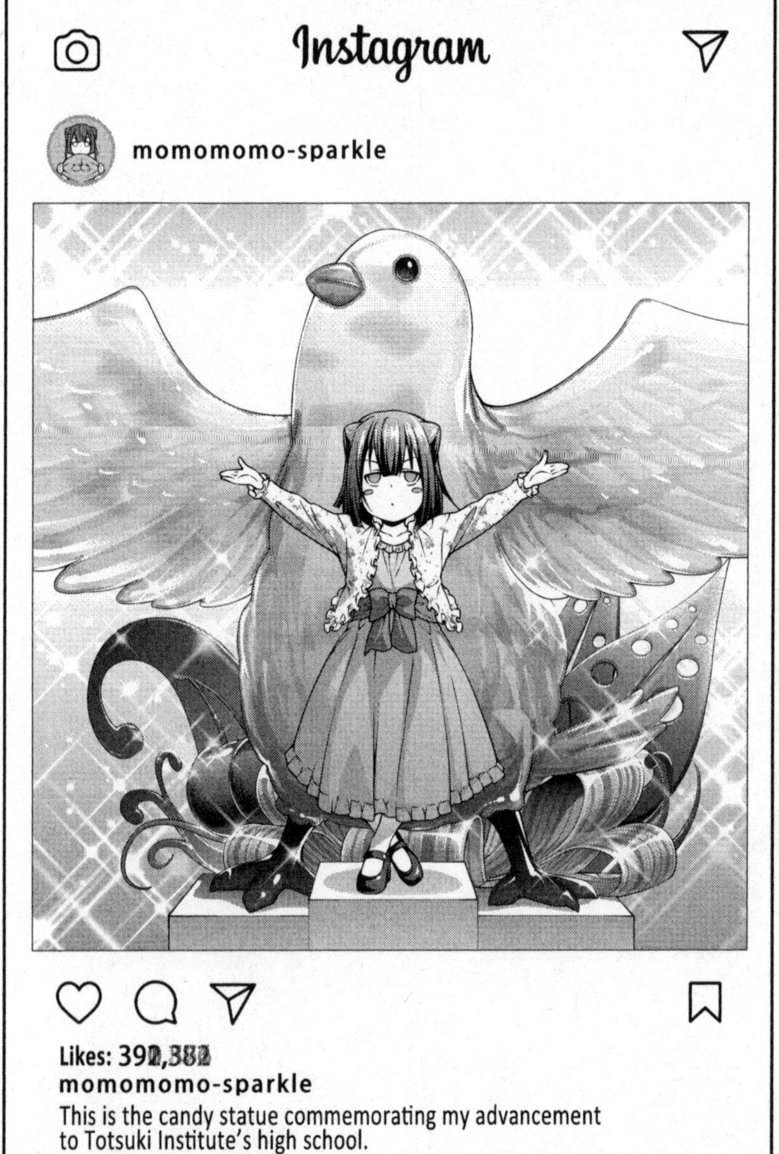
Instagram
momomomo-sparkle
Likes: 392,382
momomomo-sparkle
This is the candy statue commemorating my advancement to Totsuki Institute's high school.

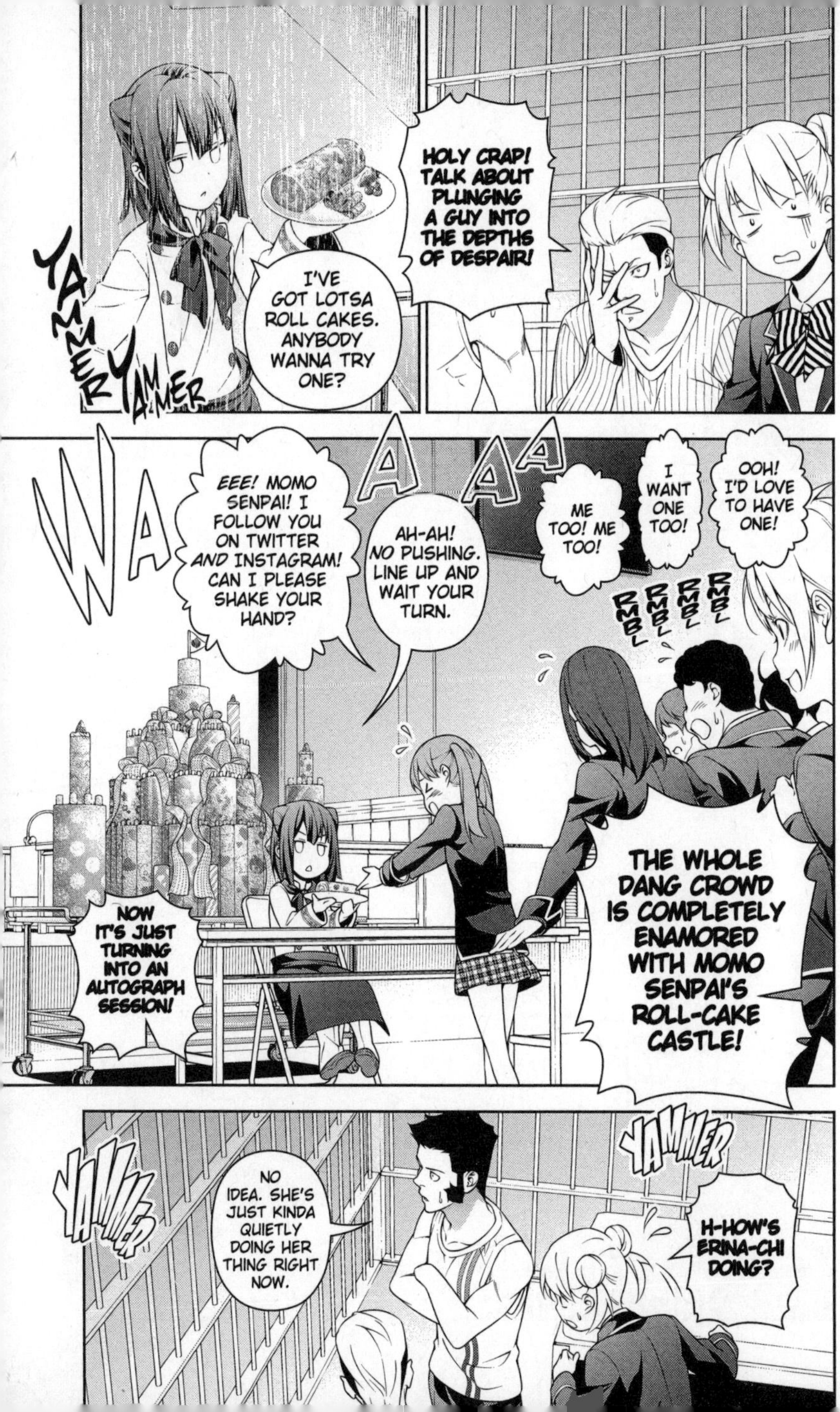

HOLY CRAP! TALK ABOUT PLUNGING A GUY INTO THE DEPTHS OF DESPAIR!
I'VE GOT LOTSA ROLL CAKES. ANYBODY WANNA TRY ONE?
YAMMER YAMMER
OOH! I'D LOVE TO HAVE ONE!
I WANT ONE TOO!
ME TOO! ME TOO!
RMBL RMBL RMBL RMBL
AAA
AH-AH! NO PUSHING. LINE UP AND WAIT YOUR TURN.
EEE! MOMO SENPAI! I FOLLOW YOU ON TWITTER AND INSTAGRAM! CAN I PLEASE SHAKE YOUR HAND?
WA
THE WHOLE DANG CROWD IS COMPLETELY ENAMORED WITH MOMO SENPAI'S ROLL-CAKE CASTLE!
NOW IT'S JUST TURNING INTO AN AUTOGRAPH SESSION!
YAMMER
H-HOW'S ERINA-CHI DOING?
NO IDEA. SHE'S JUST KINDA QUIETLY DOING HER THING RIGHT NOW.
YAMMER

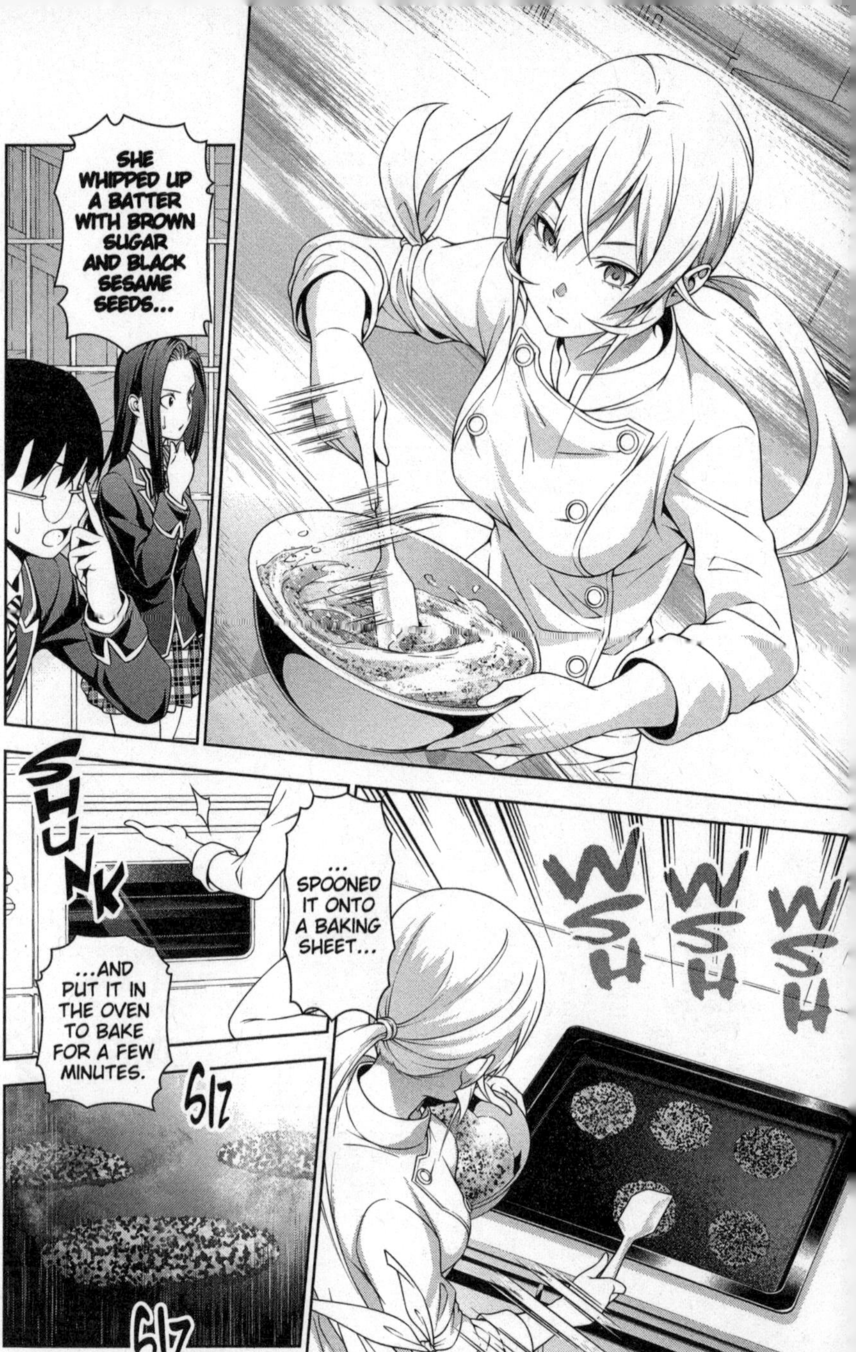
SHE WHIPPED UP A BATTER WITH BROWN SUGAR AND BLACK SESAME SEEDS...
WSH
WSH
WSH
... SPOONED IT ONTO A BAKING SHEET...
SHUNK
...AND PUT IT IN THE OVEN TO BAKE FOR A FEW MINUTES.
SIZ
SIZ

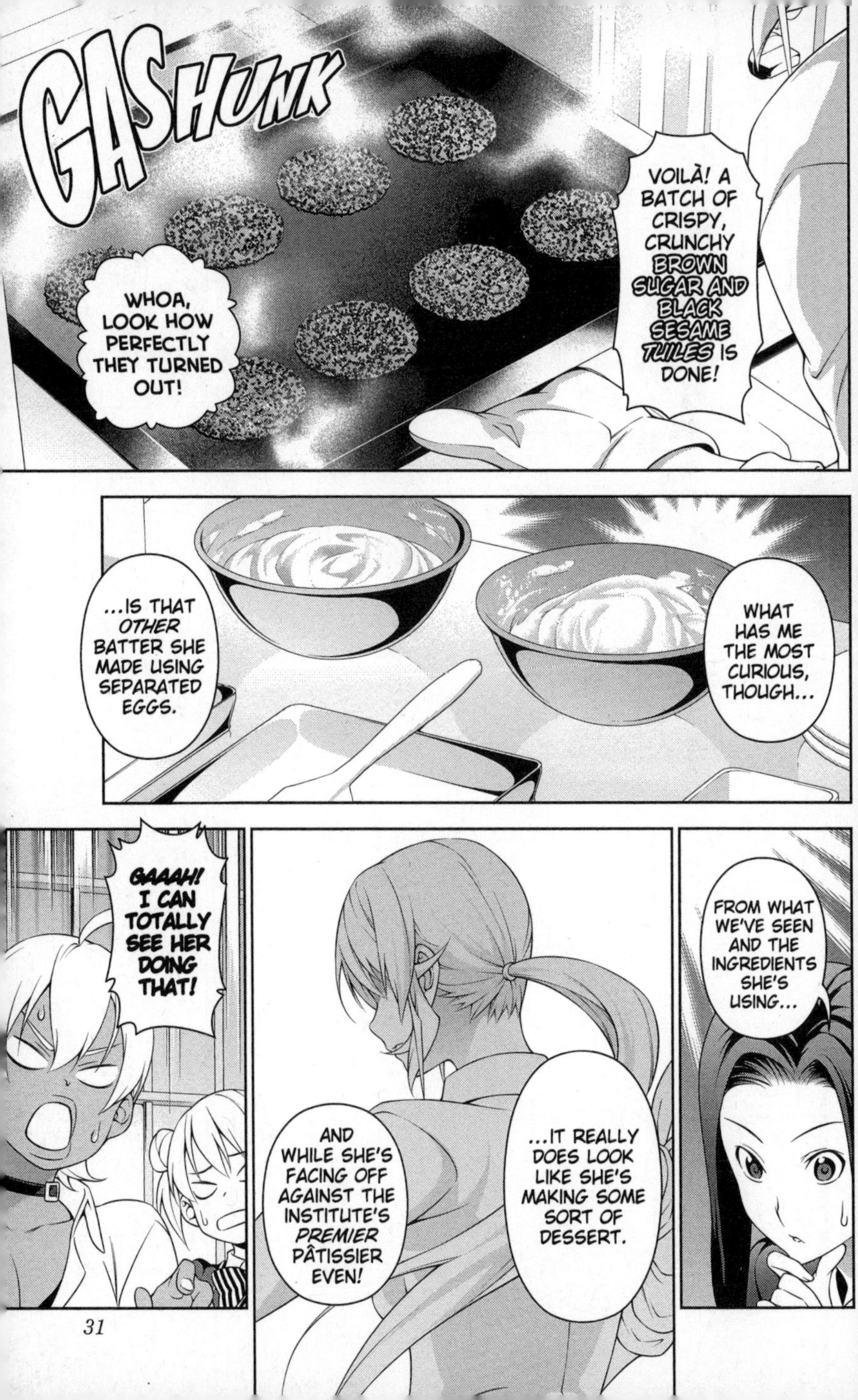
VOILÀ! A BATCH OF CRISPY, CRUNCHY BROWN SUGAR AND BLACK SESAME *TUILES* IS DONE!
GASHUNK
WHOA, LOOK HOW PERFECTLY THEY TURNED OUT!
WHAT HAS ME THE MOST CURIOUS, THOUGH...
...IS THAT *OTHER* BATTER SHE MADE USING SEPARATED EGGS.
FROM WHAT WE'VE SEEN AND THE INGREDIENTS SHE'S USING...
...IT REALLY DOES LOOK LIKE SHE'S MAKING SOME SORT OF DESSERT.
AND WHILE SHE'S FACING OFF AGAINST THE INSTITUTE'S *PREMIER* PÂTISSIER EVEN!
GAAAH! I CAN TOTALLY SEE HER DOING THAT!

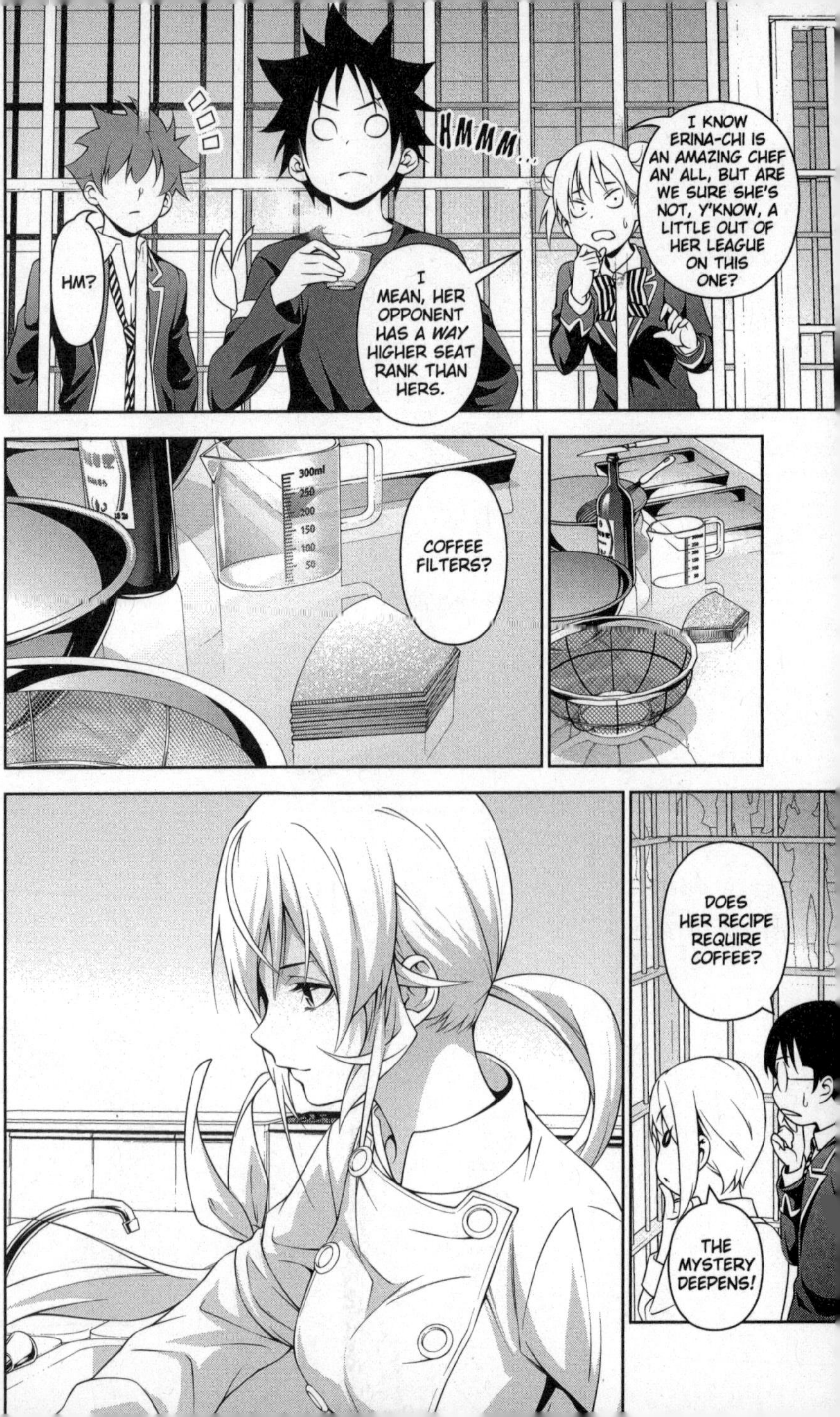
I KNOW ERINA-CHI IS AN AMAZING CHEF AN' ALL, BUT ARE WE SURE SHE'S NOT, Y'KNOW, A LITTLE OUT OF HER LEAGUE ON THIS ONE?
HMMM...
I MEAN, HER OPPONENT HAS A *WAY* HIGHER SEAT RANK THAN HERS.
HM?
COFFEE FILTERS?
DOES HER RECIPE REQUIRE COFFEE?
THE MYSTERY DEEPENS!

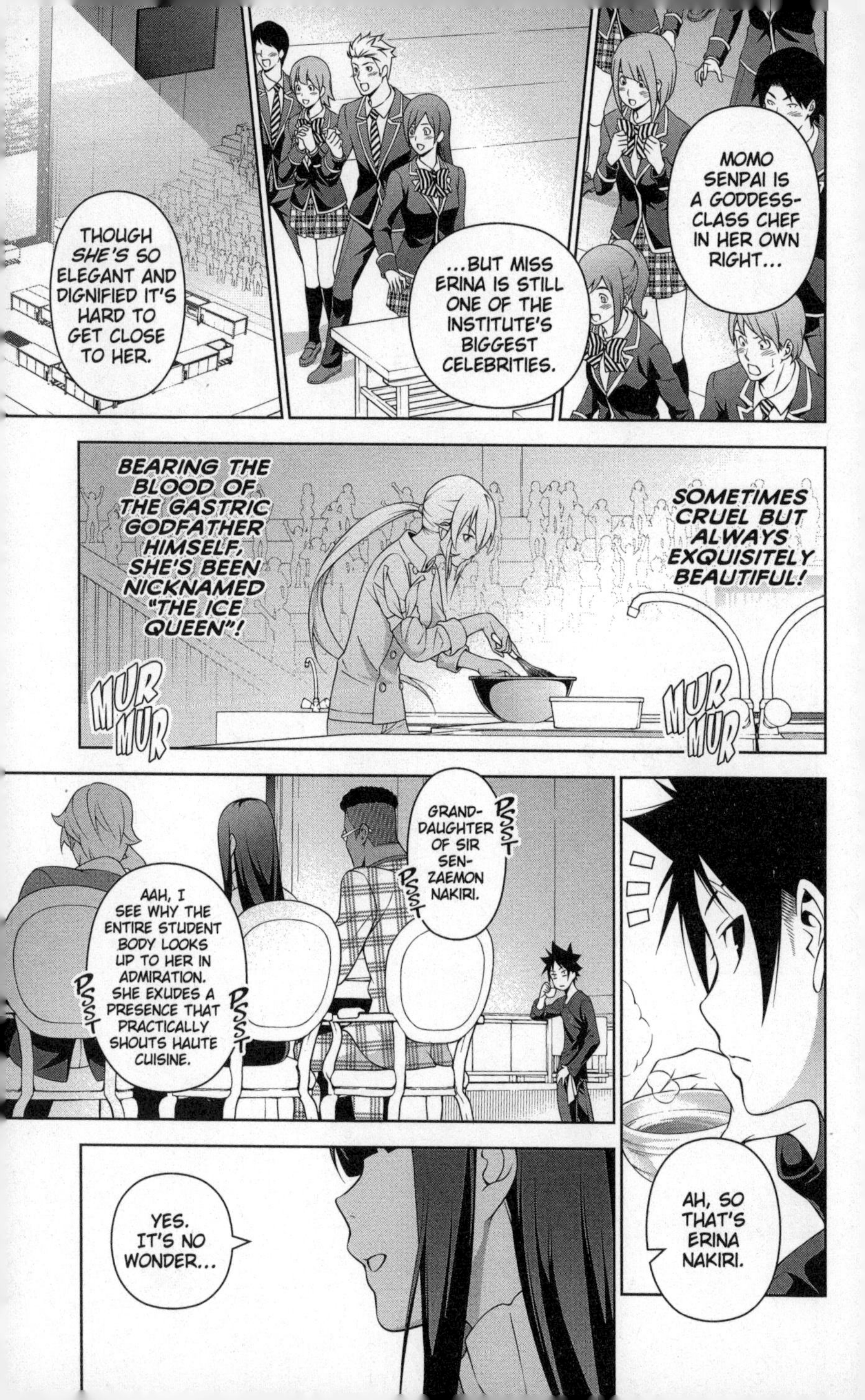
MOMO SENPAI IS A GODDESS-CLASS CHEF IN HER OWN RIGHT...
...BUT MISS ERINA IS STILL ONE OF THE INSTITUTE'S BIGGEST CELEBRITIES.
THOUGH SHE'S SO ELEGANT AND DIGNIFIED IT'S HARD TO GET CLOSE TO HER.
SOMETIMES CRUEL BUT ALWAYS EXQUISITELY BEAUTIFUL!
BEARING THE BLOOD OF THE GASTRIC GODFATHER HIMSELF, SHE'S BEEN NICKNAMED "THE ICE QUEEN"!
MUR MUR
MUR MUR
AH, SO THAT'S ERINA NAKIRI.
PSST
GRAND-DAUGHTER OF SIR SEN-ZAEMON NAKIRI.
PSST
AAH, I SEE WHY THE ENTIRE STUDENT BODY LOOKS UP TO HER IN ADMIRATION. SHE EXUDES A PRESENCE THAT PRACTICALLY SHOUTS HAUTE CUISINE.
PSST
PSST
YES. IT'S NO WONDER...

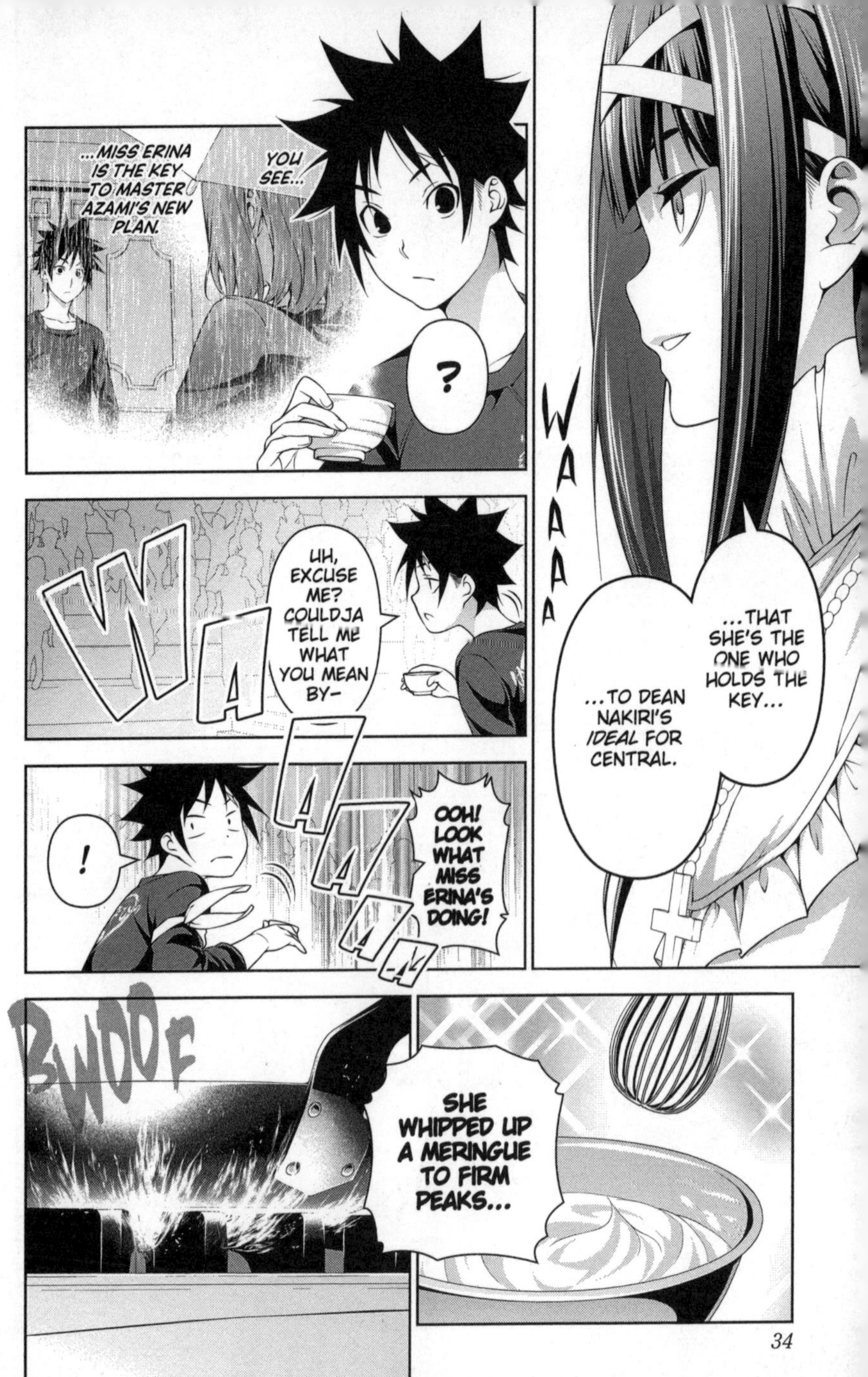
WAAAA
...THAT SHE'S THE ONE WHO HOLDS THE KEY...
...TO DEAN NAKIRI'S *IDEAL* FOR CENTRAL.
YOU SEE...
...MISS ERINA IS THE KEY TO MASTER AZAMI'S NEW PLAN.
?
UH, EXCUSE ME? COULDJA TELL ME WHAT YOU MEAN BY-
WA
AAAAA
OOH! LOOK WHAT MISS ERINA'S DOING!
!
SHE WHIPPED UP A MERINGUE TO FIRM PEAKS...
BWOOF

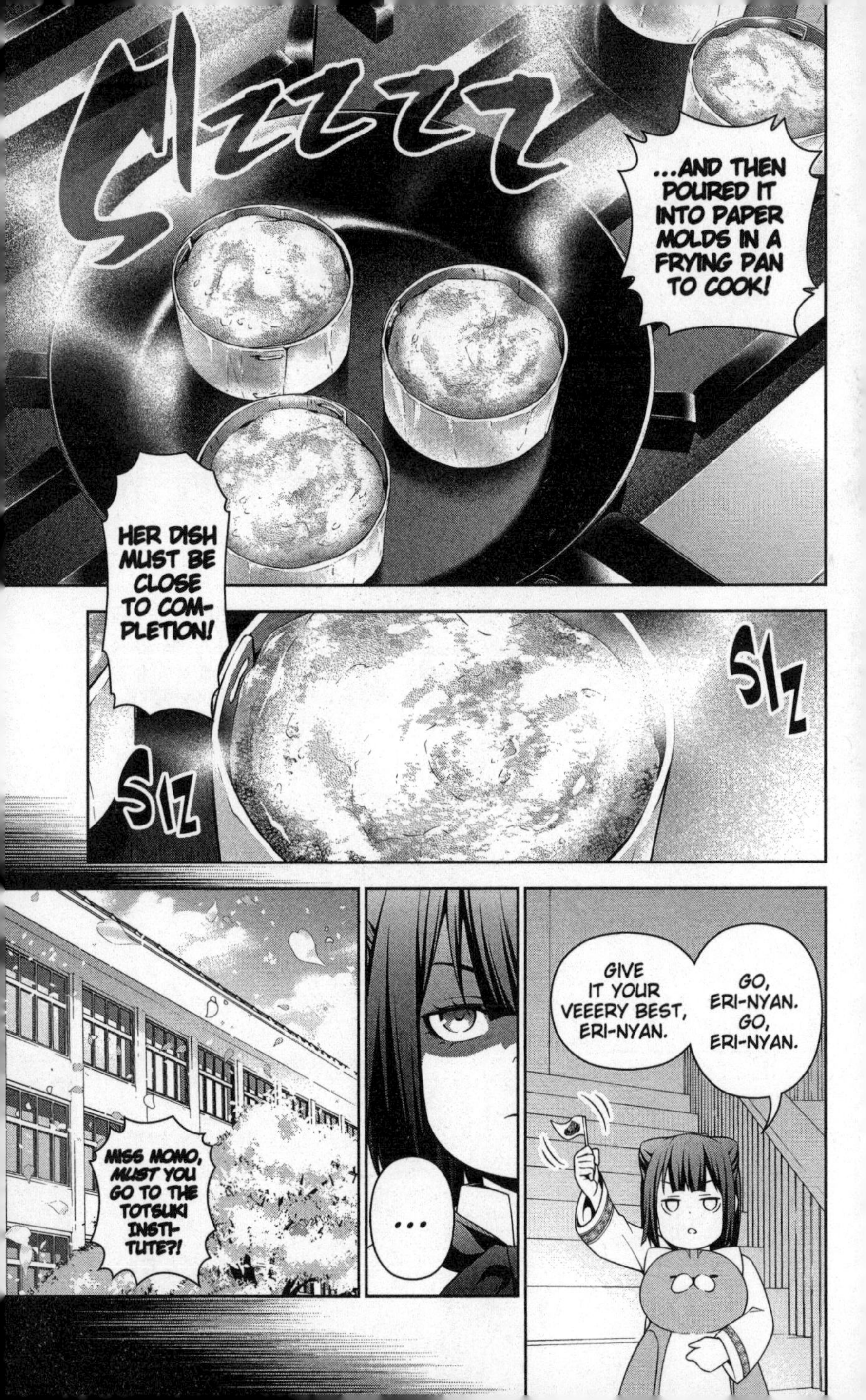
SIZZZZ
...AND THEN POURED IT INTO PAPER MOLDS IN A FRYING PAN TO COOK!
HER DISH MUST BE CLOSE TO COMPLETION!
SIZ
SIZ
GO, ERI-NYAN. GO, ERI-NYAN.
GIVE IT YOUR VEEERY BEST, ERI-NYAN.
...
MISS MOMO, MUST YOU GO TO THE TOTSUKI INSTITUTE?!

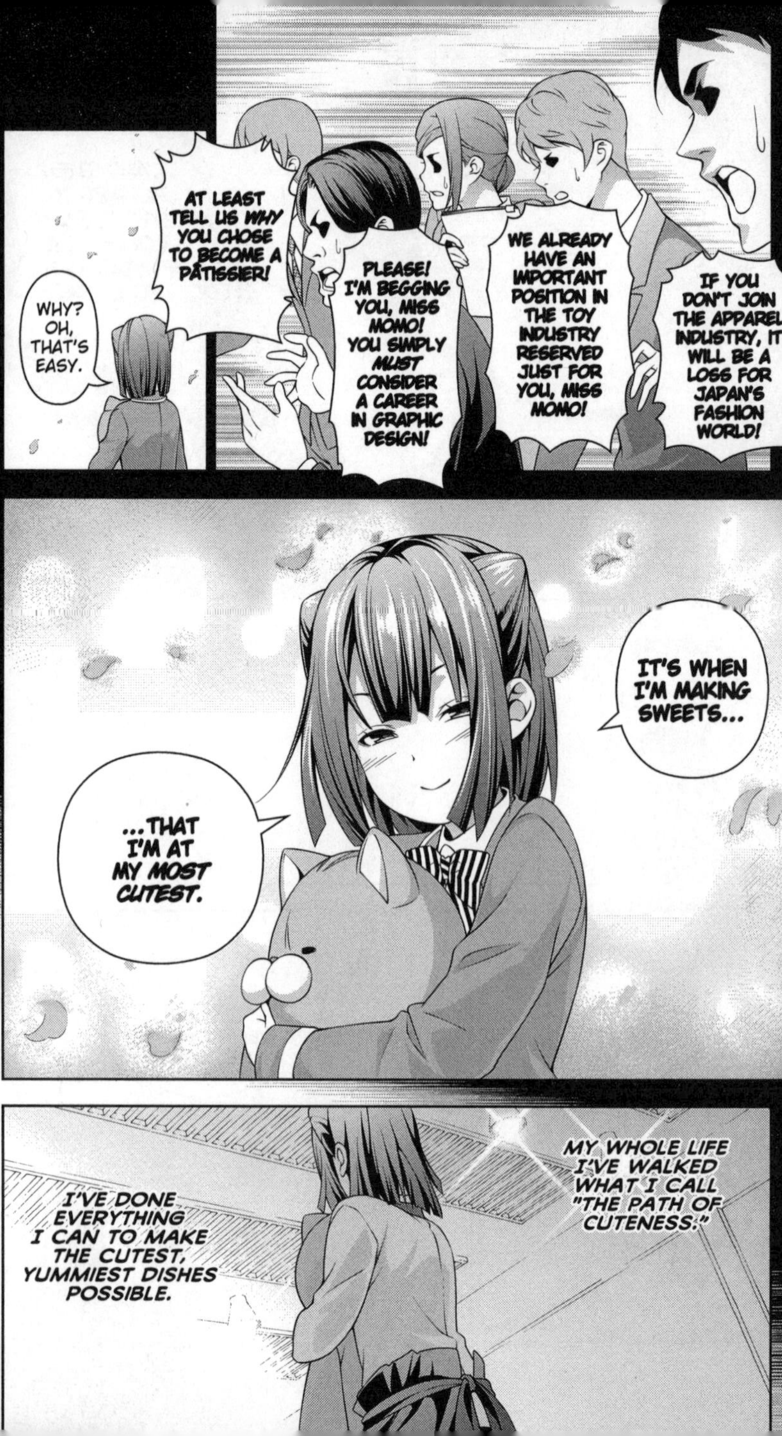
IF YOU DON'T JOIN THE APPAREL INDUSTRY, IT WILL BE A LOSS FOR JAPAN'S FASHION WORLD!
WE ALREADY HAVE AN IMPORTANT POSITION IN THE TOY INDUSTRY RESERVED JUST FOR YOU, MISS MOMO!
PLEASE! I'M BEGGING YOU, MISS MOMO! YOU SIMPLY *MUST* CONSIDER A CAREER IN GRAPHIC DESIGN!
AT LEAST TELL US *WHY* YOU CHOSE TO BECOME A PÂTISSIER!
WHY? OH, THAT'S EASY.
IT'S WHEN I'M MAKING SWEETS...
...THAT I'M AT MY *MOST CUTEST*.
MY WHOLE LIFE I'VE WALKED WHAT I CALL "THE PATH OF CUTENESS."
I'VE DONE EVERYTHING I CAN TO MAKE THE CUTEST, YUMMIEST DISHES POSSIBLE.

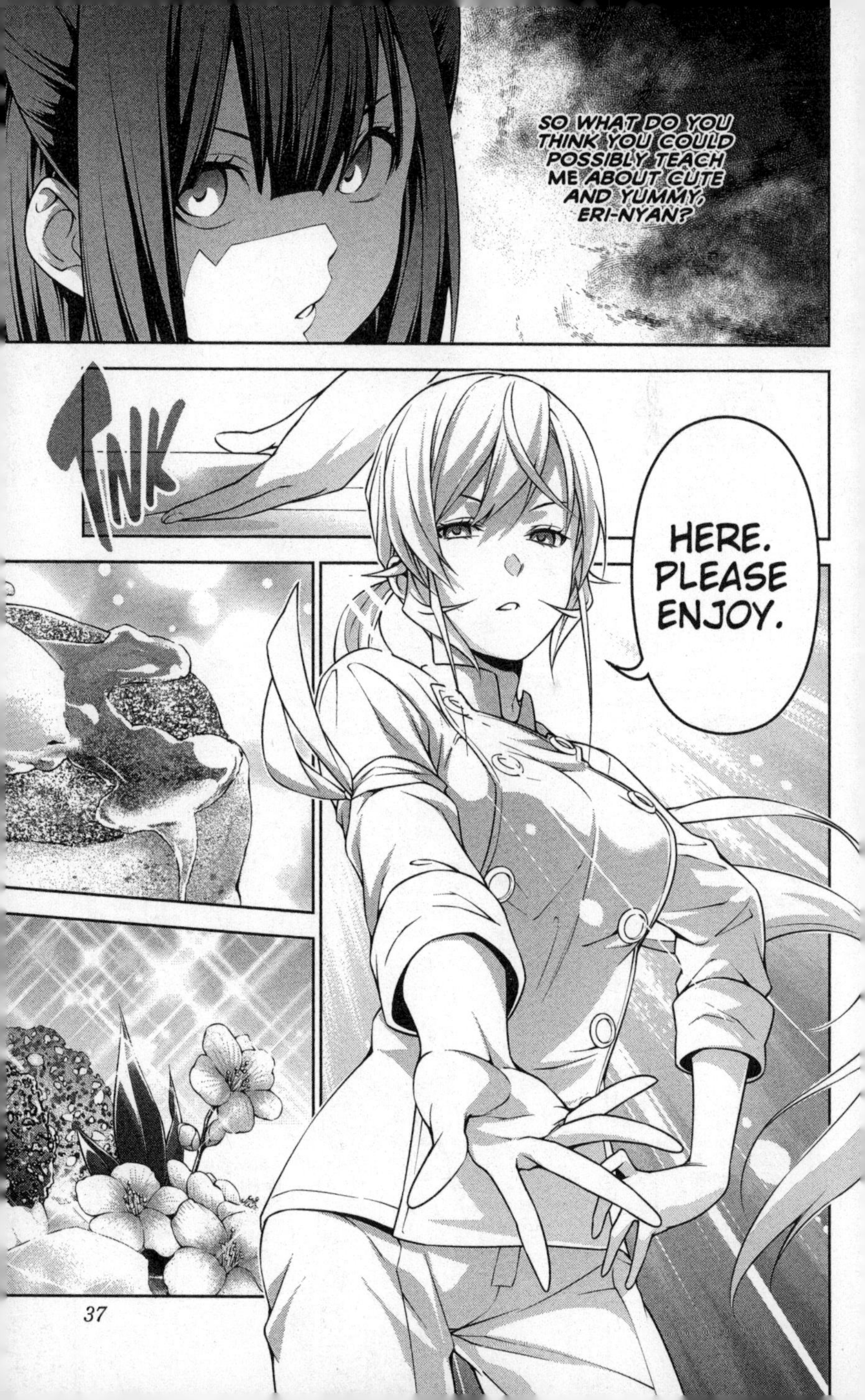
SO WHAT DO YOU THINK YOU COULD POSSIBLY TEACH ME ABOUT CUTE AND YUMMY, ERI-NYAN?
TINK
HERE. PLEASE ENJOY.

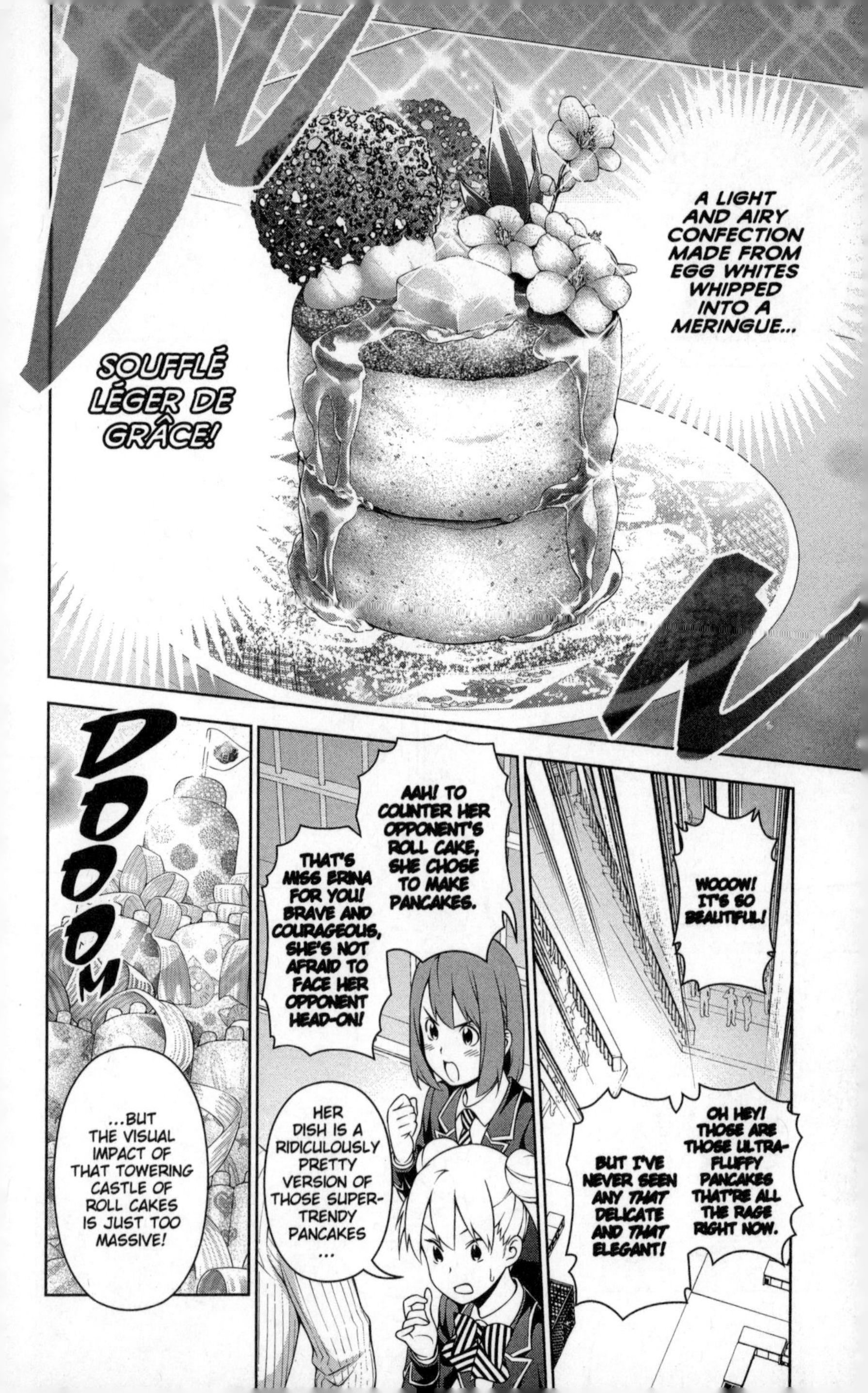
A LIGHT AND AIRY CONFECTION MADE FROM EGG WHITES WHIPPED INTO A MERINGUE...
SOUFFLÉ LÉGER DE GRÂCE!
WOOOW! IT'S SO BEAUTIFUL!
OH HEY! THOSE ARE THOSE ULTRA-FLUFFY PANCAKES THAT'RE ALL THE RAGE RIGHT NOW.
BUT I'VE NEVER SEEN ANY THAT DELICATE AND THAT ELEGANT!
AAH! TO COUNTER HER OPPONENT'S ROLL CAKE, SHE CHOSE TO MAKE PANCAKES.
THAT'S MISS ERINA FOR YOU! BRAVE AND COURAGEOUS, SHE'S NOT AFRAID TO FACE HER OPPONENT HEAD-ON!
HER DISH IS A RIDICULOUSLY PRETTY VERSION OF THOSE SUPER-TRENDY PANCAKES ...
...BUT THE VISUAL IMPACT OF THAT TOWERING CASTLE OF ROLL CAKES IS JUST TOO MASSIVE!

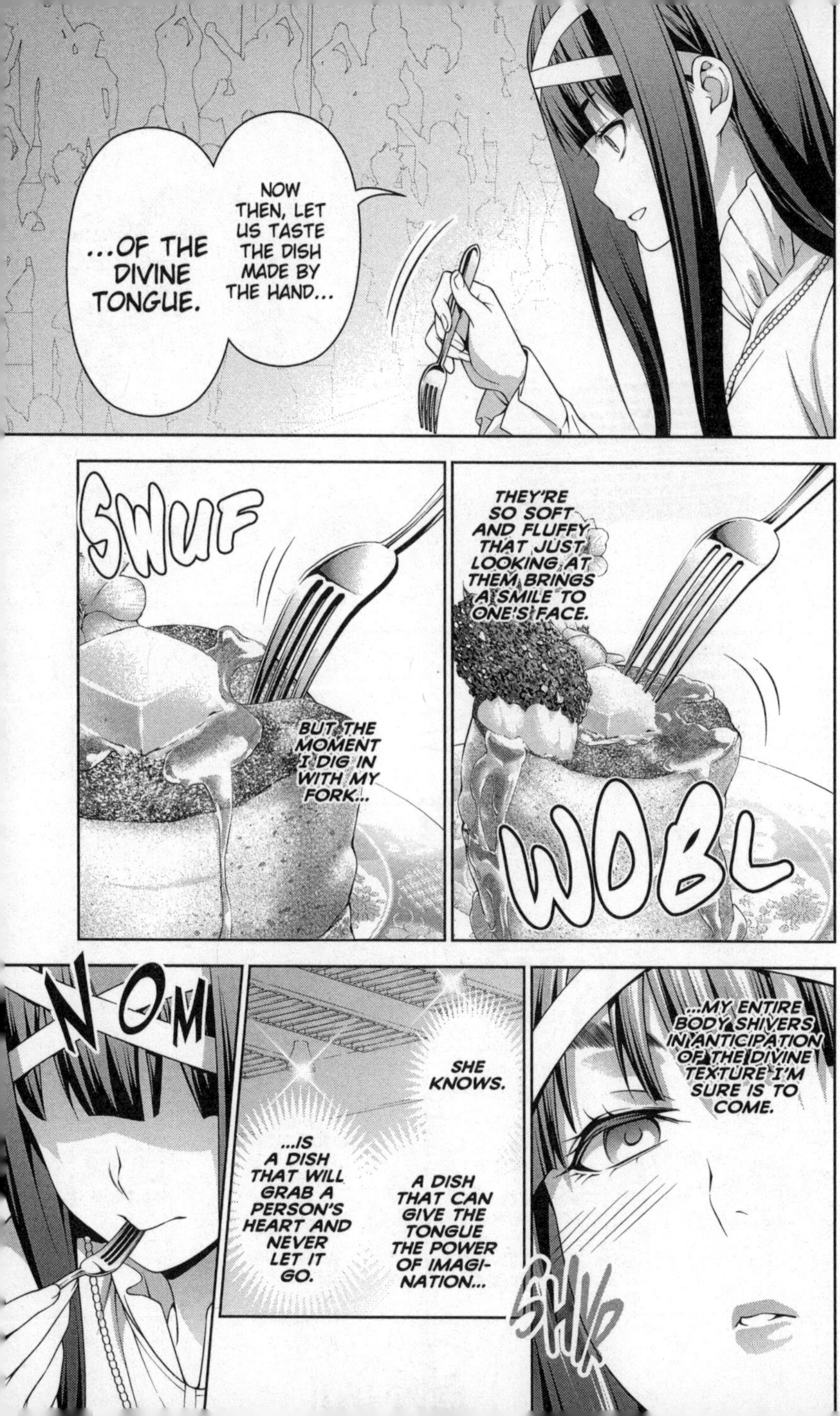
NOW THEN, LET US TASTE THE DISH MADE BY THE HAND...
...OF THE DIVINE TONGUE.
THEY'RE SO SOFT AND FLUFFY THAT JUST LOOKING AT THEM BRINGS A SMILE TO ONE'S FACE.
WOBL
SWUF
BUT THE MOMENT I DIG IN WITH MY FORK...
...MY ENTIRE BODY SHIVERS IN ANTICIPATION OF THE DIVINE TEXTURE I'M SURE IS TO COME.
SHE KNOWS.
A DISH THAT CAN GIVE THE TONGUE THE POWER OF IMAGI-NATION...
...IS A DISH THAT WILL GRAB A PERSON'S HEART AND NEVER LET IT GO.
NOM

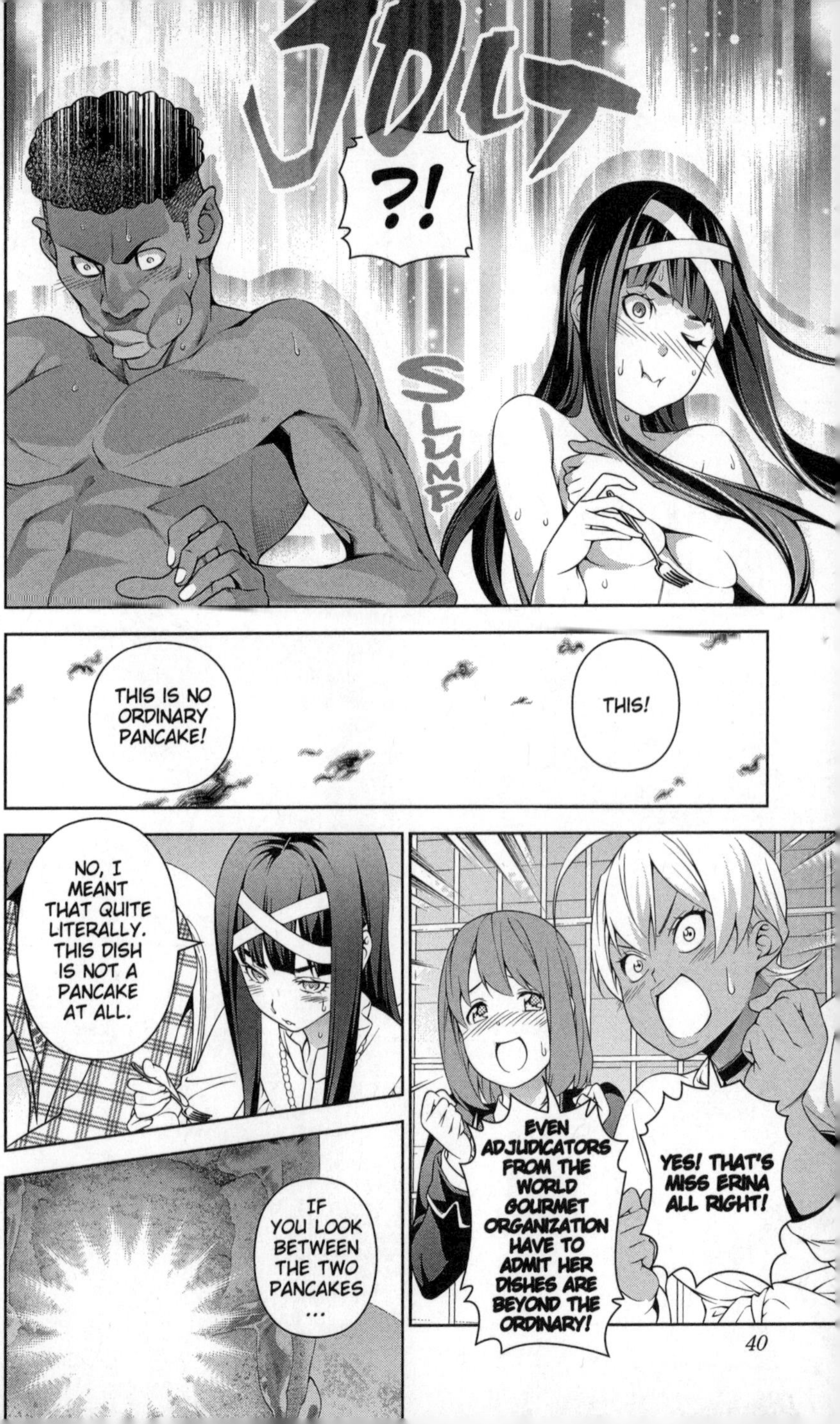
?!
SLUMP
THIS!
THIS IS NO ORDINARY PANCAKE!
YES! THAT'S MISS ERINA ALL RIGHT!
EVEN ADJUDICATORS FROM THE WORLD GOURMET ORGANIZATION HAVE TO ADMIT HER DISHES ARE BEYOND THE ORDINARY!
NO, I MEANT THAT QUITE LITERALLY. THIS DISH IS NOT A PANCAKE AT ALL.
IF YOU LOOK BETWEEN THE TWO PANCAKES ...

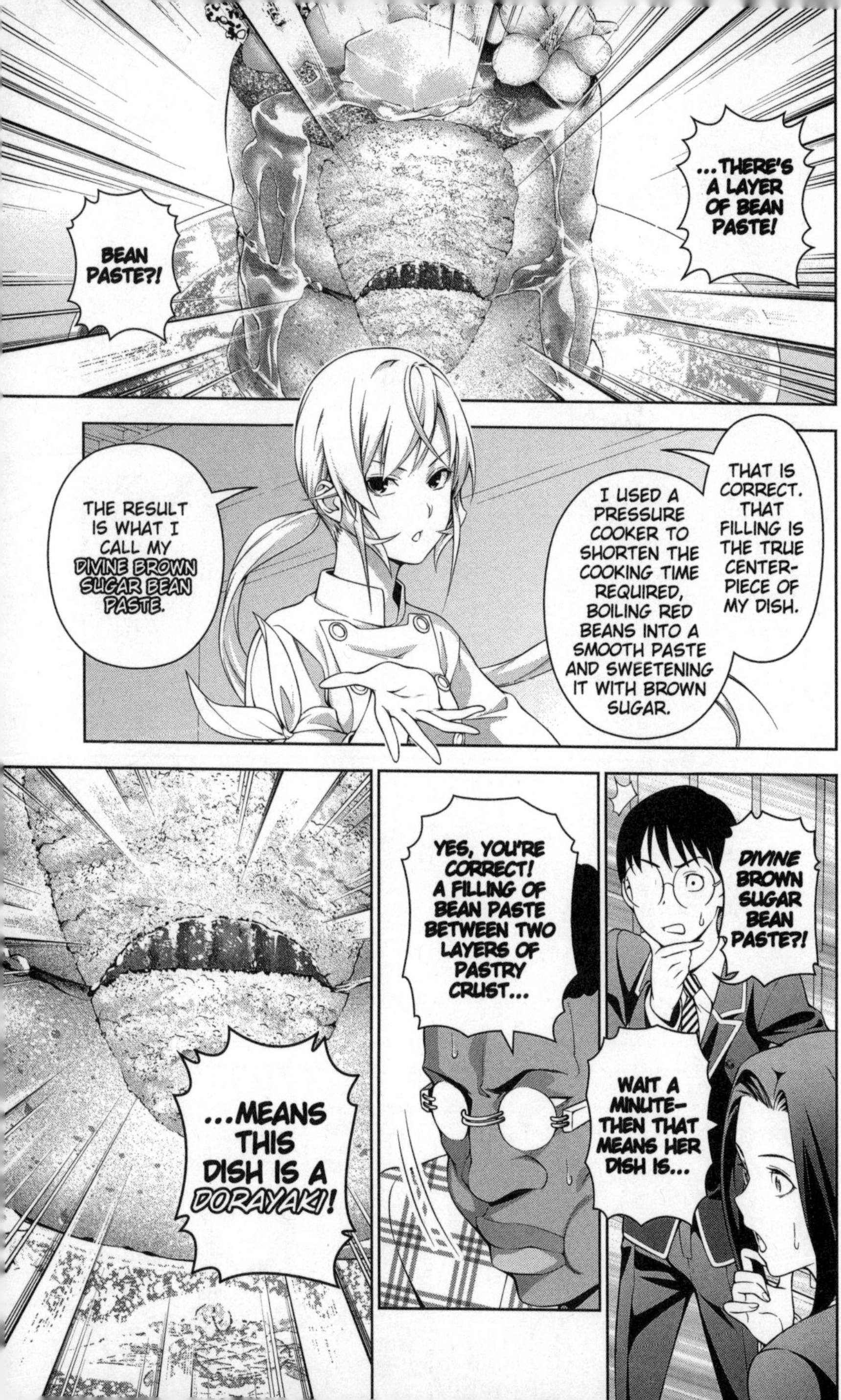
...THERE'S A LAYER OF BEAN PASTE!
BEAN PASTE?!
THAT IS CORRECT. THAT FILLING IS THE TRUE CENTER-PIECE OF MY DISH.
I USED A PRESSURE COOKER TO SHORTEN THE COOKING TIME REQUIRED, BOILING RED BEANS INTO A SMOOTH PASTE AND SWEETENING IT WITH BROWN SUGAR.
THE RESULT IS WHAT I CALL MY DIVINE BROWN SUGAR BEAN PASTE.
DIVINE BROWN SUGAR BEAN PASTE?!
WAIT A MINUTE–THEN THAT MEANS HER DISH IS...
YES, YOU'RE CORRECT! A FILLING OF BEAN PASTE BETWEEN TWO LAYERS OF PASTRY CRUST...
...MEANS THIS DISH IS A DORAYAKI!

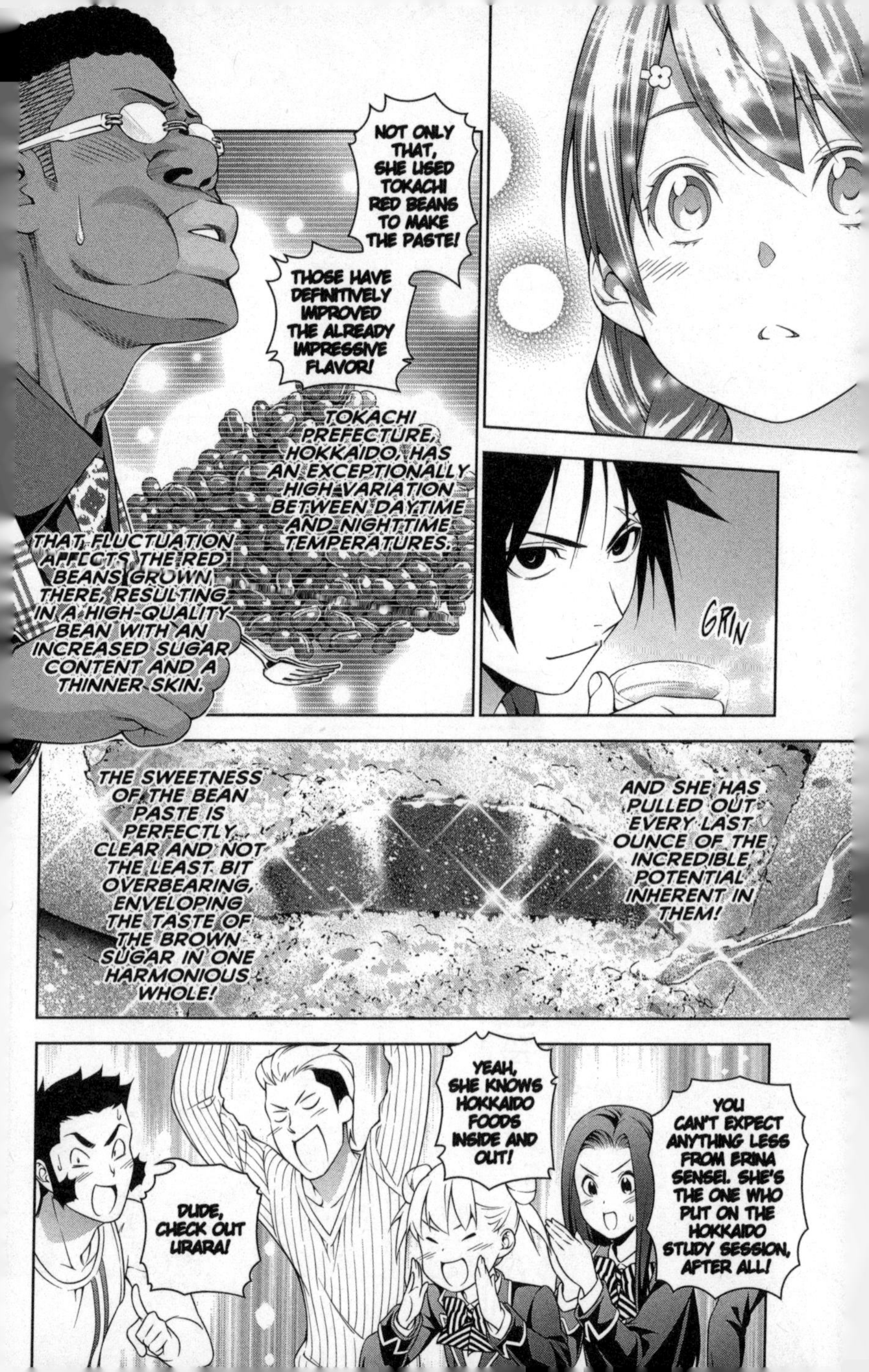
GRIN
NOT ONLY THAT, SHE USED TOKACHI RED BEANS TO MAKE THE PASTE!
THOSE HAVE DEFINITIVELY IMPROVED THE ALREADY IMPRESSIVE FLAVOR!
TOKACHI PREFECTURE, HOKKAIDO, HAS AN EXCEPTIONALLY HIGH VARIATION BETWEEN DAYTIME AND NIGHTTIME TEMPERATURES.
THAT FLUCTUATION AFFECTS THE RED BEANS GROWN THERE, RESULTING IN A HIGH-QUALITY BEAN WITH AN INCREASED SUGAR CONTENT AND A THINNER SKIN.
AND SHE HAS PULLED OUT EVERY LAST OUNCE OF THE INCREDIBLE POTENTIAL INHERENT IN THEM!
THE SWEETNESS OF THE BEAN PASTE IS PERFECTLY CLEAR AND NOT THE LEAST BIT OVERBEARING, ENVELOPING THE TASTE OF THE BROWN SUGAR IN ONE HARMONIOUS WHOLE!
YOU CAN'T EXPECT ANYTHING LESS FROM ERINA SENSEI. SHE'S THE ONE WHO PUT ON THE HOKKAIDO STUDY SESSION, AFTER ALL!
YEAH, SHE KNOWS HOKKAIDO FOODS INSIDE AND OUT!
DUDE, CHECK OUT URARA!

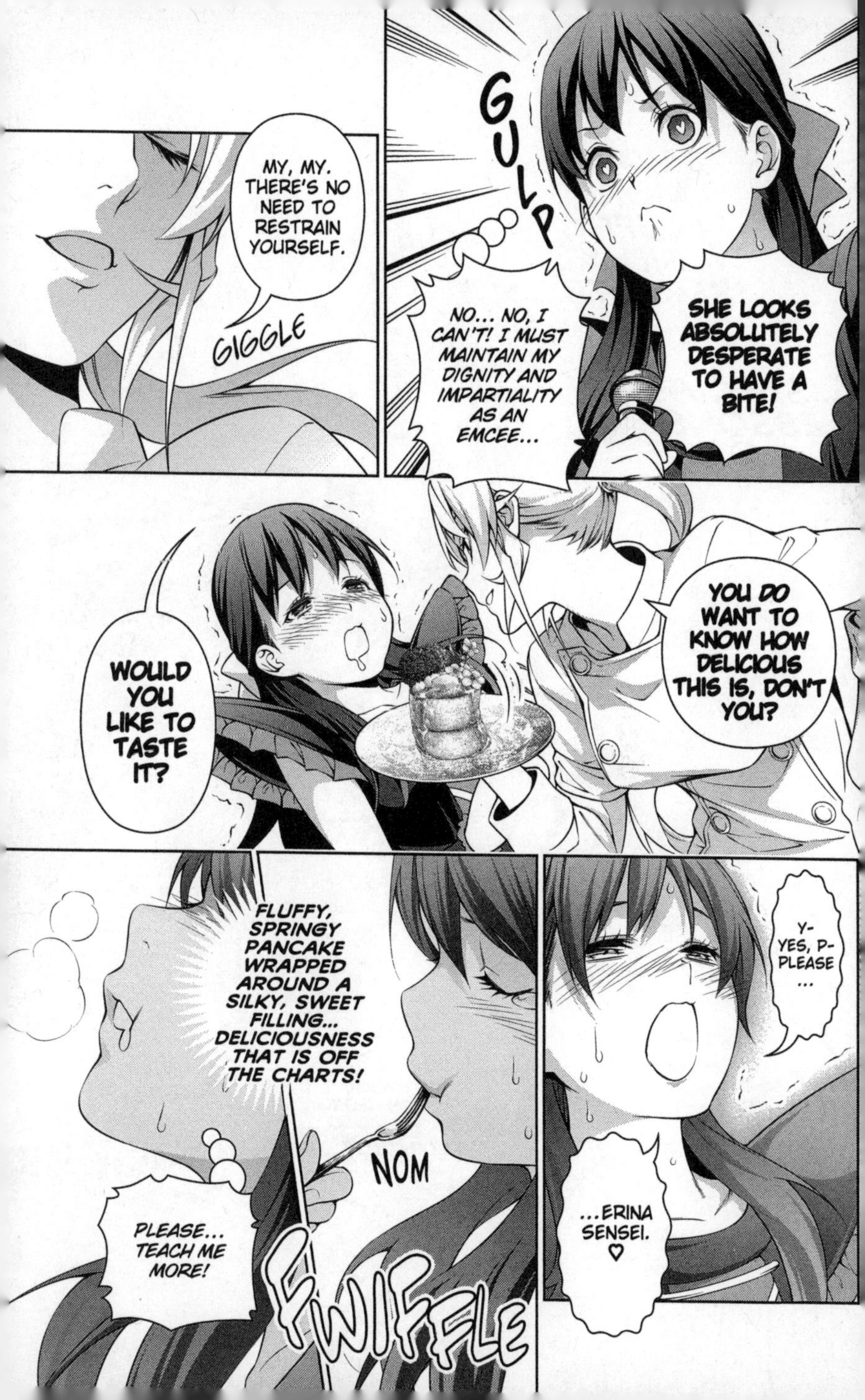
GULP
SHE LOOKS ABSOLUTELY DESPERATE TO HAVE A BITE!
NO... NO, I CAN'T! I MUST MAINTAIN MY DIGNITY AND IMPARTIALITY AS AN EMCEE...
MY, MY. THERE'S NO NEED TO RESTRAIN YOURSELF.
GIGGLE
YOU DO WANT TO KNOW HOW DELICIOUS THIS IS, DON'T YOU?
WOULD YOU LIKE TO TASTE IT?
Y- YES, P- PLEASE ...
...ERINA SENSEI. ♡
FLUFFY, SPRINGY PANCAKE WRAPPED AROUND A SILKY, SWEET FILLING... DELICIOUSNESS THAT IS OFF THE CHARTS!
NOM
PLEASE... TEACH ME MORE!
FWIFFLE

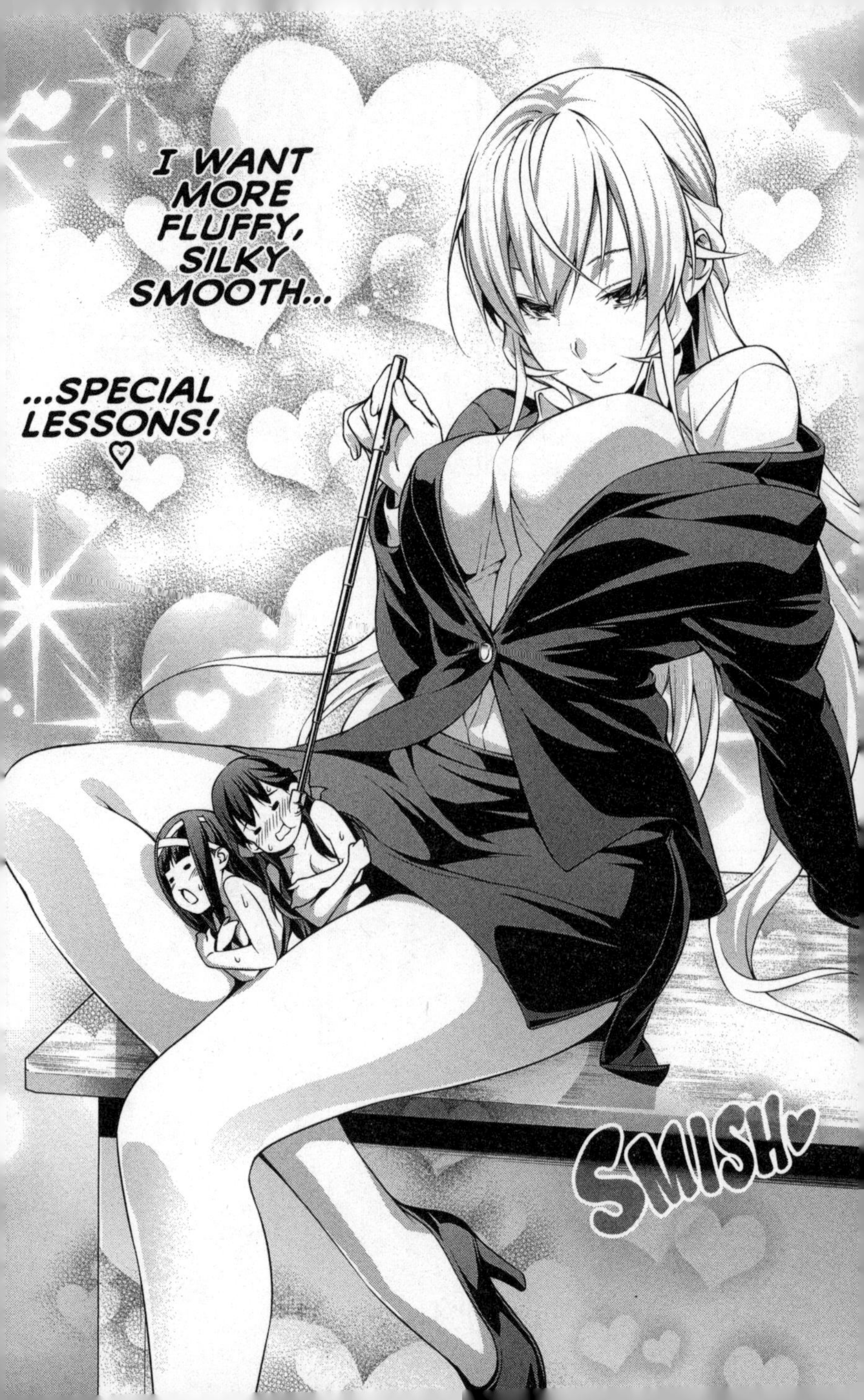
I WANT MORE FLUFFY, SILKY SMOOTH...
...SPECIAL LESSONS! ♡
SMISH♡

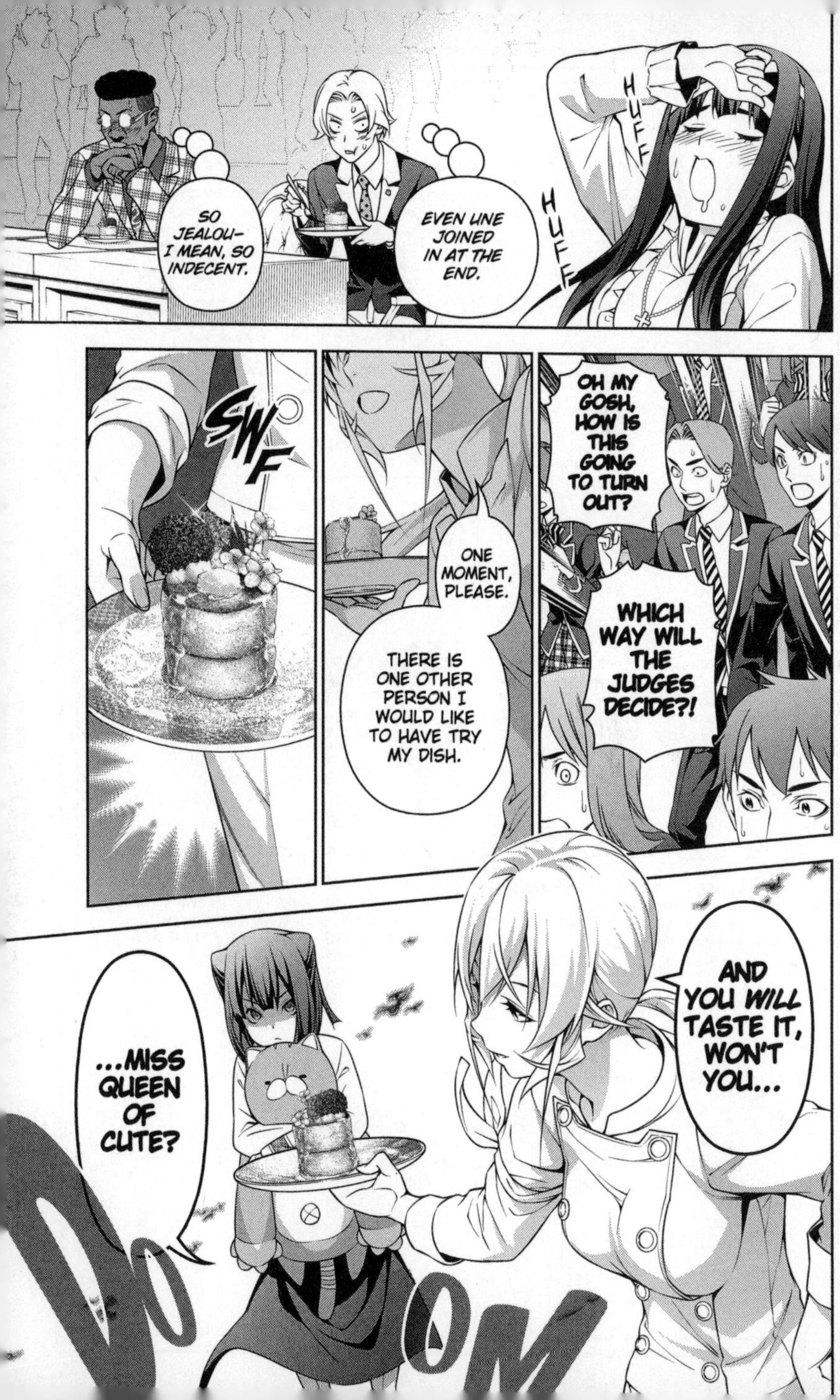
HUFF
HUFF
EVEN UNE JOINED IN AT THE END.
SO JEALOU- I MEAN, SO INDECENT.
OH MY GOSH, HOW IS THIS GOING TO TURN OUT?
WHICH WAY WILL THE JUDGES DECIDE?!
ONE MOMENT, PLEASE.
THERE IS ONE OTHER PERSON I WOULD LIKE TO HAVE TRY MY DISH.
SWF
AND YOU WILL TASTE IT, WON'T YOU...
...MISS QUEEN OF CUTE?

ARTIST: YUTO TSUKUDA RECIPE BY: YUKI MORISAKI

PRACTICAL RECIPE #1

VOLUME 29 SPECIAL SUPPLEMENT!

CHEF MOMO'S CANDY SHOP SOY SAUCE & BROWN SUGAR ROLL CAKE

PLUNK
WELCOME, COME ON IN.

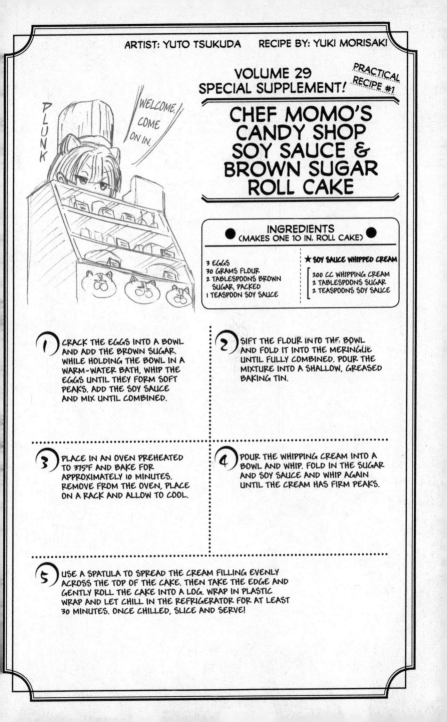

INGREDIENTS
(MAKES ONE 10 IN. ROLL CAKE)

3 EGGS
30 GRAMS FLOUR
2 TABLESPOONS BROWN SUGAR, PACKED
1 TEASPOON SOY SAUCE

★ SOY SAUCE WHIPPED CREAM

200 CC WHIPPING CREAM
2 TABLESPOONS SUGAR
2 TEASPOONS SOY SAUCE

1. CRACK THE EGGS INTO A BOWL AND ADD THE BROWN SUGAR. WHILE HOLDING THE BOWL IN A WARM-WATER BATH, WHIP THE EGGS UNTIL THEY FORM SOFT PEAKS. ADD THE SOY SAUCE AND MIX UNTIL COMBINED.

2. SIFT THE FLOUR INTO THE BOWL AND FOLD IT INTO THE MERINGUE UNTIL FULLY COMBINED. POUR THE MIXTURE INTO A SHALLOW, GREASED BAKING TIN.

3. PLACE IN AN OVEN PREHEATED TO 375°F AND BAKE FOR APPROXIMATELY 10 MINUTES. REMOVE FROM THE OVEN, PLACE ON A RACK AND ALLOW TO COOL.

4. POUR THE WHIPPING CREAM INTO A BOWL AND WHIP. FOLD IN THE SUGAR AND SOY SAUCE AND WHIP AGAIN UNTIL THE CREAM HAS FIRM PEAKS.

5. USE A SPATULA TO SPREAD THE CREAM FILLING EVENLY ACROSS THE TOP OF THE CAKE. THEN TAKE THE EDGE AND GENTLY ROLL THE CAKE INTO A LOG. WRAP IN PLASTIC WRAP AND LET CHILL IN THE REFRIGERATOR FOR AT LEAST 30 MINUTES. ONCE CHILLED, SLICE AND SERVE!

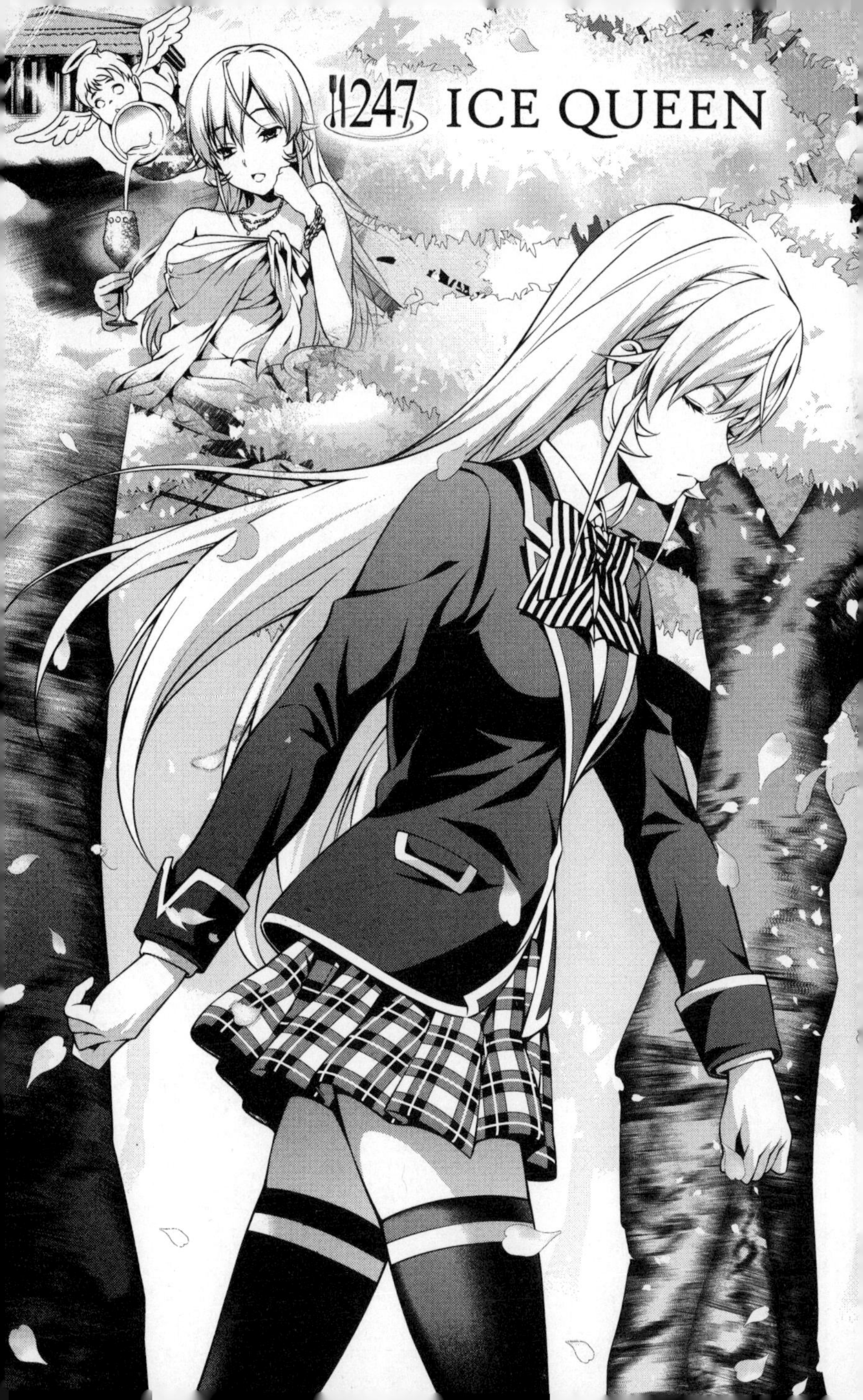

247 ICE QUEEN

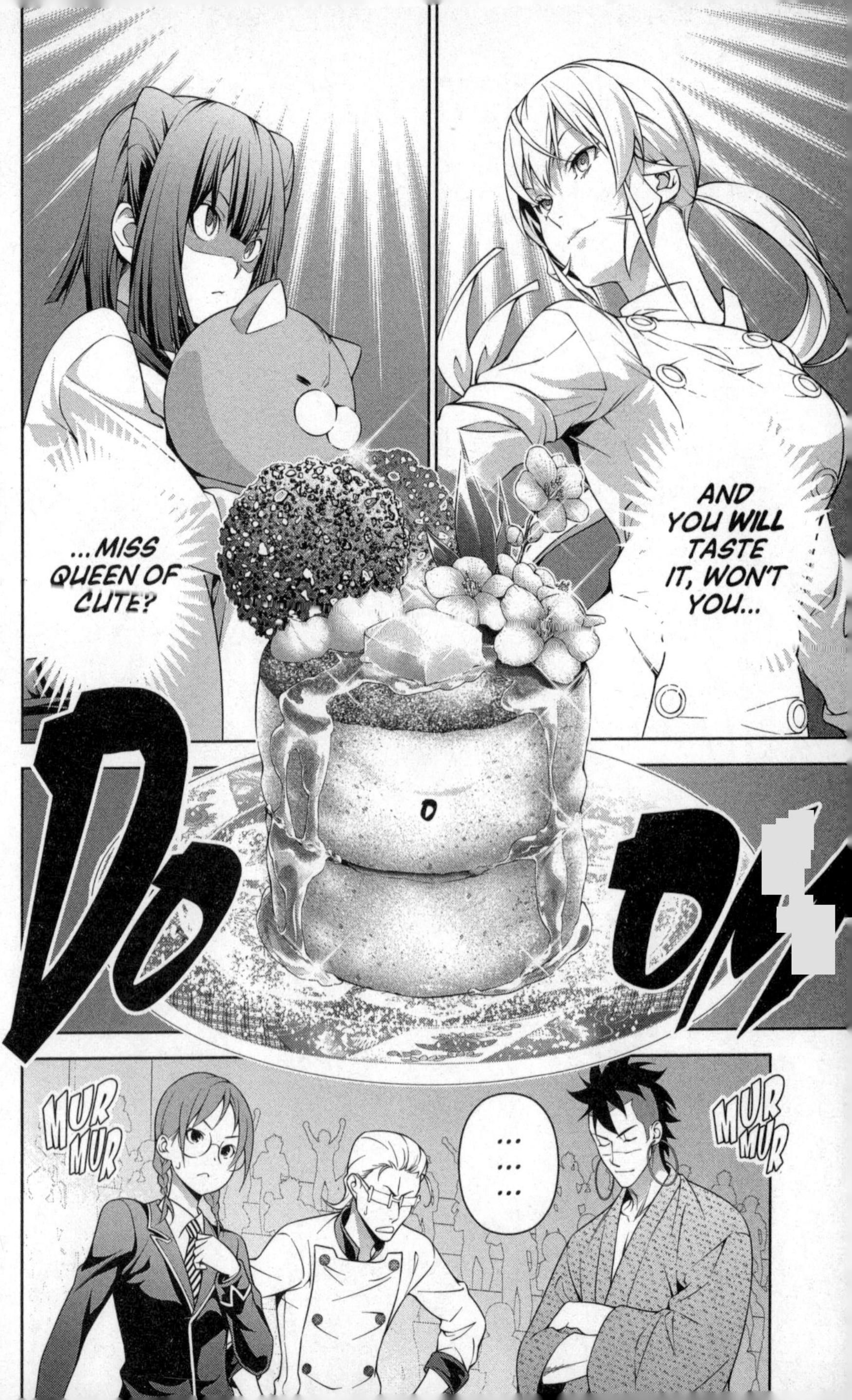
AND YOU WILL TASTE IT, WON'T YOU...
...MISS QUEEN OF CUTE?
DO DOM
MUR MUR
...
...
...
MUR MUR

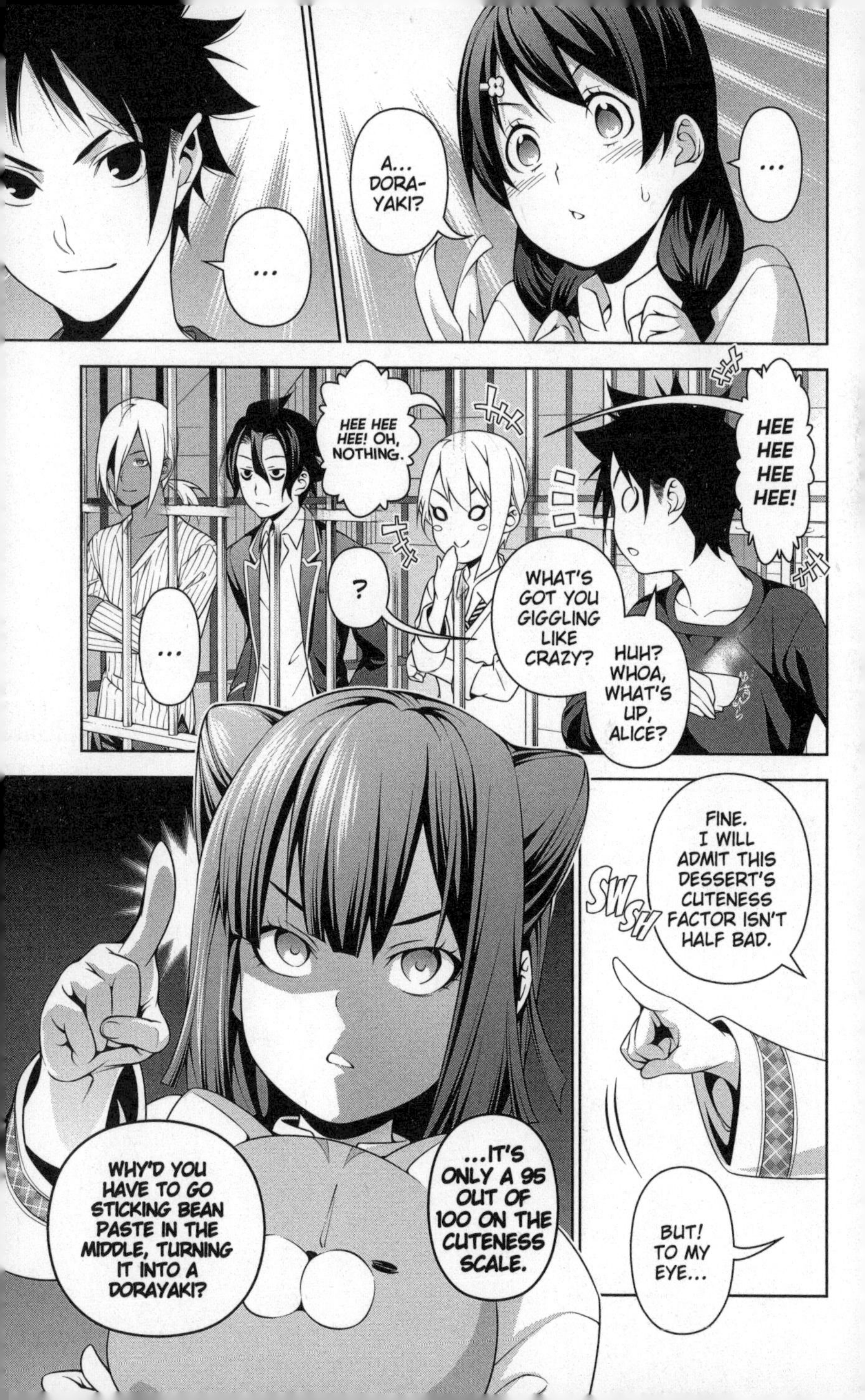
...
A... DORA-YAKI?
...
HEE HEE HEE HEE!
HUH? WHOA, WHAT'S UP, ALICE?
WHAT'S GOT YOU GIGGLING LIKE CRAZY?
HEE HEE HEE! OH, NOTHING.
?
...
FINE. I WILL ADMIT THIS DESSERT'S CUTENESS FACTOR ISN'T HALF BAD.
SWSH
BUT! TO MY EYE...
...IT'S ONLY A 95 OUT OF 100 ON THE CUTENESS SCALE.
WHY'D YOU HAVE TO GO STICKING BEAN PASTE IN THE MIDDLE, TURNING IT INTO A DORAYAKI?

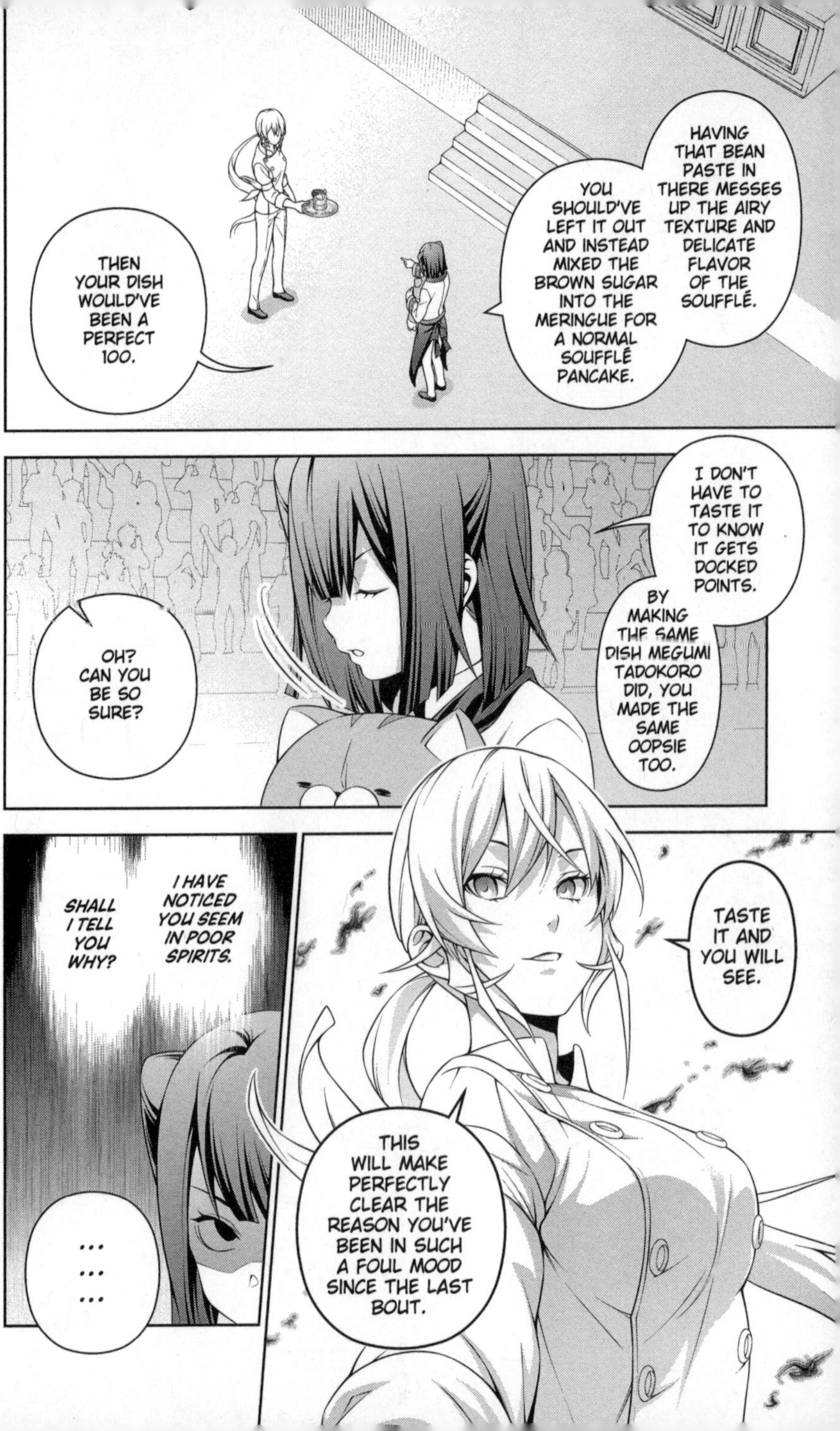
HAVING THAT BEAN PASTE IN THERE MESSES UP THE AIRY TEXTURE AND DELICATE FLAVOR OF THE SOUFFLÉ.
YOU SHOULD'VE LEFT IT OUT AND INSTEAD MIXED THE BROWN SUGAR INTO THE MERINGUE FOR A NORMAL SOUFFLÉ PANCAKE.
THEN YOUR DISH WOULD'VE BEEN A PERFECT 100.
I DON'T HAVE TO TASTE IT TO KNOW IT GETS DOCKED POINTS.
BY MAKING THE SAME DISH MEGUMI TADOKORO DID, YOU MADE THE SAME OOPSIE TOO.
OH? CAN YOU BE SO SURE?
TASTE IT AND YOU WILL SEE.
THIS WILL MAKE PERFECTLY CLEAR THE REASON YOU'VE BEEN IN SUCH A FOUL MOOD SINCE THE LAST BOUT.
I HAVE NOTICED YOU SEEM IN POOR SPIRITS.
SHALL I TELL YOU WHY?
... ...

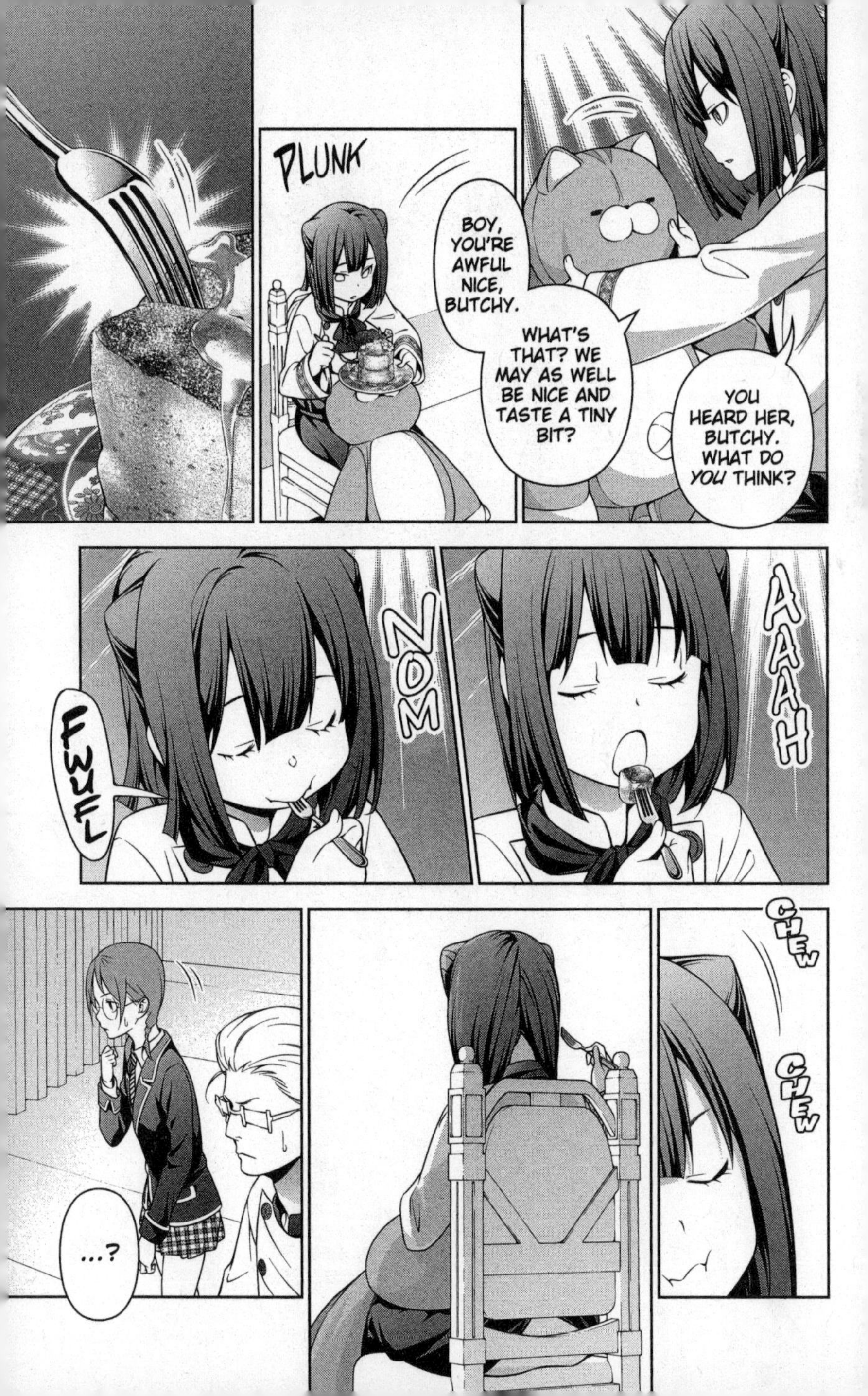
YOU HEARD HER, BUTCHY. WHAT DO *YOU* THINK?
WHAT'S THAT? WE MAY AS WELL BE NICE AND TASTE A TINY BIT?
BOY, YOU'RE AWFUL NICE, BUTCHY.
PLUNK
AAAAH
NOM
FWUFL
CHEW
CHEW
...?

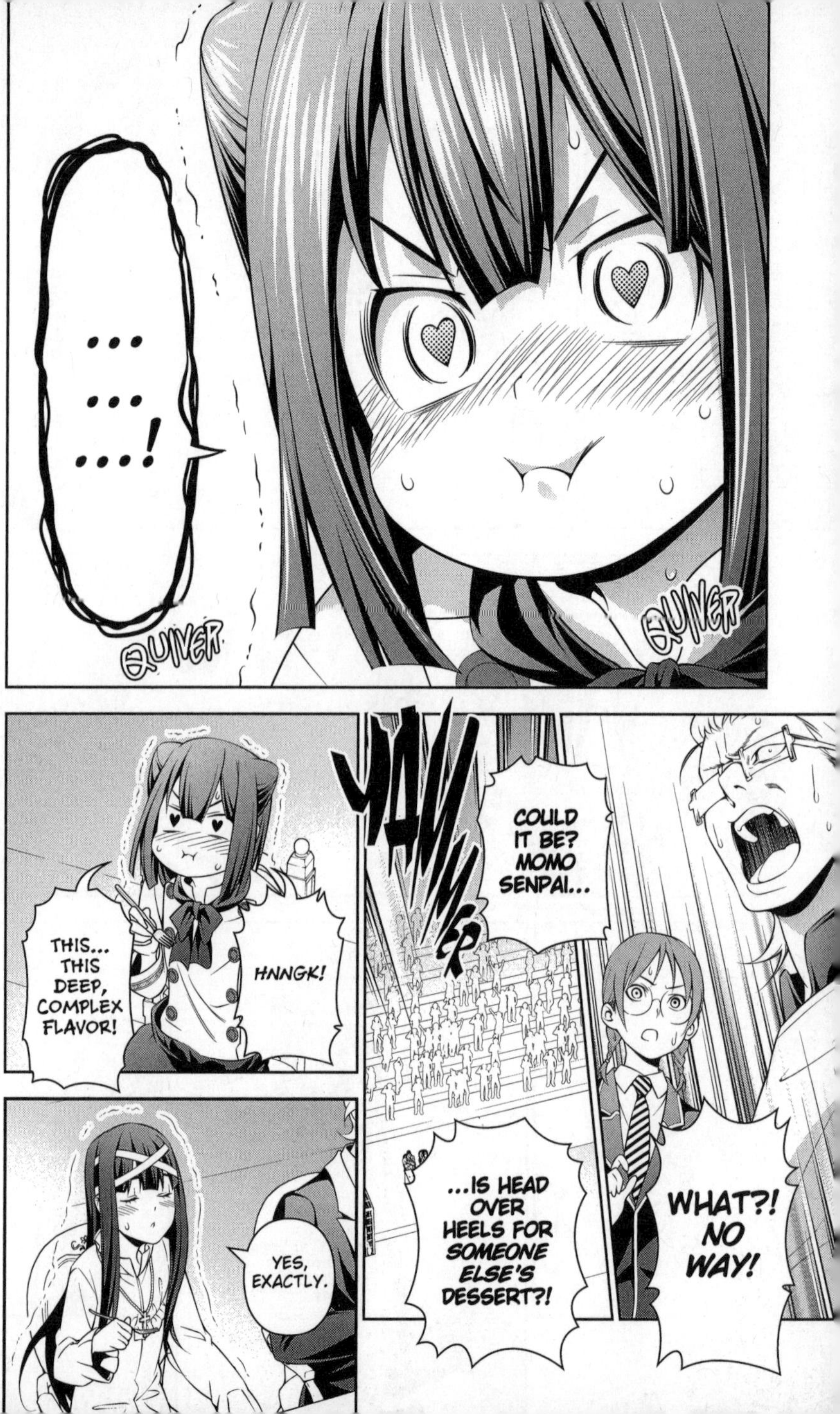
......!
QUIVER
QUIVER
YAMMER
COULD IT BE? MOMO SENPAI...
...IS HEAD OVER HEELS FOR SOMEONE ELSE'S DESSERT?!
WHAT?! NO WAY!
HNNGK!
THIS... THIS DEEP, COMPLEX FLAVOR!
YES, EXACTLY.

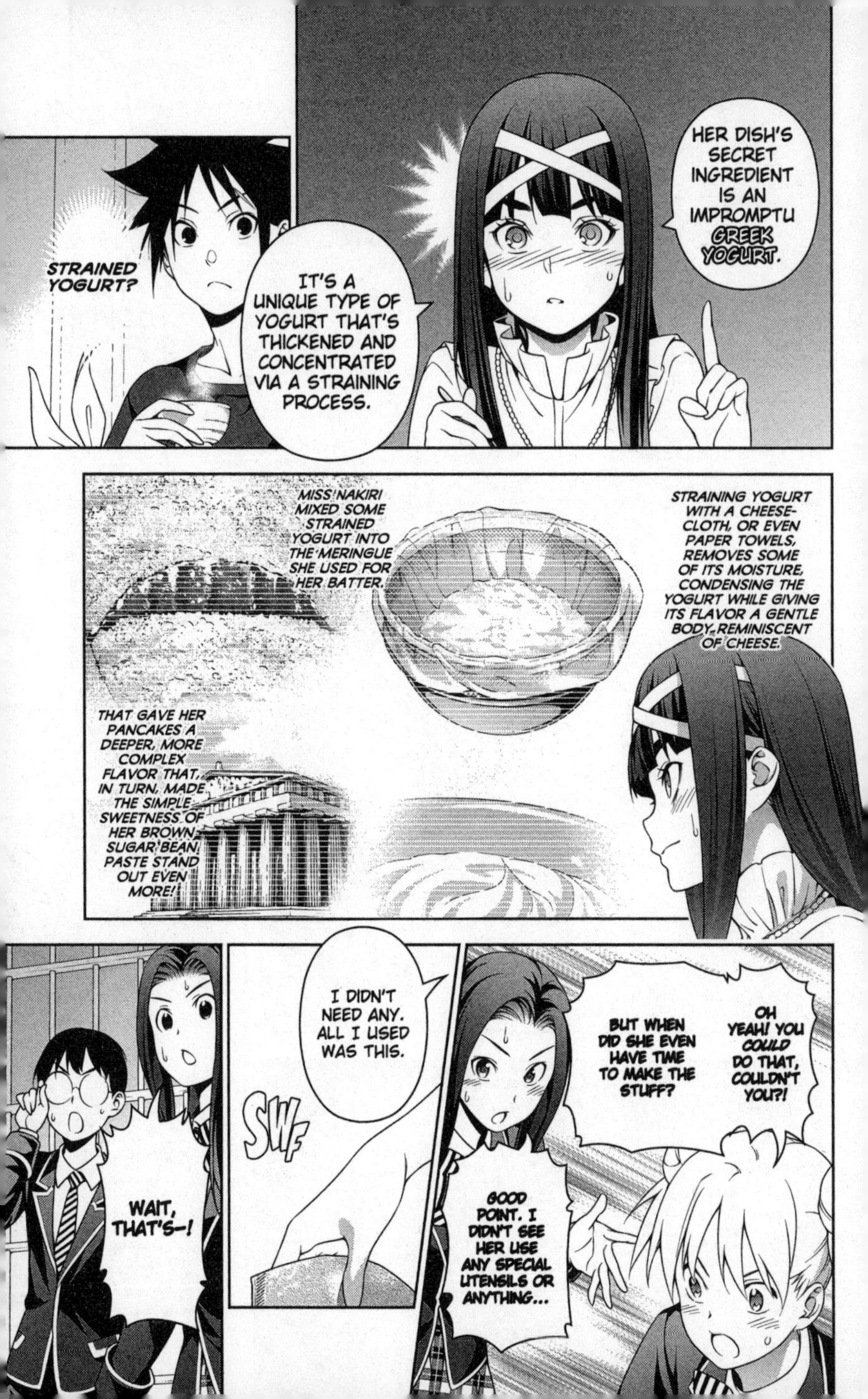
HER DISH'S SECRET INGREDIENT IS AN IMPROMPTU GREEK YOGURT.
STRAINED YOGURT?
IT'S A UNIQUE TYPE OF YOGURT THAT'S THICKENED AND CONCENTRATED VIA A STRAINING PROCESS.
STRAINING YOGURT WITH A CHEESE-CLOTH, OR EVEN PAPER TOWELS, REMOVES SOME OF ITS MOISTURE, CONDENSING THE YOGURT WHILE GIVING ITS FLAVOR A GENTLE BODY REMINISCENT OF CHEESE.
MISS NAKIRI MIXED SOME STRAINED YOGURT INTO THE MERINGUE SHE USED FOR HER BATTER.
THAT GAVE HER PANCAKES A DEEPER, MORE COMPLEX FLAVOR THAT, IN TURN, MADE THE SIMPLE SWEETNESS OF HER BROWN SUGAR BEAN PASTE STAND OUT EVEN MORE!
OH YEAH! YOU COULD DO THAT, COULDN'T YOU?!
BUT WHEN DID SHE EVEN HAVE TIME TO MAKE THE STUFF?
GOOD POINT. I DIDN'T SEE HER USE ANY SPECIAL UTENSILS OR ANYTHING...
I DIDN'T NEED ANY. ALL I USED WAS THIS.
SWF
WAIT, THAT'S-!

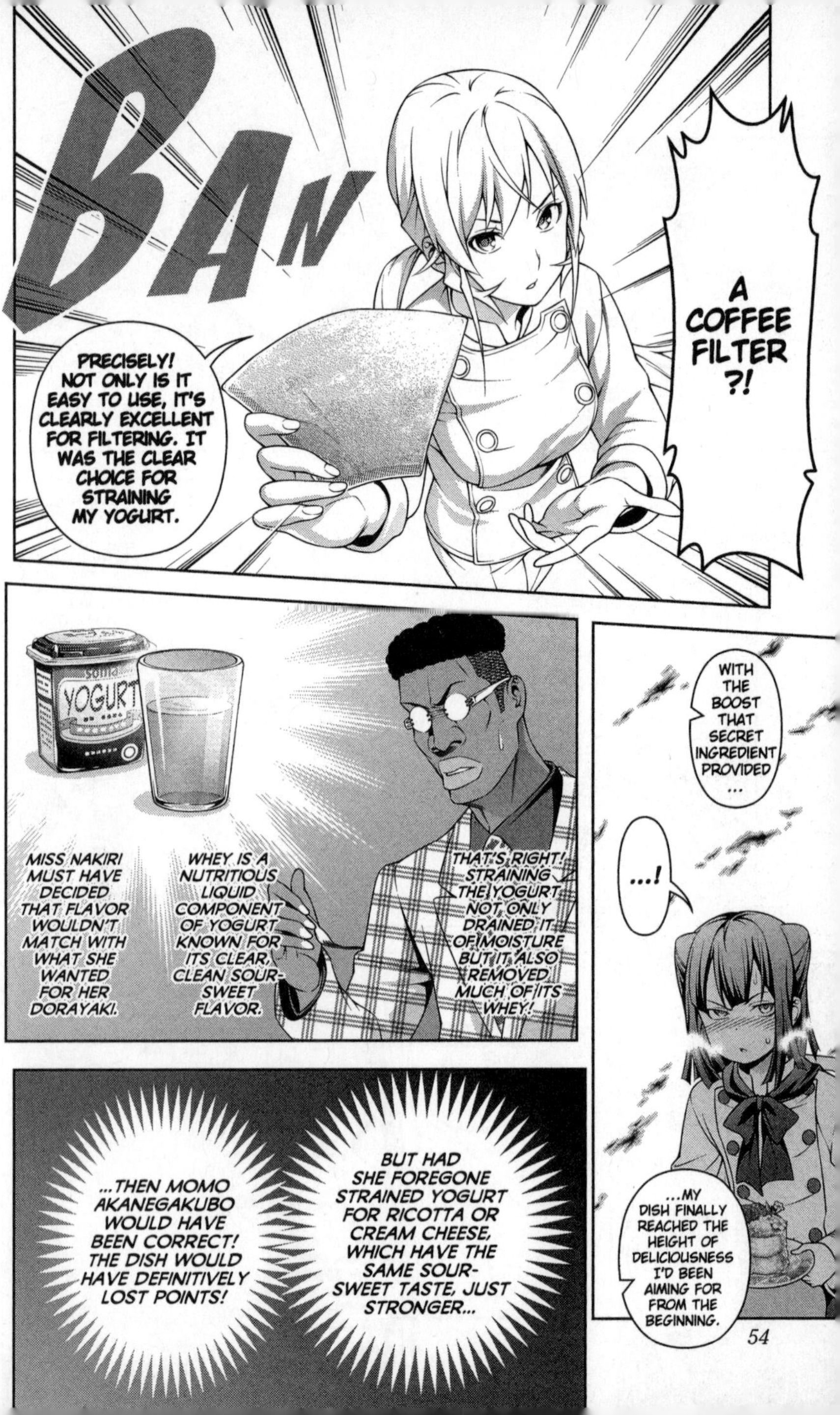
A COFFEE FILTER ?!
BAN
PRECISELY! NOT ONLY IS IT EASY TO USE, IT'S CLEARLY EXCELLENT FOR FILTERING. IT WAS THE CLEAR CHOICE FOR STRAINING MY YOGURT.
WITH THE BOOST THAT SECRET INGREDIENT PROVIDED ...
...!
...MY DISH FINALLY REACHED THE HEIGHT OF DELICIOUSNESS I'D BEEN AIMING FOR FROM THE BEGINNING.
YOGURT
THAT'S RIGHT! STRAINING THE YOGURT NOT ONLY DRAINED IT OF MOISTURE BUT IT ALSO REMOVED MUCH OF ITS WHEY!
WHEY IS A NUTRITIOUS LIQUID COMPONENT OF YOGURT KNOWN FOR ITS CLEAR, CLEAN SOUR-SWEET FLAVOR.
MISS NAKIRI MUST HAVE DECIDED THAT FLAVOR WOULDN'T MATCH WITH WHAT SHE WANTED FOR HER DORAYAKI.
BUT HAD SHE FOREGONE STRAINED YOGURT FOR RICOTTA OR CREAM CHEESE, WHICH HAVE THE SAME SOUR-SWEET TASTE, JUST STRONGER...
...THEN MOMO AKANEGAKUBO WOULD HAVE BEEN CORRECT! THE DISH WOULD HAVE DEFINITIVELY LOST POINTS!

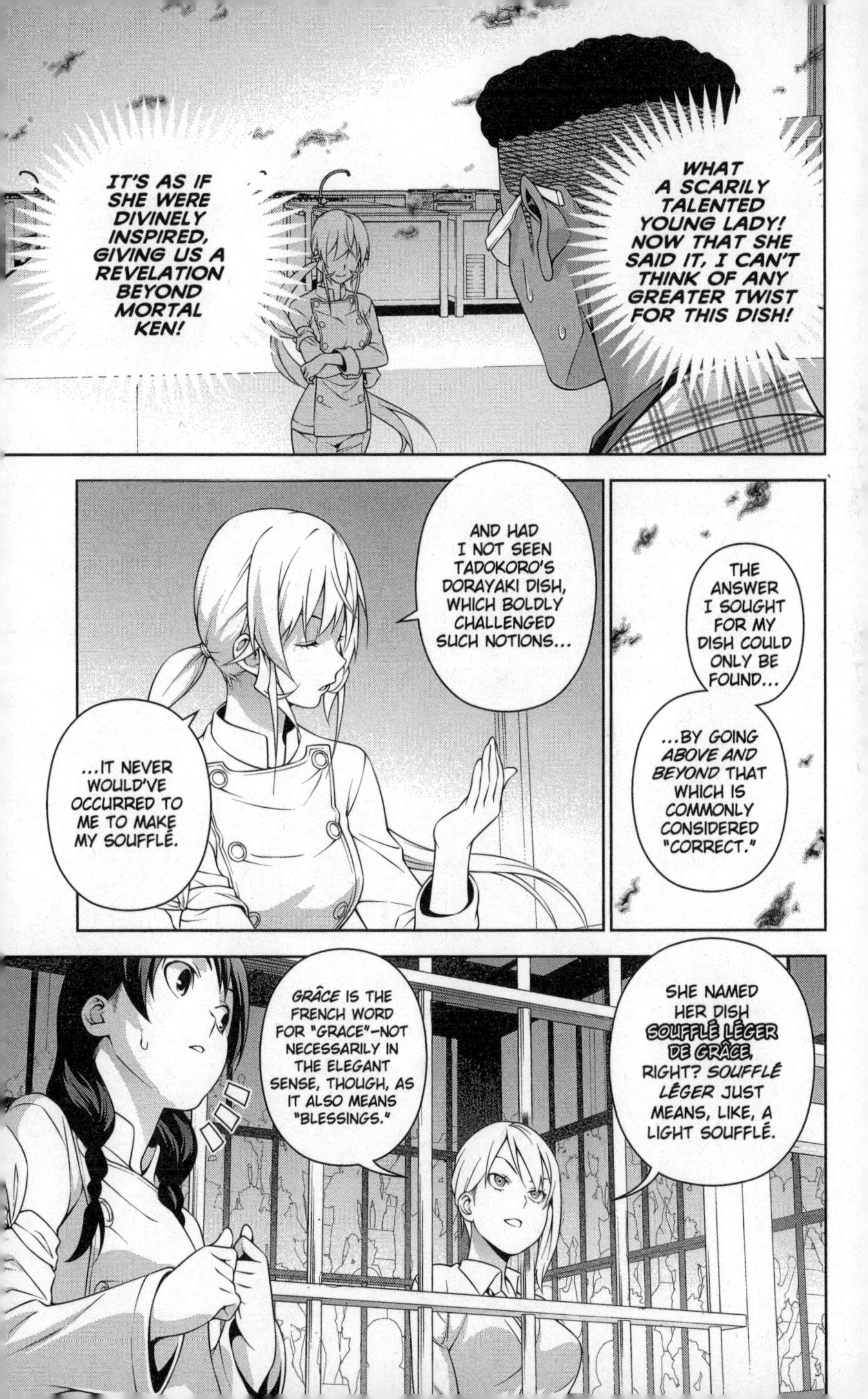
WHAT A SCARILY TALENTED YOUNG LADY! NOW THAT SHE SAID IT, I CAN'T THINK OF ANY GREATER TWIST FOR THIS DISH!
IT'S AS IF SHE WERE DIVINELY INSPIRED, GIVING US A REVELATION BEYOND MORTAL KEN!
THE ANSWER I SOUGHT FOR MY DISH COULD ONLY BE FOUND...
...BY GOING *ABOVE AND BEYOND* THAT WHICH IS COMMONLY CONSIDERED "CORRECT."
AND HAD I NOT SEEN TADOKORO'S DORAYAKI DISH, WHICH BOLDLY CHALLENGED SUCH NOTIONS...
...IT NEVER WOULD'VE OCCURRED TO ME TO MAKE MY SOUFFLÉ.
SHE NAMED HER DISH SOUFFLÉ LÉGER DE GRÂCE, RIGHT? *SOUFFLÉ LÉGER* JUST MEANS, LIKE, A LIGHT SOUFFLÉ.
GRÂCE IS THE FRENCH WORD FOR "GRACE"—NOT NECESSARILY IN THE ELEGANT SENSE, THOUGH, AS IT ALSO MEANS "BLESSINGS."

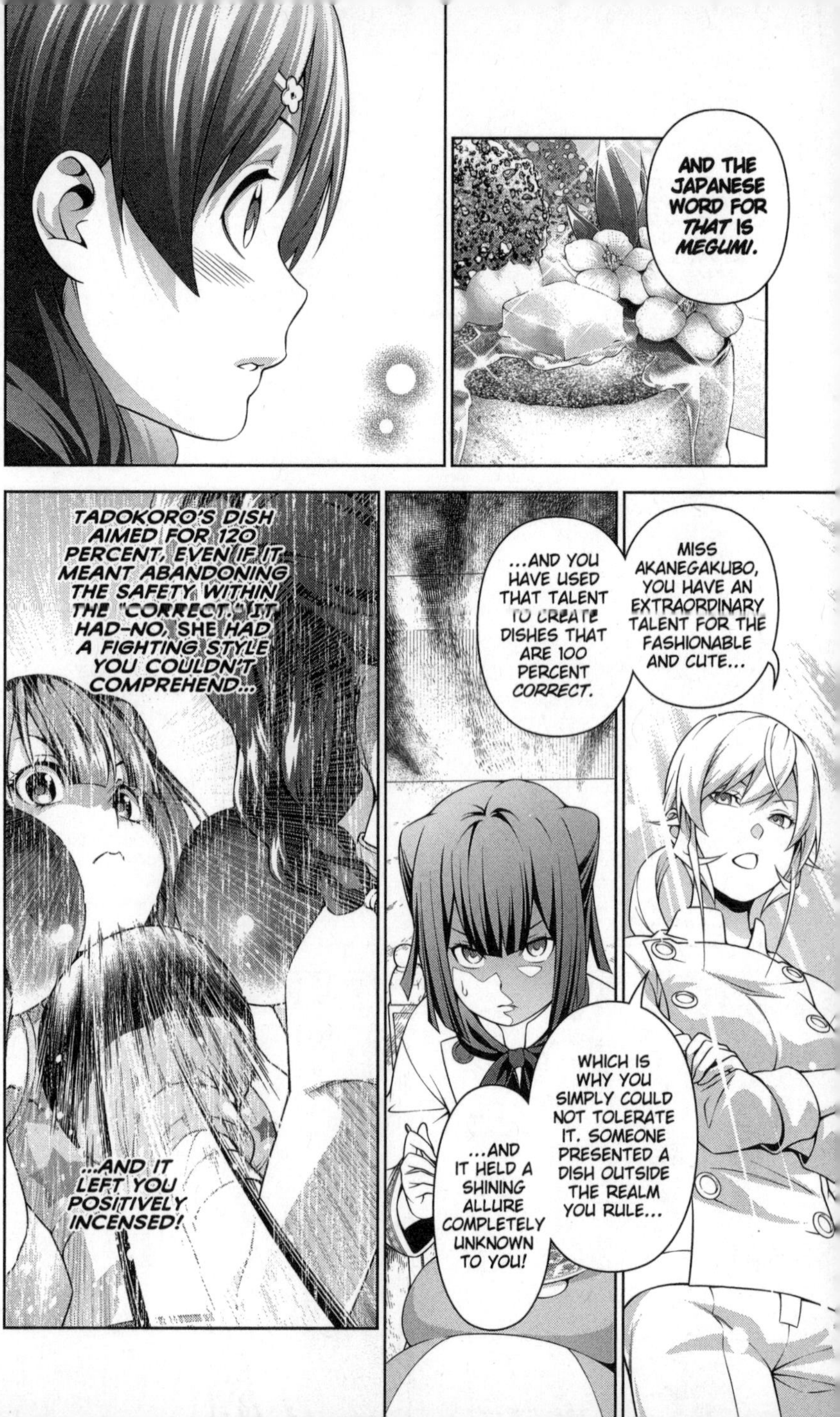
AND THE JAPANESE WORD FOR THAT IS MEGUMI.
MISS AKANEGAKUBO, YOU HAVE AN EXTRAORDINARY TALENT FOR THE FASHIONABLE AND CUTE...
...AND YOU HAVE USED THAT TALENT TO CREATE DISHES THAT ARE 100 PERCENT CORRECT.
TADOKORO'S DISH AIMED FOR 120 PERCENT, EVEN IF IT MEANT ABANDONING THE SAFETY WITHIN THE "CORRECT." IT HAD-NO, SHE HAD A FIGHTING STYLE YOU COULDN'T COMPREHEND...
WHICH IS WHY YOU SIMPLY COULD NOT TOLERATE IT. SOMEONE PRESENTED A DISH OUTSIDE THE REALM YOU RULE...
...AND IT HELD A SHINING ALLURE COMPLETELY UNKNOWN TO YOU!
...AND IT LEFT YOU POSITIVELY INCENSED!

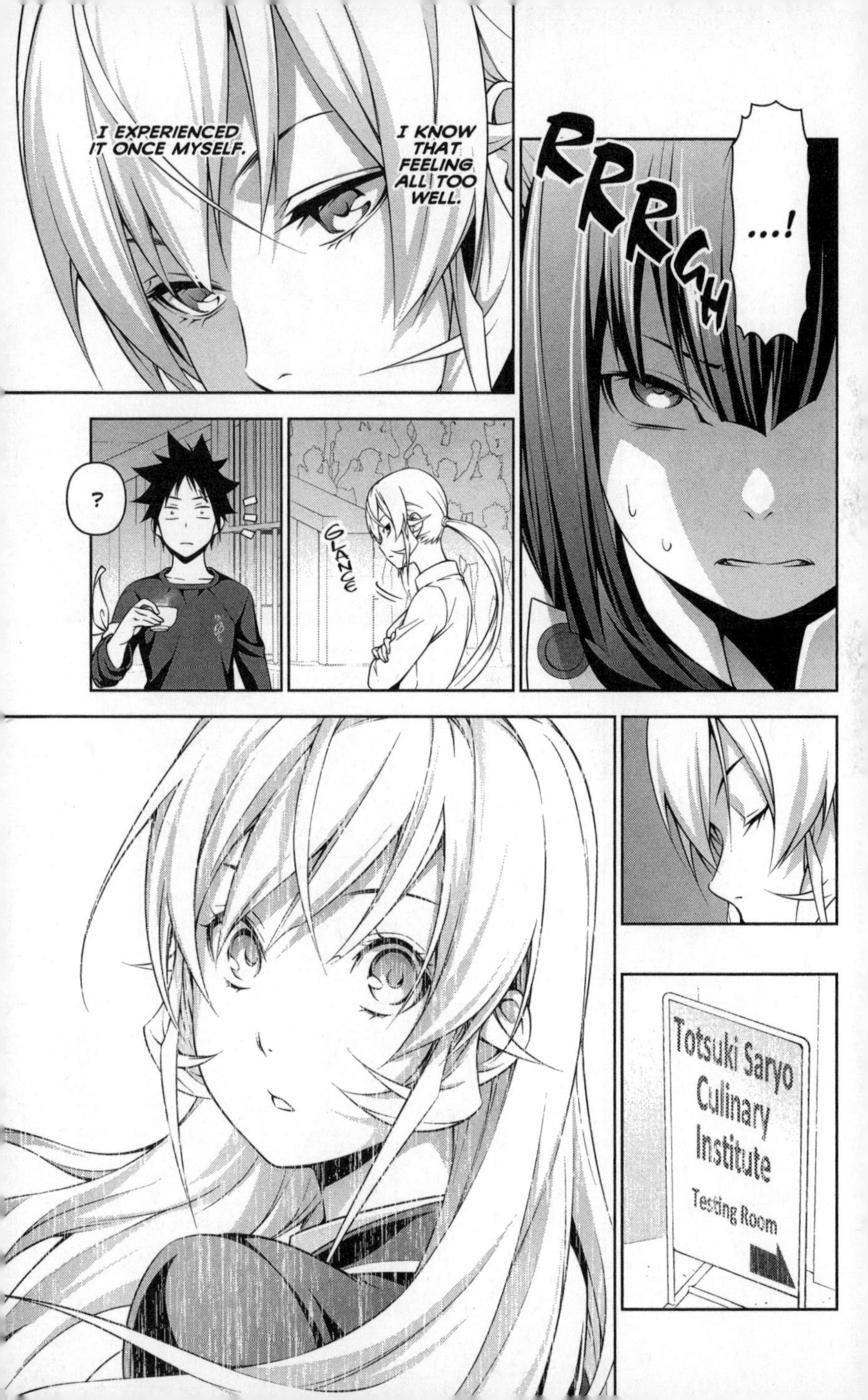
RRRGH
...!
I KNOW THAT FEELING ALL TOO WELL.
I EXPERIENCED IT ONCE MYSELF.
GLANCE
?
Totsuki Saryo Culinary Institute
Testing Room

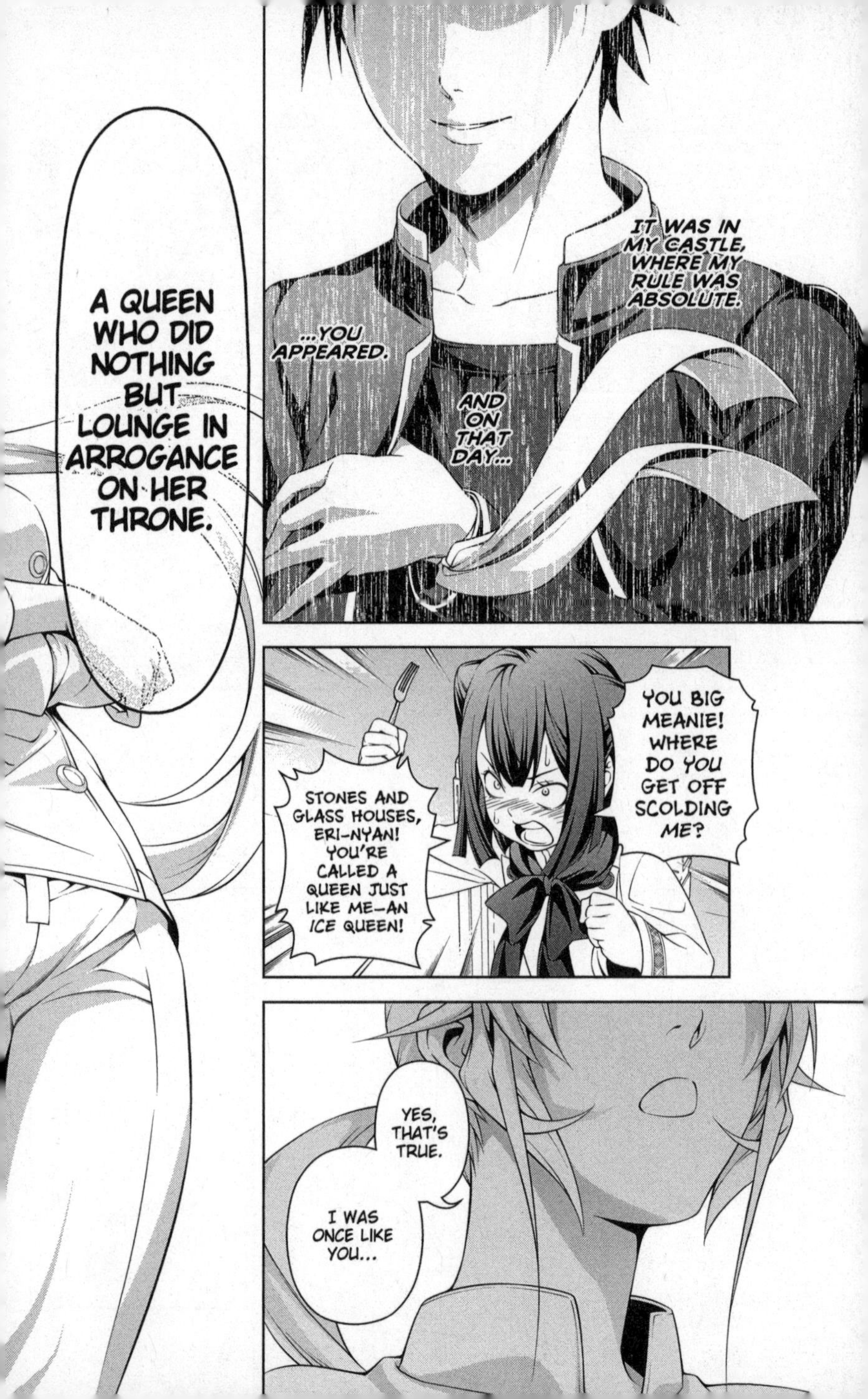
IT WAS IN MY CASTLE, WHERE MY RULE WAS ABSOLUTE.
AND ON THAT DAY...
...YOU APPEARED.
YOU BIG MEANIE! WHERE DO YOU GET OFF SCOLDING ME?
STONES AND GLASS HOUSES, ERI-NYAN! YOU'RE CALLED A QUEEN JUST LIKE ME—AN ICE QUEEN!
YES, THAT'S TRUE.
I WAS ONCE LIKE YOU...
A QUEEN WHO DID NOTHING BUT LOUNGE IN ARROGANCE ON HER THRONE.

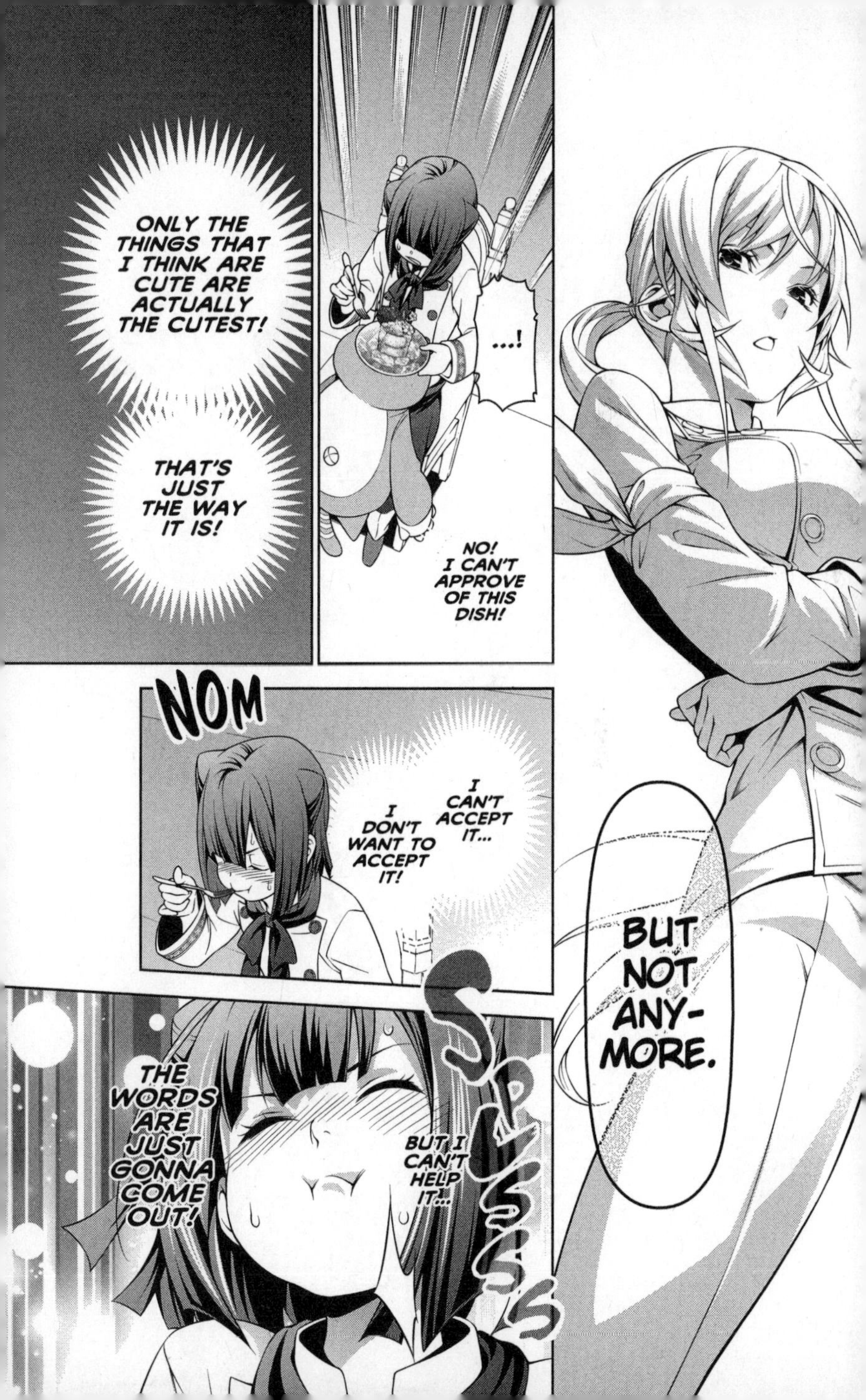
BUT NOT ANY-MORE.
...!
NO! I CAN'T APPROVE OF THIS DISH!
ONLY THE THINGS THAT I THINK ARE CUTE ARE ACTUALLY THE CUTEST!
THAT'S JUST THE WAY IT IS!
NOM
I CAN'T ACCEPT IT...
I DON'T WANT TO ACCEPT IT!
BUT I CAN'T HELP IT...
THE WORDS ARE JUST GONNA COME OUT!

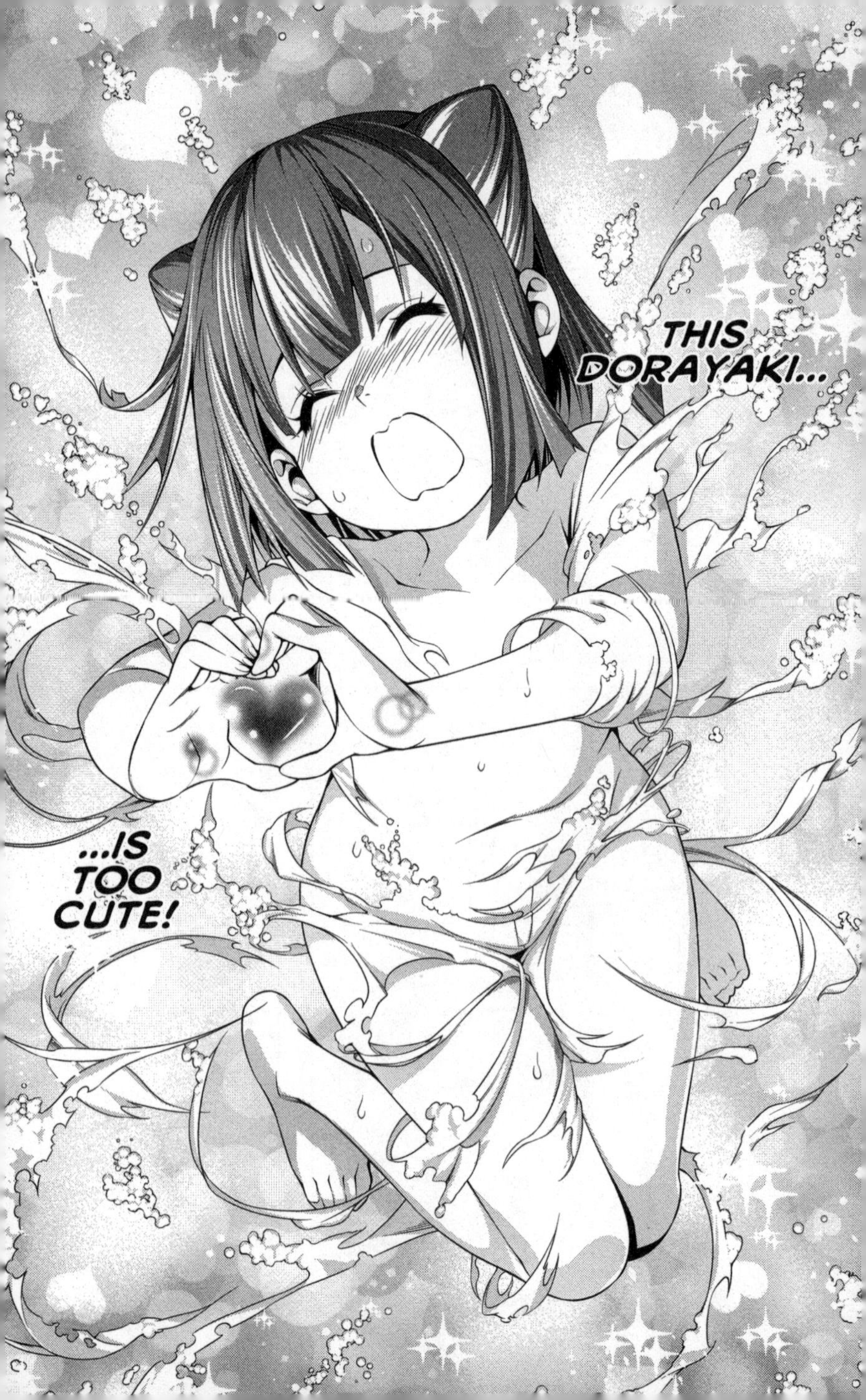
THIS DORAYAKI...
...IS TOO CUTE!

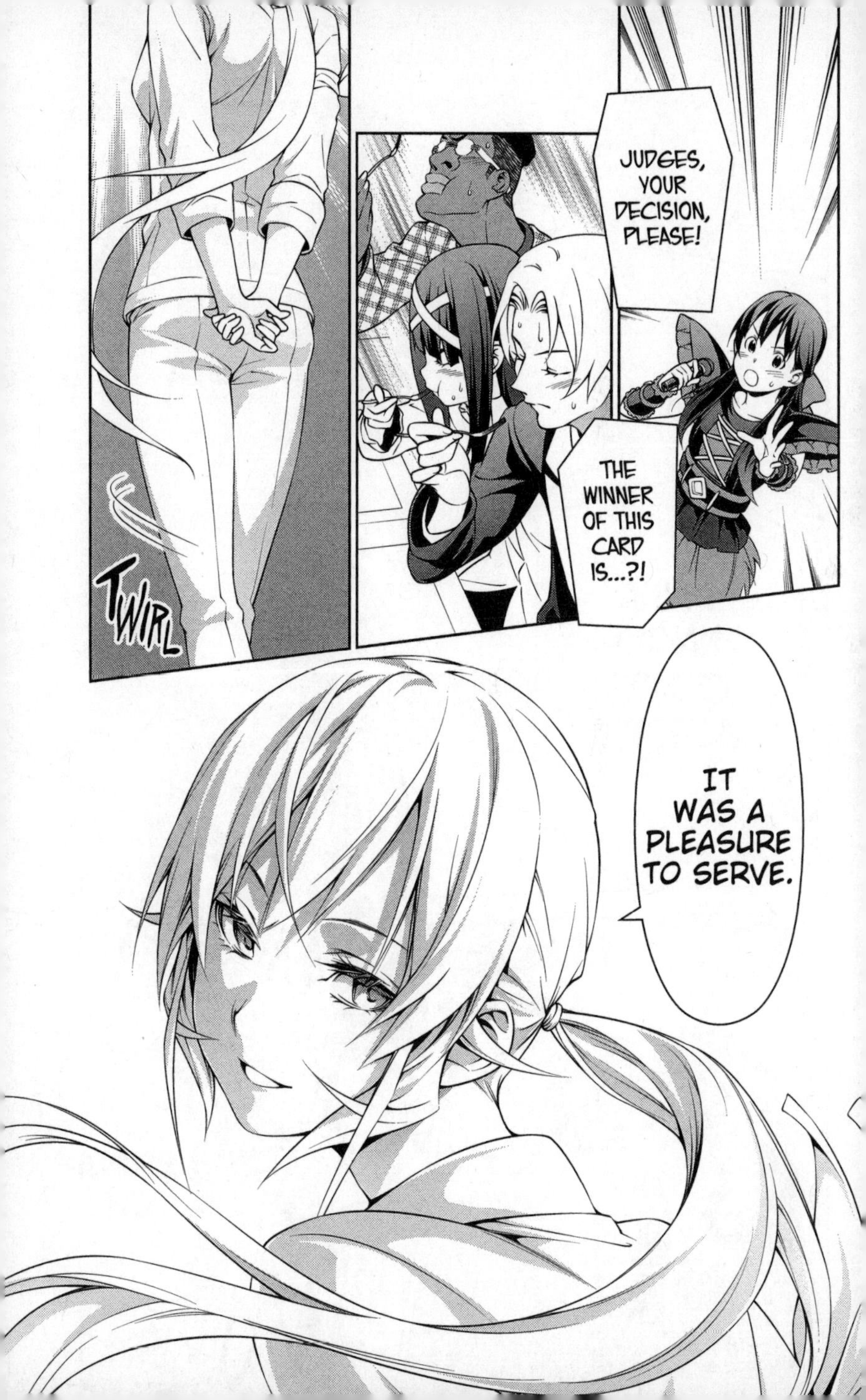
JUDGES, YOUR DECISION, PLEASE!
THE WINNER OF THIS CARD IS...?!
TWIRL
IT WAS A PLEASURE TO SERVE.

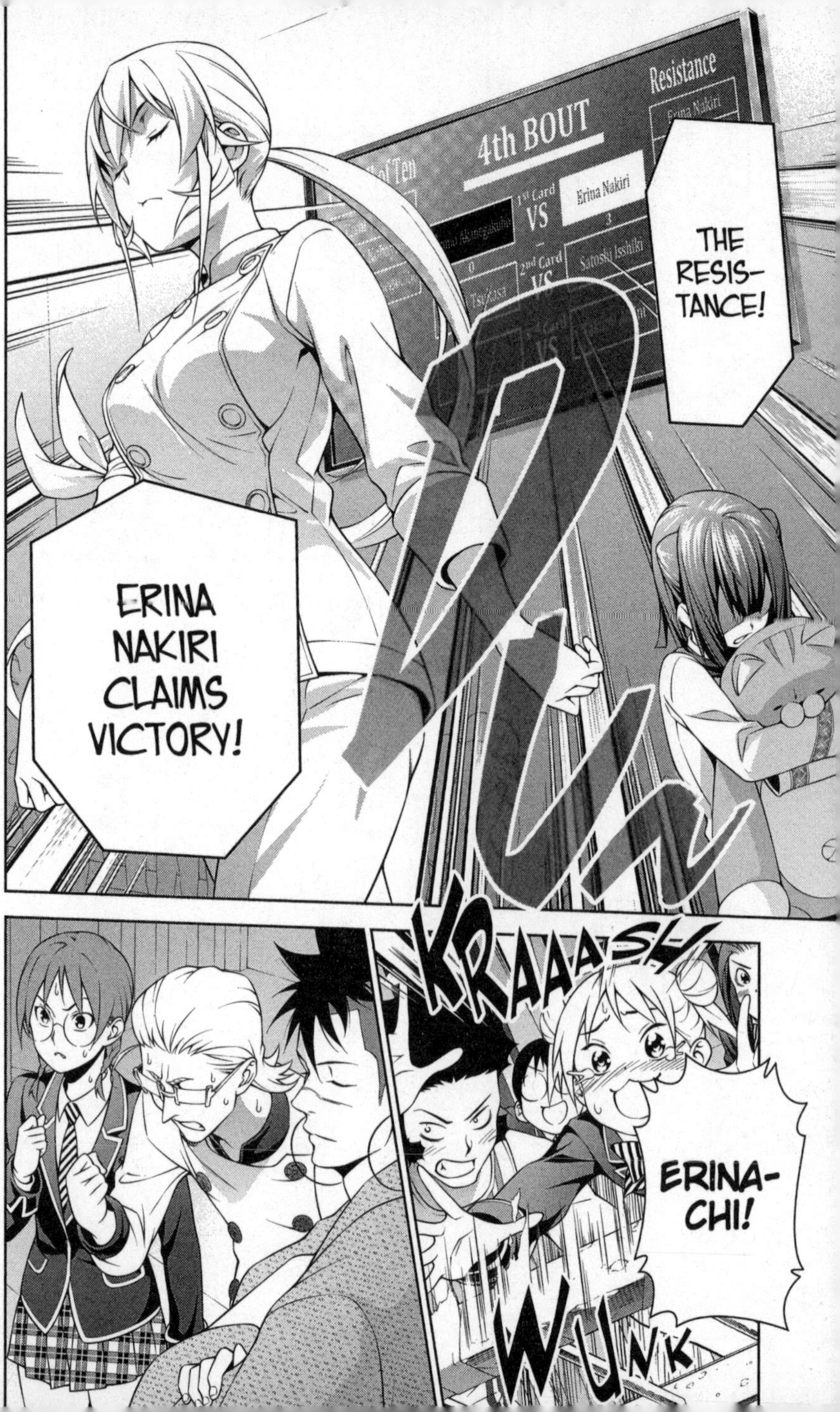
Resistance
4th BOUT
Erina Nakiri
VS
THE RESISTANCE!
ERINA NAKIRI CLAIMS VICTORY!
KRAAASH
ERINA-CHI!
WUNK

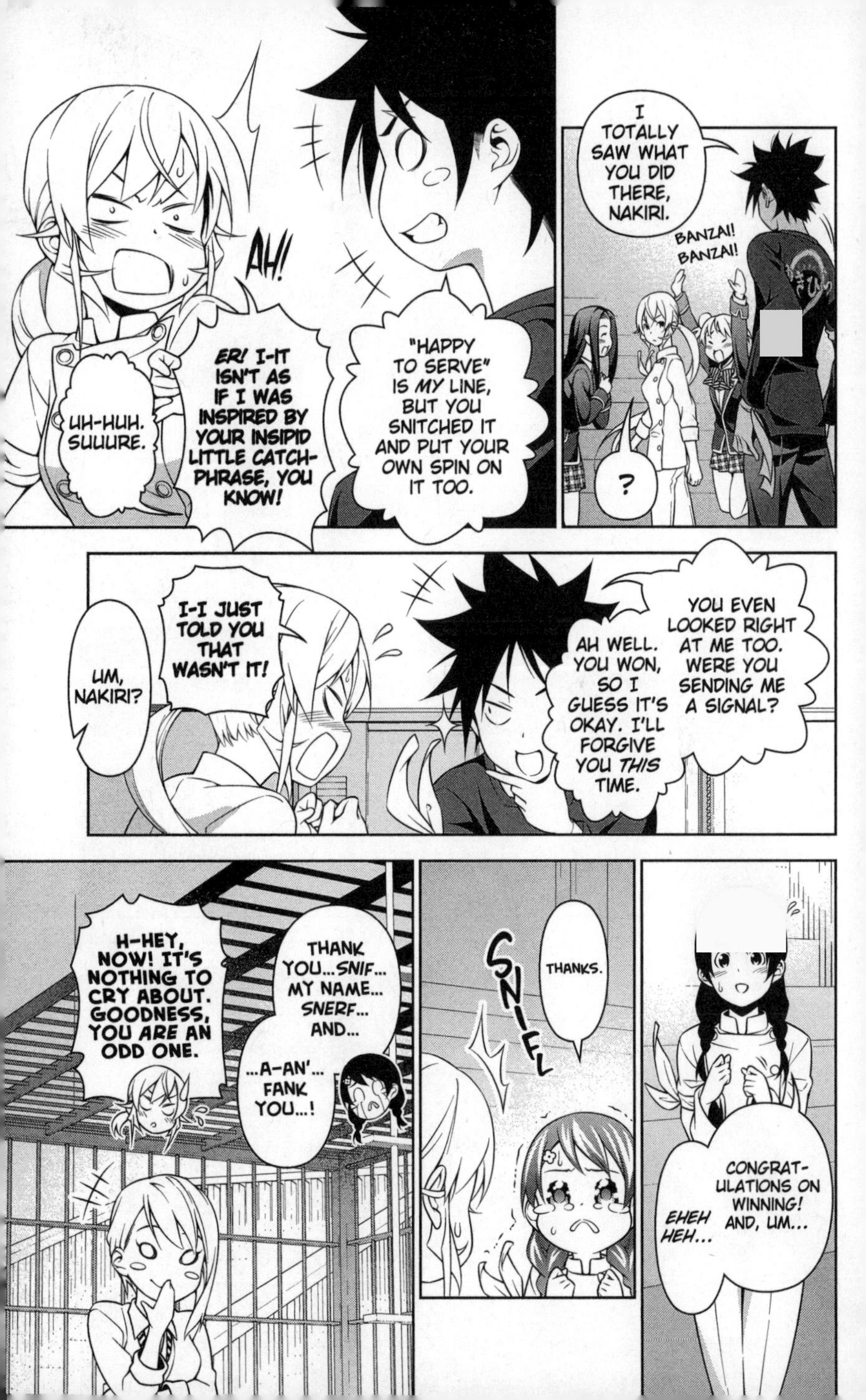
I TOTALLY SAW WHAT YOU DID THERE, NAKIRI.
BANZAI! BANZAI!
?
AH!
"HAPPY TO SERVE" IS MY LINE, BUT YOU SNITCHED IT AND PUT YOUR OWN SPIN ON IT TOO.
ER! I-IT ISN'T AS IF I WAS INSPIRED BY YOUR INSIPID LITTLE CATCH-PHRASE, YOU KNOW!
UH-HUH. SUUURE.
YOU EVEN LOOKED RIGHT AT ME TOO. WERE YOU SENDING ME A SIGNAL?
AH WELL. YOU WON, SO I GUESS IT'S OKAY. I'LL FORGIVE YOU THIS TIME.
I-I JUST TOLD YOU THAT WASN'T IT!
UM, NAKIRI?
CONGRAT-ULATIONS ON WINNING! AND, UM...
EHEH HEH...
SNIFL
THANKS.
THANK YOU...SNIF... MY NAME... SNERF... AND...
...A-AN'... FANK YOU...!
H-HEY, NOW! IT'S NOTHING TO CRY ABOUT. GOODNESS, YOU ARE AN ODD ONE.

HOW WILL THE OTHER TWO CARDS PLAY OUT?

NOW...

LOSE VS WIN

?

RIGHT!

WE'VE SECURED ONE CRITICAL VICTORY.

ANY-WAY...

Council of Ten	4th BOUT		Resistance
Tsukasa	Momo Akanegakubo	1st Card VS	Erina Nakiri
Kobayashi	0		Satoshi Isshiki
Akanegakubo	Eishi Tsukasa	2nd Card VS	Soma Yuk
			Takumi
Rindo Kobayashi	3rd Card VS	Satoshi Isshiki	

Council of Ten	4th BOUT		Resistance
			Erina Nakiri
	Momo Akanegakubo	1st Card VS	Satoshi Isshiki
	0	Erina Nakiri	Soma Yuk
		3	Takumi
	Eishi Tsukasa	2nd Card VS	Satoshi Isshiki
	Rindo Kobayashi	3rd Card VS	Takumi Aldini

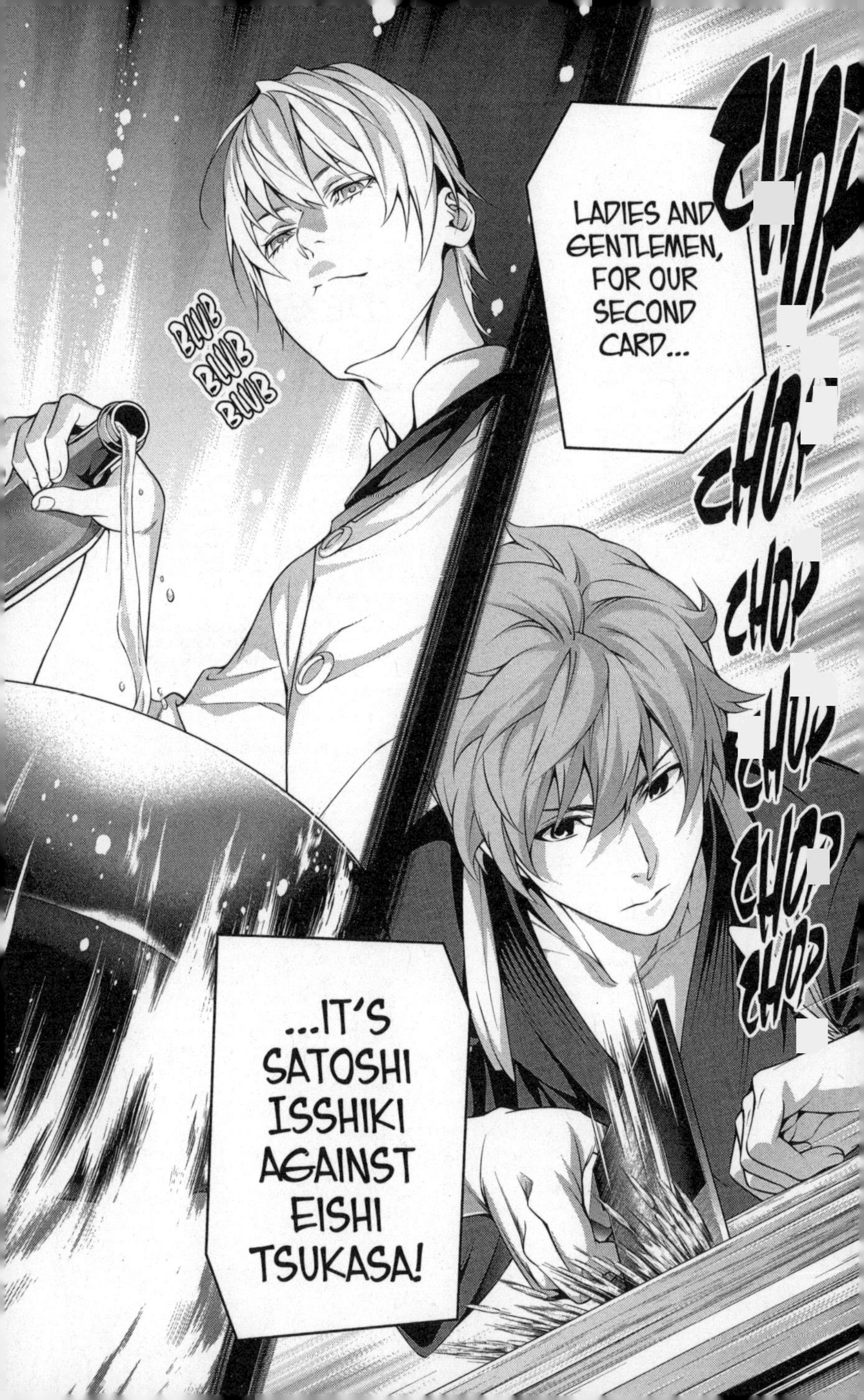
CHOP
CHOP
CHOP
CHOP
CHOP
CHOP
LADIES AND GENTLEMEN, FOR OUR SECOND CARD...
BLUB BLUB BLUB
...IT'S SATOSHI ISSHIKI AGAINST EISHI TSUKASA!

ARTIST: YUTO TSUKUDA RECIPE BY: YUKI MORISAKI

VOLUME 29 SPECIAL SUPPLEMENT!

PRACTICAL RECIPE #2

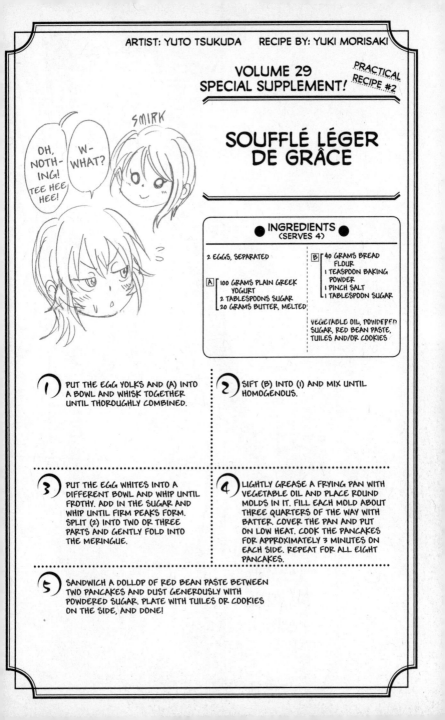

SMIRK
OH, NOTHING! TEE HEE HEE!
W-WHAT?

SOUFFLÉ LÉGER DE GRÂCE

INGREDIENTS
(SERVES 4)

2 EGGS, SEPARATED

A
- 100 GRAMS PLAIN GREEK YOGURT
- 2 TABLESPOONS SUGAR
- 20 GRAMS BUTTER, MELTED

B
- 40 GRAMS BREAD FLOUR
- 1 TEASPOON BAKING POWDER
- 1 PINCH SALT
- 1 TABLESPOON SUGAR

VEGETABLE OIL, POWDERED SUGAR, RED BEAN PASTE, TUILES AND/OR COOKIES

1. PUT THE EGG YOLKS AND (A) INTO A BOWL AND WHISK TOGETHER UNTIL THOROUGHLY COMBINED.

2. SIFT (B) INTO (1) AND MIX UNTIL HOMOGENOUS.

3. PUT THE EGG WHITES INTO A DIFFERENT BOWL AND WHIP UNTIL FROTHY. ADD IN THE SUGAR AND WHIP UNTIL FIRM PEAKS FORM. SPLIT (2) INTO TWO OR THREE PARTS AND GENTLY FOLD INTO THE MERINGUE.

4. LIGHTLY GREASE A FRYING PAN WITH VEGETABLE OIL AND PLACE ROUND MOLDS IN IT. FILL EACH MOLD ABOUT THREE QUARTERS OF THE WAY WITH BATTER. COVER THE PAN AND PUT ON LOW HEAT. COOK THE PANCAKES FOR APPROXIMATELY 3 MINUTES ON EACH SIDE. REPEAT FOR ALL EIGHT PANCAKES.

5. SANDWICH A DOLLOP OF RED BEAN PASTE BETWEEN TWO PANCAKES AND DUST GENEROUSLY WITH POWDERED SUGAR. PLATE WITH TUILES OR COOKIES ON THE SIDE, AND DONE!

#248 WHAT THE AVERAGE FEEL

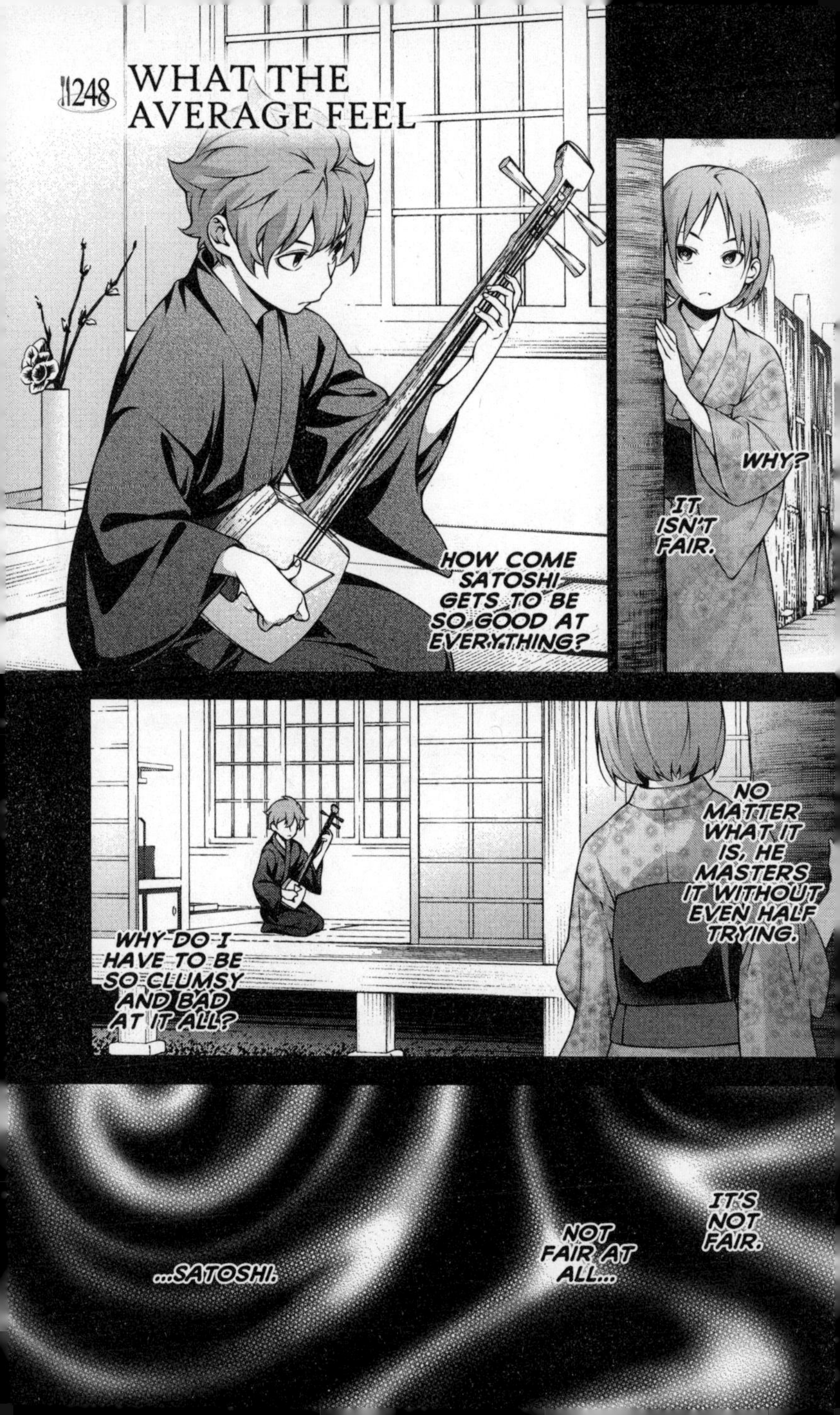
WHY?
IT ISN'T FAIR.
HOW COME SATOSHI GETS TO BE SO GOOD AT EVERYTHING?
NO MATTER WHAT IT IS, HE MASTERS IT WITHOUT EVEN HALF TRYING.
WHY DO I HAVE TO BE SO CLUMSY AND BAD AT IT ALL?
IT'S NOT FAIR.
NOT FAIR AT ALL...
...SATOSHI.

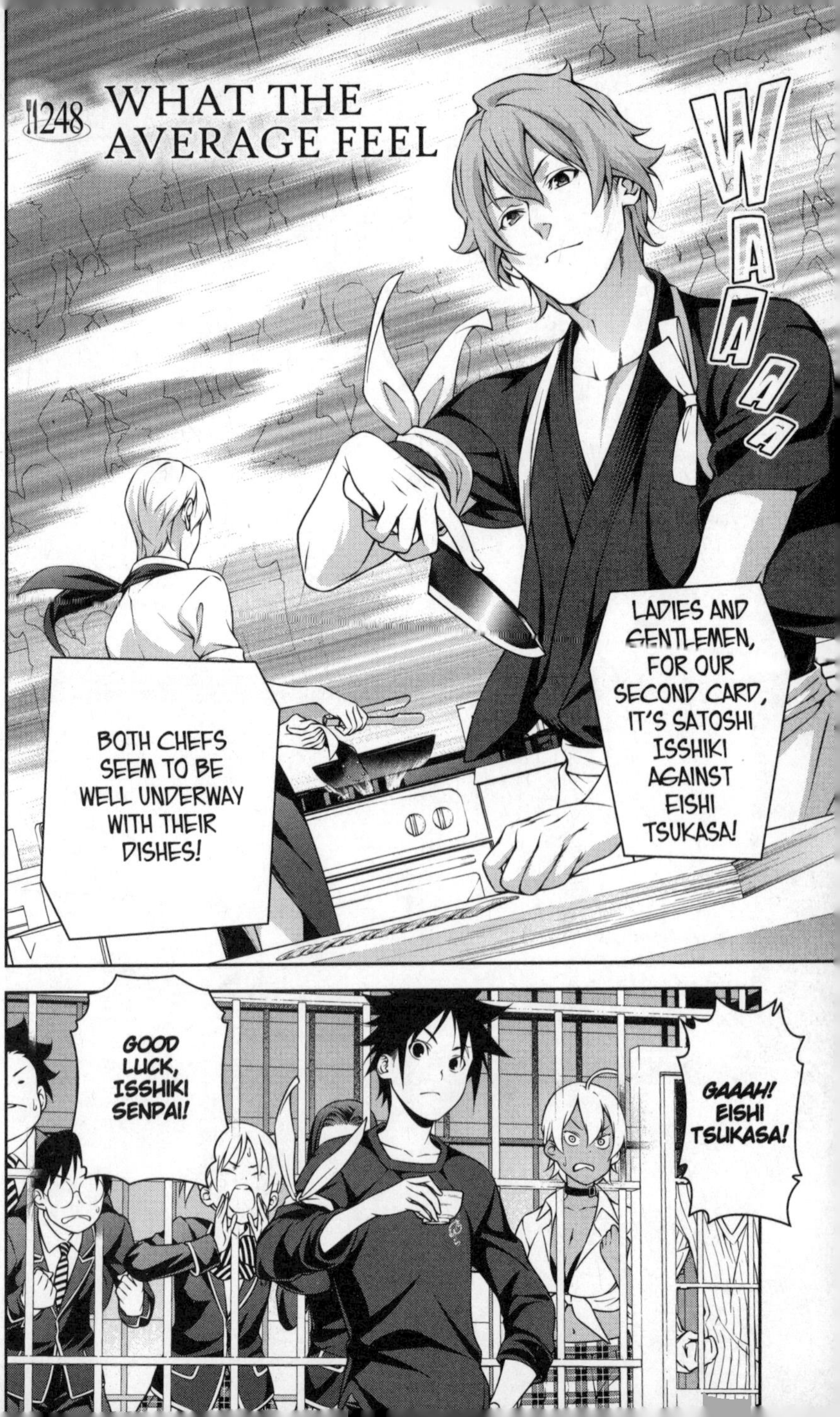
248 WHAT THE AVERAGE FEEL
WAAAAA
LADIES AND GENTLEMEN, FOR OUR SECOND CARD, IT'S SATOSHI ISSHIKI AGAINST EISHI TSUKASA!
BOTH CHEFS SEEM TO BE WELL UNDERWAY WITH THEIR DISHES!
GAAAH! EISHI TSUKASA!
GOOD LUCK, ISSHIKI SENPAI!

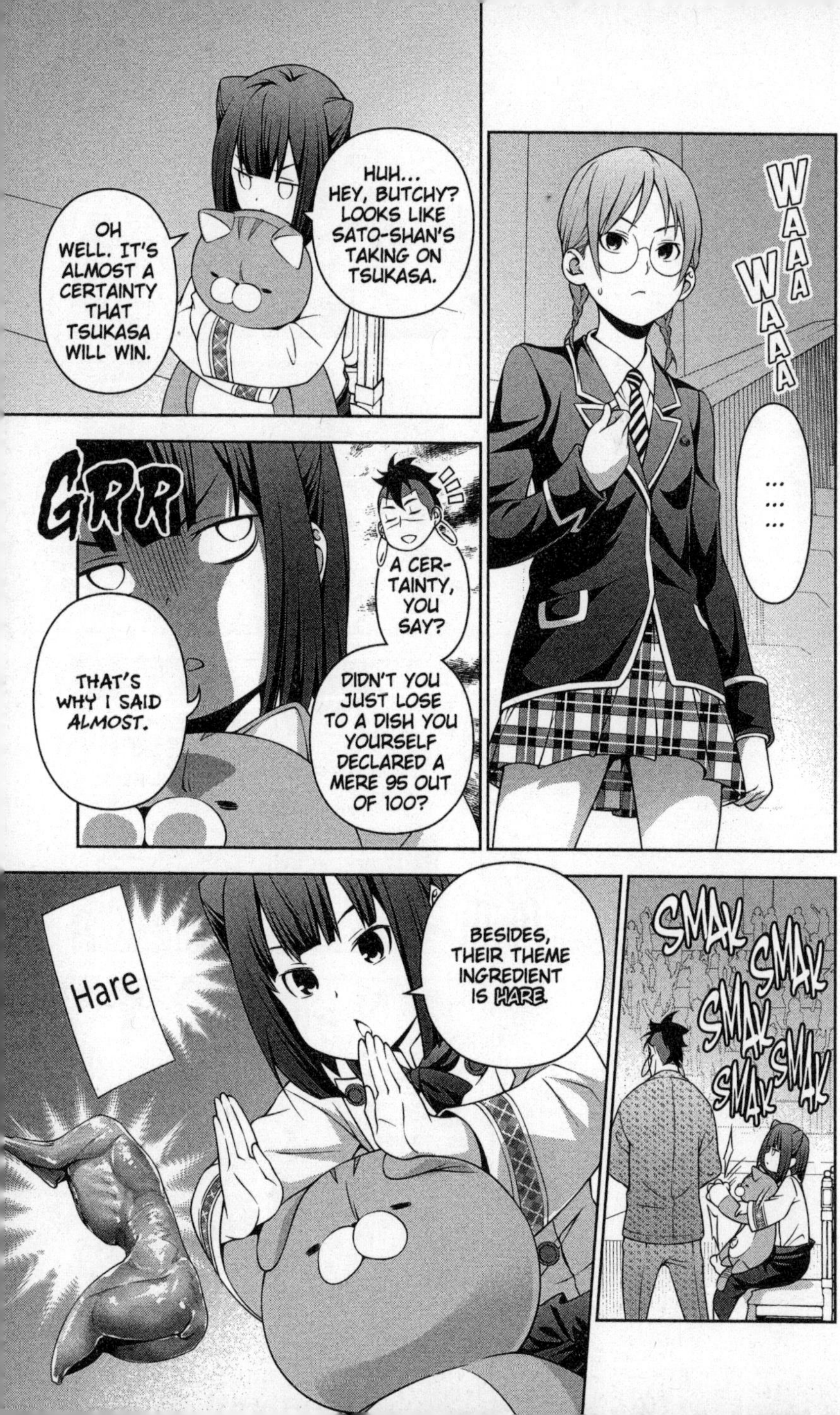
WAAAA WAAAA
......
HUH... HEY, BUTCHY? LOOKS LIKE SATO-SHAN'S TAKING ON TSUKASA.
OH WELL. IT'S ALMOST A CERTAINTY THAT TSUKASA WILL WIN.
A CERTAINTY, YOU SAY?
DIDN'T YOU JUST LOSE TO A DISH YOU YOURSELF DECLARED A MERE 95 OUT OF 100?
GRR
THAT'S WHY I SAID *ALMOST*.
SMAK SMAK SMAK SMAK SMAK SMAK
BESIDES, THEIR THEME INGREDIENT IS HARE.
Hare

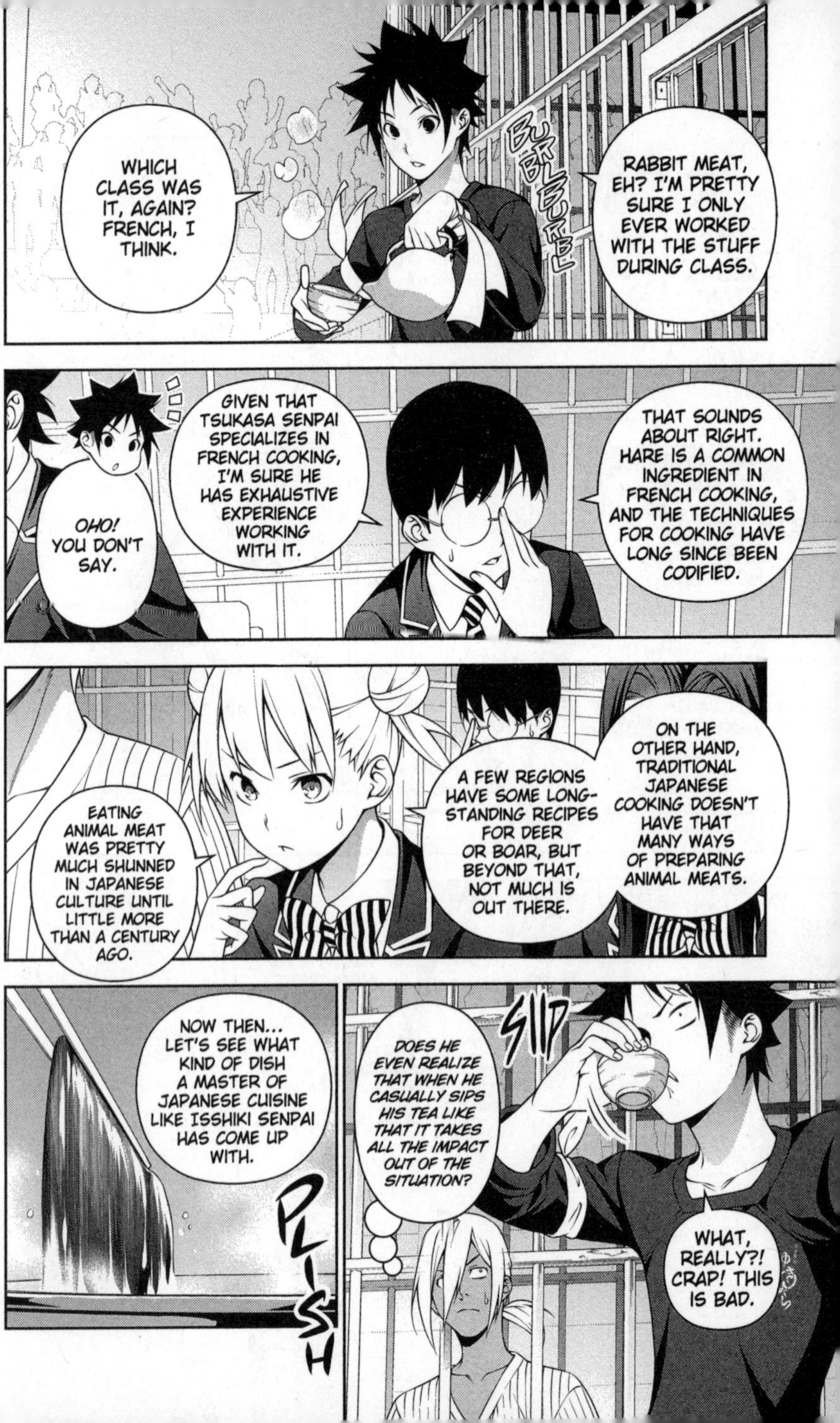
RABBIT MEAT, EH? I'M PRETTY SURE I ONLY EVER WORKED WITH THE STUFF DURING CLASS.
WHICH CLASS WAS IT, AGAIN? FRENCH, I THINK.
THAT SOUNDS ABOUT RIGHT. HARE IS A COMMON INGREDIENT IN FRENCH COOKING, AND THE TECHNIQUES FOR COOKING HAVE LONG SINCE BEEN CODIFIED.
GIVEN THAT TSUKASA SENPAI SPECIALIZES IN FRENCH COOKING, I'M SURE HE HAS EXHAUSTIVE EXPERIENCE WORKING WITH IT.
OHO! YOU DON'T SAY.
ON THE OTHER HAND, TRADITIONAL JAPANESE COOKING DOESN'T HAVE THAT MANY WAYS OF PREPARING ANIMAL MEATS.
A FEW REGIONS HAVE SOME LONG-STANDING RECIPES FOR DEER OR BOAR, BUT BEYOND THAT, NOT MUCH IS OUT THERE.
EATING ANIMAL MEAT WAS PRETTY MUCH SHUNNED IN JAPANESE CULTURE UNTIL LITTLE MORE THAN A CENTURY AGO.
SIP
DOES HE EVEN REALIZE THAT WHEN HE CASUALLY SIPS HIS TEA LIKE THAT IT TAKES ALL THE IMPACT OUT OF THE SITUATION?
WHAT, REALLY?! CRAP! THIS IS BAD.
NOW THEN... LET'S SEE WHAT KIND OF DISH A MASTER OF JAPANESE CUISINE LIKE ISSHIKI SENPAI HAS COME UP WITH.
PLISH

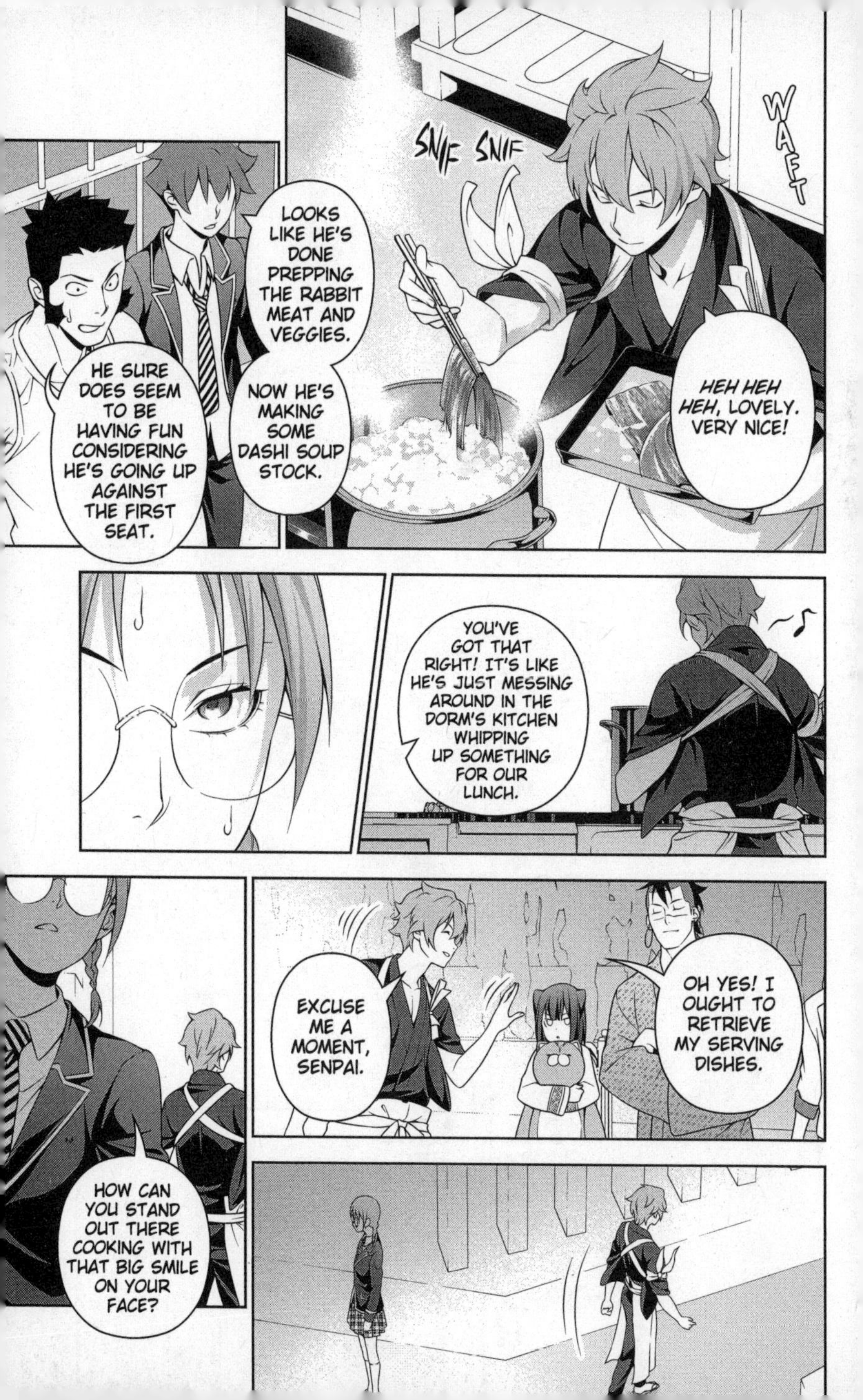
WAFT
SNIF SNIF
HEH HEH HEH, LOVELY. VERY NICE!
LOOKS LIKE HE'S DONE PREPPING THE RABBIT MEAT AND VEGGIES.
NOW HE'S MAKING SOME DASHI SOUP STOCK.
HE SURE DOES SEEM TO BE HAVING FUN CONSIDERING HE'S GOING UP AGAINST THE FIRST SEAT.
YOU'VE GOT THAT RIGHT! IT'S LIKE HE'S JUST MESSING AROUND IN THE DORM'S KITCHEN WHIPPING UP SOMETHING FOR OUR LUNCH.
OH YES! I OUGHT TO RETRIEVE MY SERVING DISHES.
EXCUSE ME A MOMENT, SENPAI.
HOW CAN YOU STAND OUT THERE COOKING WITH THAT BIG SMILE ON YOUR FACE?

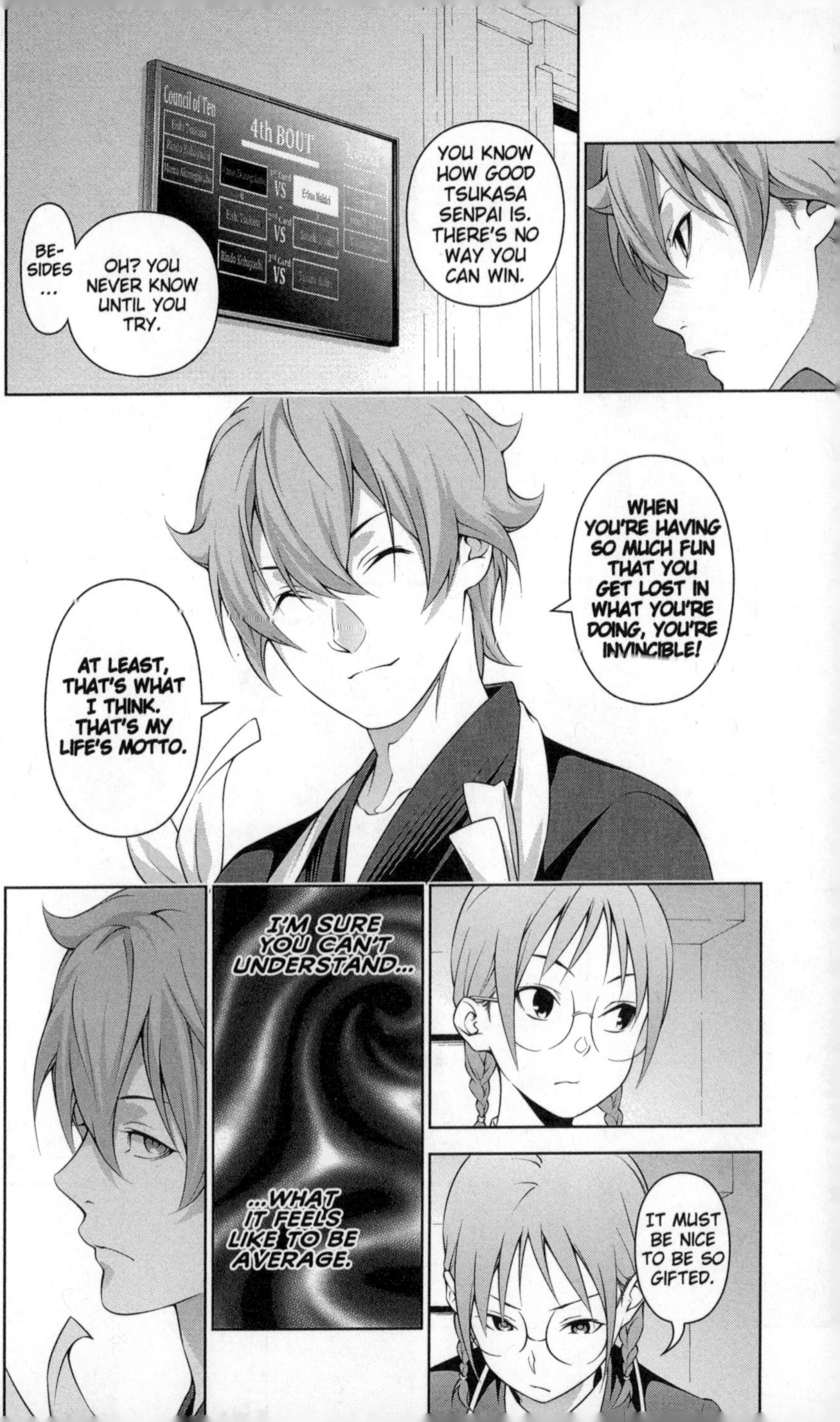
Council of Ten
4th BOUT
VS
VS
VS
YOU KNOW HOW GOOD TSUKASA SENPAI IS. THERE'S NO WAY YOU CAN WIN.
OH? YOU NEVER KNOW UNTIL YOU TRY.
BE-SIDES...
WHEN YOU'RE HAVING SO MUCH FUN THAT YOU GET LOST IN WHAT YOU'RE DOING, YOU'RE INVINCIBLE!
AT LEAST, THAT'S WHAT I THINK. THAT'S MY LIFE'S MOTTO.
IT MUST BE NICE TO BE SO GIFTED.
I'M SURE YOU CAN'T UNDERSTAND...
...WHAT IT FEELS LIKE TO BE AVERAGE.

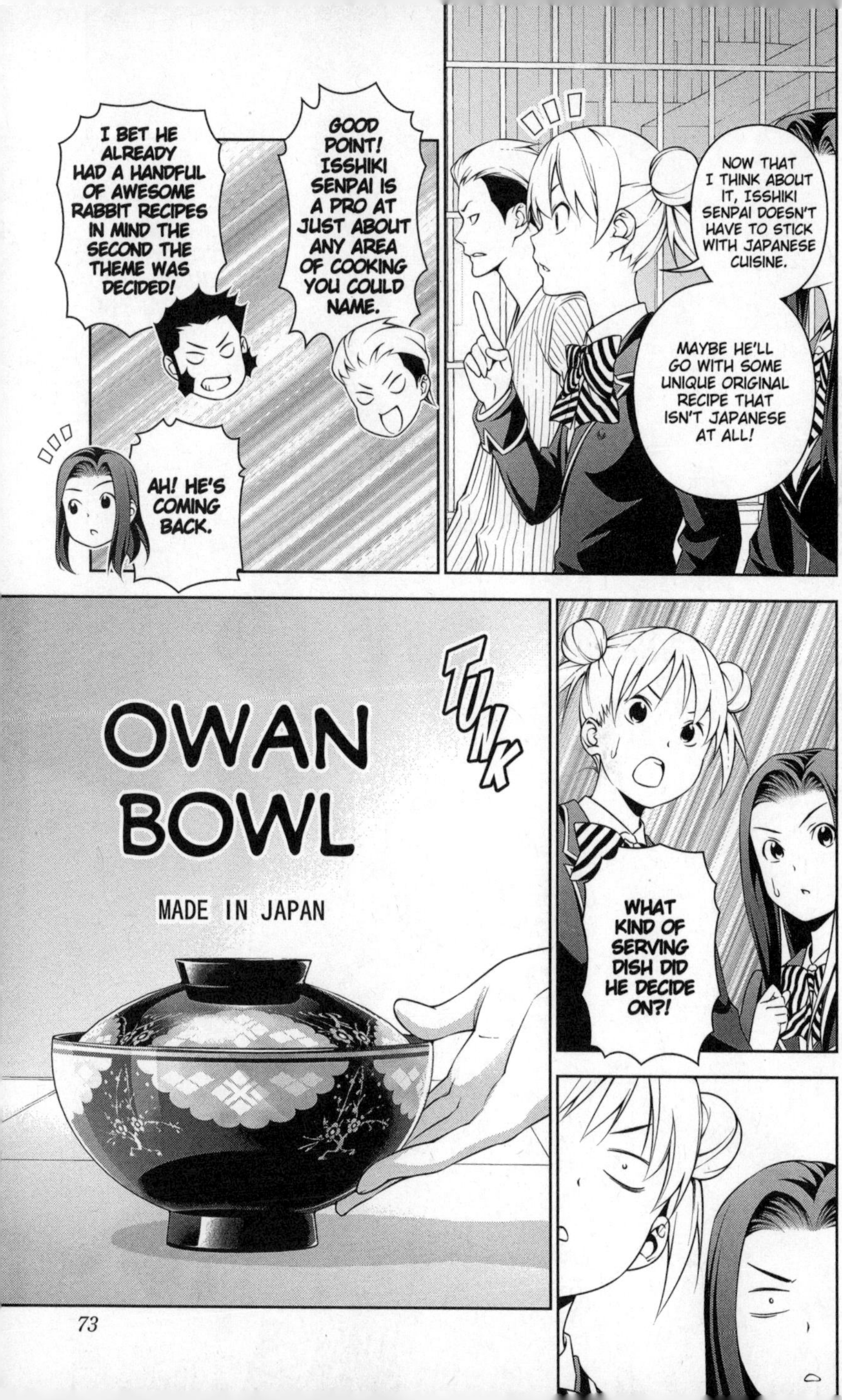
NOW THAT I THINK ABOUT IT, ISSHIKI SENPAI DOESN'T HAVE TO STICK WITH JAPANESE CUISINE.
MAYBE HE'LL GO WITH SOME UNIQUE ORIGINAL RECIPE THAT ISN'T JAPANESE AT ALL!
GOOD POINT! ISSHIKI SENPAI IS A PRO AT JUST ABOUT ANY AREA OF COOKING YOU COULD NAME.
I BET HE ALREADY HAD A HANDFUL OF AWESOME RABBIT RECIPES IN MIND THE SECOND THE THEME WAS DECIDED!
AH! HE'S COMING BACK.
WHAT KIND OF SERVING DISH DID HE DECIDE ON?!
TUNK
OWAN BOWL
MADE IN JAPAN

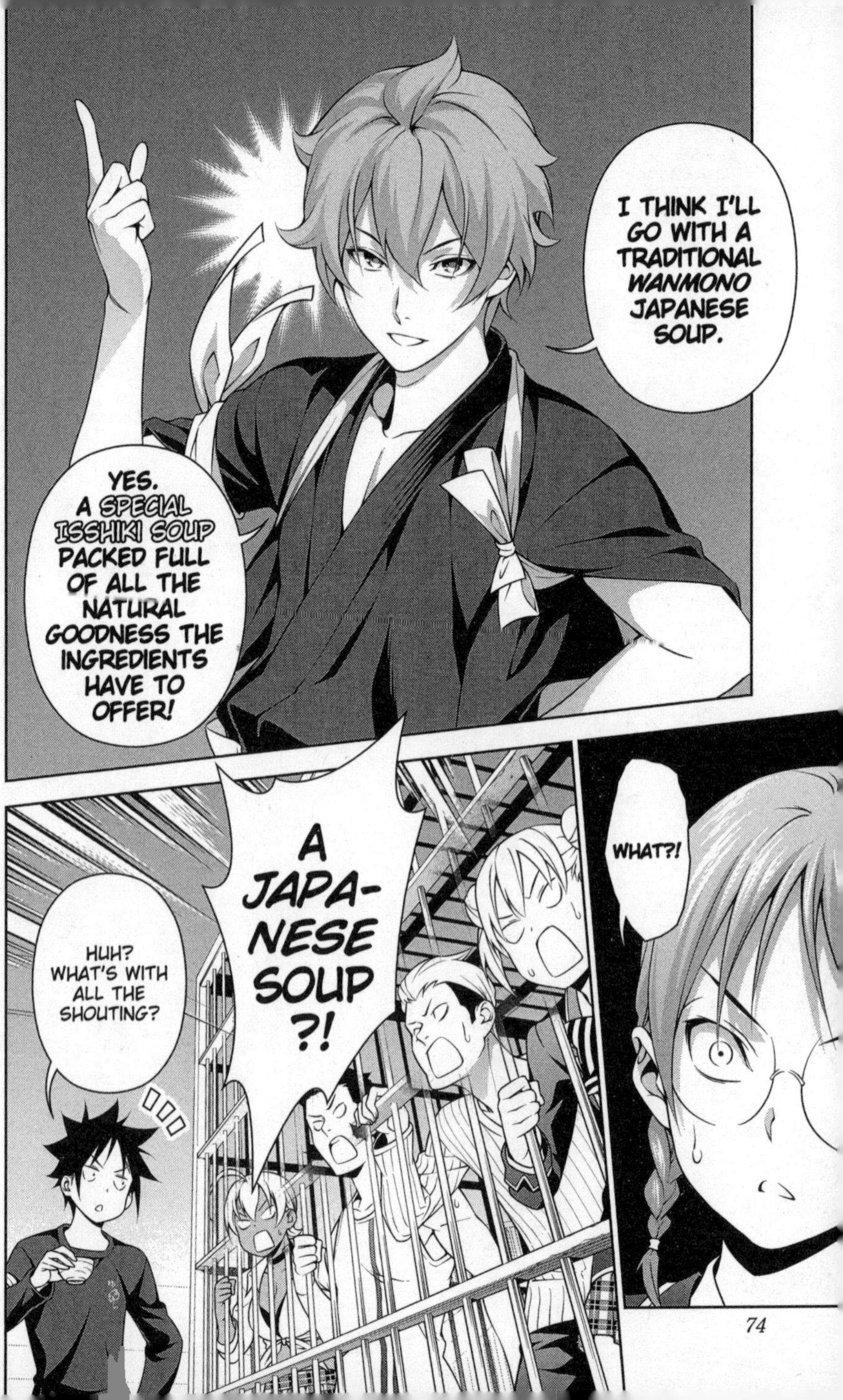
I THINK I'LL GO WITH A TRADITIONAL *WANMONO* JAPANESE SOUP.
YES. A SPECIAL ISSHIKI SOUP PACKED FULL OF ALL THE NATURAL GOODNESS THE INGREDIENTS HAVE TO OFFER!
WHAT?!
A JAPA-NESE SOUP ?!
HUH? WHAT'S WITH ALL THE SHOUTING?

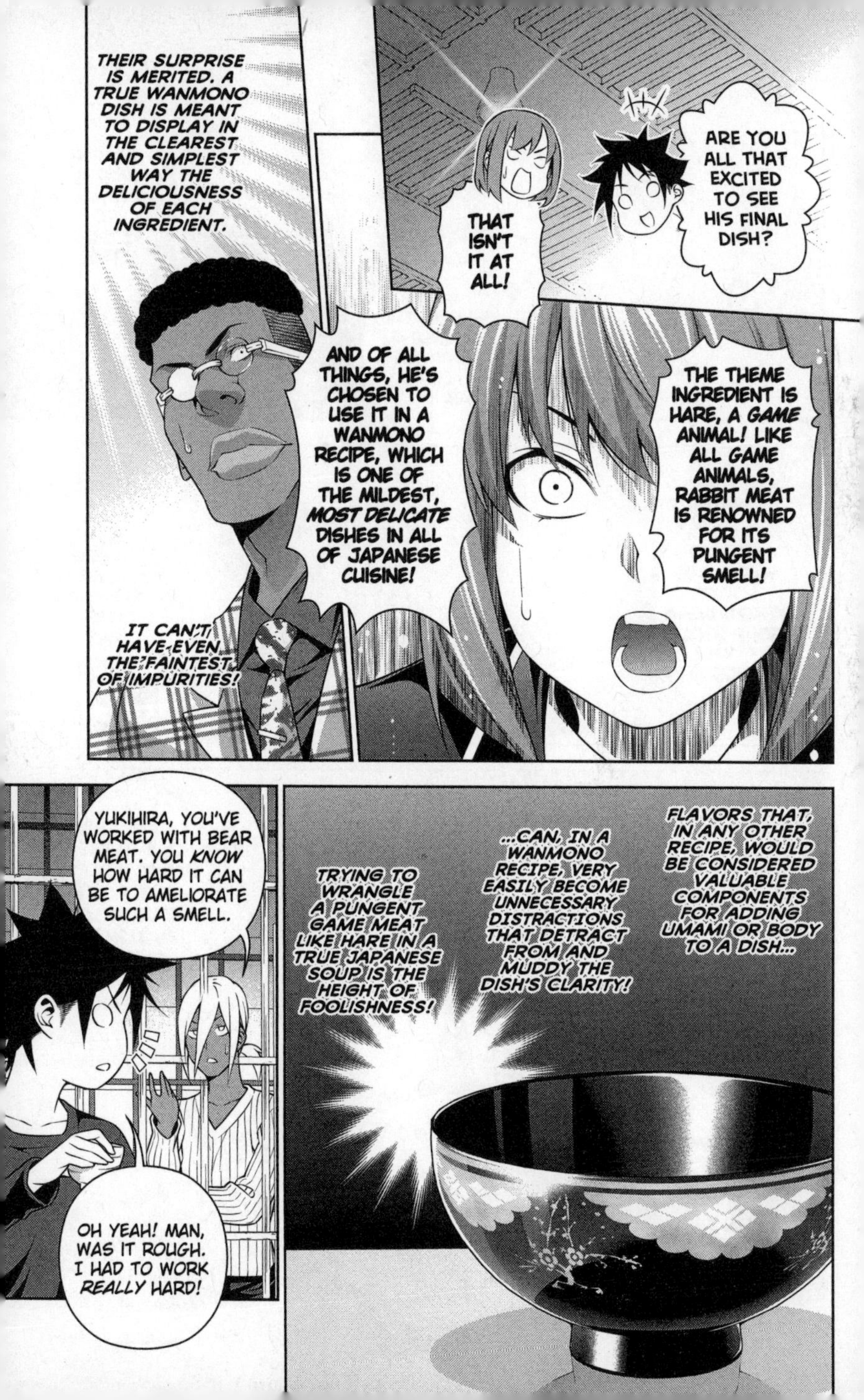
ARE YOU ALL THAT EXCITED TO SEE HIS FINAL DISH?
THAT ISN'T IT AT ALL!
THE THEME INGREDIENT IS HARE, A *GAME* ANIMAL! LIKE ALL GAME ANIMALS, RABBIT MEAT IS RENOWNED FOR ITS PUNGENT SMELL!
AND OF ALL THINGS, HE'S CHOSEN TO USE IT IN A WANMONO RECIPE, WHICH IS ONE OF THE MILDEST, *MOST DELICATE* DISHES IN ALL OF JAPANESE CUISINE!
THEIR SURPRISE IS MERITED. A TRUE WANMONO DISH IS MEANT TO DISPLAY IN THE CLEAREST AND SIMPLEST WAY THE DELICIOUSNESS OF EACH INGREDIENT.
IT CAN'T HAVE EVEN THE FAINTEST OF IMPURITIES!
FLAVORS THAT, IN ANY OTHER RECIPE, WOULD BE CONSIDERED VALUABLE COMPONENTS FOR ADDING UMAMI OR BODY TO A DISH...
...CAN, IN A WANMONO RECIPE, VERY EASILY BECOME UNNECESSARY DISTRACTIONS THAT DETRACT FROM AND MUDDY THE DISH'S CLARITY!
TRYING TO WRANGLE A PUNGENT GAME MEAT LIKE HARE IN A TRUE JAPANESE SOUP IS THE HEIGHT OF FOOLISHNESS!
YUKIHIRA, YOU'VE WORKED WITH BEAR MEAT. YOU *KNOW* HOW HARD IT CAN BE TO AMELIORATE SUCH A SMELL.
OH YEAH! MAN, WAS IT ROUGH. I HAD TO WORK *REALLY* HARD!

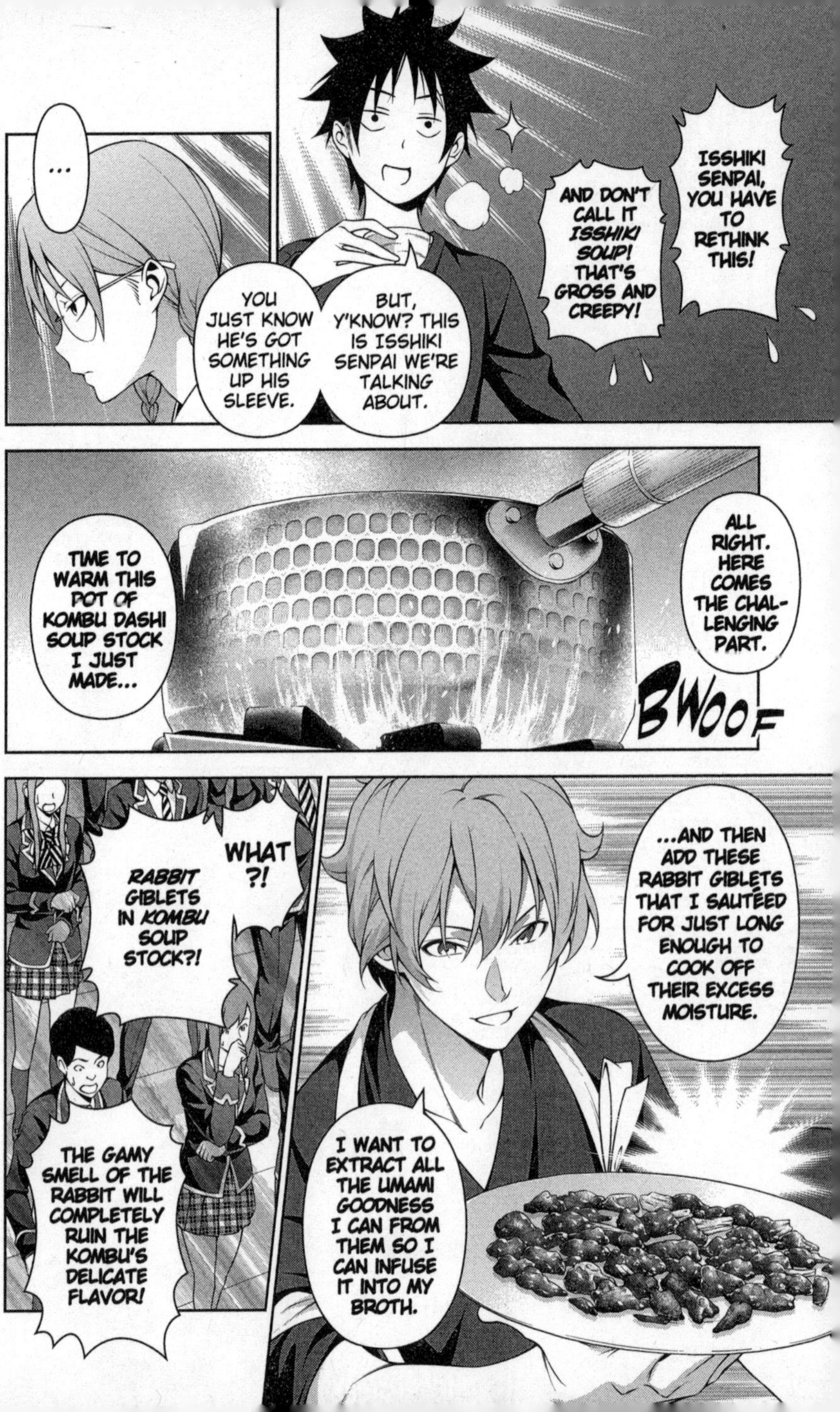
ISSHIKI SENPAI, YOU HAVE TO RETHINK THIS!
AND DON'T CALL IT *ISSHIKI SOUP!* THAT'S GROSS AND CREEPY!
BUT, Y'KNOW? THIS IS ISSHIKI SENPAI WE'RE TALKING ABOUT.
YOU JUST KNOW HE'S GOT SOMETHING UP HIS SLEEVE.
...
ALL RIGHT. HERE COMES THE CHAL-LENGING PART.
BWOOF
TIME TO WARM THIS POT OF KOMBU DASHI SOUP STOCK I JUST MADE...
...AND THEN ADD THESE RABBIT GIBLETS THAT I SAUTÉED FOR JUST LONG ENOUGH TO COOK OFF THEIR EXCESS MOISTURE.
I WANT TO EXTRACT ALL THE UMAMI GOODNESS I CAN FROM THEM SO I CAN INFUSE IT INTO MY BROTH.
WHAT?!
RABBIT GIBLETS IN *KOMBU* SOUP STOCK?!
THE GAMY SMELL OF THE RABBIT WILL COMPLETELY RUIN THE KOMBU'S DELICATE FLAVOR!

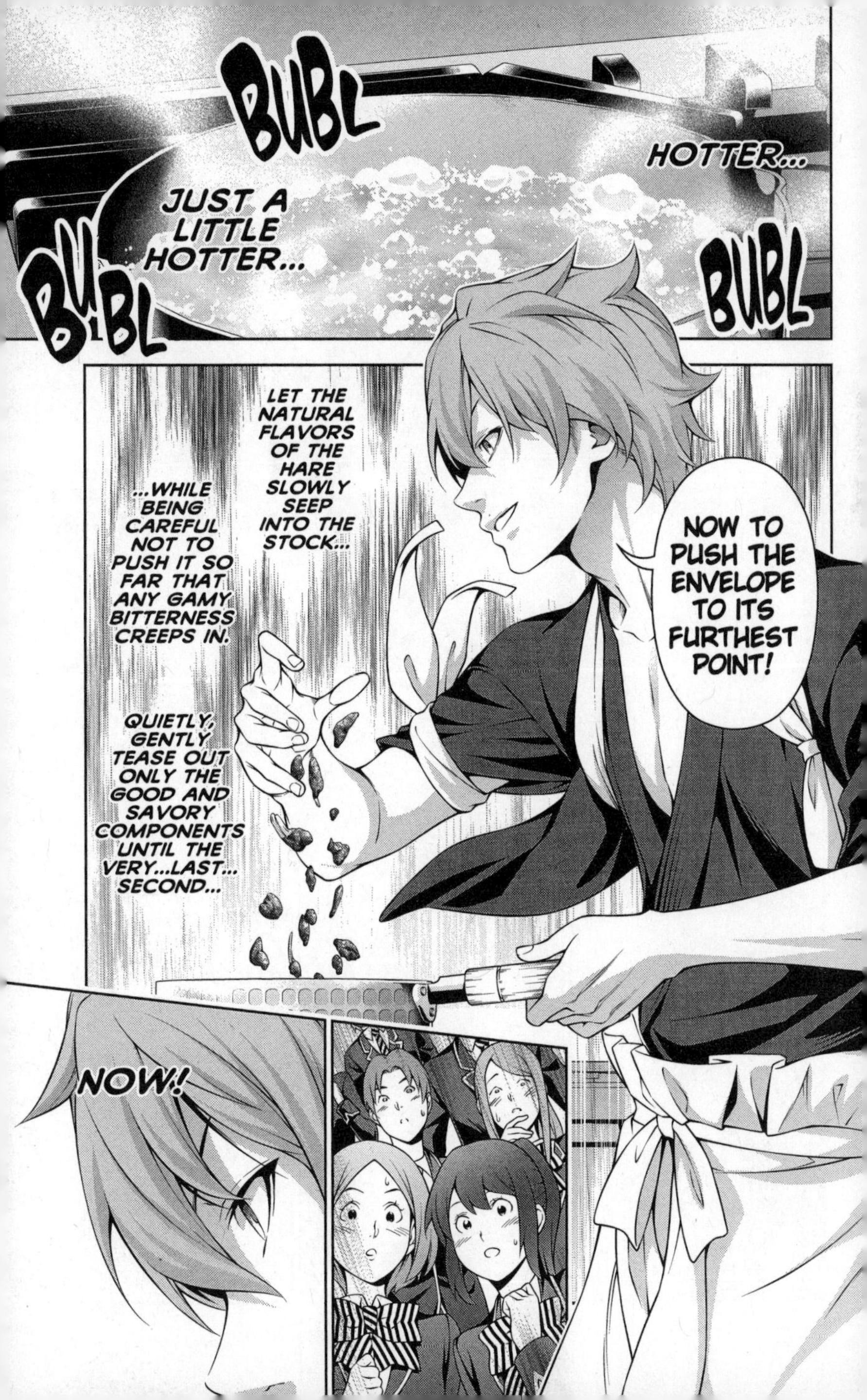
BUBL
HOTTER...
BUBL
JUST A LITTLE HOTTER...
BUBL
NOW TO PUSH THE ENVELOPE TO ITS FURTHEST POINT!
LET THE NATURAL FLAVORS OF THE HARE SLOWLY SEEP INTO THE STOCK...
...WHILE BEING CAREFUL NOT TO PUSH IT SO FAR THAT ANY GAMY BITTERNESS CREEPS IN.
QUIETLY, GENTLY TEASE OUT ONLY THE GOOD AND SAVORY COMPONENTS UNTIL THE VERY...LAST... SECOND...
NOW!

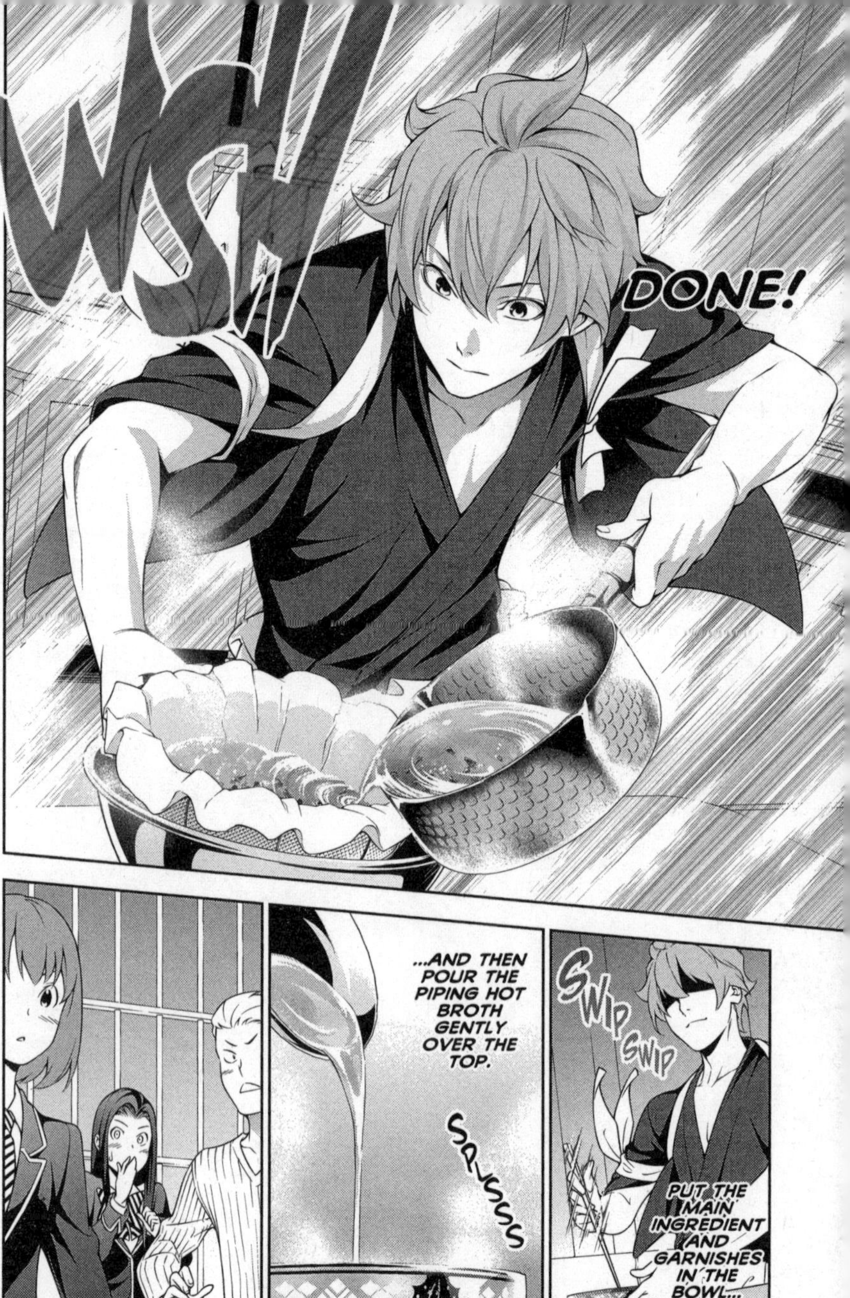
WSH!
DONE!
SWIP SWIP
PUT THE MAIN INGREDIENT AND GARNISHES IN THE BOWL...
...AND THEN POUR THE PIPING HOT BROTH GENTLY OVER THE TOP.

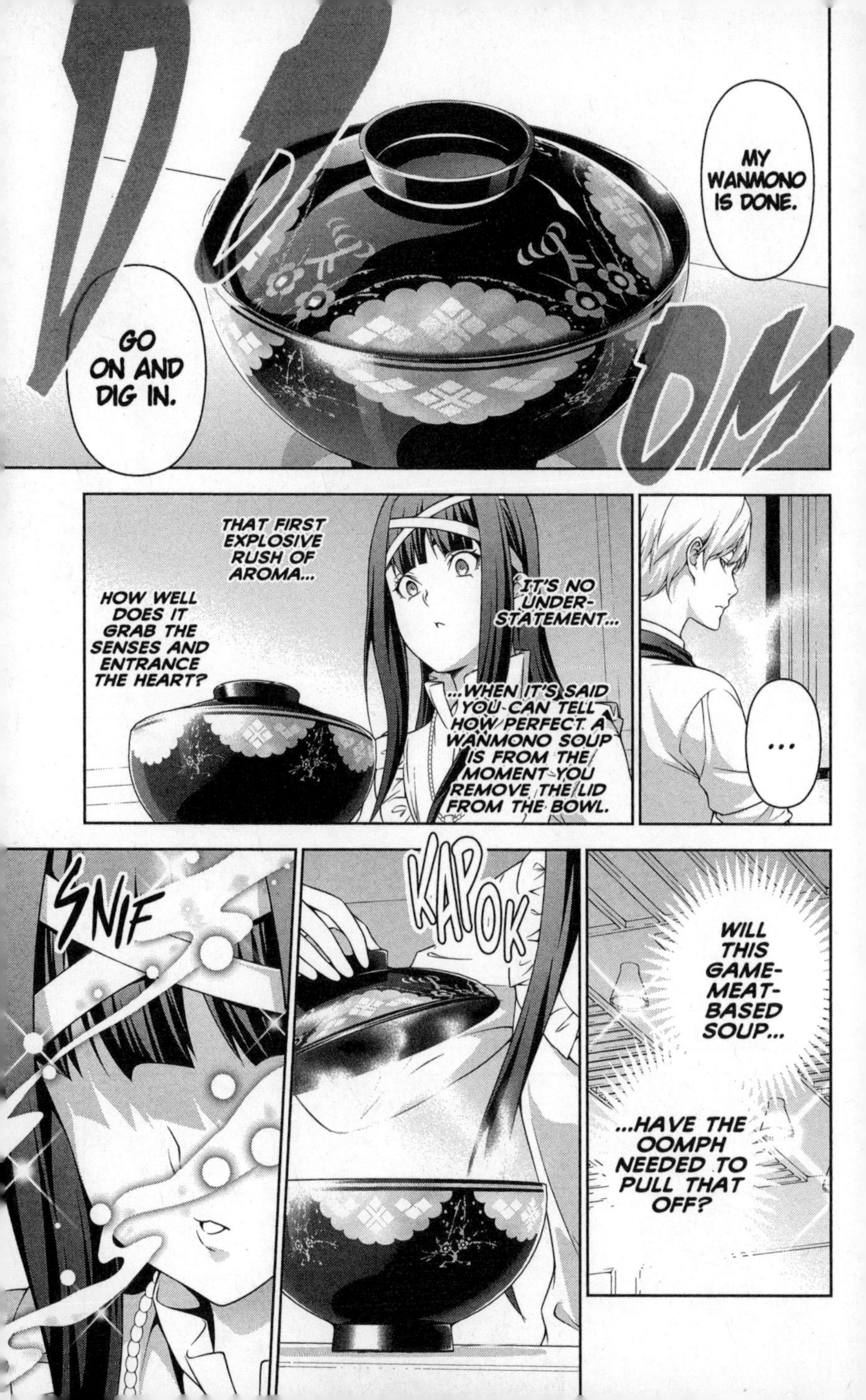
MY WANMONO IS DONE.
GO ON AND DIG IN.
DOM
...
IT'S NO UNDERSTATEMENT...
...WHEN IT'S SAID YOU CAN TELL HOW PERFECT A WANMONO SOUP IS FROM THE MOMENT YOU REMOVE THE LID FROM THE BOWL.
THAT FIRST EXPLOSIVE RUSH OF AROMA...
HOW WELL DOES IT GRAB THE SENSES AND ENTRANCE THE HEART?
WILL THIS GAME-MEAT-BASED SOUP...
...HAVE THE OOMPH NEEDED TO PULL THAT OFF?
KAPOK
SNIF

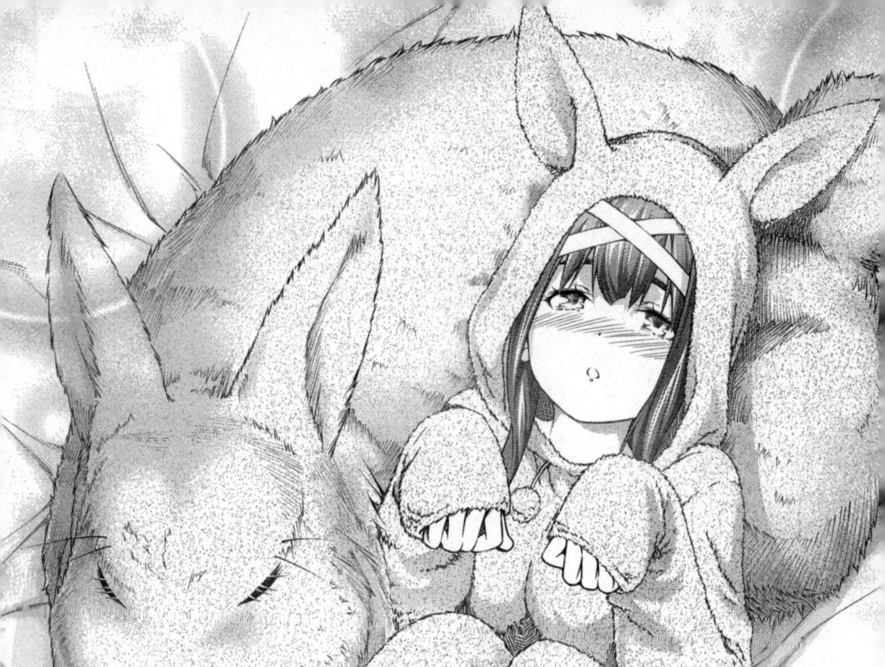
IT'S SO WARM!

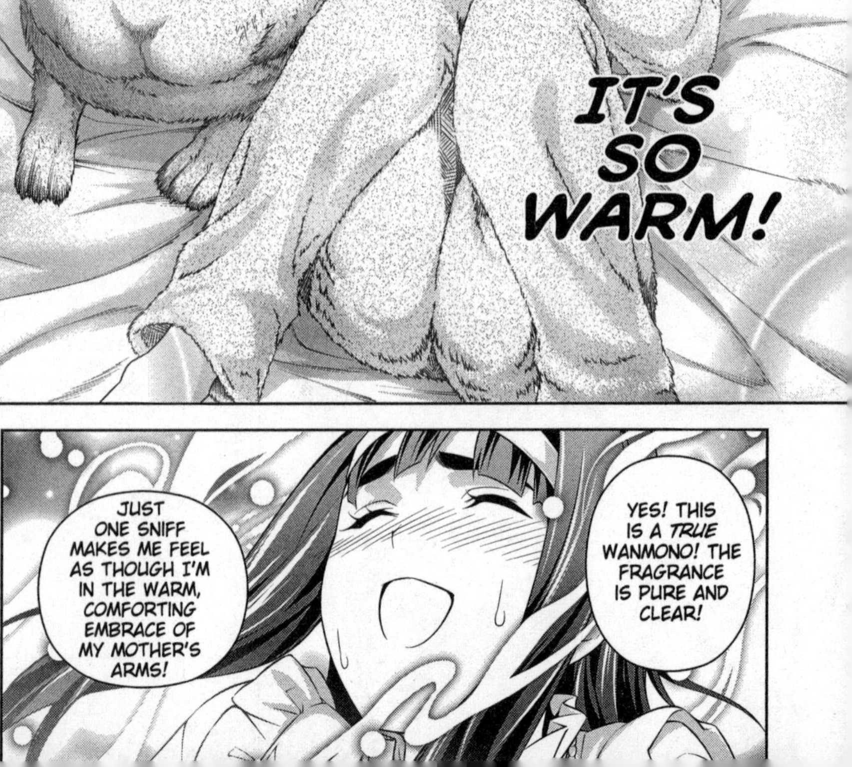
YES! THIS IS A *TRUE* WANMONO! THE FRAGRANCE IS PURE AND CLEAR!
JUST ONE SNIFF MAKES ME FEEL AS THOUGH I'M IN THE WARM, COMFORTING EMBRACE OF MY MOTHER'S ARMS!

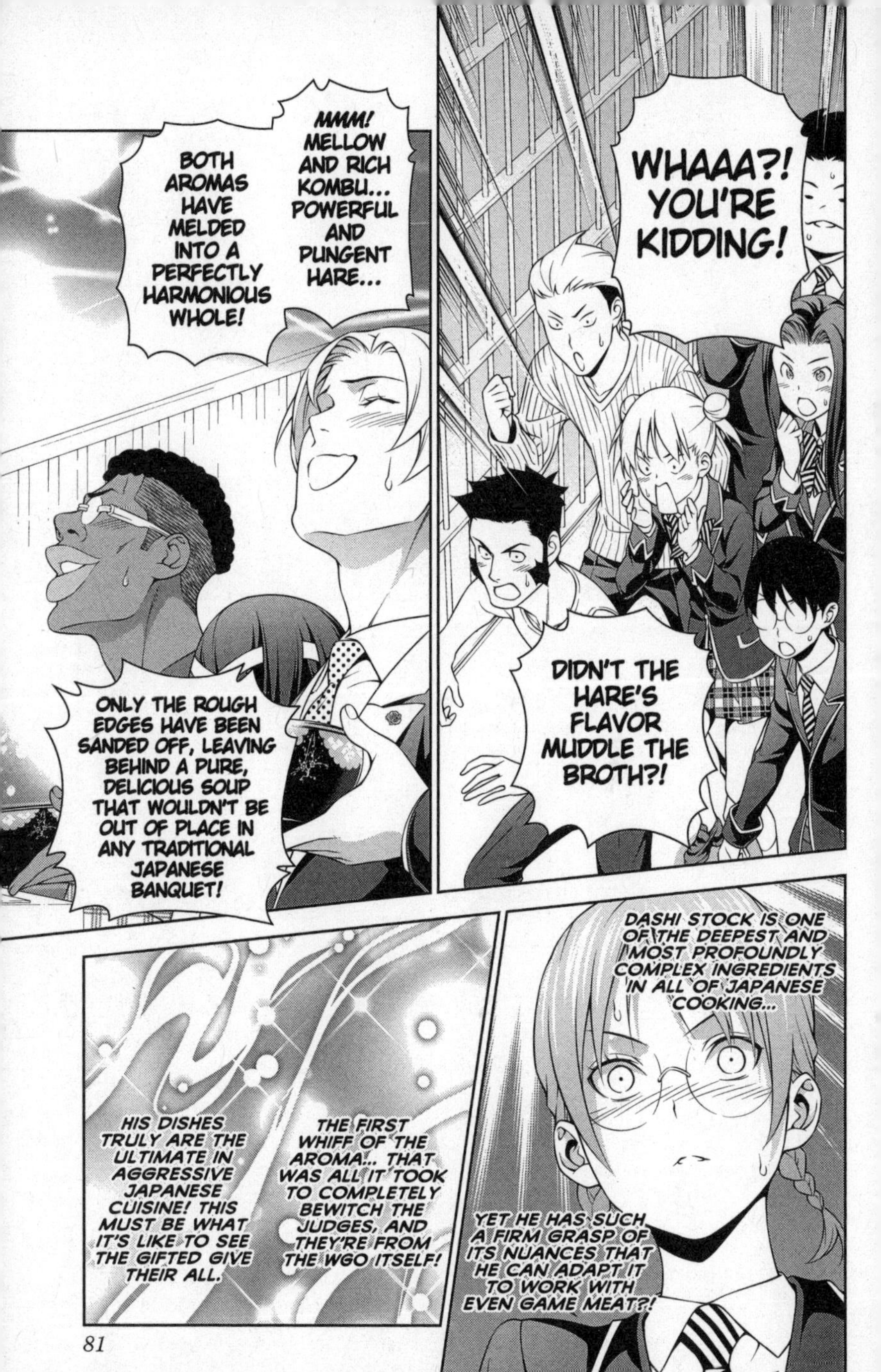
WHAAA?! YOU'RE KIDDING!
DIDN'T THE HARE'S FLAVOR MUDDLE THE BROTH?!
MMM! MELLOW AND RICH KOMBU... POWERFUL AND PUNGENT HARE...
BOTH AROMAS HAVE MELDED INTO A PERFECTLY HARMONIOUS WHOLE!
ONLY THE ROUGH EDGES HAVE BEEN SANDED OFF, LEAVING BEHIND A PURE, DELICIOUS SOUP THAT WOULDN'T BE OUT OF PLACE IN ANY TRADITIONAL JAPANESE BANQUET!
DASHI STOCK IS ONE OF THE DEEPEST AND MOST PROFOUNDLY COMPLEX INGREDIENTS IN ALL OF JAPANESE COOKING...
YET HE HAS SUCH A FIRM GRASP OF ITS NUANCES THAT HE CAN ADAPT IT TO WORK WITH EVEN GAME MEAT?!
THE FIRST WHIFF OF THE AROMA... THAT WAS ALL IT TOOK TO COMPLETELY BEWITCH THE JUDGES, AND THEY'RE FROM THE WGO ITSELF!
HIS DISHES TRULY ARE THE ULTIMATE IN AGGRESSIVE JAPANESE CUISINE! THIS MUST BE WHAT IT'S LIKE TO SEE THE GIFTED GIVE THEIR ALL.

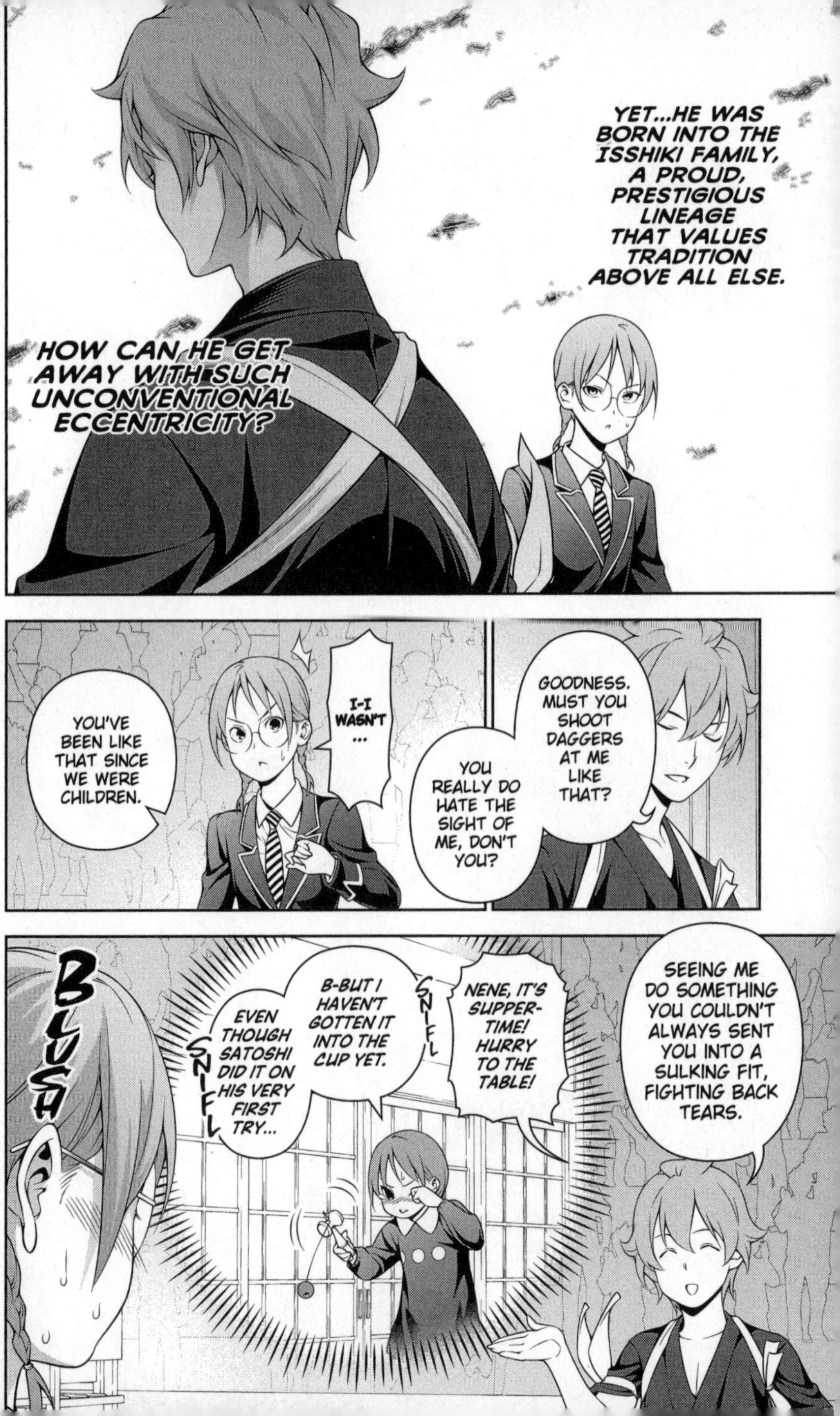
YET...HE WAS BORN INTO THE ISSHIKI FAMILY, A PROUD, PRESTIGIOUS LINEAGE THAT VALUES TRADITION ABOVE ALL ELSE.
HOW CAN HE GET AWAY WITH SUCH UNCONVENTIONAL ECCENTRICITY?
GOODNESS. MUST YOU SHOOT DAGGERS AT ME LIKE THAT?
YOU REALLY DO HATE THE SIGHT OF ME, DON'T YOU?
I-I WASN'T ...
YOU'VE BEEN LIKE THAT SINCE WE WERE CHILDREN.
SEEING ME DO SOMETHING YOU COULDN'T ALWAYS SENT YOU INTO A SULKING FIT, FIGHTING BACK TEARS.
NENE, IT'S SUPPER-TIME! HURRY TO THE TABLE!
SNIFL
B-BUT I HAVEN'T GOTTEN IT INTO THE CUP YET.
EVEN THOUGH SATOSHI DID IT ON HIS VERY FIRST TRY...
SNIFL
BLUSH

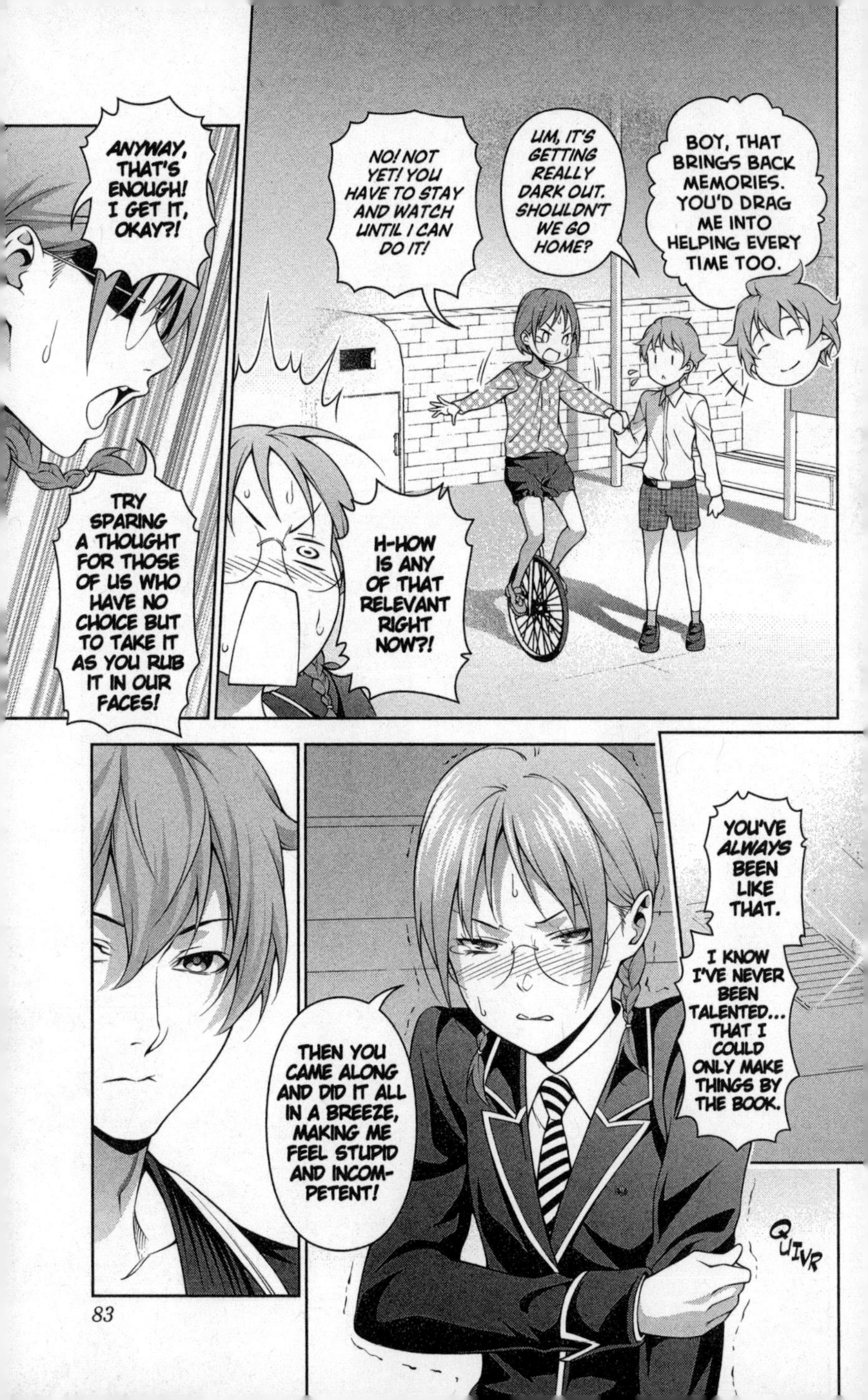
BOY, THAT BRINGS BACK MEMORIES. YOU'D DRAG ME INTO HELPING EVERY TIME TOO.
UM, IT'S GETTING REALLY DARK OUT. SHOULDN'T WE GO HOME?
NO! NOT YET! YOU HAVE TO STAY AND WATCH UNTIL I CAN DO IT!
H-HOW IS ANY OF THAT RELEVANT RIGHT NOW?!
ANYWAY, THAT'S ENOUGH! I GET IT, OKAY?!
TRY SPARING A THOUGHT FOR THOSE OF US WHO HAVE NO CHOICE BUT TO TAKE IT AS YOU RUB IT IN OUR FACES!
YOU'VE ALWAYS BEEN LIKE THAT.
I KNOW I'VE NEVER BEEN TALENTED... THAT I COULD ONLY MAKE THINGS BY THE BOOK.
QUIVR
THEN YOU CAME ALONG AND DID IT ALL IN A BREEZE, MAKING ME FEEL STUPID AND INCOMPETENT!

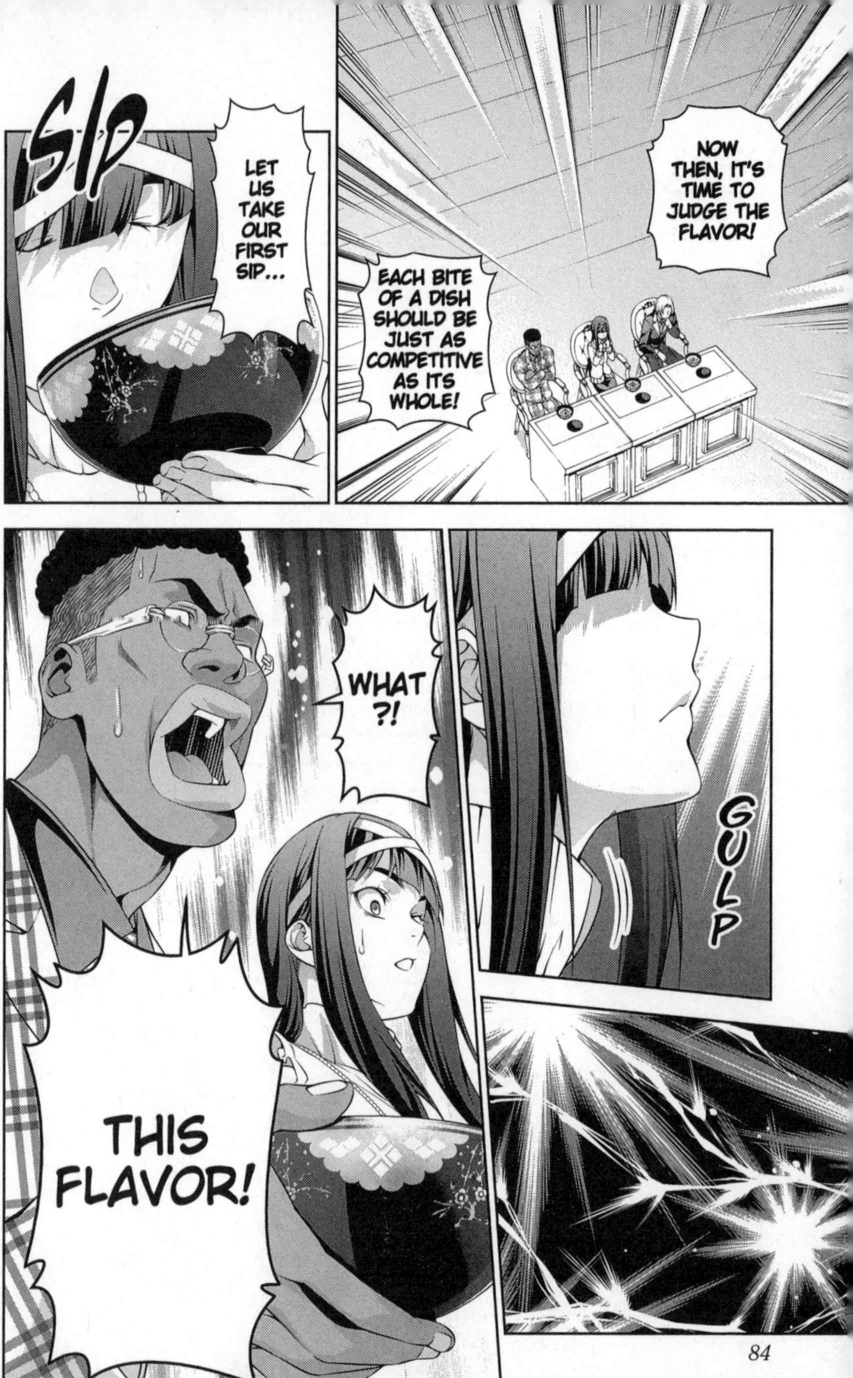
NOW THEN, IT'S TIME TO JUDGE THE FLAVOR!
EACH BITE OF A DISH SHOULD BE JUST AS COMPETITIVE AS ITS WHOLE!
SIP
LET US TAKE OUR FIRST SIP...
GULP
WHAT?!
THIS FLAVOR!

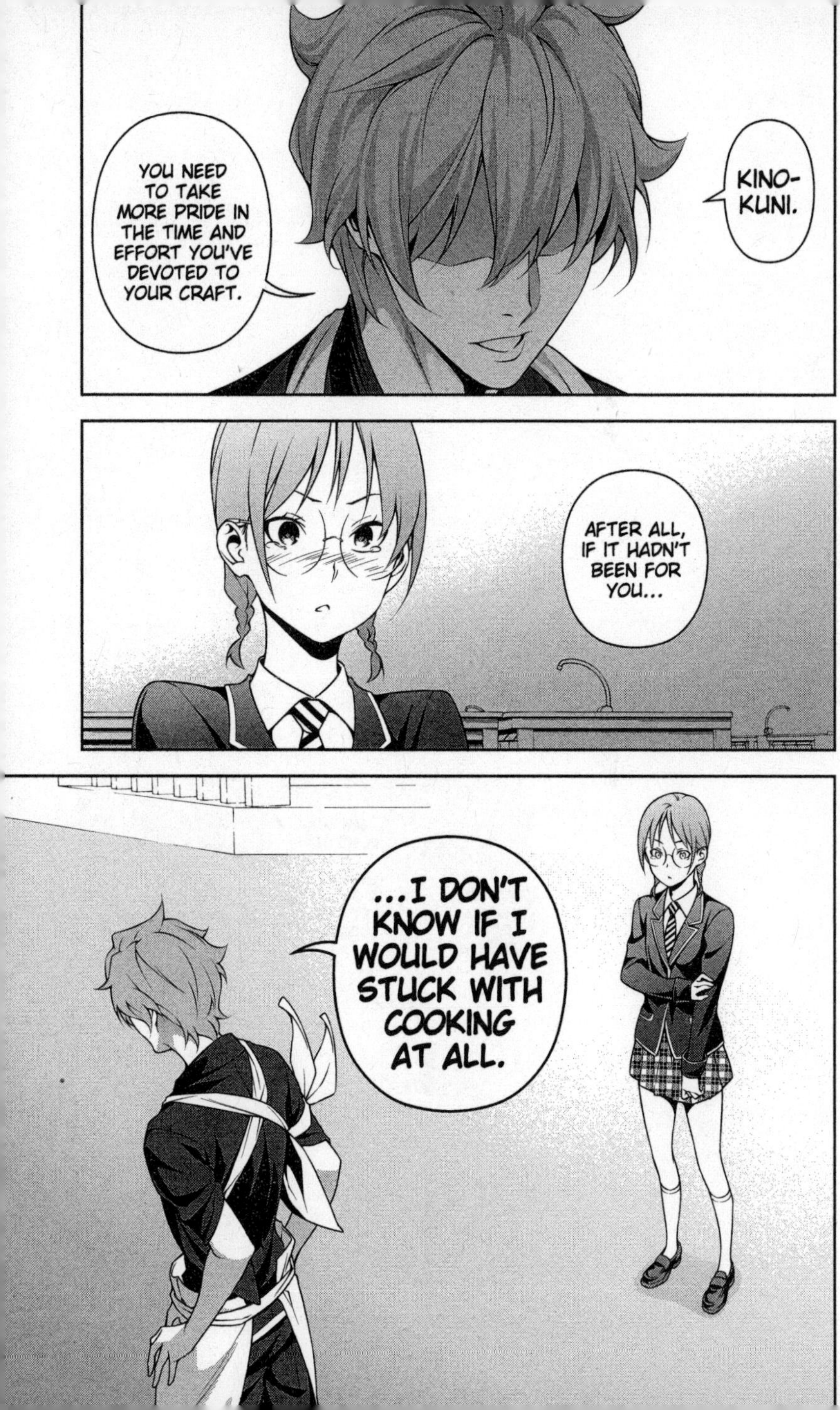
KINO-KUNI.
YOU NEED TO TAKE MORE PRIDE IN THE TIME AND EFFORT YOU'VE DEVOTED TO YOUR CRAFT.
AFTER ALL, IF IT HADN'T BEEN FOR YOU...
...I DON'T KNOW IF I WOULD HAVE STUCK WITH COOKING AT ALL.

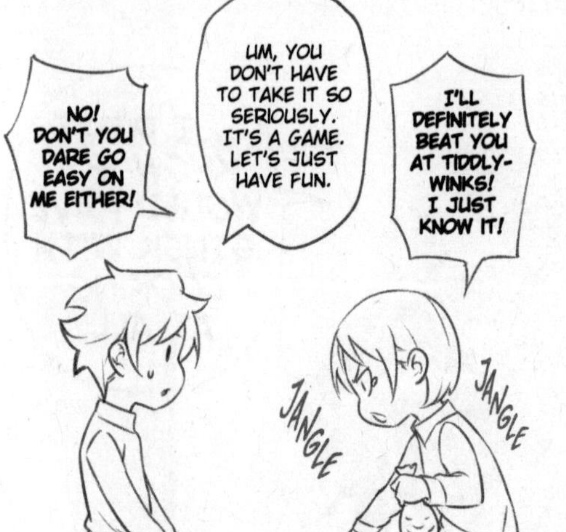
I'LL DEFINITELY BEAT YOU AT TIDDLY-WINKS! I JUST KNOW IT!
UM, YOU DON'T HAVE TO TAKE IT SO SERIOUSLY. IT'S A GAME. LET'S JUST HAVE FUN.
NO! DON'T YOU DARE GO EASY ON ME EITHER!
JANGLE
JANGLE

249
WATCHING FROM BESIDE YOU
GO 5
SHOKUGEKI NO SOMA
GO 50
WEEKLY JUMP

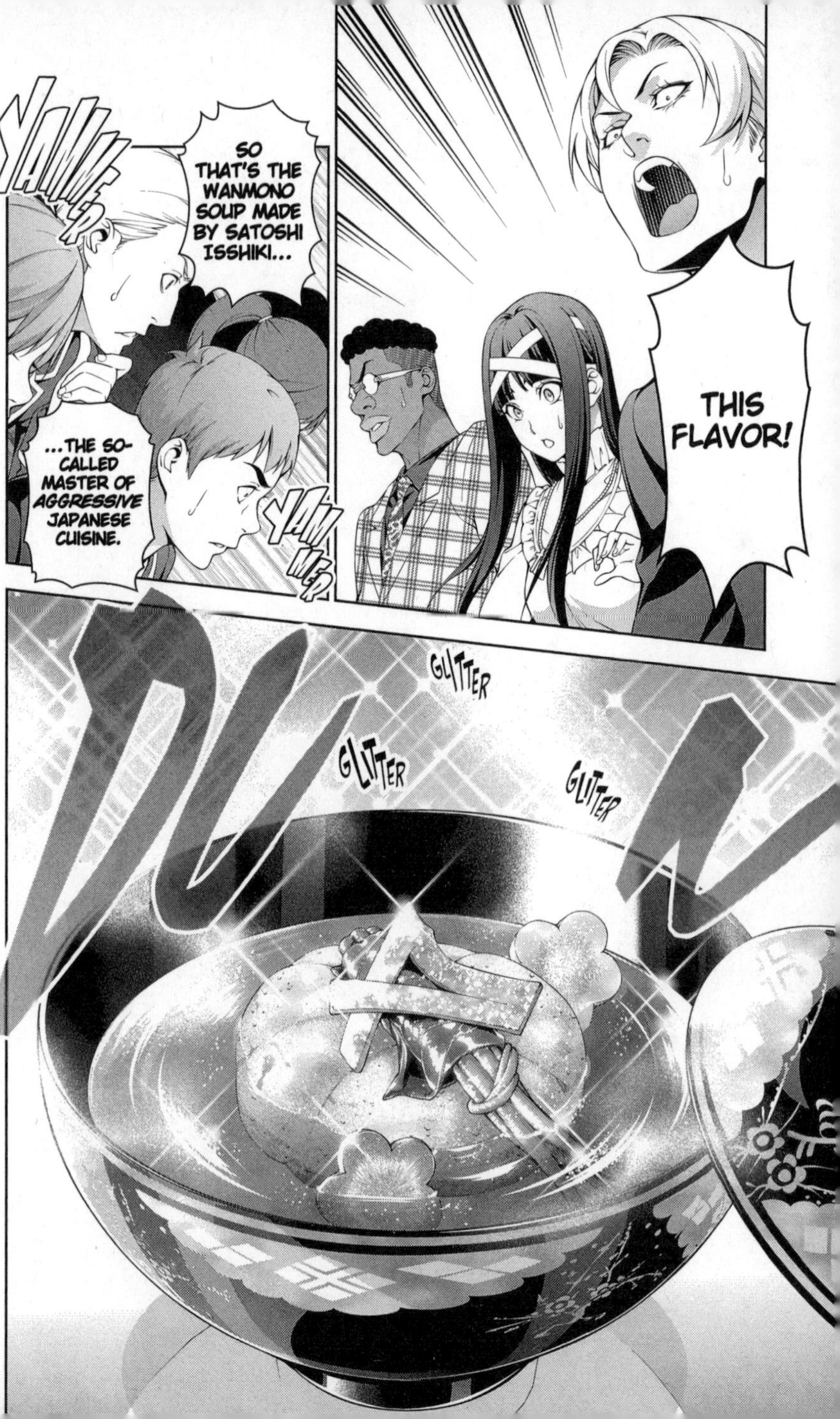
THIS FLAVOR!
SO THAT'S THE WANMONO SOUP MADE BY SATOSHI ISSHIKI...
YAMMER
...THE SO-CALLED MASTER OF *AGGRESSIVE* JAPANESE CUISINE.
YAMMER
GLITTER
GLITTER
GLITTER

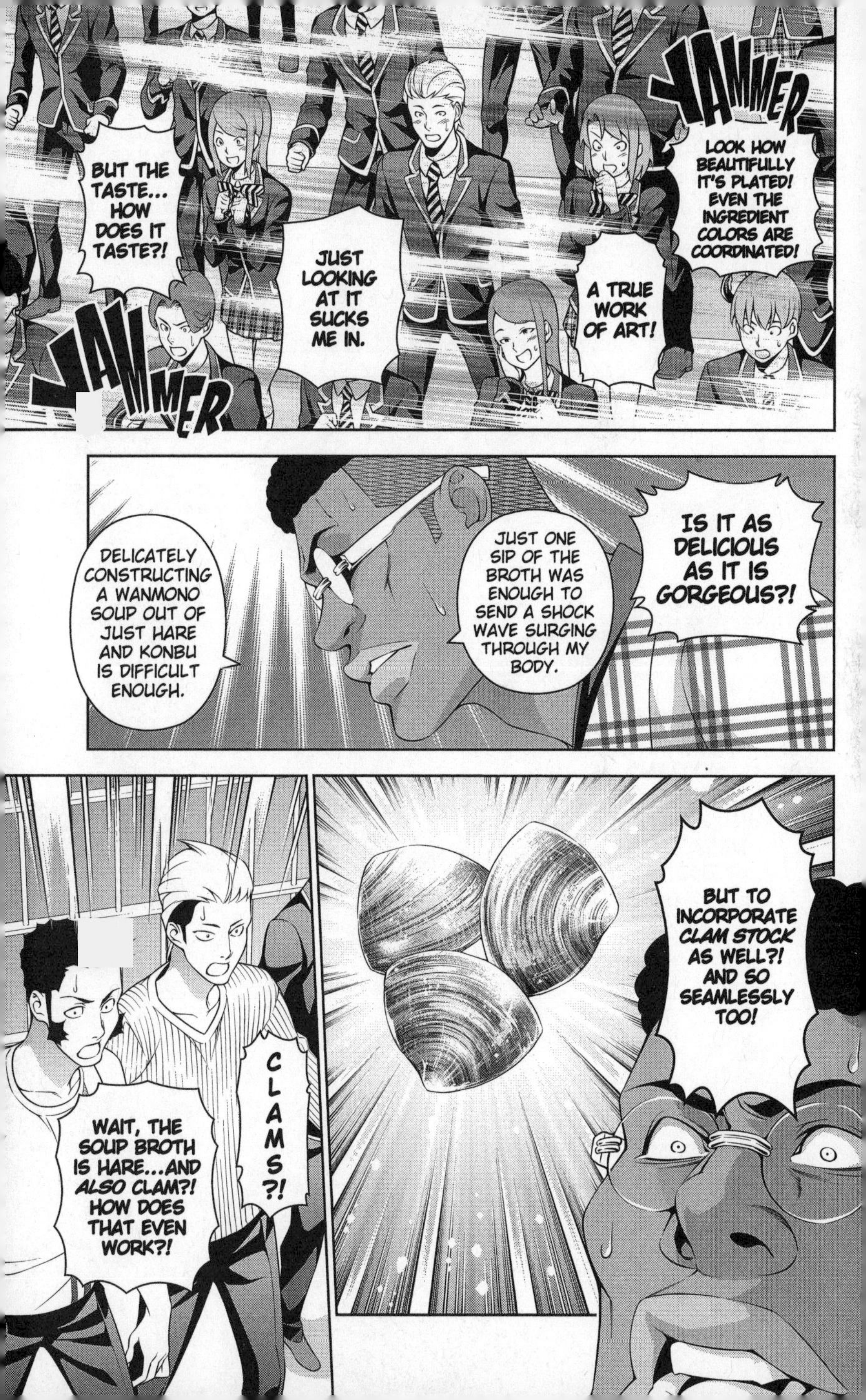
HAMMER
LOOK HOW BEAUTIFULLY IT'S PLATED! EVEN THE INGREDIENT COLORS ARE COORDINATED!
A TRUE WORK OF ART!
JUST LOOKING AT IT SUCKS ME IN.
BUT THE TASTE... HOW DOES IT TASTE?!
HAMMER
IS IT AS DELICIOUS AS IT IS GORGEOUS?!
JUST ONE SIP OF THE BROTH WAS ENOUGH TO SEND A SHOCK WAVE SURGING THROUGH MY BODY.
DELICATELY CONSTRUCTING A WANMONO SOUP OUT OF JUST HARE AND KONBU IS DIFFICULT ENOUGH.
BUT TO INCORPORATE *CLAM STOCK* AS WELL?! AND SO SEAMLESSLY TOO!
CLAMS?!
WAIT, THE SOUP BROTH IS HARE...AND *ALSO CLAM*?! HOW DOES THAT EVEN WORK?!

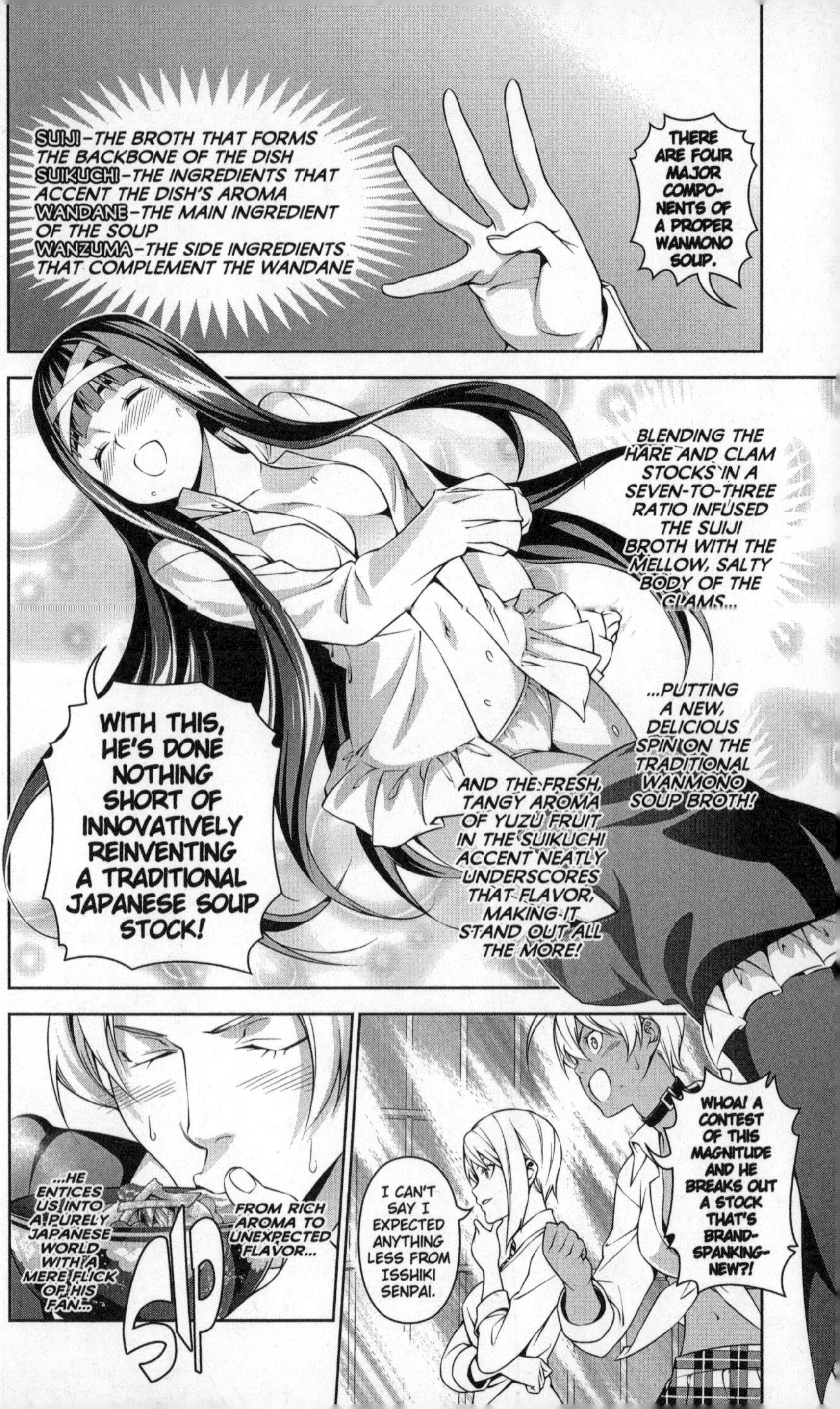
THERE ARE FOUR MAJOR COMPONENTS OF A PROPER WANMONO SOUP.
SUIJI—THE BROTH THAT FORMS THE BACKBONE OF THE DISH
SUIKUCHI—THE INGREDIENTS THAT ACCENT THE DISH'S AROMA
WANDANE—THE MAIN INGREDIENT OF THE SOUP
WANZUMA—THE SIDE INGREDIENTS THAT COMPLEMENT THE WANDANE
BLENDING THE HARE AND CLAM STOCKS IN A SEVEN-TO-THREE RATIO INFUSED THE SUIJI BROTH WITH THE MELLOW, SALTY BODY OF THE CLAMS...
...PUTTING A NEW, DELICIOUS SPIN ON THE TRADITIONAL WANMONO SOUP BROTH!
AND THE FRESH, TANGY AROMA OF YUZU FRUIT IN THE SUIKUCHI ACCENT NEATLY UNDERSCORES THAT FLAVOR, MAKING IT STAND OUT ALL THE MORE!
WITH THIS, HE'S DONE NOTHING SHORT OF INNOVATIVELY REINVENTING A TRADITIONAL JAPANESE SOUP STOCK!
WHOA! A CONTEST OF THIS MAGNITUDE AND HE BREAKS OUT A STOCK THAT'S BRAND-SPANKING-NEW?!
I CAN'T SAY I EXPECTED ANYTHING LESS FROM ISSHIKI SENPAI.
FROM RICH AROMA TO UNEXPECTED FLAVOR...
...HE ENTICES US INTO A PURELY JAPANESE WORLD WITH A MERE FLICK OF HIS FAN...
SIP

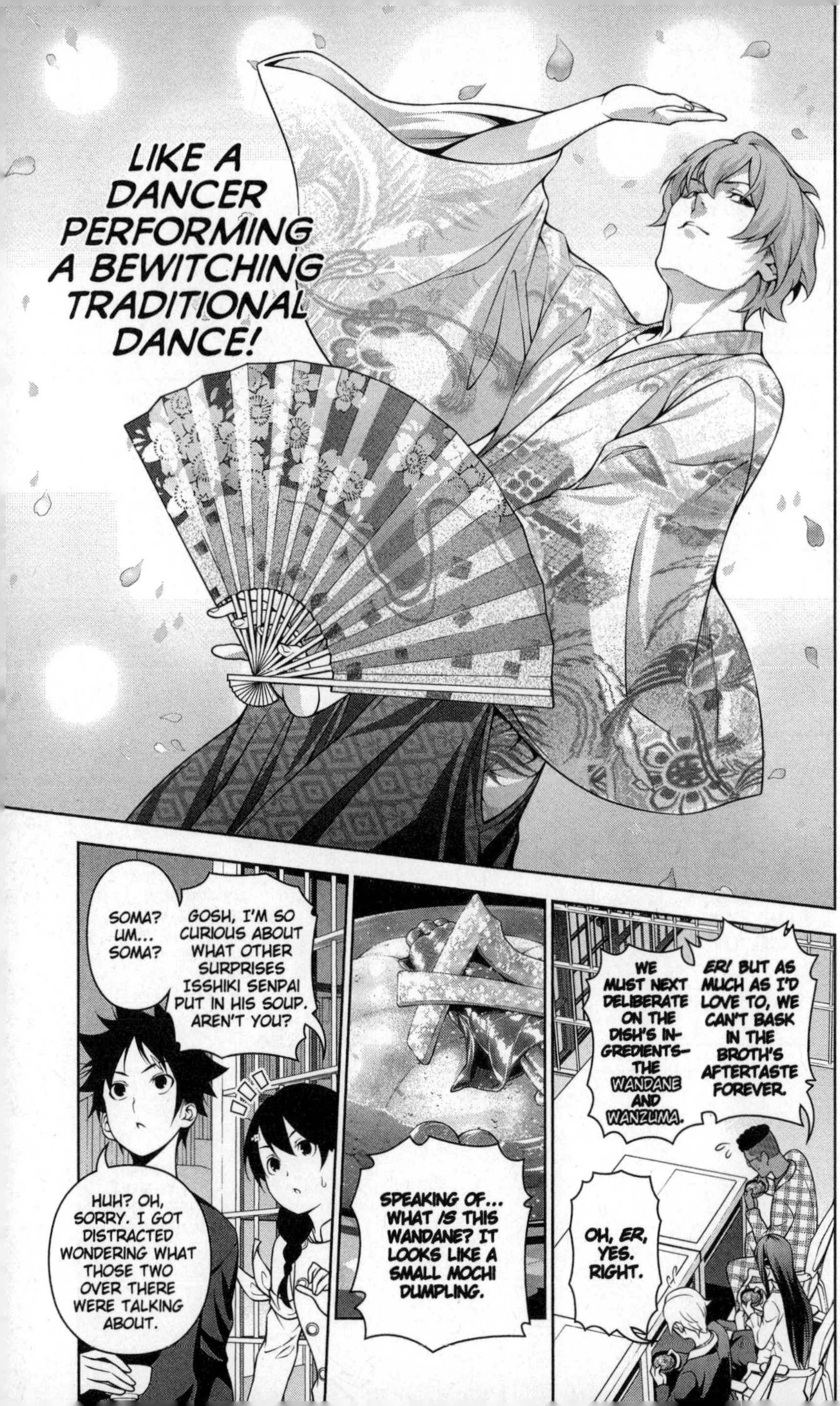
LIKE A DANCER PERFORMING A BEWITCHING TRADITIONAL DANCE!
ER! BUT AS MUCH AS I'D LOVE TO, WE CAN'T BASK IN THE BROTH'S AFTERTASTE FOREVER.
WE MUST NEXT DELIBERATE ON THE DISH'S INGREDIENTS—THE WANDANE AND WANZUMA.
OH, ER, YES. RIGHT.
SPEAKING OF... WHAT IS THIS WANDANE? IT LOOKS LIKE A SMALL MOCHI DUMPLING.
GOSH, I'M SO CURIOUS ABOUT WHAT OTHER SURPRISES ISSHIKI SENPAI PUT IN HIS SOUP. AREN'T YOU?
SOMA? UM... SOMA?
HUH? OH, SORRY. I GOT DISTRACTED WONDERING WHAT THOSE TWO OVER THERE WERE TALKING ABOUT.

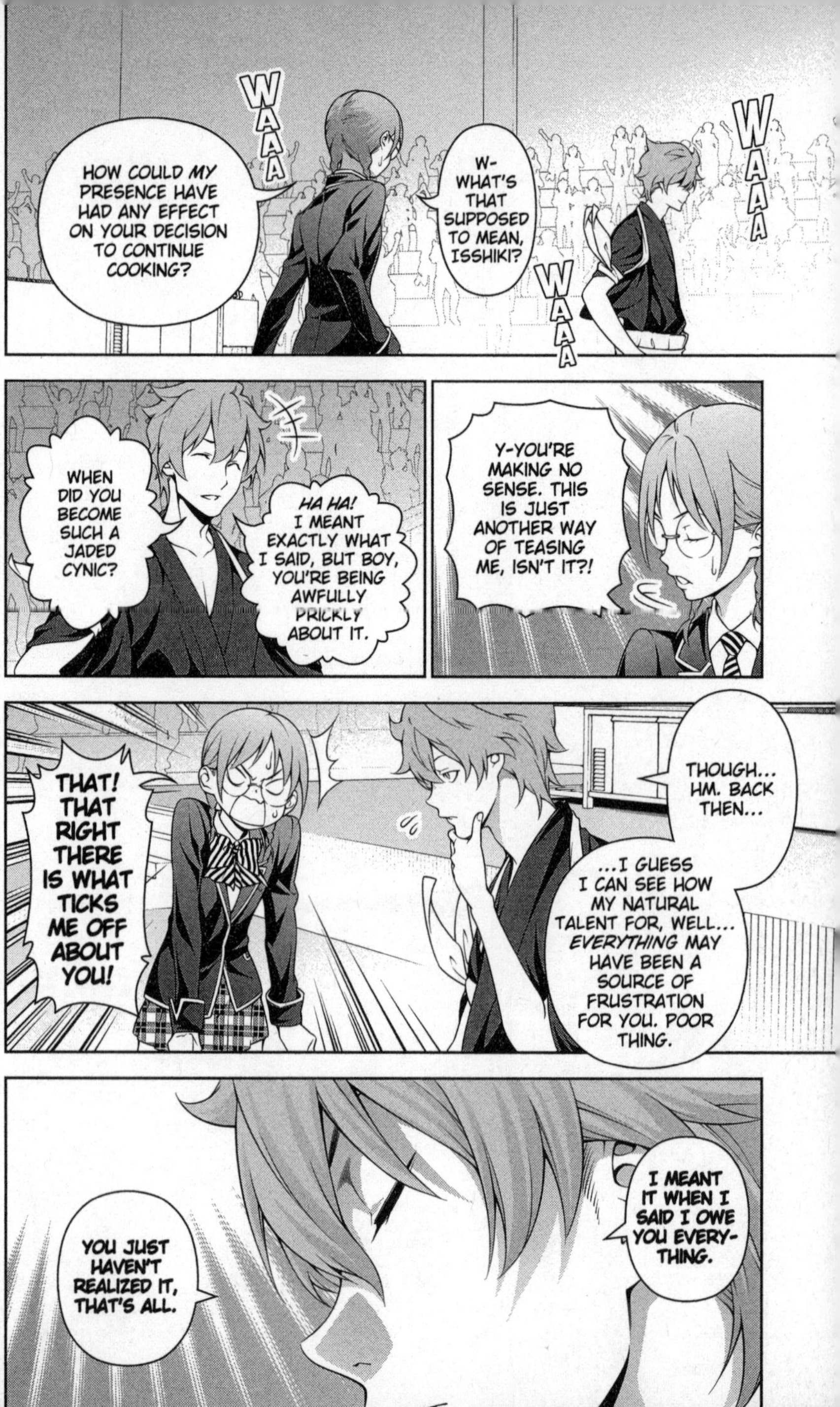
WAAAA
W- WHAT'S THAT SUPPOSED TO MEAN, ISSHIKI?
WAAAA
HOW COULD *MY* PRESENCE HAVE HAD ANY EFFECT ON YOUR DECISION TO CONTINUE COOKING?
WAAAA
Y-YOU'RE MAKING NO SENSE. THIS IS JUST ANOTHER WAY OF TEASING ME, ISN'T IT?!
HA HA! I MEANT EXACTLY WHAT I SAID, BUT BOY, YOU'RE BEING AWFULLY PRICKLY ABOUT IT.
WHEN DID YOU BECOME SUCH A JADED CYNIC?
THOUGH... HM. BACK THEN...
...I GUESS I CAN SEE HOW MY NATURAL TALENT FOR, WELL... *EVERYTHING* MAY HAVE BEEN A SOURCE OF FRUSTRATION FOR YOU. POOR THING.
THAT! THAT RIGHT THERE IS WHAT TICKS ME OFF ABOUT YOU!
I MEANT IT WHEN I SAID I OWE YOU EVERYTHING.
YOU JUST HAVEN'T REALIZED IT, THAT'S ALL.

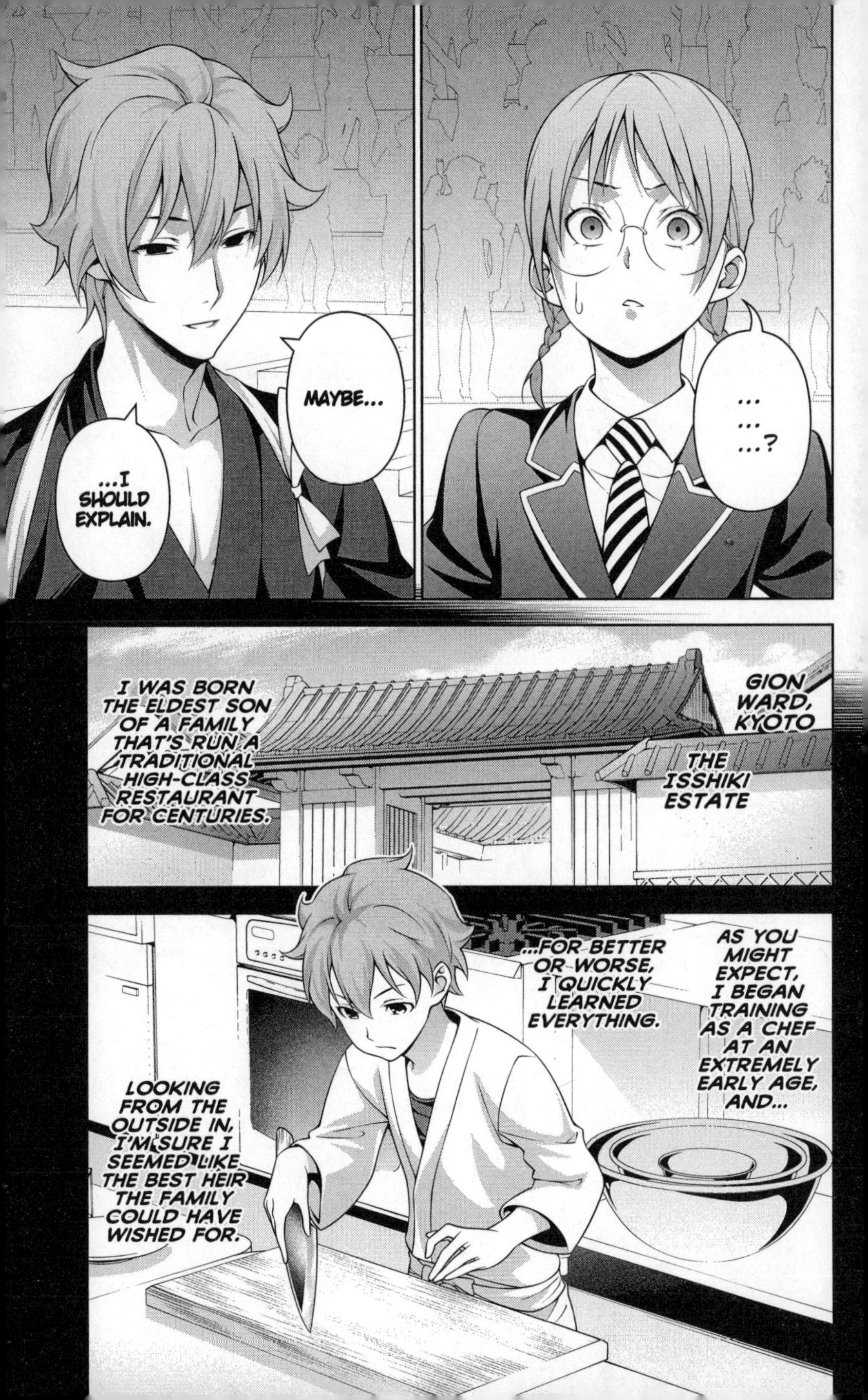

... ...?
MAYBE...
...I SHOULD EXPLAIN.
GION WARD, KYOTO
THE ISSHIKI ESTATE
I WAS BORN THE ELDEST SON OF A FAMILY THAT'S RUN A TRADITIONAL HIGH-CLASS RESTAURANT FOR CENTURIES.
AS YOU MIGHT EXPECT, I BEGAN TRAINING AS A CHEF AT AN EXTREMELY EARLY AGE, AND...
...FOR BETTER OR WORSE, I QUICKLY LEARNED EVERYTHING.
LOOKING FROM THE OUTSIDE IN, I'M SURE I SEEMED LIKE THE BEST HEIR THE FAMILY COULD HAVE WISHED FOR.

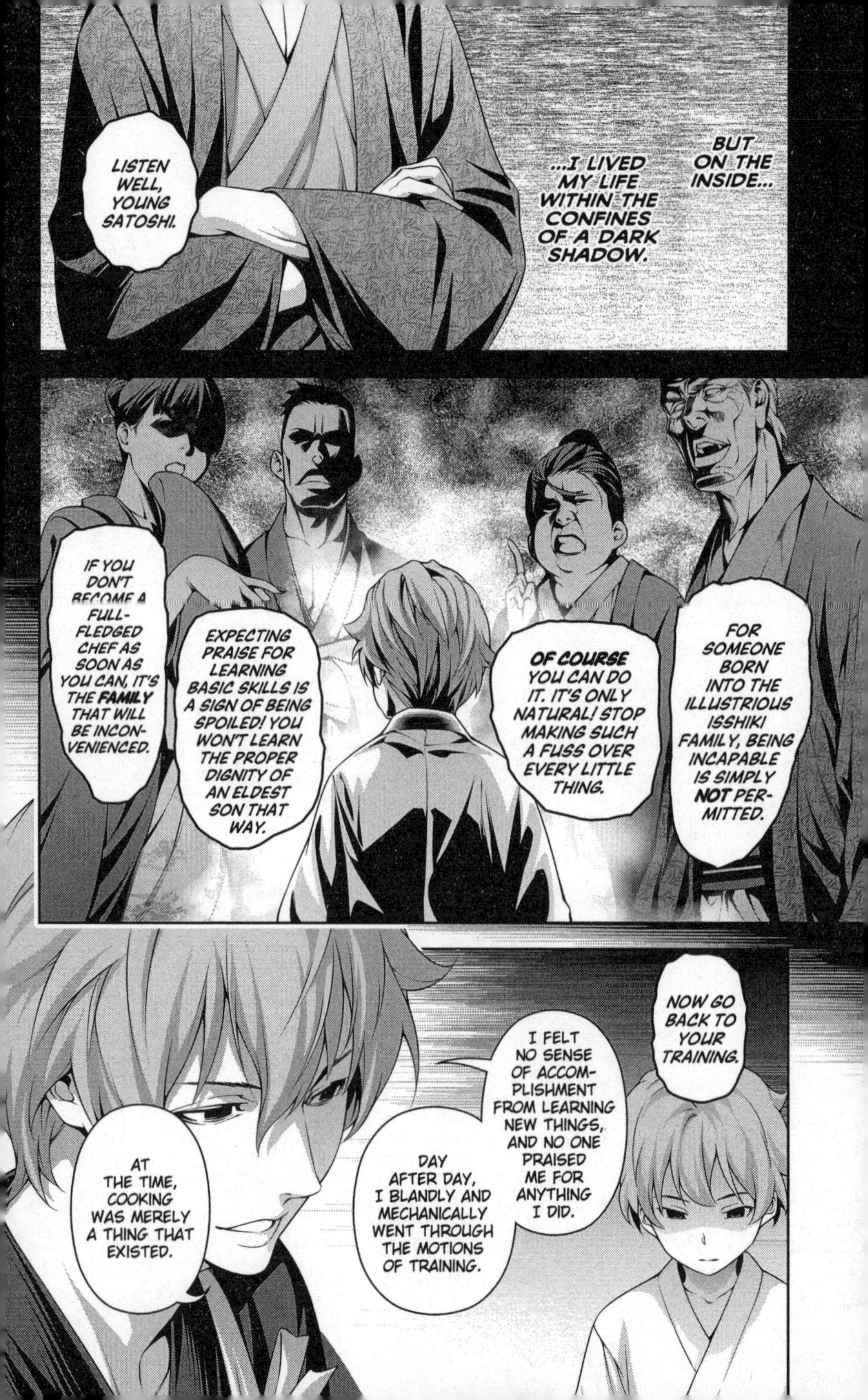
BUT ON THE INSIDE...
...I LIVED MY LIFE WITHIN THE CONFINES OF A DARK SHADOW.
LISTEN WELL, YOUNG SATOSHI.
FOR SOMEONE BORN INTO THE ILLUSTRIOUS ISSHIKI FAMILY, BEING INCAPABLE IS SIMPLY **NOT** PERMITTED.
OF COURSE YOU CAN DO IT. IT'S ONLY NATURAL! STOP MAKING SUCH A FUSS OVER EVERY LITTLE THING.
EXPECTING PRAISE FOR LEARNING BASIC SKILLS IS A SIGN OF BEING SPOILED! YOU WON'T LEARN THE PROPER DIGNITY OF AN ELDEST SON THAT WAY.
IF YOU DON'T BECOME A FULL-FLEDGED CHEF AS SOON AS YOU CAN, IT'S THE **FAMILY** THAT WILL BE INCONVENIENCED.
NOW GO BACK TO YOUR TRAINING.
I FELT NO SENSE OF ACCOMPLISHMENT FROM LEARNING NEW THINGS, AND NO ONE PRAISED ME FOR ANYTHING I DID.
DAY AFTER DAY, I BLANDLY AND MECHANICALLY WENT THROUGH THE MOTIONS OF TRAINING.
AT THE TIME, COOKING WAS MERELY A THING THAT EXISTED.

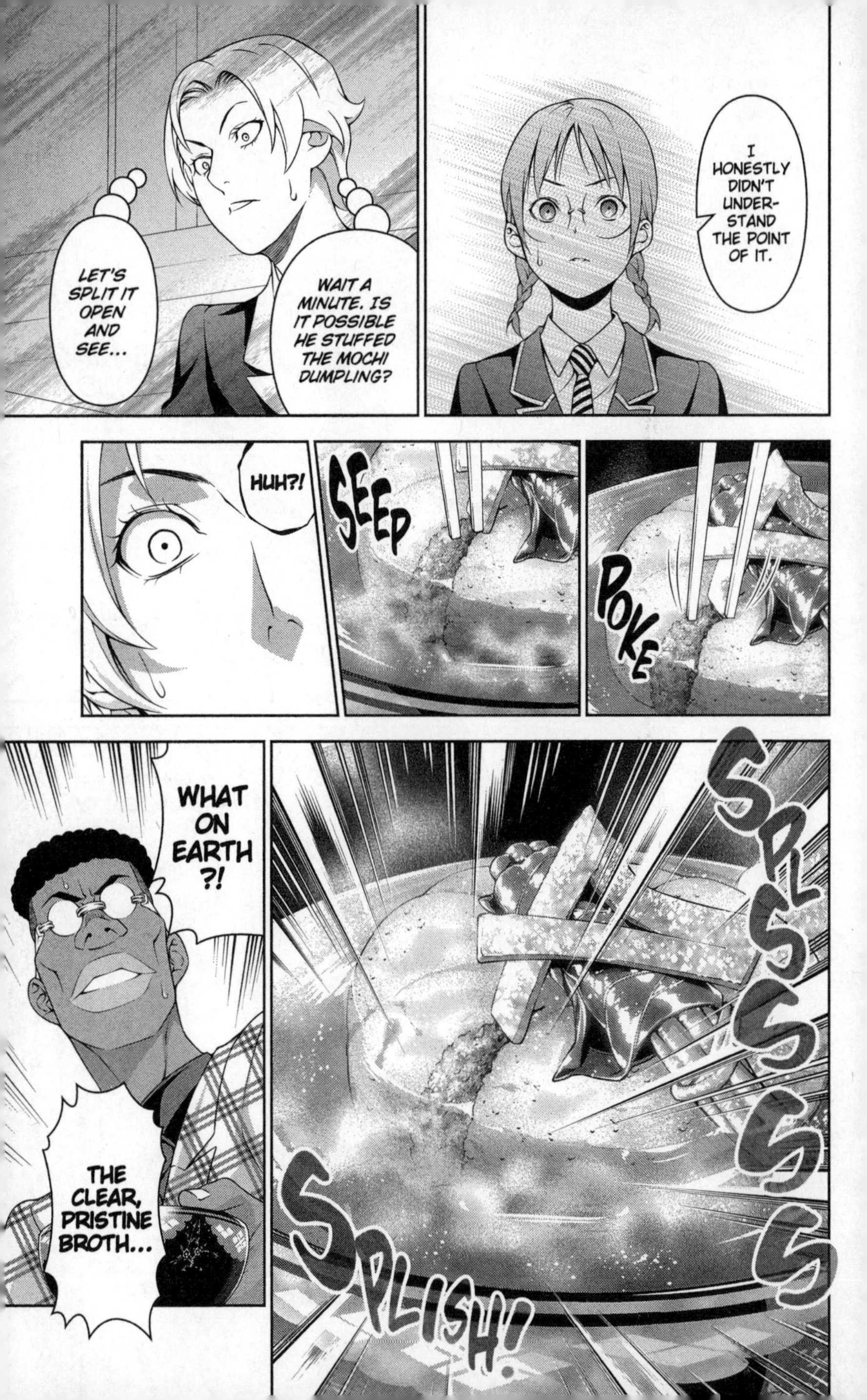
I HONESTLY DIDN'T UNDER-STAND THE POINT OF IT.
WAIT A MINUTE. IS IT POSSIBLE HE STUFFED THE MOCHI DUMPLING?
LET'S SPLIT IT OPEN AND SEE...
POKE
SEEP
HUH?!
SPLSSSSS
SPLISH!
WHAT ON EARTH ?!
THE CLEAR, PRISTINE BROTH...

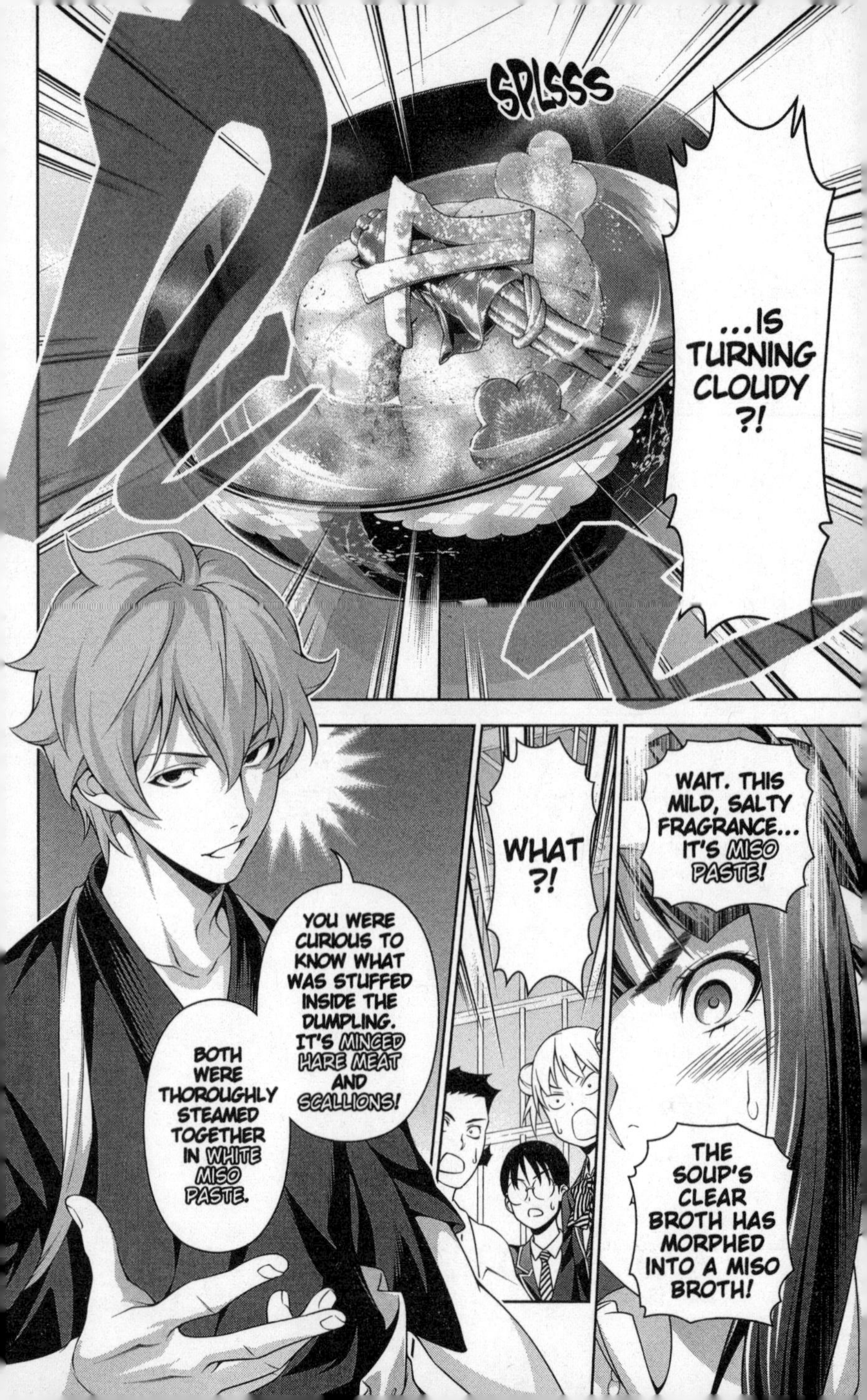
SPLSSS
...IS TURNING CLOUDY ?!
WAIT. THIS MILD, SALTY FRAGRANCE... IT'S MISO PASTE!
THE SOUP'S CLEAR BROTH HAS MORPHED INTO A MISO BROTH!
WHAT ?!
YOU WERE CURIOUS TO KNOW WHAT WAS STUFFED INSIDE THE DUMPLING. IT'S MINCED HARE MEAT AND SCALLIONS!
BOTH WERE THOROUGHLY STEAMED TOGETHER IN WHITE MISO PASTE.

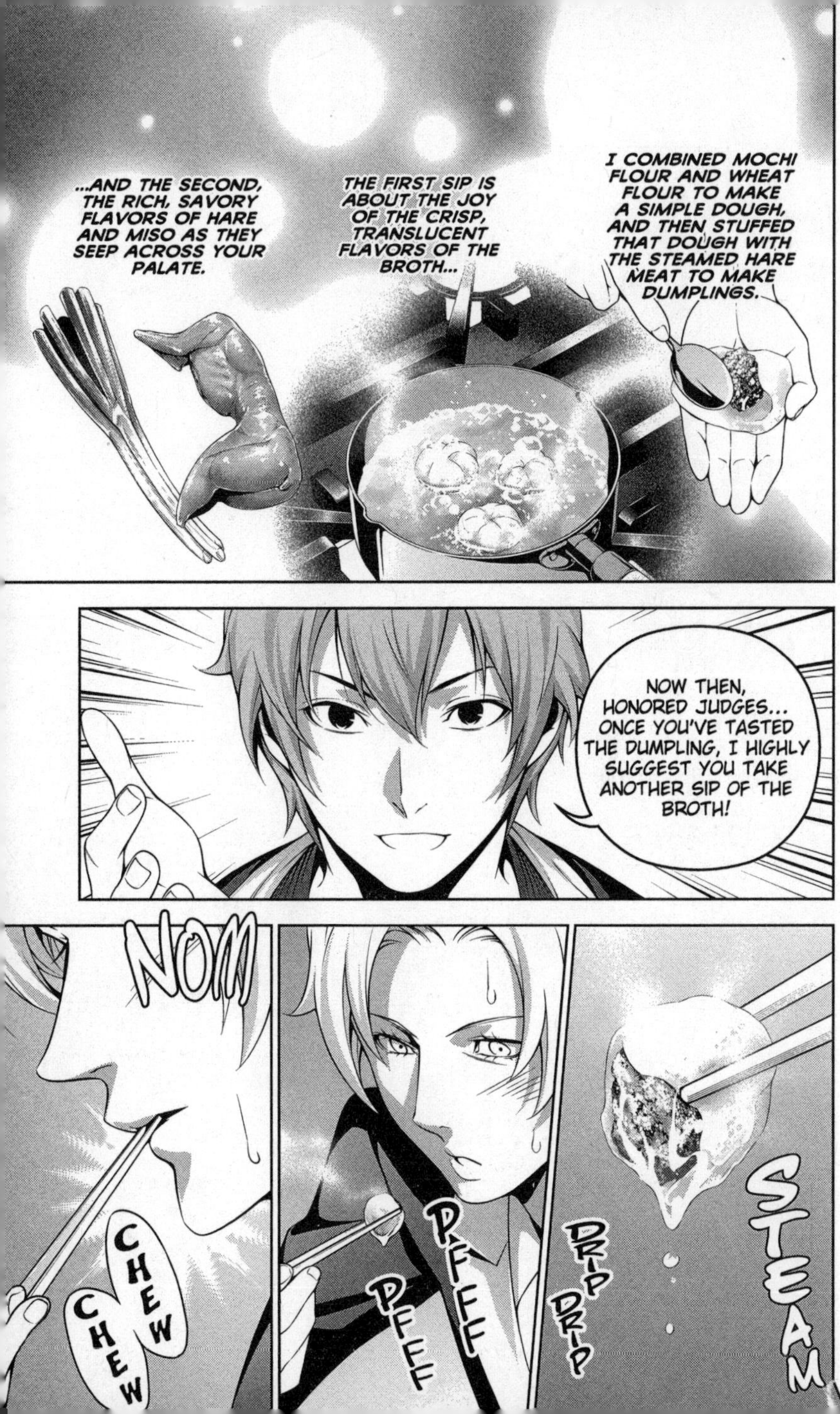
I COMBINED MOCHI FLOUR AND WHEAT FLOUR TO MAKE A SIMPLE DOUGH, AND THEN STUFFED THAT DOUGH WITH THE STEAMED HARE MEAT TO MAKE DUMPLINGS.
THE FIRST SIP IS ABOUT THE JOY OF THE CRISP, TRANSLUCENT FLAVORS OF THE BROTH...
...AND THE SECOND, THE RICH, SAVORY FLAVORS OF HARE AND MISO AS THEY SEEP ACROSS YOUR PALATE.
NOW THEN, HONORED JUDGES... ONCE YOU'VE TASTED THE DUMPLING, I HIGHLY SUGGEST YOU TAKE ANOTHER SIP OF THE BROTH!
STEAM
DRIP DRIP
PFFF PFFF
NOM
CHEW CHEW

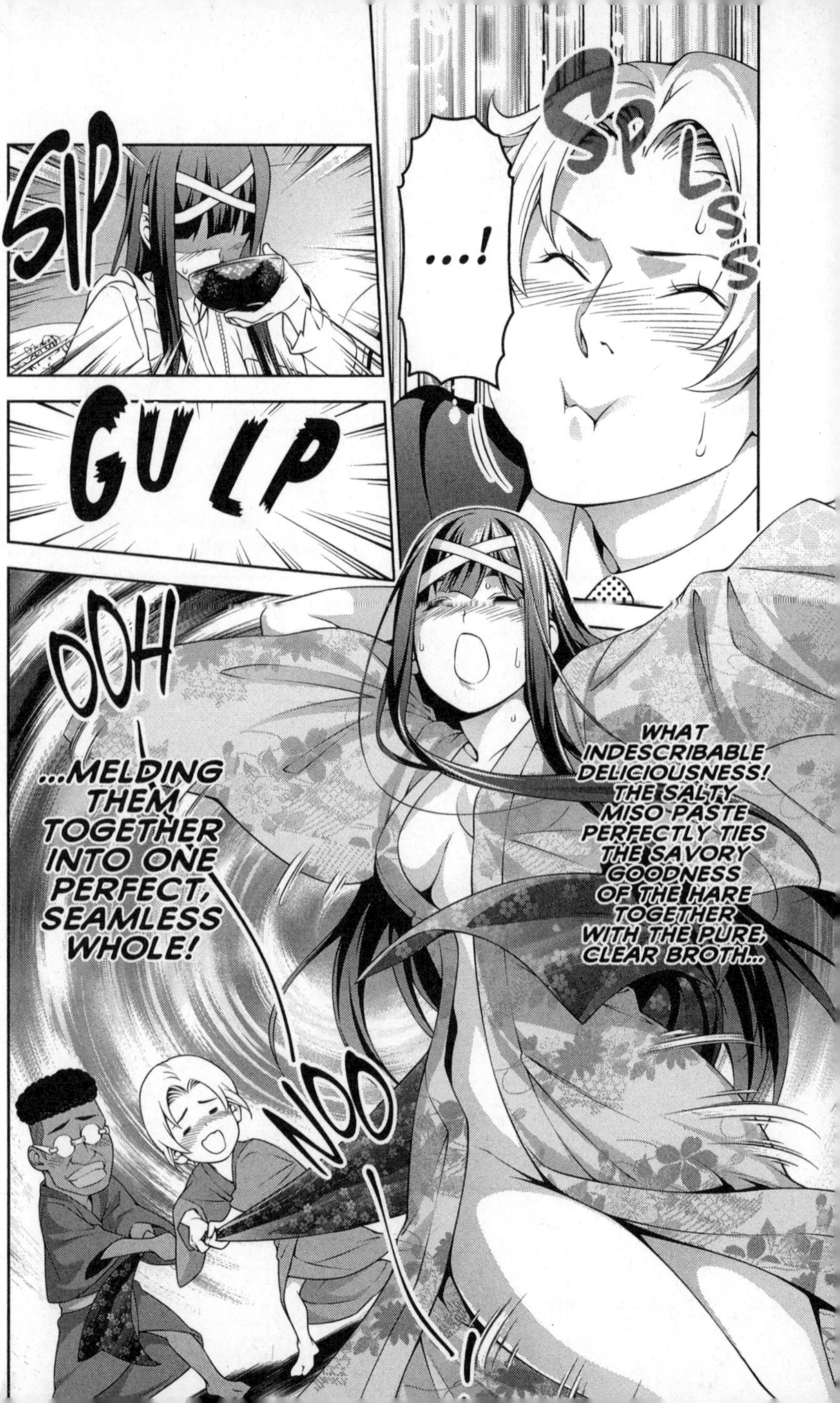
SPLSS
...!
SIP
GULP
WHAT INDESCRIBABLE DELICIOUSNESS! THE SALTY MISO PASTE PERFECTLY TIES THE SAVORY GOODNESS OF THE HARE TOGETHER WITH THE PURE, CLEAR BROTH...
OOH
...MELDING THEM TOGETHER INTO ONE PERFECT, SEAMLESS WHOLE!
NOO—!

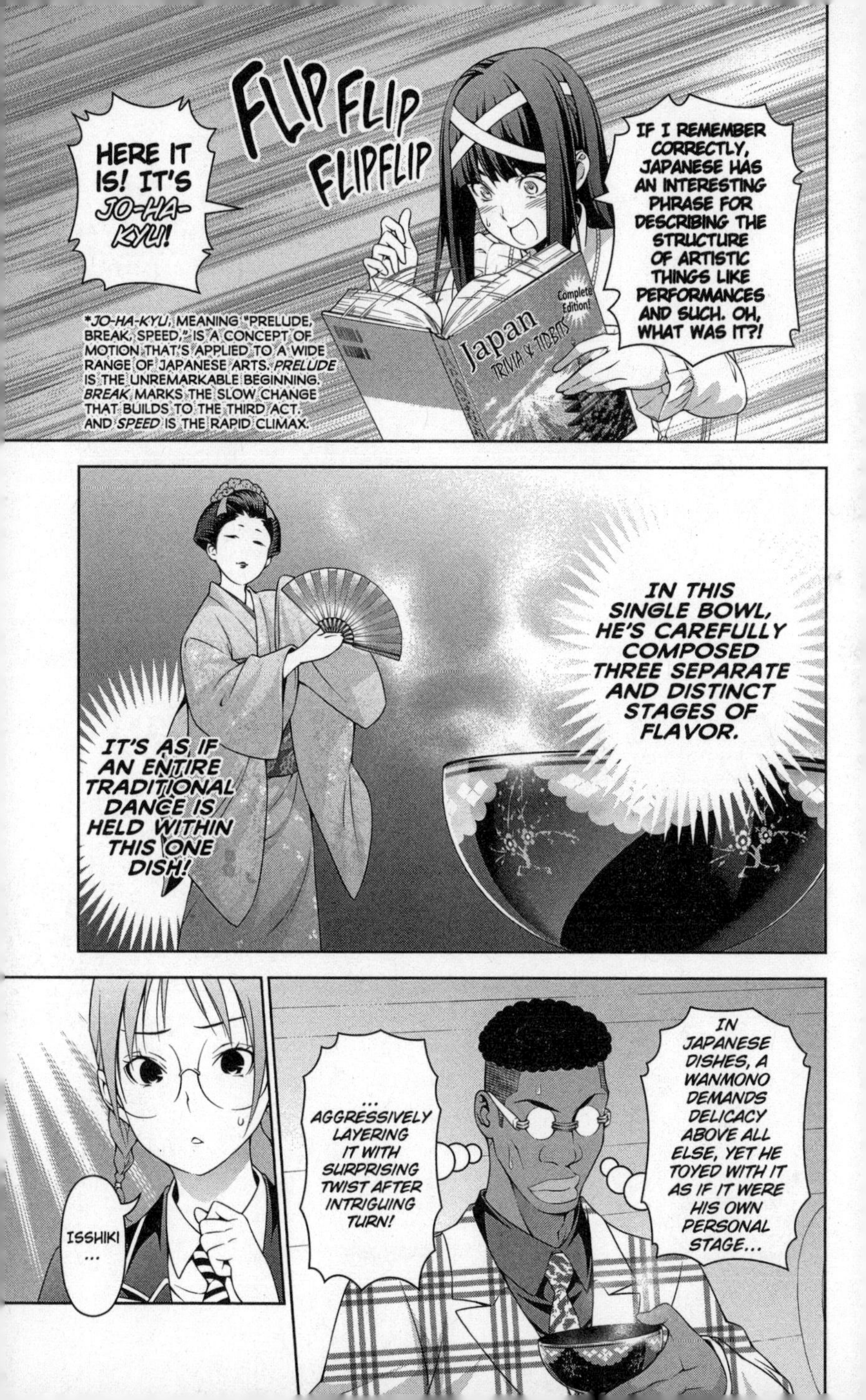
IF I REMEMBER CORRECTLY, JAPANESE HAS AN INTERESTING PHRASE FOR DESCRIBING THE STRUCTURE OF ARTISTIC THINGS LIKE PERFORMANCES AND SUCH. OH, WHAT WAS IT?!
FLIP FLIP FLIPFLIP
Complete Edition!
Japan TRIVIA & TIDBITS
HERE IT IS! IT'S JO-HA-KYU!
*JO-HA-KYU, MEANING "PRELUDE, BREAK, SPEED," IS A CONCEPT OF MOTION THAT'S APPLIED TO A WIDE RANGE OF JAPANESE ARTS. PRELUDE IS THE UNREMARKABLE BEGINNING. BREAK MARKS THE SLOW CHANGE THAT BUILDS TO THE THIRD ACT. AND SPEED IS THE RAPID CLIMAX.
IN THIS SINGLE BOWL, HE'S CAREFULLY COMPOSED THREE SEPARATE AND DISTINCT STAGES OF FLAVOR.
IT'S AS IF AN ENTIRE TRADITIONAL DANCE IS HELD WITHIN THIS ONE DISH!
IN JAPANESE DISHES, A WANMONO DEMANDS DELICACY ABOVE ALL ELSE, YET HE TOYED WITH IT AS IF IT WERE HIS OWN PERSONAL STAGE...
...AGGRESSIVELY LAYERING IT WITH SURPRISING TWIST AFTER INTRIGUING TURN!
ISSHIKI...

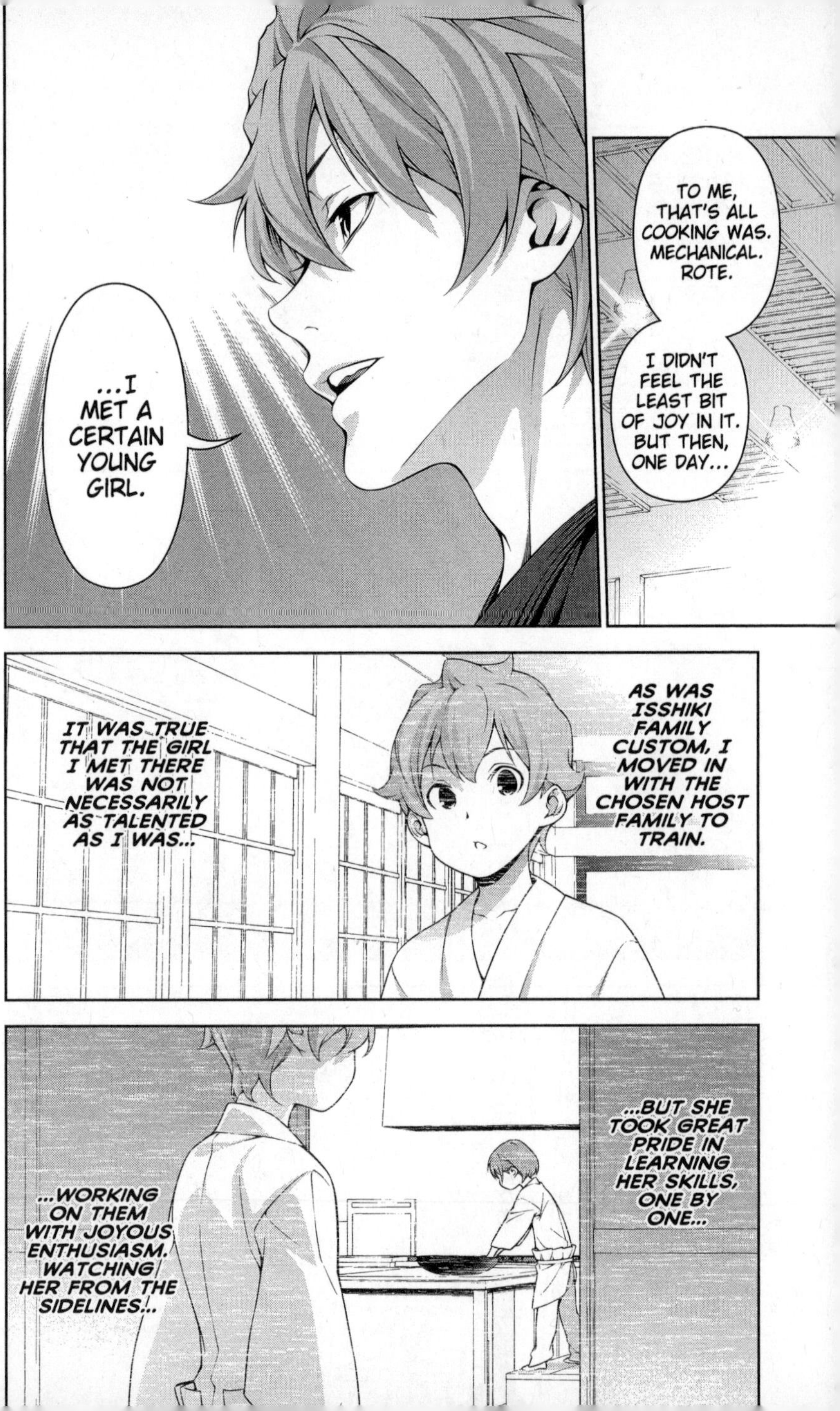
TO ME, THAT'S ALL COOKING WAS. MECHANICAL. ROTE.
I DIDN'T FEEL THE LEAST BIT OF JOY IN IT. BUT THEN, ONE DAY...
...I MET A CERTAIN YOUNG GIRL.
AS WAS ISSHIKI FAMILY CUSTOM, I MOVED IN WITH THE CHOSEN HOST FAMILY TO TRAIN.
IT WAS TRUE THAT THE GIRL I MET THERE WAS NOT NECESSARILY AS TALENTED AS I WAS...
...BUT SHE TOOK GREAT PRIDE IN LEARNING HER SKILLS, ONE BY ONE...
...WORKING ON THEM WITH JOYOUS ENTHUSIASM. WATCHING HER FROM THE SIDELINES...

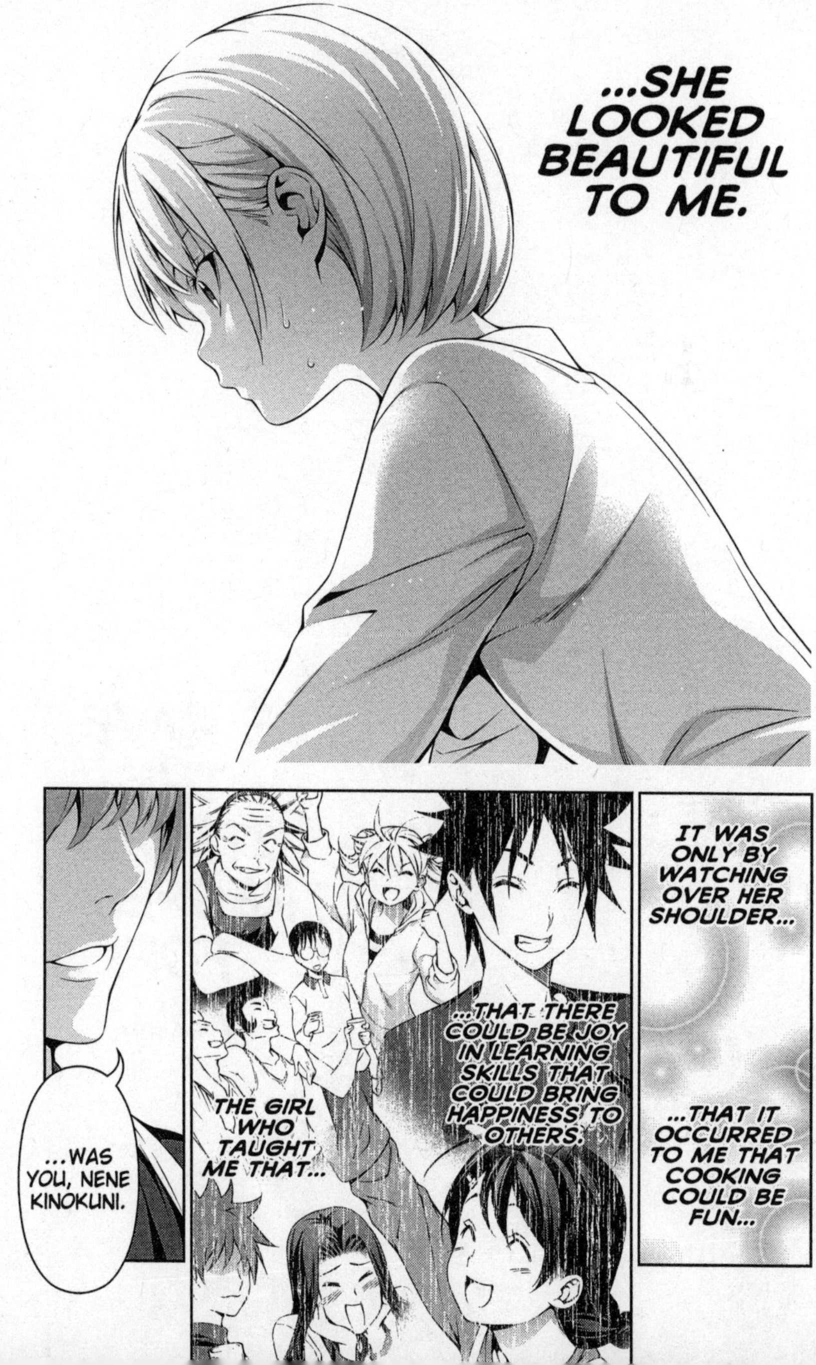
...SHE LOOKED BEAUTIFUL TO ME.
IT WAS ONLY BY WATCHING OVER HER SHOULDER...
...THAT IT OCCURRED TO ME THAT COOKING COULD BE FUN...
...THAT THERE COULD BE JOY IN LEARNING SKILLS THAT COULD BRING HAPPINESS TO OTHERS.
THE GIRL WHO TAUGHT ME THAT...
...WAS YOU, NENE KINOKUNI.

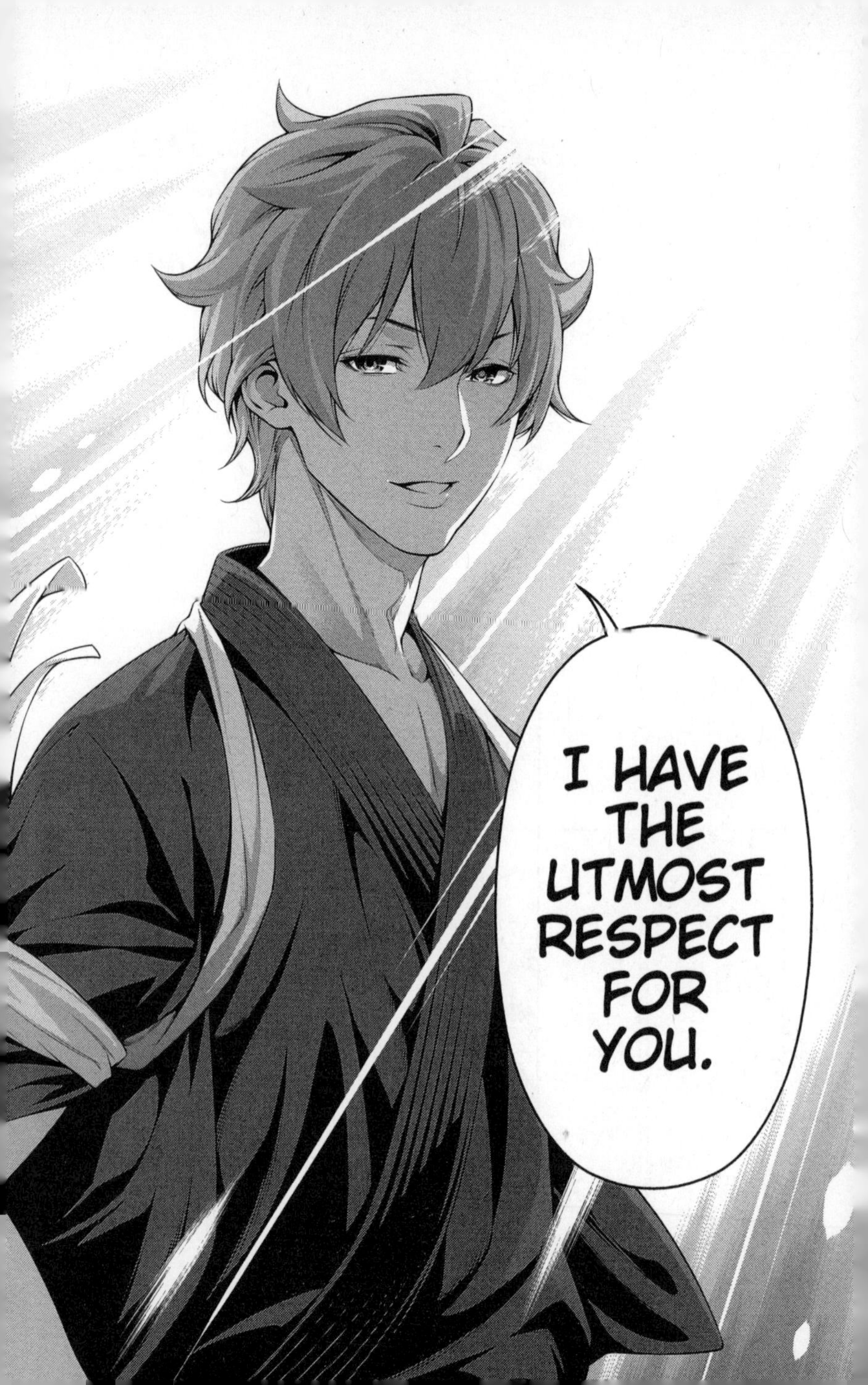
I HAVE THE UTMOST RESPECT FOR YOU.

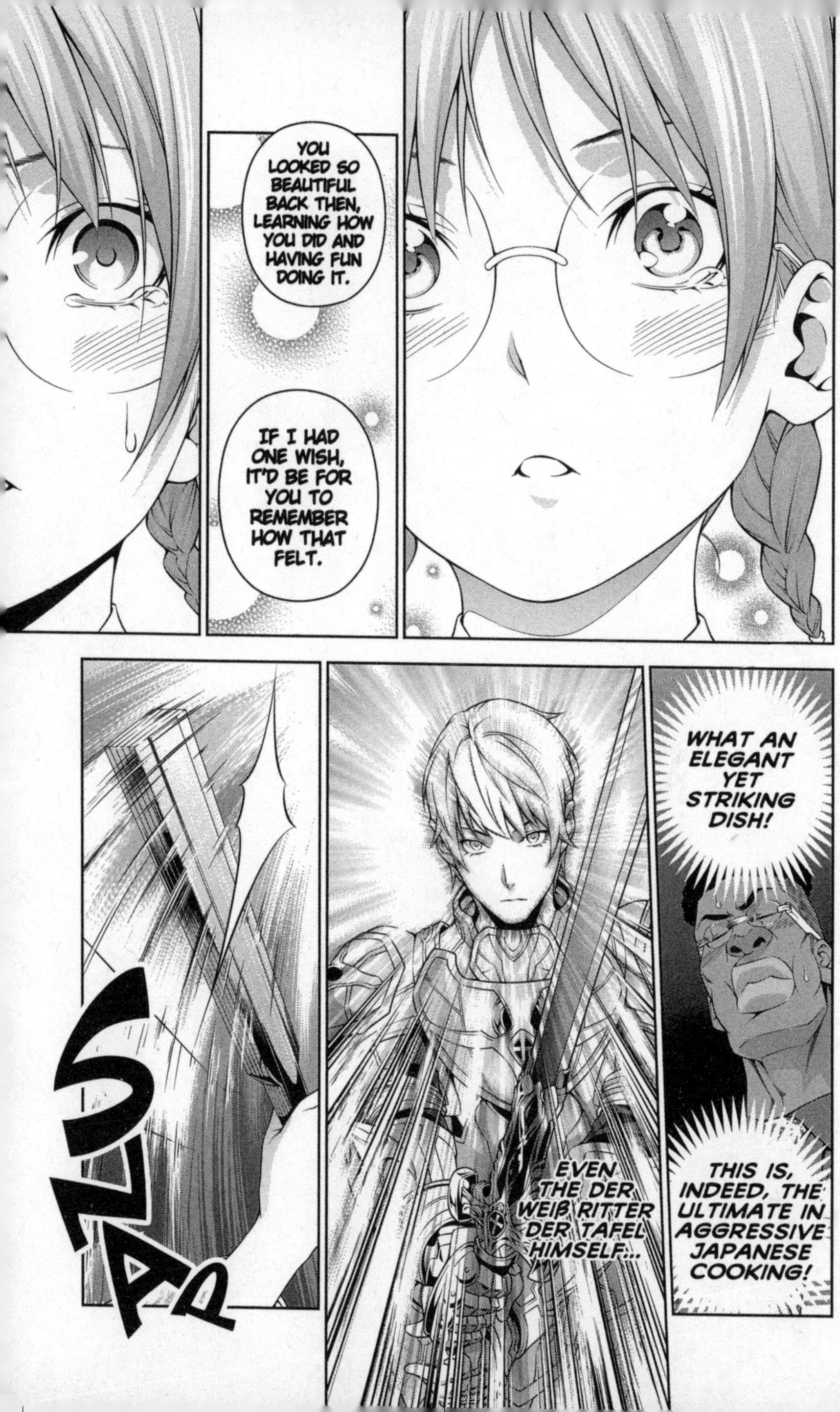
YOU LOOKED SO BEAUTIFUL BACK THEN, LEARNING HOW YOU DID AND HAVING FUN DOING IT.
IF I HAD ONE WISH, IT'D BE FOR YOU TO REMEMBER HOW THAT FELT.
WHAT AN ELEGANT YET STRIKING DISH!
THIS IS, INDEED, THE ULTIMATE IN AGGRESSIVE JAPANESE COOKING!
EVEN THE DER WEIß RITTER DER TAFEL HIMSELF...
SNAP

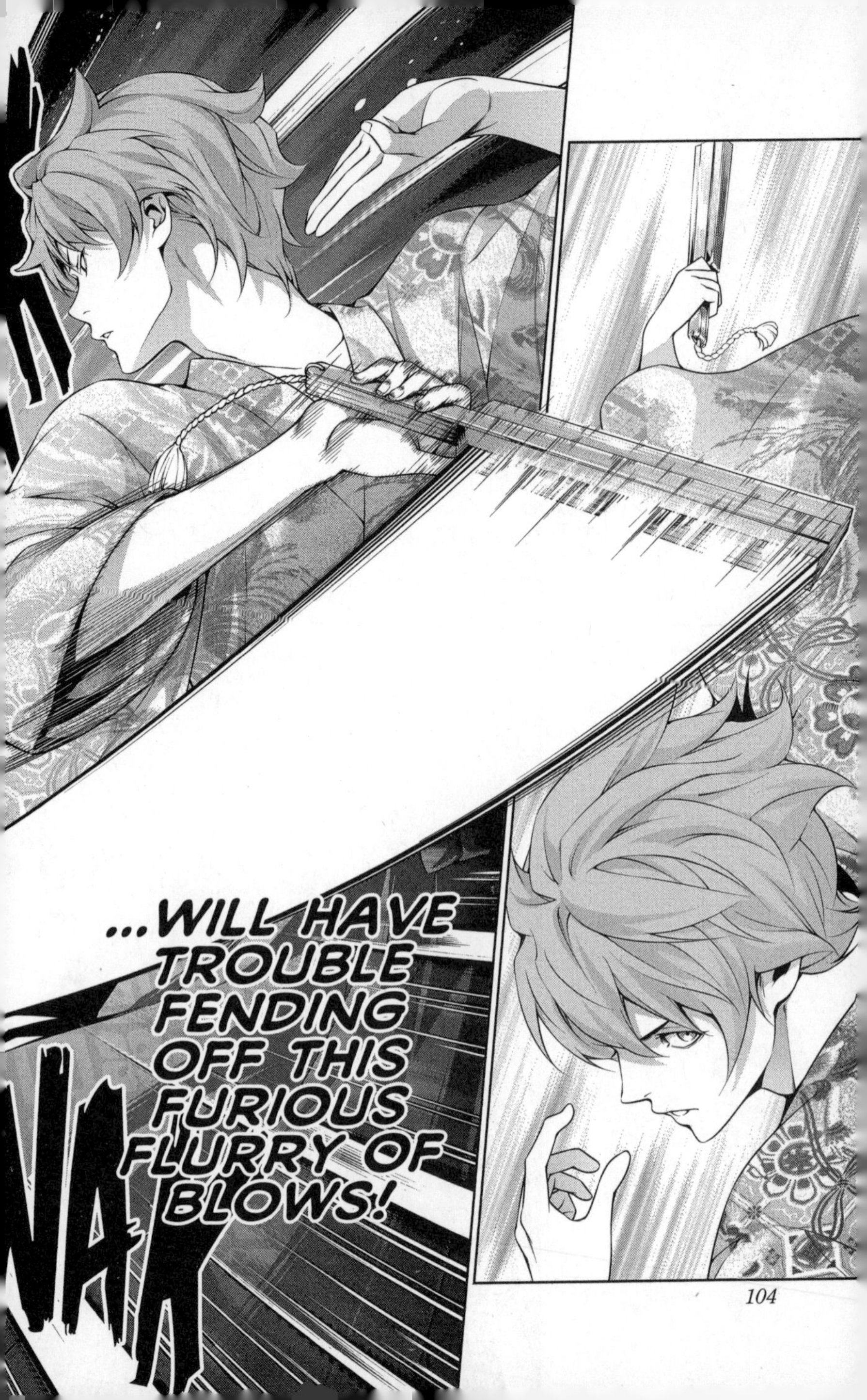
...WILL HAVE TROUBLE FENDING OFF THIS FURIOUS FLURRY OF BLOWS!

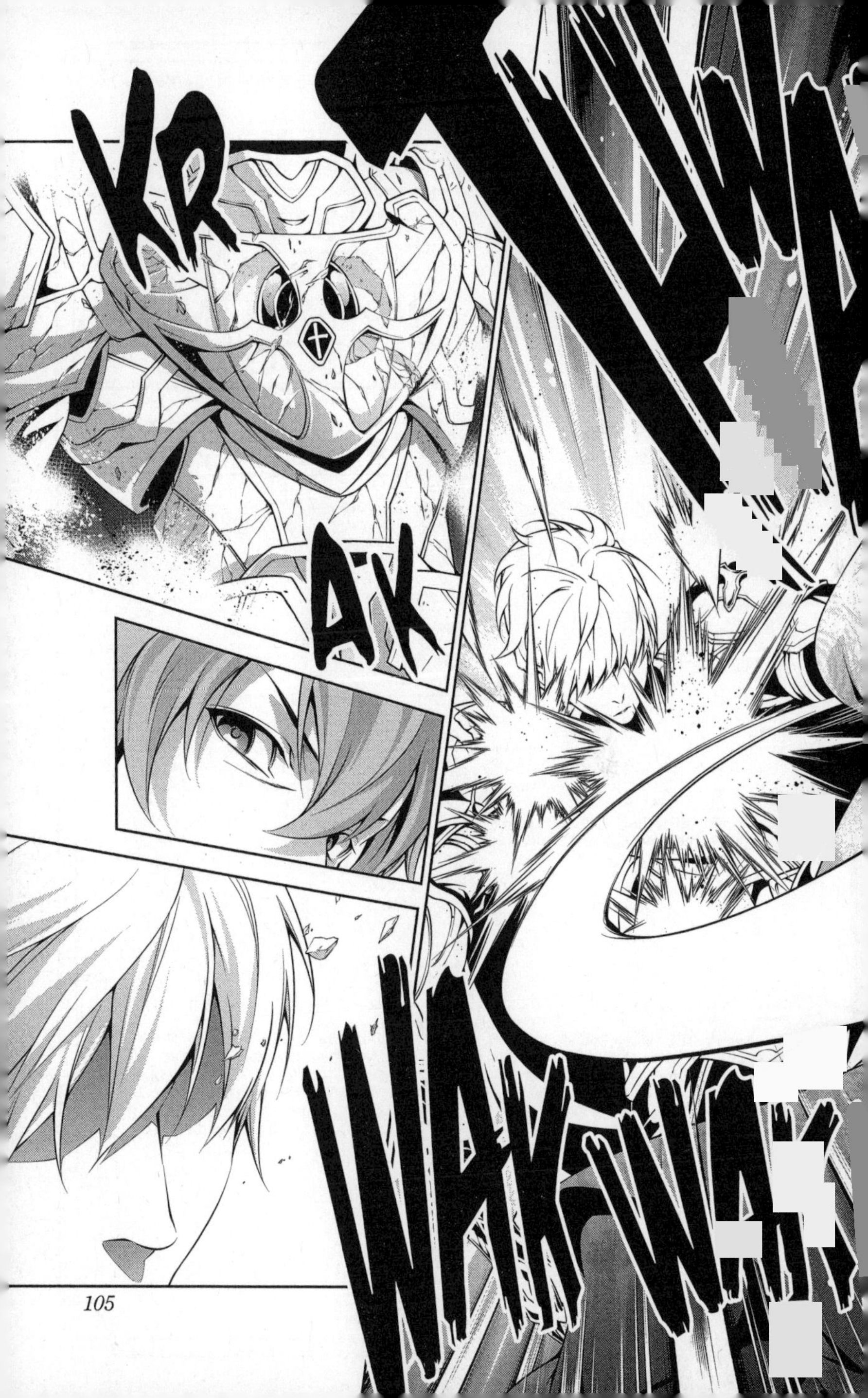
KRAK

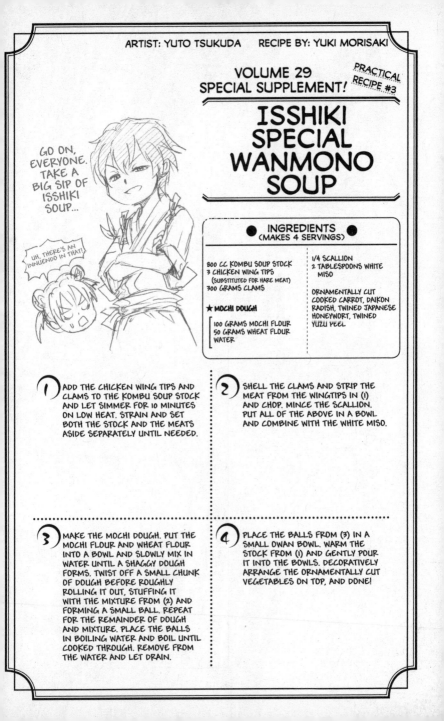

ARTIST: YUTO TSUKUDA   RECIPE BY: YUKI MORISAKI

VOLUME 29
SPECIAL SUPPLEMENT! PRACTICAL RECIPE #3

ISSHIKI SPECIAL WANMONO SOUP

GO ON, EVERYONE. TAKE A BIG SIP OF ISSHIKI SOUP...

UH, THERE'S AN INNUENDO IN THAT!

● INGREDIENTS ●
(MAKES 4 SERVINGS)

800 CC KOMBU SOUP STOCK
3 CHICKEN WING TIPS
(SUBSTITUTED FOR HARE MEAT)
300 GRAMS CLAMS

★ MOCHI DOUGH

100 GRAMS MOCHI FLOUR
50 GRAMS WHEAT FLOUR
WATER

1/4 SCALLION
2 TABLESPOONS WHITE MISO

ORNAMENTALLY CUT COOKED CARROT, DAIKON RADISH, TWINED JAPANESE HONEYWORT, TWINED YUZU PEEL

1 ADD THE CHICKEN WING TIPS AND CLAMS TO THE KOMBU SOUP STOCK AND LET SIMMER FOR 10 MINUTES ON LOW HEAT. STRAIN AND SET BOTH THE STOCK AND THE MEATS ASIDE SEPARATELY UNTIL NEEDED.

2 SHELL THE CLAMS AND STRIP THE MEAT FROM THE WINGTIPS IN (1) AND CHOP. MINCE THE SCALLION. PUT ALL OF THE ABOVE IN A BOWL AND COMBINE WITH THE WHITE MISO.

3 MAKE THE MOCHI DOUGH. PUT THE MOCHI FLOUR AND WHEAT FLOUR INTO A BOWL AND SLOWLY MIX IN WATER UNTIL A SHAGGY DOUGH FORMS. TWIST OFF A SMALL CHUNK OF DOUGH BEFORE ROUGHLY ROLLING IT OUT, STUFFING IT WITH THE MIXTURE FROM (2) AND FORMING A SMALL BALL. REPEAT FOR THE REMAINDER OF DOUGH AND MIXTURE. PLACE THE BALLS IN BOILING WATER AND BOIL UNTIL COOKED THROUGH. REMOVE FROM THE WATER AND LET DRAIN.

4 PLACE THE BALLS FROM (3) IN A SMALL OWAN BOWL. WARM THE STOCK FROM (1) AND GENTLY POUR IT INTO THE BOWLS. DECORATIVELY ARRANGE THE ORNAMENTALLY CUT VEGETABLES ON TOP, AND DONE!

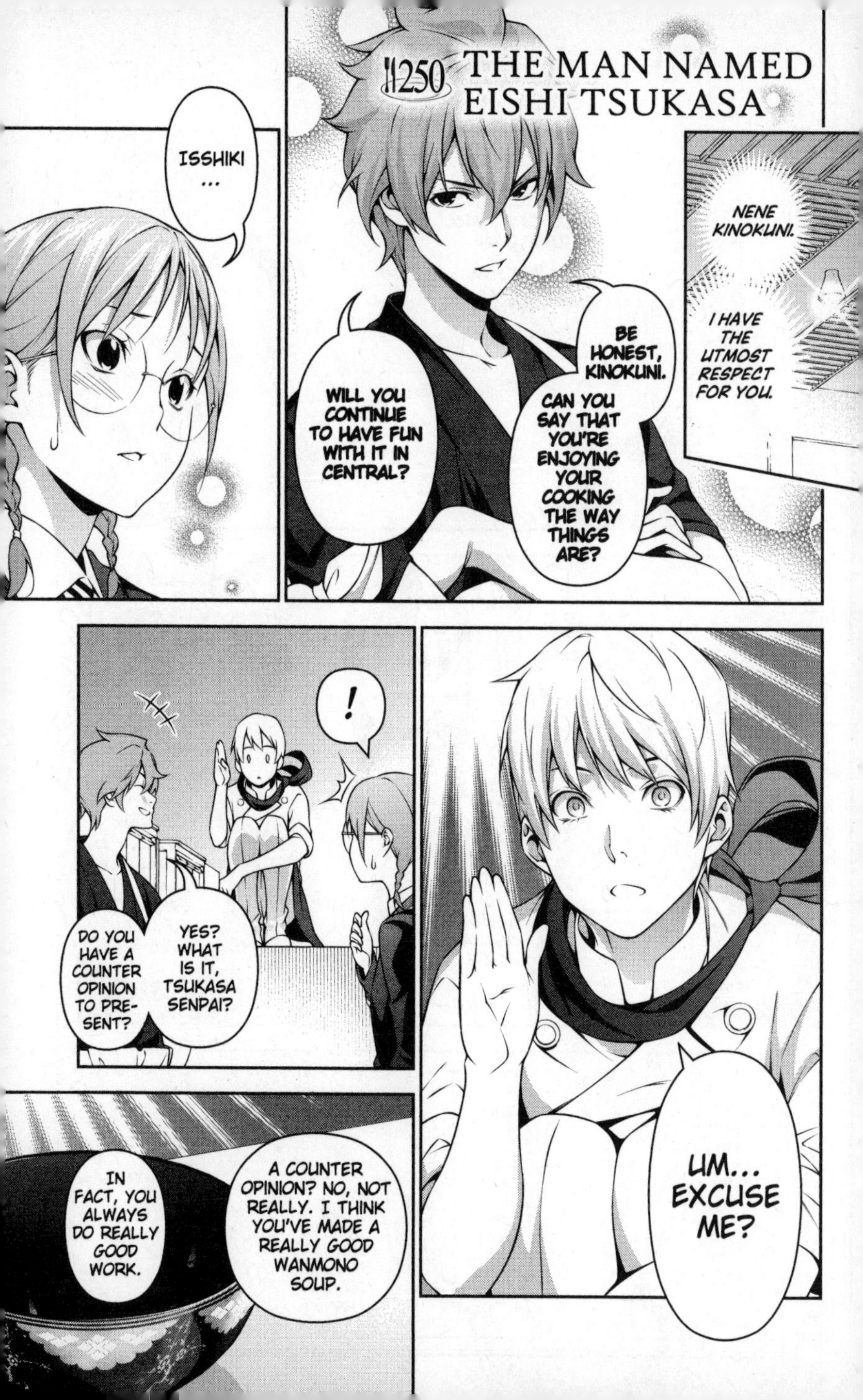

250 THE MAN NAMED EISHI TSUKASA
NENE KINOKUNI.
I HAVE THE UTMOST RESPECT FOR YOU.
BE HONEST, KINOKUNI.
CAN YOU SAY THAT YOU'RE ENJOYING YOUR COOKING THE WAY THINGS ARE?
WILL YOU CONTINUE TO HAVE FUN WITH IT IN CENTRAL?
ISSHIKI...
UM... EXCUSE ME?
!
YES? WHAT IS IT, TSUKASA SENPAI?
DO YOU HAVE A COUNTER OPINION TO PRE-SENT?
A COUNTER OPINION? NO, NOT REALLY. I THINK YOU'VE MADE A REALLY GOOD WANMONO SOUP.
IN FACT, YOU ALWAYS DO REALLY GOOD WORK.

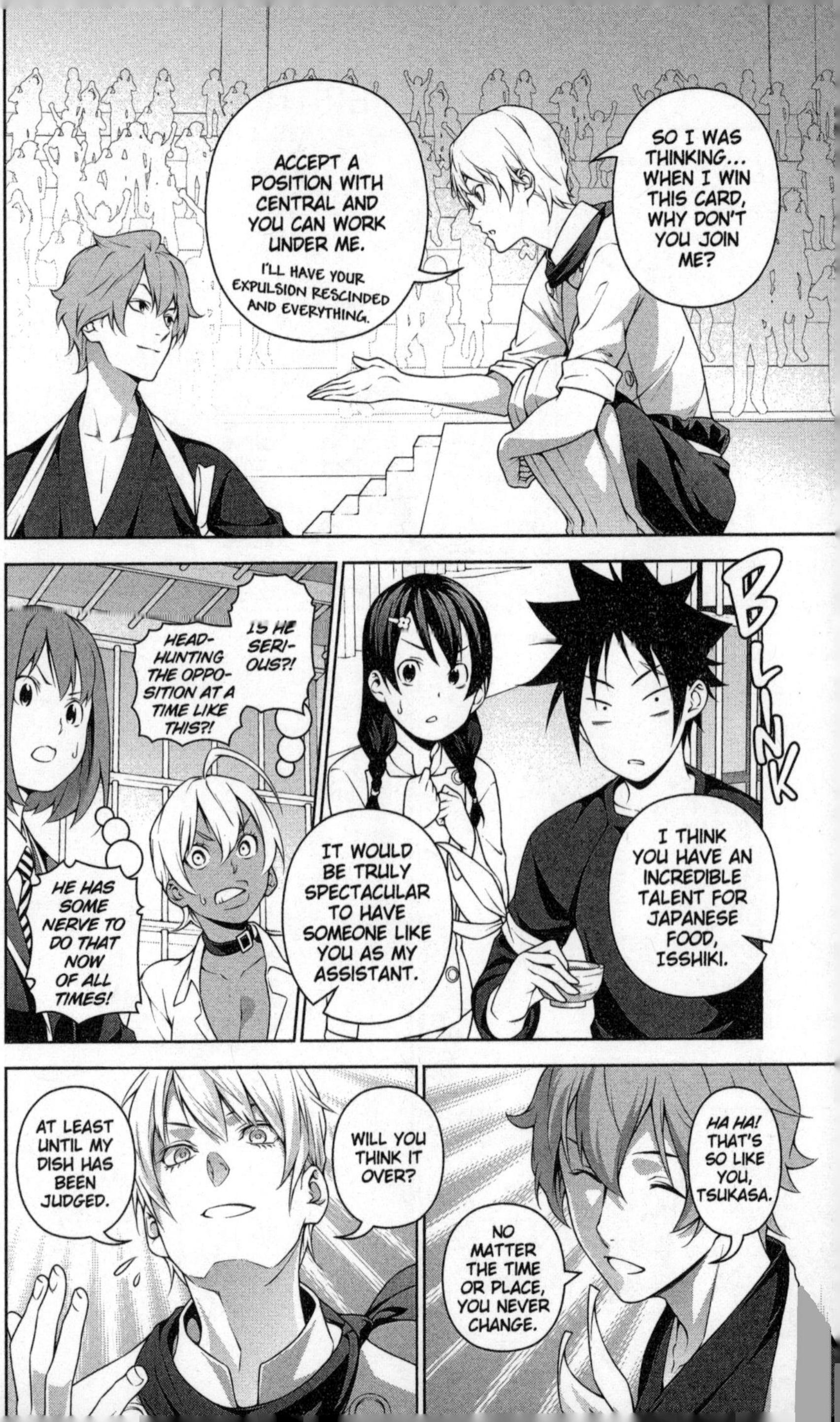
SO I WAS THINKING... WHEN I WIN THIS CARD, WHY DON'T YOU JOIN ME?
ACCEPT A POSITION WITH CENTRAL AND YOU CAN WORK UNDER ME.
I'LL HAVE YOUR EXPULSION RESCINDED AND EVERYTHING.
BLINK
I THINK YOU HAVE AN INCREDIBLE TALENT FOR JAPANESE FOOD, ISSHIKI.
IT WOULD BE TRULY SPECTACULAR TO HAVE SOMEONE LIKE YOU AS MY ASSISTANT.
IS HE SERIOUS?!
HEAD-HUNTING THE OPPOSITION AT A TIME LIKE THIS?!
HE HAS SOME NERVE TO DO THAT NOW OF ALL TIMES!
HA HA! THAT'S SO LIKE YOU, TSUKASA.
NO MATTER THE TIME OR PLACE, YOU NEVER CHANGE.
WILL YOU THINK IT OVER?
AT LEAST UNTIL MY DISH HAS BEEN JUDGED.

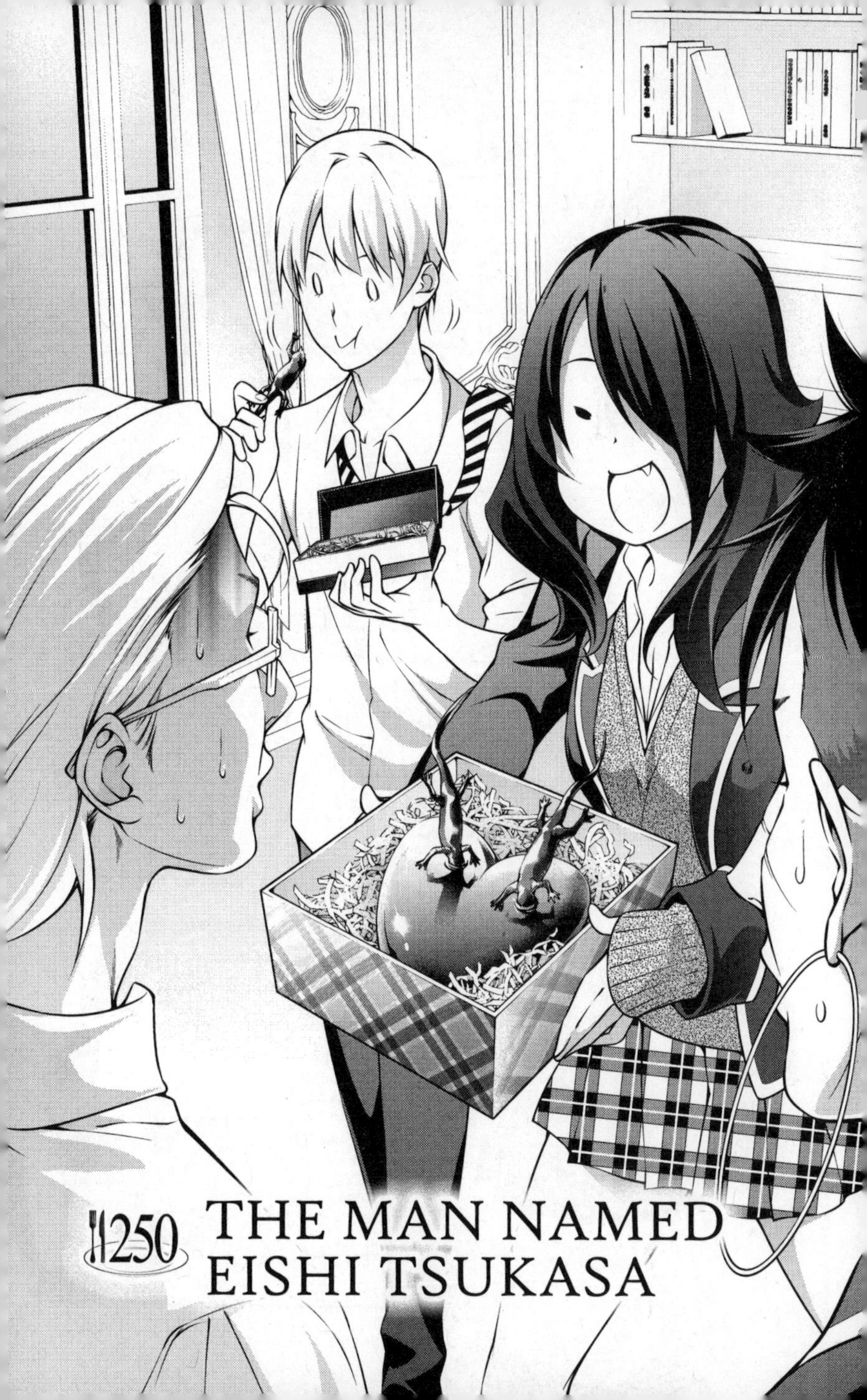
250
THE MAN NAMED
EISHI TSUKASA

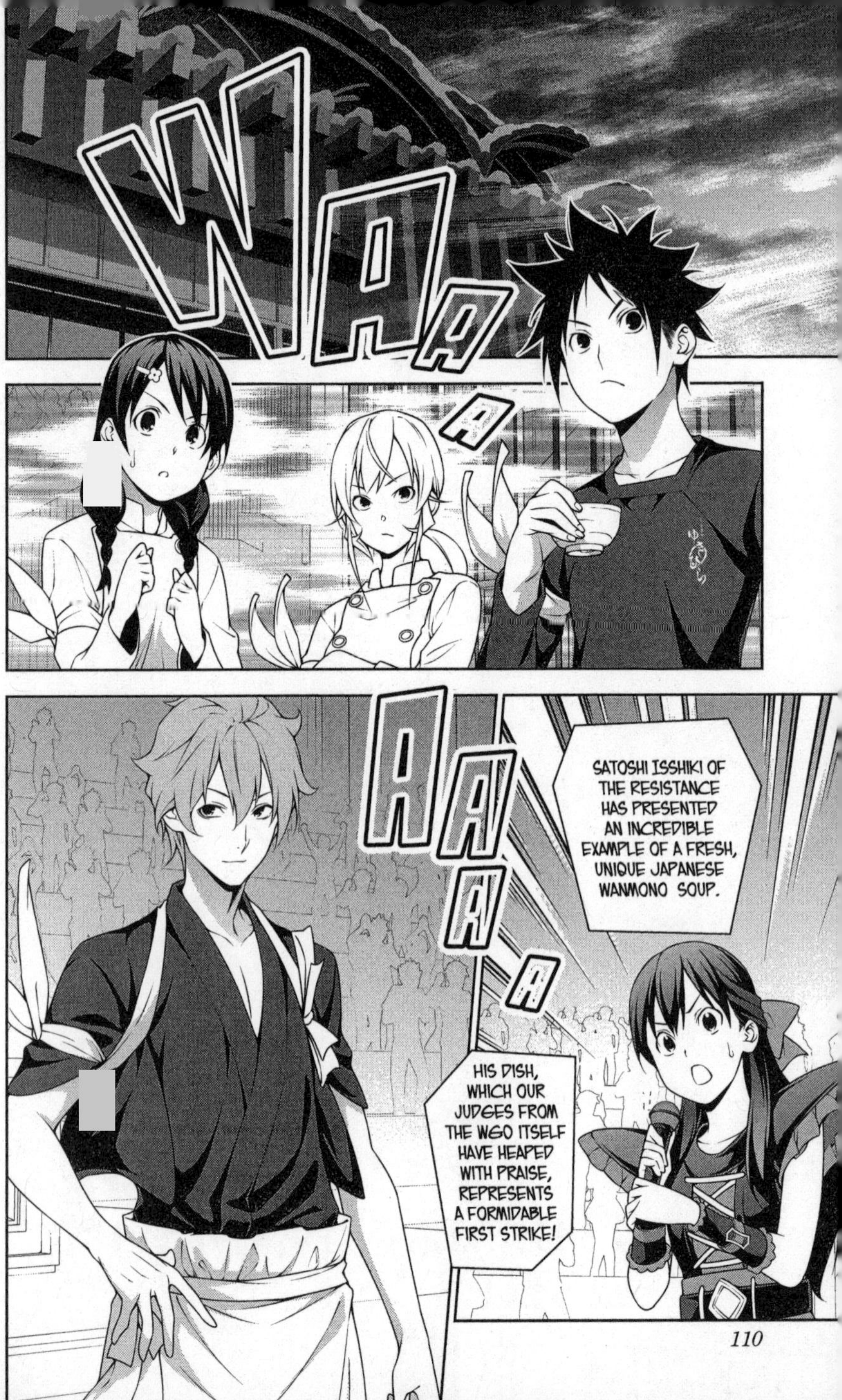
WAAA
A
AAAAA
SATOSHI ISSHIKI OF THE RESISTANCE HAS PRESENTED AN INCREDIBLE EXAMPLE OF A FRESH, UNIQUE JAPANESE WANMONO SOUP.
HIS DISH, WHICH OUR JUDGES FROM THE WGO ITSELF HAVE HEAPED WITH PRAISE, REPRESENTS A FORMIDABLE FIRST STRIKE!

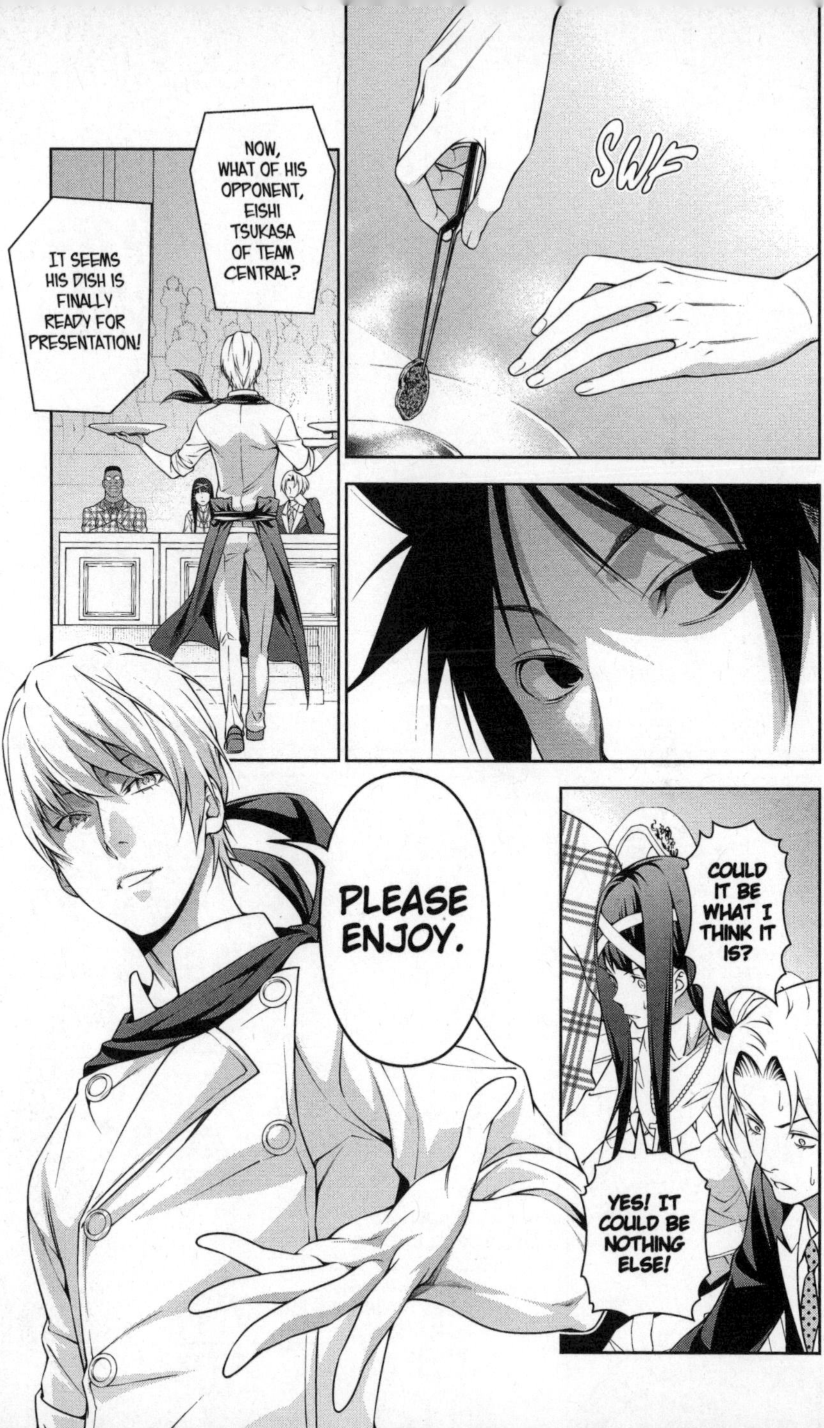
SWF
NOW, WHAT OF HIS OPPONENT, EISHI TSUKASA OF TEAM CENTRAL?
IT SEEMS HIS DISH IS FINALLY READY FOR PRESENTATION!
COULD IT BE WHAT I THINK IT IS?
YES! IT COULD BE NOTHING ELSE!
PLEASE ENJOY.

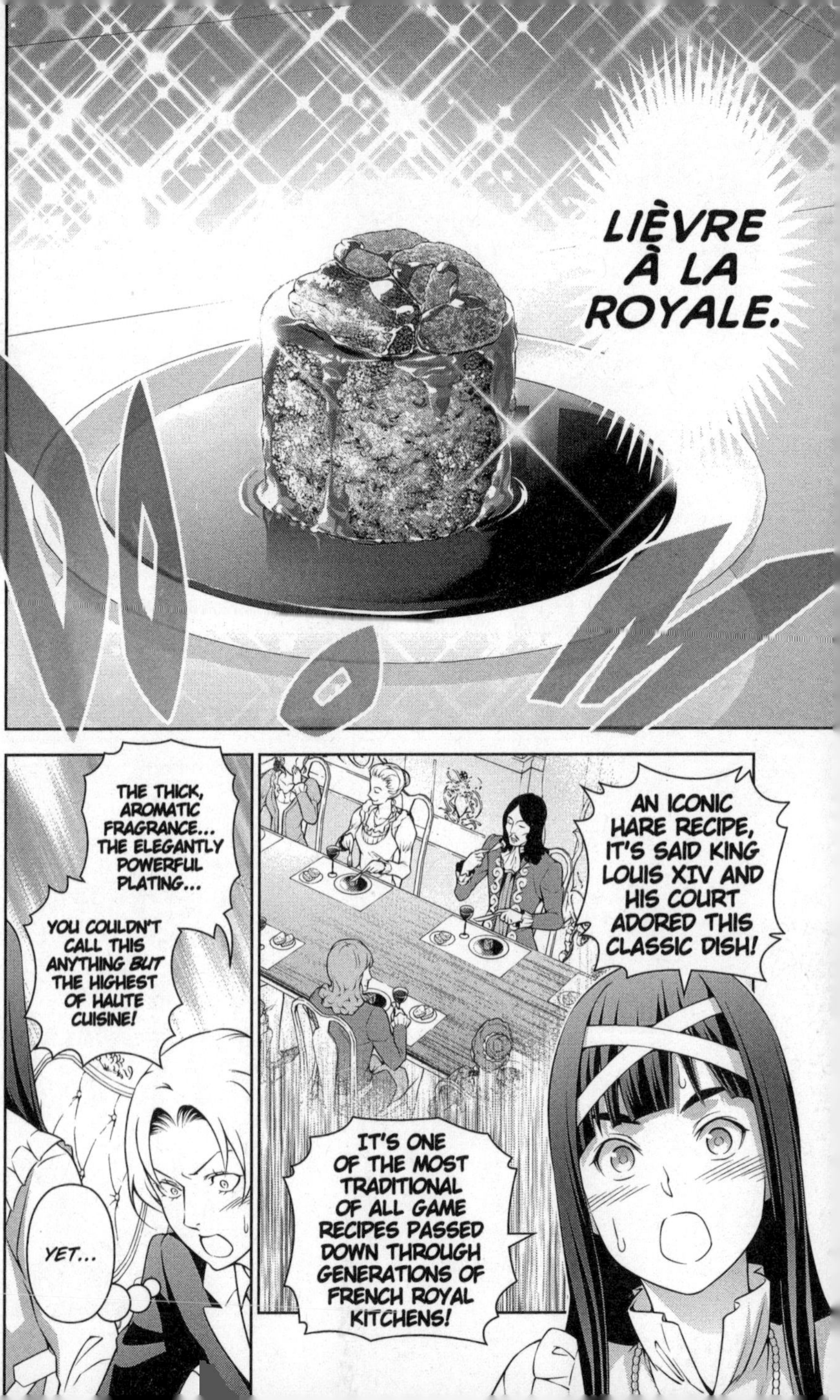
LIÈVRE À LA ROYALE.
AN ICONIC HARE RECIPE, IT'S SAID KING LOUIS XIV AND HIS COURT ADORED THIS CLASSIC DISH!
IT'S ONE OF THE MOST TRADITIONAL OF ALL GAME RECIPES PASSED DOWN THROUGH GENERATIONS OF FRENCH ROYAL KITCHENS!
THE THICK, AROMATIC FRAGRANCE... THE ELEGANTLY POWERFUL PLATING...
YOU COULDN'T CALL THIS ANYTHING *BUT* THE HIGHEST OF HAUTE CUISINE!
YET...

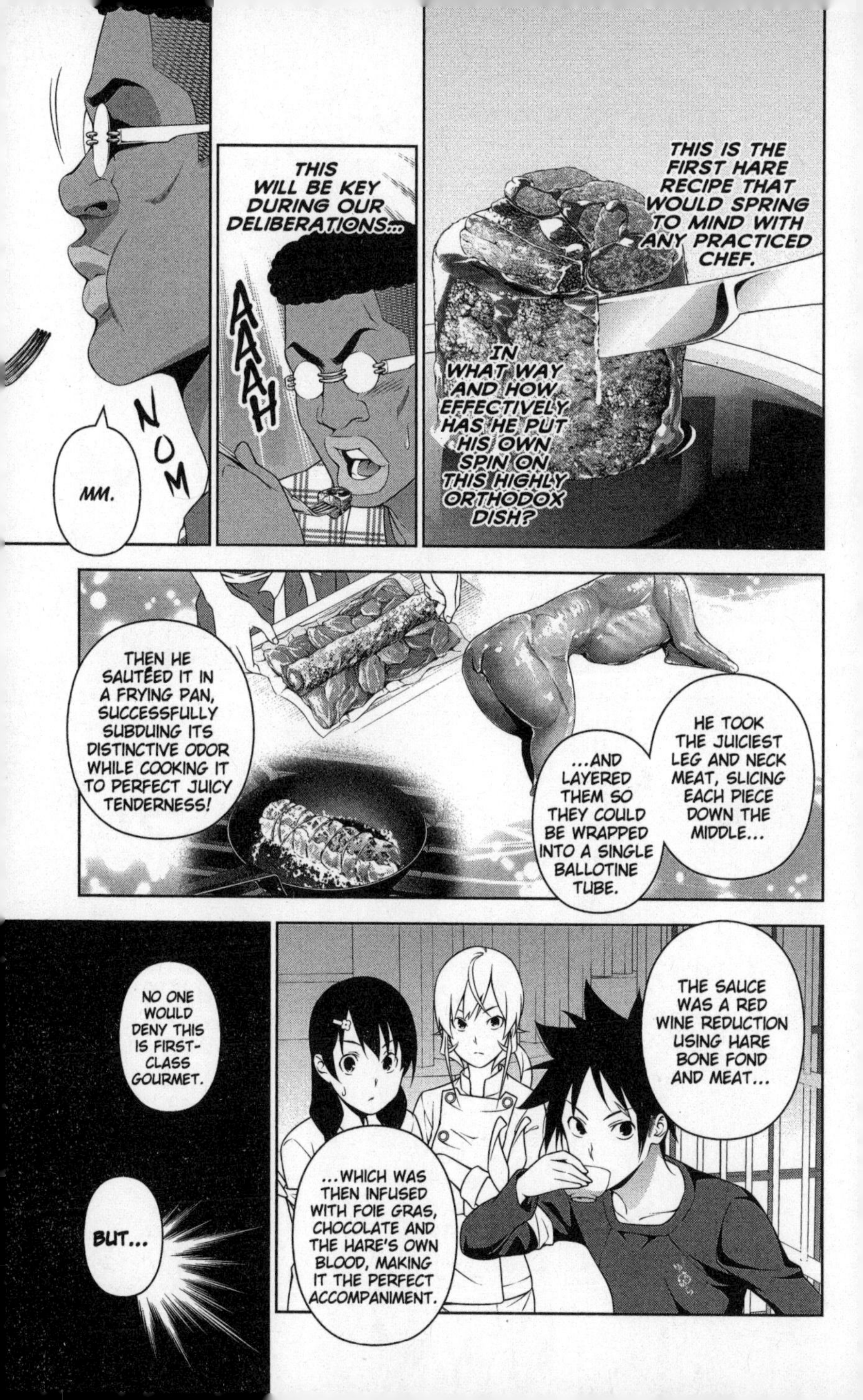
THIS IS THE FIRST HARE RECIPE THAT WOULD SPRING TO MIND WITH ANY PRACTICED CHEF.
IN WHAT WAY AND HOW EFFECTIVELY HAS HE PUT HIS OWN SPIN ON THIS HIGHLY ORTHODOX DISH?
THIS WILL BE KEY DURING OUR DELIBERATIONS...
AAAH
NOM
MM.
HE TOOK THE JUICIEST LEG AND NECK MEAT, SLICING EACH PIECE DOWN THE MIDDLE...
...AND LAYERED THEM SO THEY COULD BE WRAPPED INTO A SINGLE BALLOTINE TUBE.
THEN HE SAUTÉED IT IN A FRYING PAN, SUCCESSFULLY SUBDUING ITS DISTINCTIVE ODOR WHILE COOKING IT TO PERFECT JUICY TENDERNESS!
THE SAUCE WAS A RED WINE REDUCTION USING HARE BONE FOND AND MEAT...
...WHICH WAS THEN INFUSED WITH FOIE GRAS, CHOCOLATE AND THE HARE'S OWN BLOOD, MAKING IT THE PERFECT ACCOMPANIMENT.
NO ONE WOULD DENY THIS IS FIRST-CLASS GOURMET.
BUT...

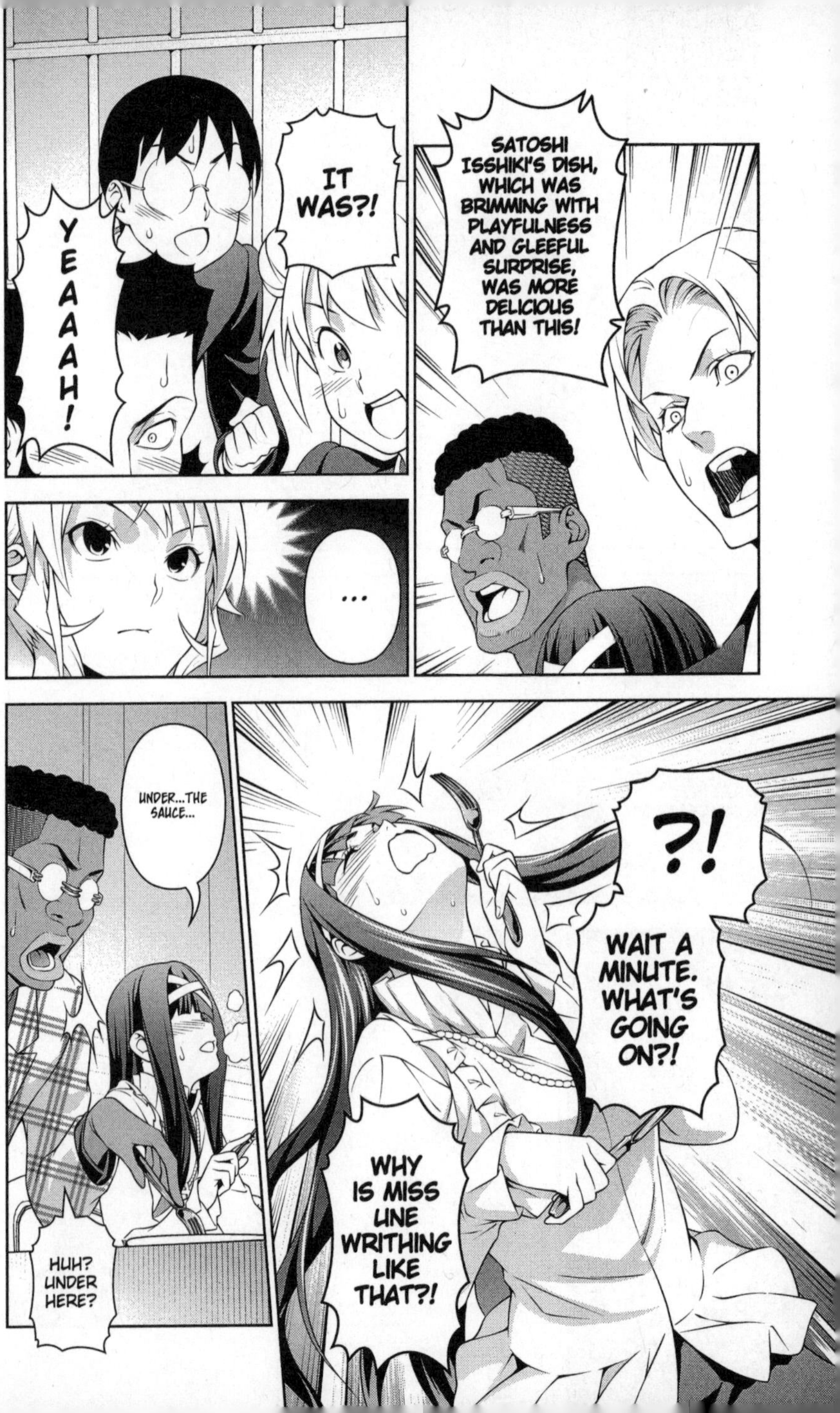
SATOSHI ISSHIKI'S DISH, WHICH WAS BRIMMING WITH PLAYFULNESS AND GLEEFUL SURPRISE, WAS MORE DELICIOUS THAN THIS!
IT WAS?!
YEAAAAH!
...
?!
WAIT A MINUTE. WHAT'S GOING ON?!
WHY IS MISS UNE WRITHING LIKE THAT?!
UNDER...THE SAUCE...
HUH? UNDER HERE?

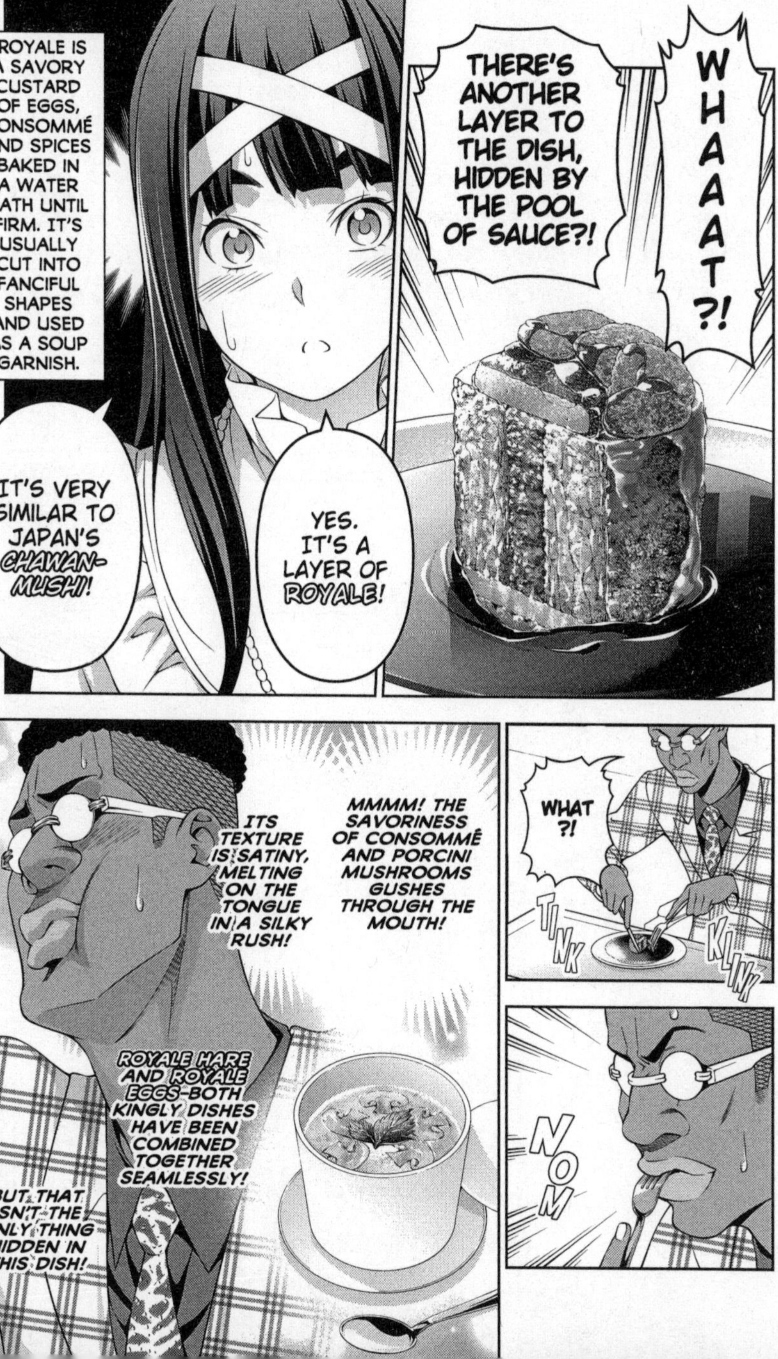
WHAAAAT?!
THERE'S ANOTHER LAYER TO THE DISH, HIDDEN BY THE POOL OF SAUCE?!
YES. IT'S A LAYER OF ROYALE!
IT'S VERY SIMILAR TO JAPAN'S CHAWAN-MUSHI!
*ROYALE IS A SAVORY CUSTARD OF EGGS, CONSOMMÉ AND SPICES BAKED IN A WATER BATH UNTIL FIRM. IT'S USUALLY CUT INTO FANCIFUL SHAPES AND USED AS A SOUP GARNISH.
WHAT?!
KLINK
TINK
NOM
MMMM! THE SAVORINESS OF CONSOMMÉ AND PORCINI MUSHROOMS GUSHES THROUGH THE MOUTH!
ITS TEXTURE IS SATINY, MELTING ON THE TONGUE IN A SILKY RUSH!
ROYALE HARE AND ROYALE EGGS—BOTH KINGLY DISHES HAVE BEEN COMBINED TOGETHER SEAMLESSLY!
BUT THAT ISN'T THE ONLY THING HIDDEN IN THIS DISH!

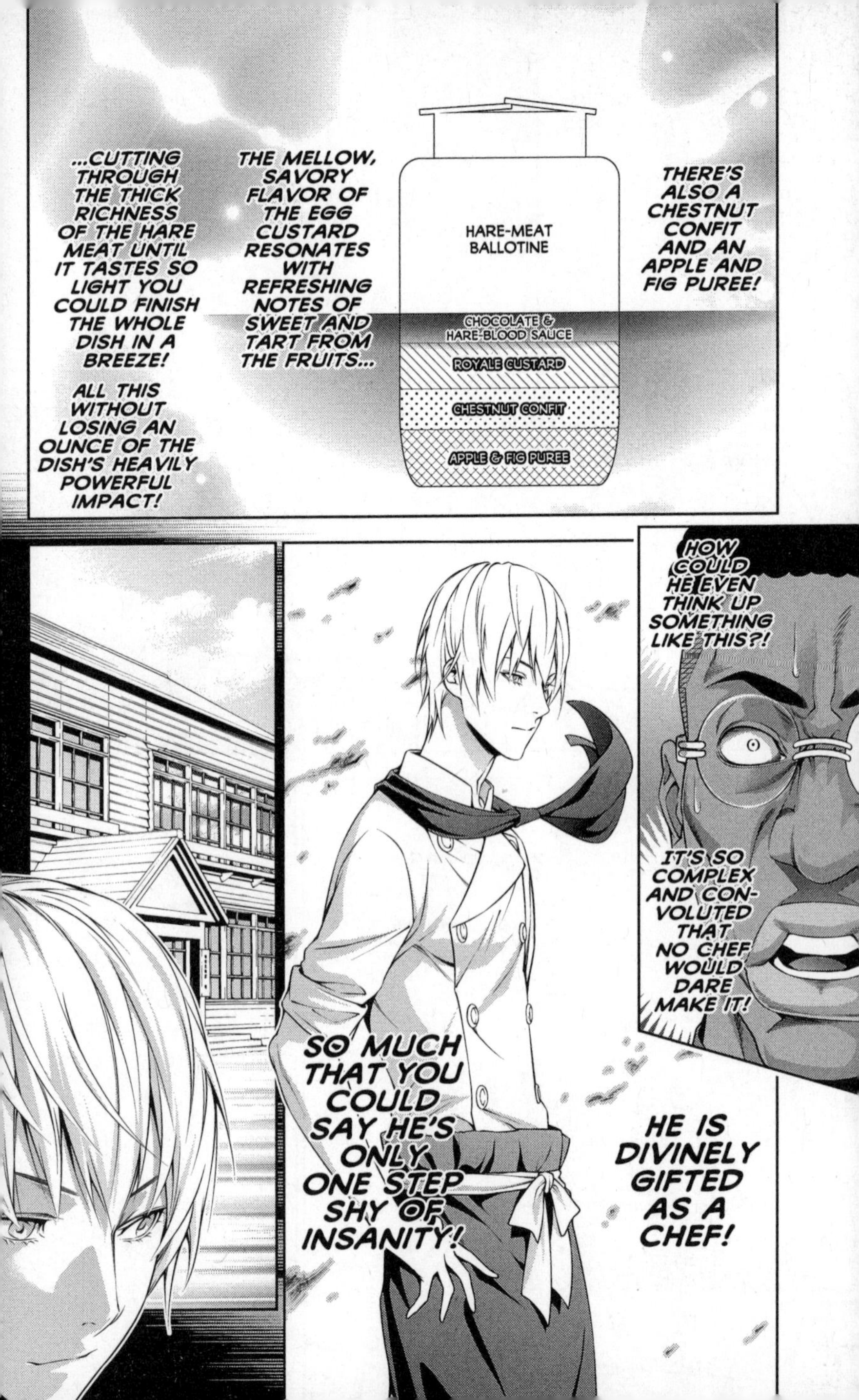

THERE'S ALSO A CHESTNUT CONFIT AND AN APPLE AND FIG PUREE!
HARE-MEAT BALLOTINE
CHOCOLATE & HARE-BLOOD SAUCE
ROYALE CUSTARD
CHESTNUT CONFIT
APPLE & FIG PUREE
THE MELLOW, SAVORY FLAVOR OF THE EGG CUSTARD RESONATES WITH REFRESHING NOTES OF SWEET AND TART FROM THE FRUITS...
...CUTTING THROUGH THE THICK RICHNESS OF THE HARE MEAT UNTIL IT TASTES SO LIGHT YOU COULD FINISH THE WHOLE DISH IN A BREEZE!
ALL THIS WITHOUT LOSING AN OUNCE OF THE DISH'S HEAVILY POWERFUL IMPACT!
HOW COULD HE EVEN THINK UP SOMETHING LIKE THIS?!
IT'S SO COMPLEX AND CON-VOLUTED THAT NO CHEF WOULD DARE MAKE IT!
HE IS DIVINELY GIFTED AS A CHEF!
SO MUCH THAT YOU COULD SAY HE'S ONLY ONE STEP SHY OF INSANITY!

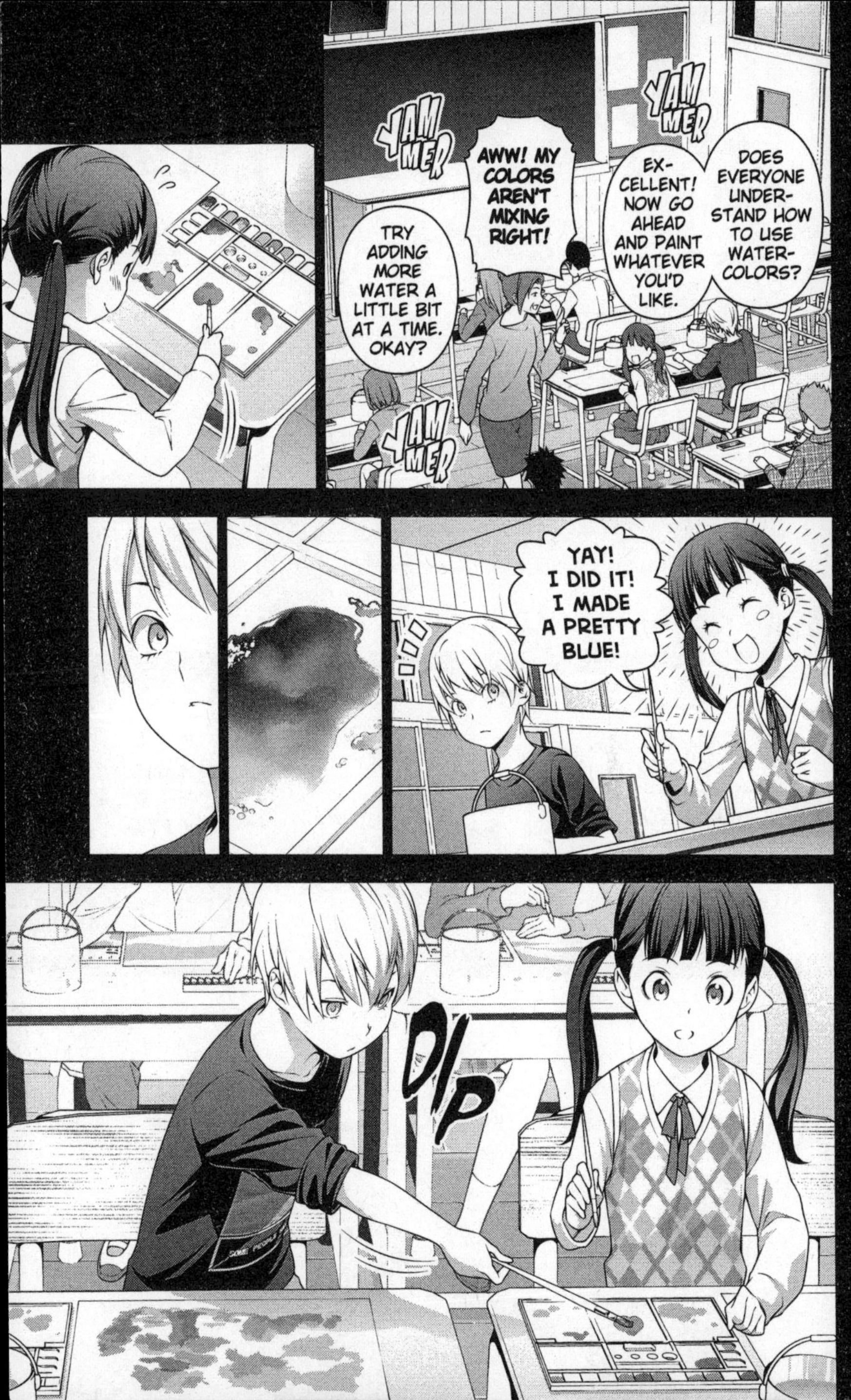
YAMMER
DOES EVERYONE UNDER-STAND HOW TO USE WATER-COLORS?
EX-CELLENT! NOW GO AHEAD AND PAINT WHATEVER YOU'D LIKE.
AWW! MY COLORS AREN'T MIXING RIGHT!
YAMMER
TRY ADDING MORE WATER A LITTLE BIT AT A TIME. OKAY?
YAMMER
YAY! I DID IT! I MADE A PRETTY BLUE!
DIP

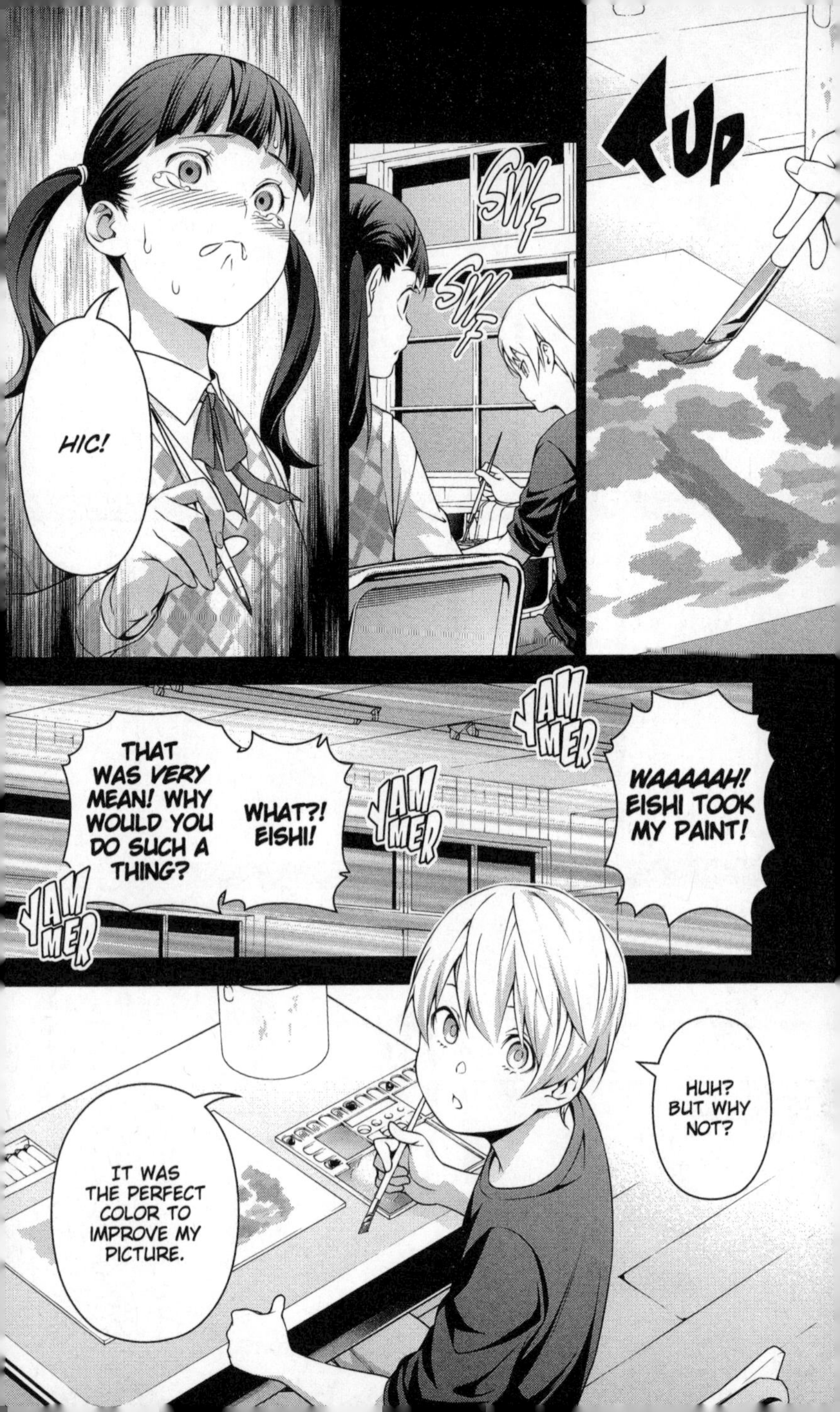
TUP
SWF
SWF
HIC!
YAMMER
WAAAAAH! EISHI TOOK MY PAINT!
YAMMER
WHAT?! EISHI!
THAT WAS VERY MEAN! WHY WOULD YOU DO SUCH A THING?
YAMMER
HUH? BUT WHY NOT?
IT WAS THE PERFECT COLOR TO IMPROVE MY PICTURE.

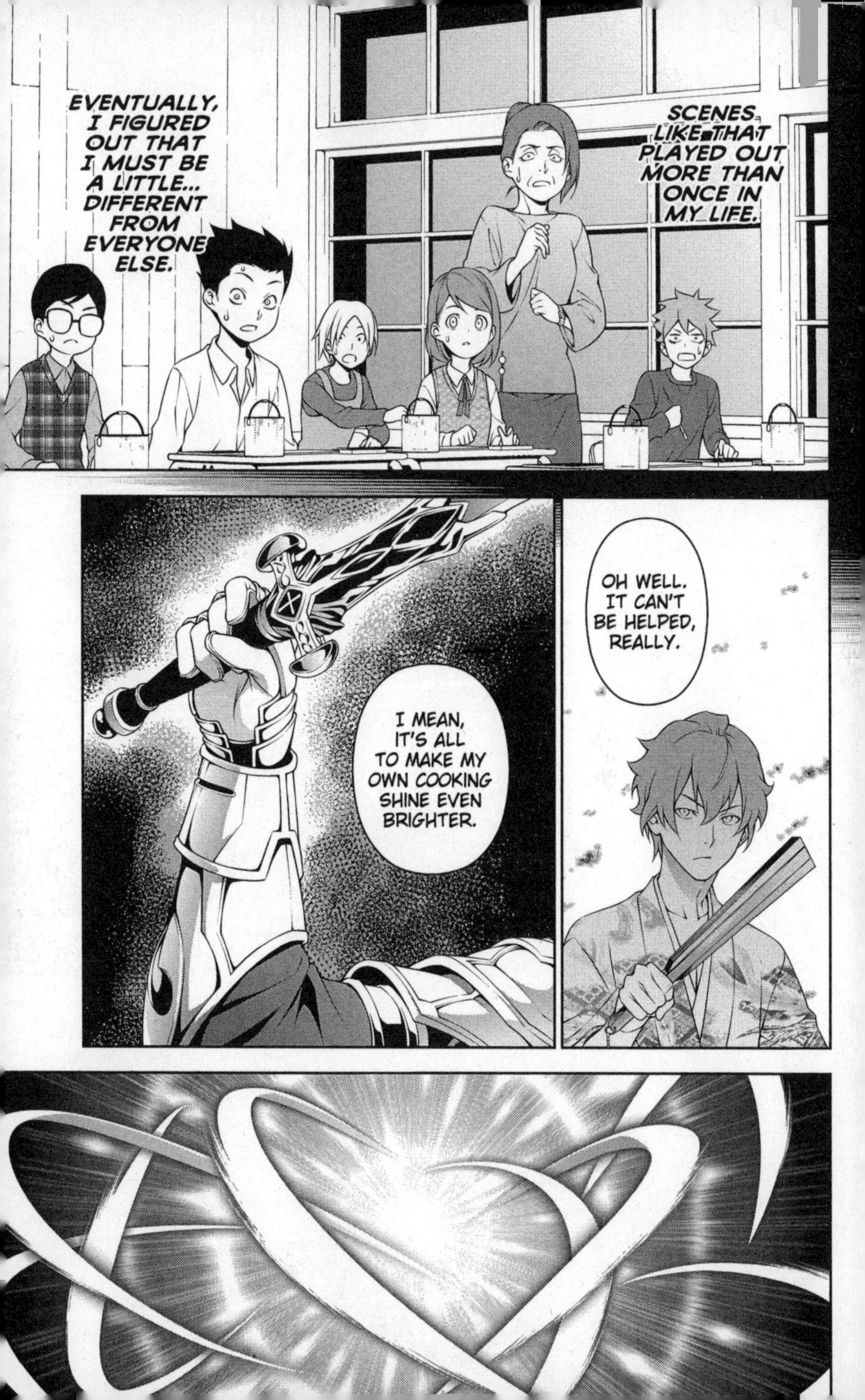
SCENES LIKE THAT PLAYED OUT MORE THAN ONCE IN MY LIFE.
EVENTUALLY, I FIGURED OUT THAT I MUST BE A LITTLE... DIFFERENT FROM EVERYONE ELSE.
OH WELL. IT CAN'T BE HELPED, REALLY.
I MEAN, IT'S ALL TO MAKE MY OWN COOKING SHINE EVEN BRIGHTER.

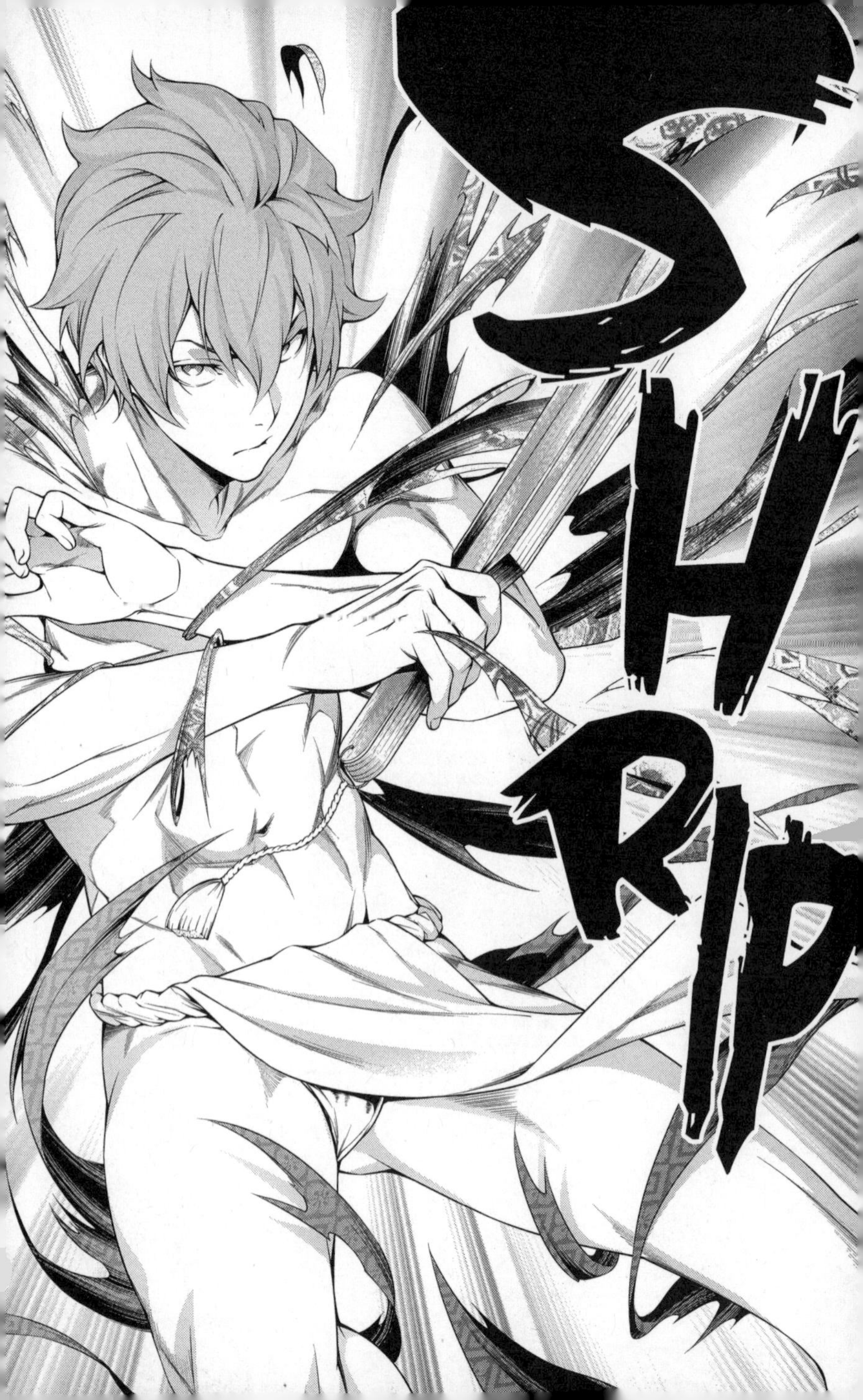
SHRIP

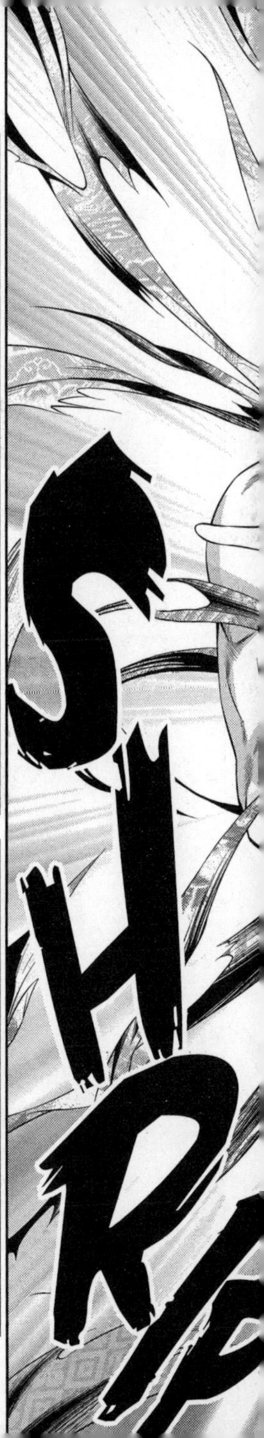
SHR

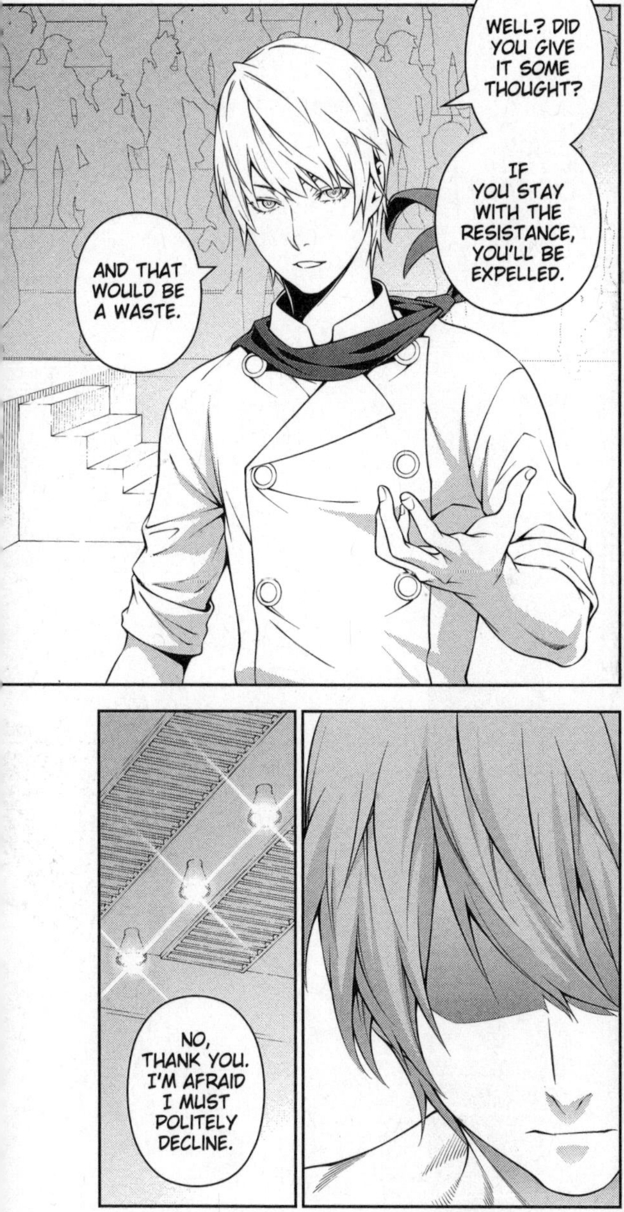
WELL? DID YOU GIVE IT SOME THOUGHT?
IF YOU STAY WITH THE RESISTANCE, YOU'LL BE EXPELLED.
AND THAT WOULD BE A WASTE.
NO, THANK YOU. I'M AFRAID I MUST POLITELY DECLINE.

...I WILL NEVER GIVE UP ENJOYING MY COOKING TO ITS FULLEST!

EVEN IF I'M STRIPPED DOWN TO NOTHING BUT A LOINCLOTH...

4th BOUT

Nene Akanegakubo	1st Card VS	Erina Nakiri
0		3
Eishi Tsukasa	2nd Card VS	Satoshi Isshiki
3		0
Rindo Kobayashi	3rd Card VS	Takumi Aldini

WOO-HOO! THE RESULTS FOR THE FOURTH BOUT'S SECOND CARD ARE IN!

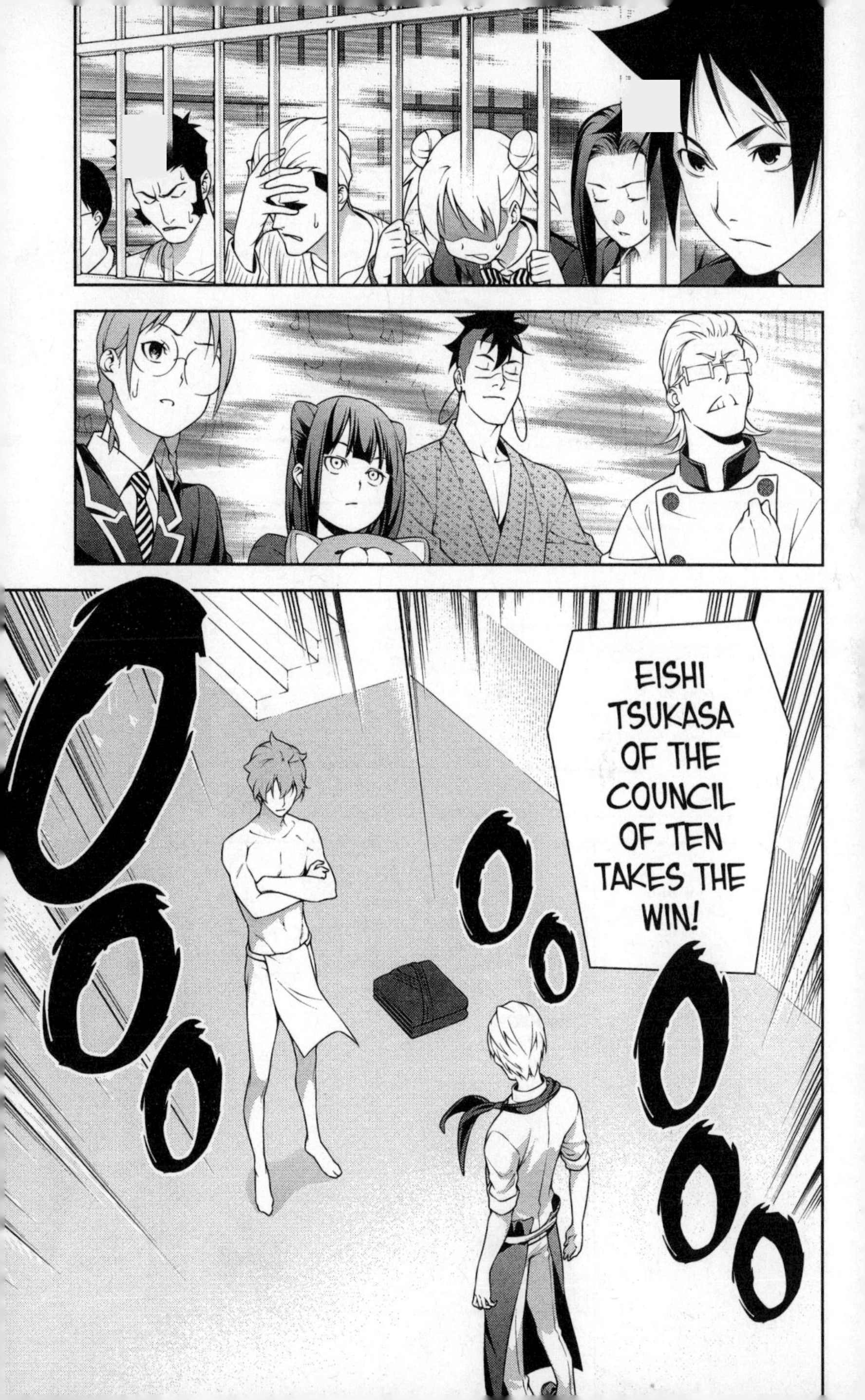
EISHI TSUKASA OF THE COUNCIL OF TEN TAKES THE WIN!

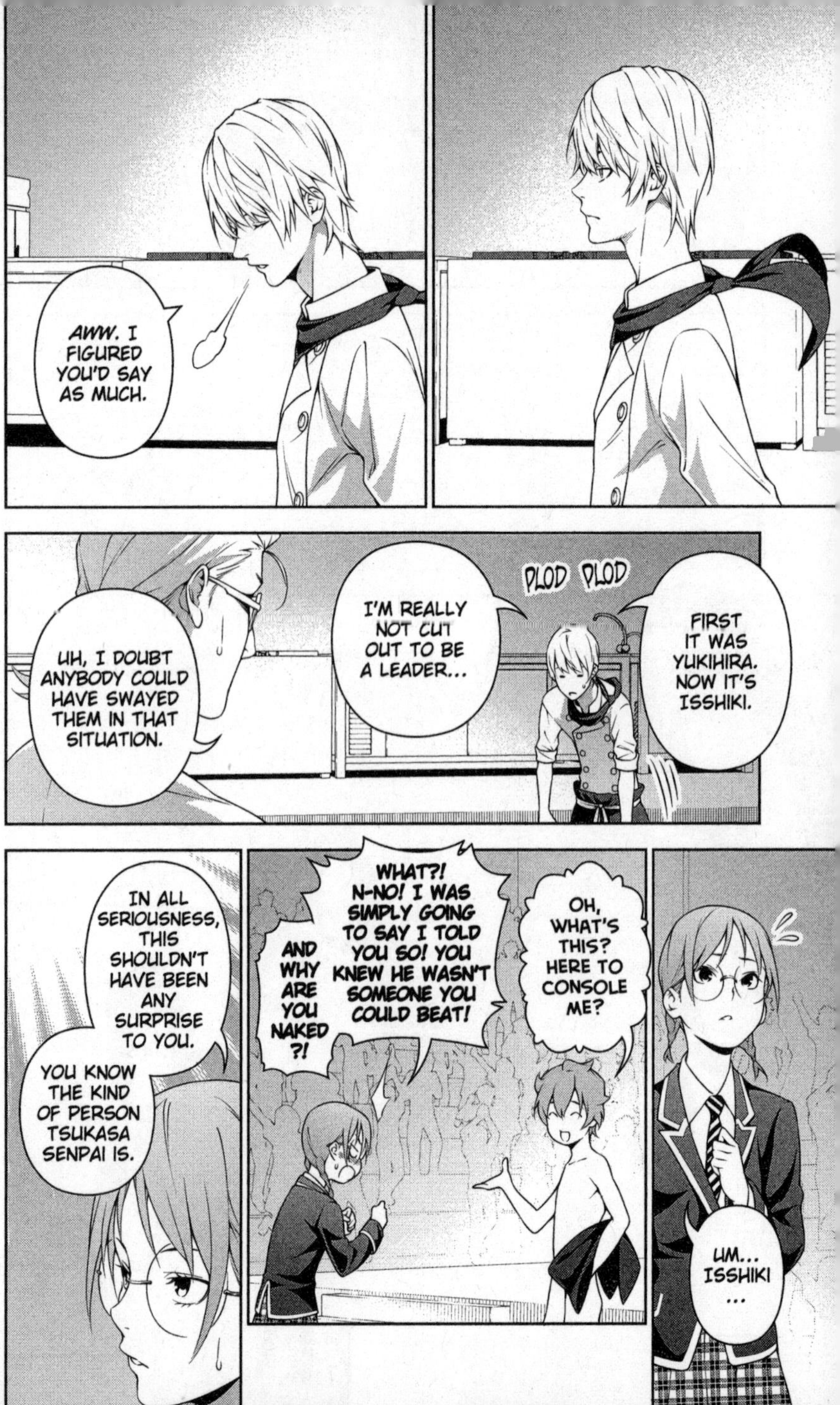
AWW. I FIGURED YOU'D SAY AS MUCH.
FIRST IT WAS YUKIHIRA. NOW IT'S ISSHIKI.
PLOD PLOD
I'M REALLY NOT CUT OUT TO BE A LEADER...
UH, I DOUBT ANYBODY COULD HAVE SWAYED THEM IN THAT SITUATION.
UM... ISSHIKI...
OH, WHAT'S THIS? HERE TO CONSOLE ME?
WHAT?! N-NO! I WAS SIMPLY GOING TO SAY I TOLD YOU SO! YOU KNEW HE WASN'T SOMEONE YOU COULD BEAT!
AND WHY ARE YOU NAKED?!
IN ALL SERIOUSNESS, THIS SHOULDN'T HAVE BEEN ANY SURPRISE TO YOU.
YOU KNOW THE KIND OF PERSON TSUKASA SENPAI IS.

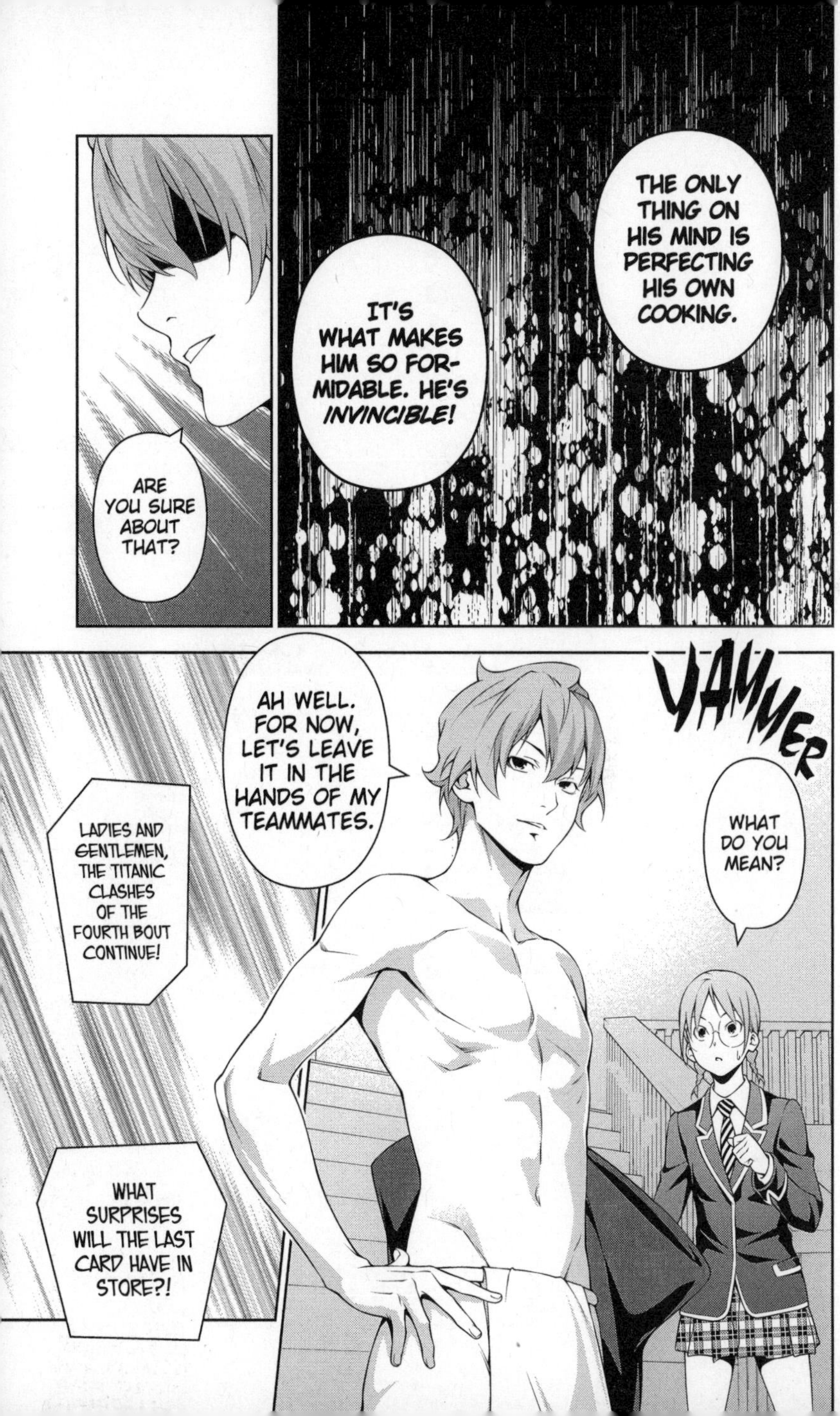
THE ONLY THING ON HIS MIND IS PERFECTING HIS OWN COOKING.
IT'S WHAT MAKES HIM SO FOR-MIDABLE. HE'S *INVINCIBLE!*
ARE YOU SURE ABOUT THAT?
VAMMER
WHAT DO YOU MEAN?
AH WELL. FOR NOW, LET'S LEAVE IT IN THE HANDS OF MY TEAMMATES.
LADIES AND GENTLEMEN, THE TITANIC CLASHES OF THE FOURTH BOUT CONTINUE!
WHAT SURPRISES WILL THE LAST CARD HAVE IN STORE?!

KUGA SENPAI'S VALENTINE'S DAY

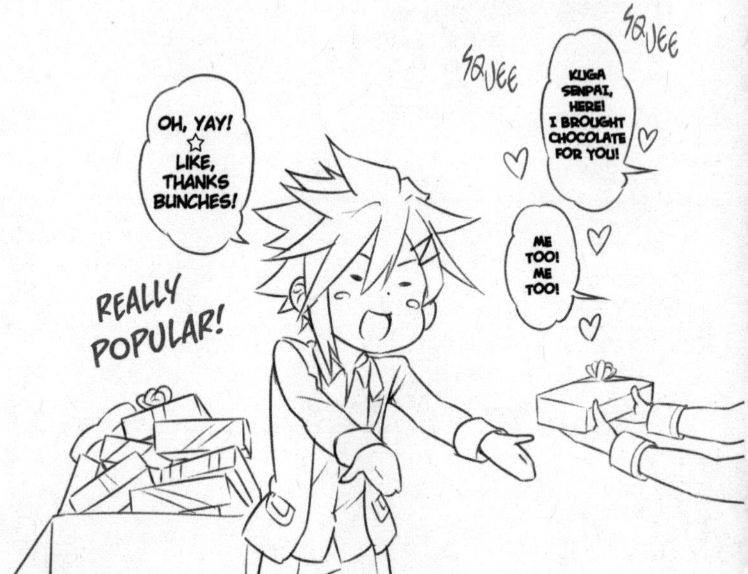
SQUEE
KUGA SENPAI, HERE! I BROUGHT CHOCOLATE FOR YOU!
SQUEE
ME TOO! ME TOO!
OH, YAY! ☆ LIKE, THANKS BUNCHES!
REALLY POPULAR!

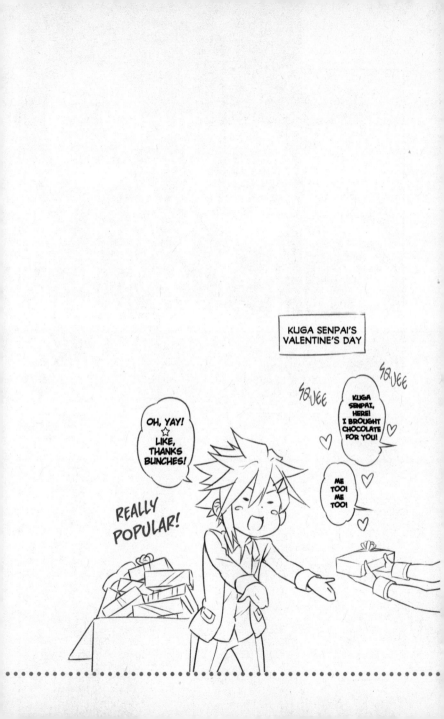

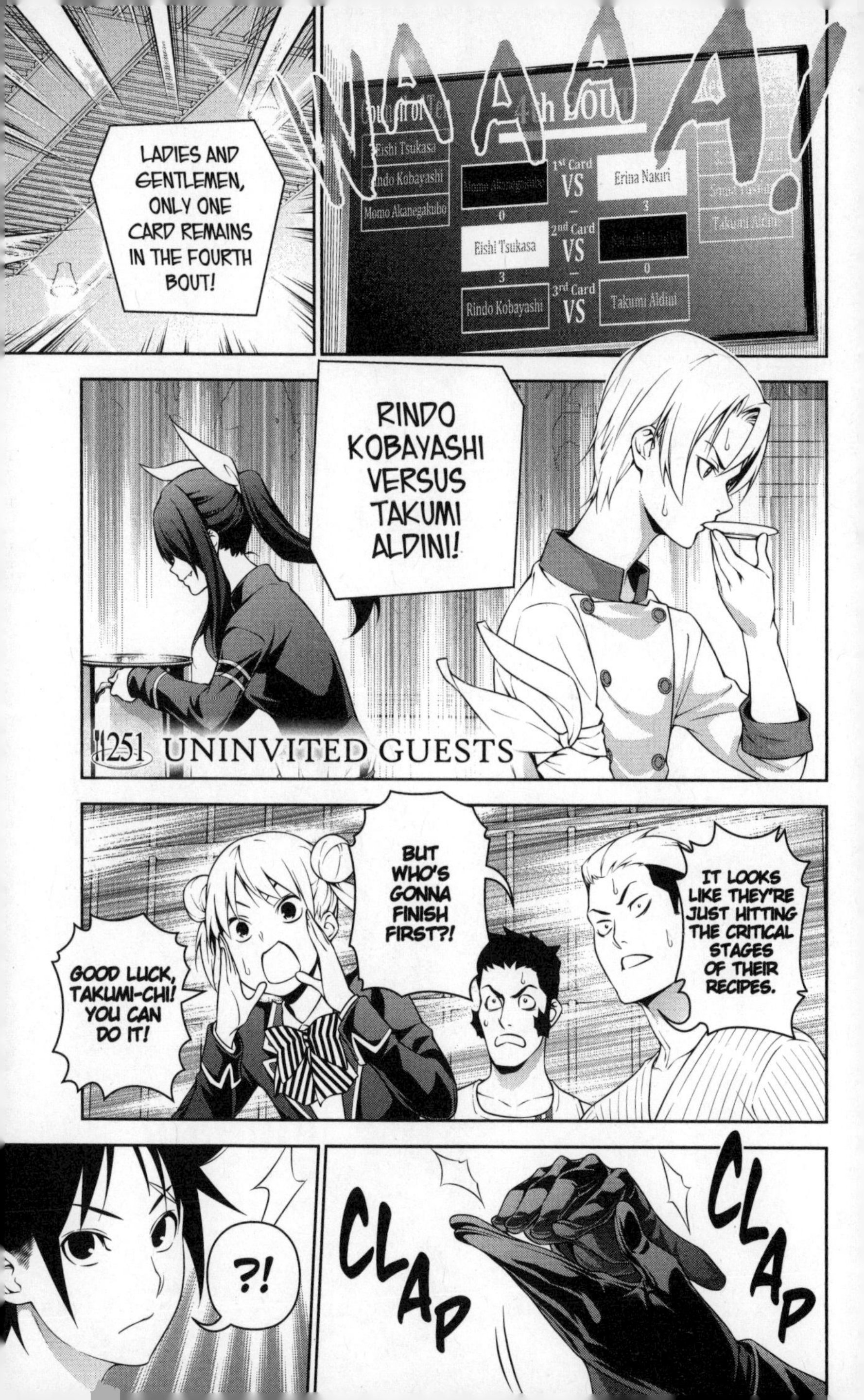
4th BOUT
Eishi Tsukasa
Rindo Kobayashi
Momo Akanegakubo
1st Card VS Erina Nakiri
0
3
Eishi Tsukasa 2nd Card VS
3
0
Rindo Kobayashi 3rd Card VS Takumi Aldini
Takumi Aldini
LADIES AND GENTLEMEN, ONLY ONE CARD REMAINS IN THE FOURTH BOUT!
RINDO KOBAYASHI VERSUS TAKUMI ALDINI!
251 UNINVITED GUESTS
IT LOOKS LIKE THEY'RE JUST HITTING THE CRITICAL STAGES OF THEIR RECIPES.
BUT WHO'S GONNA FINISH FIRST?!
GOOD LUCK, TAKUMI-CHI! YOU CAN DO IT!
CLAP
CLAP
?!

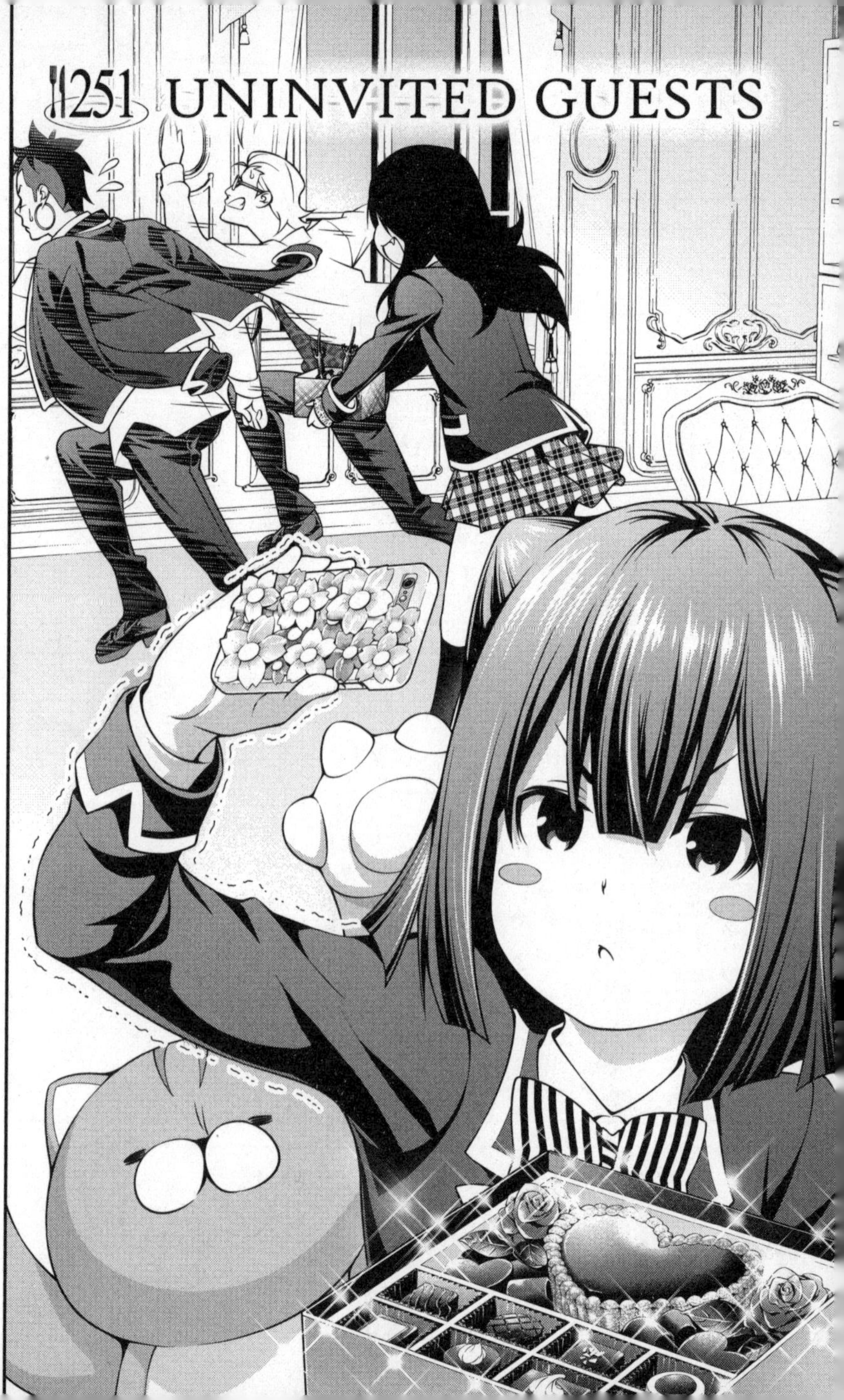
251 UNINVITED GUESTS

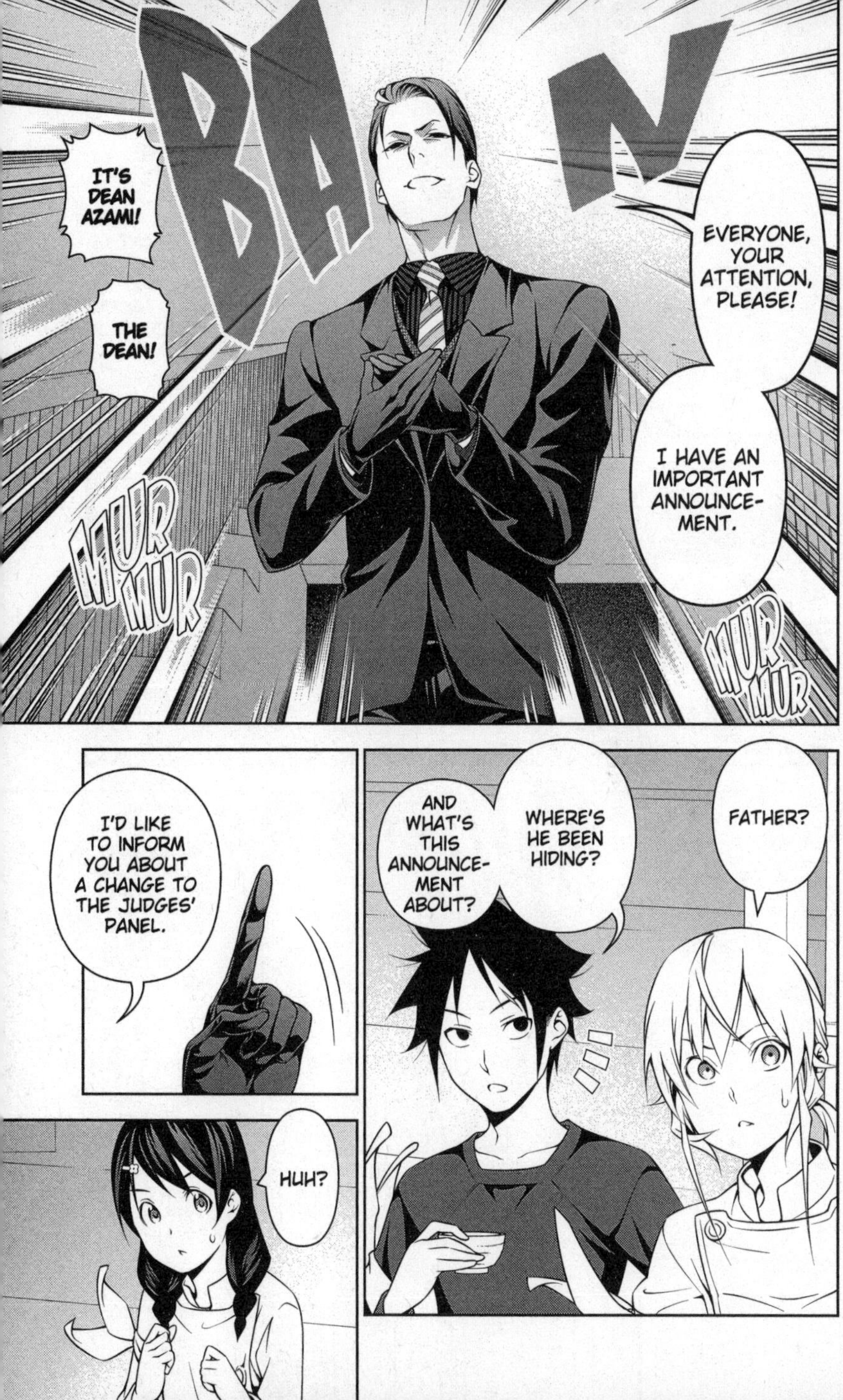
BAN
EVERYONE, YOUR ATTENTION, PLEASE!
IT'S DEAN AZAMI!
THE DEAN!
I HAVE AN IMPORTANT ANNOUNCE-MENT.
MUR MUR
MUR MUR
FATHER?
WHERE'S HE BEEN HIDING?
AND WHAT'S THIS ANNOUNCE-MENT ABOUT?
I'D LIKE TO INFORM YOU ABOUT A CHANGE TO THE JUDGES' PANEL.
HUH?

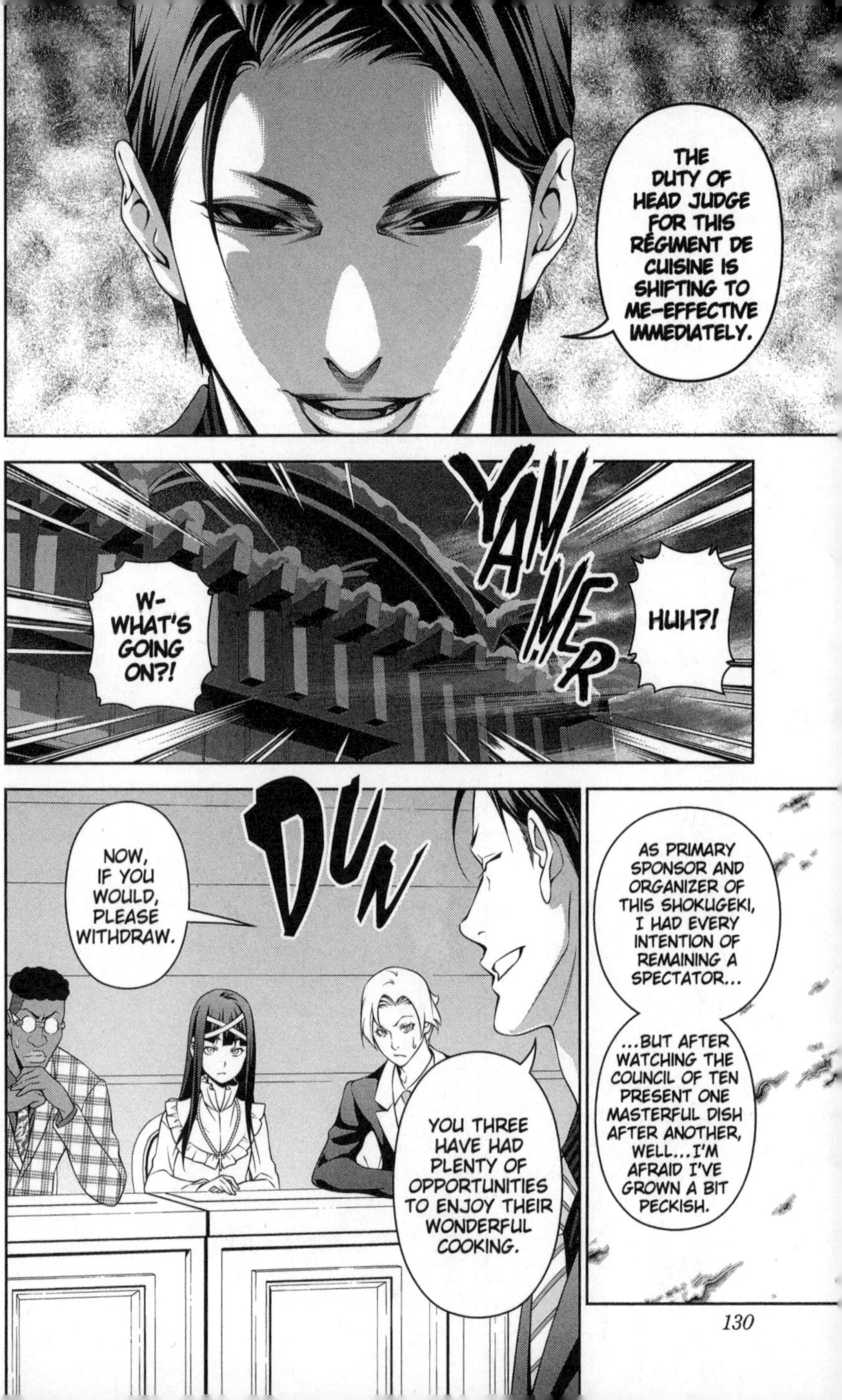
THE DUTY OF HEAD JUDGE FOR THIS RÉGIMENT DE CUISINE IS SHIFTING TO ME—EFFECTIVE IMMEDIATELY.
YAMMER
HUH?!
W-WHAT'S GOING ON?!
AS PRIMARY SPONSOR AND ORGANIZER OF THIS SHOKUGEKI, I HAD EVERY INTENTION OF REMAINING A SPECTATOR...
...BUT AFTER WATCHING THE COUNCIL OF TEN PRESENT ONE MASTERFUL DISH AFTER ANOTHER, WELL...I'M AFRAID I'VE GROWN A BIT PECKISH.
DUN
NOW, IF YOU WOULD, PLEASE WITHDRAW.
YOU THREE HAVE HAD PLENTY OF OPPORTUNITIES TO ENJOY THEIR WONDERFUL COOKING.

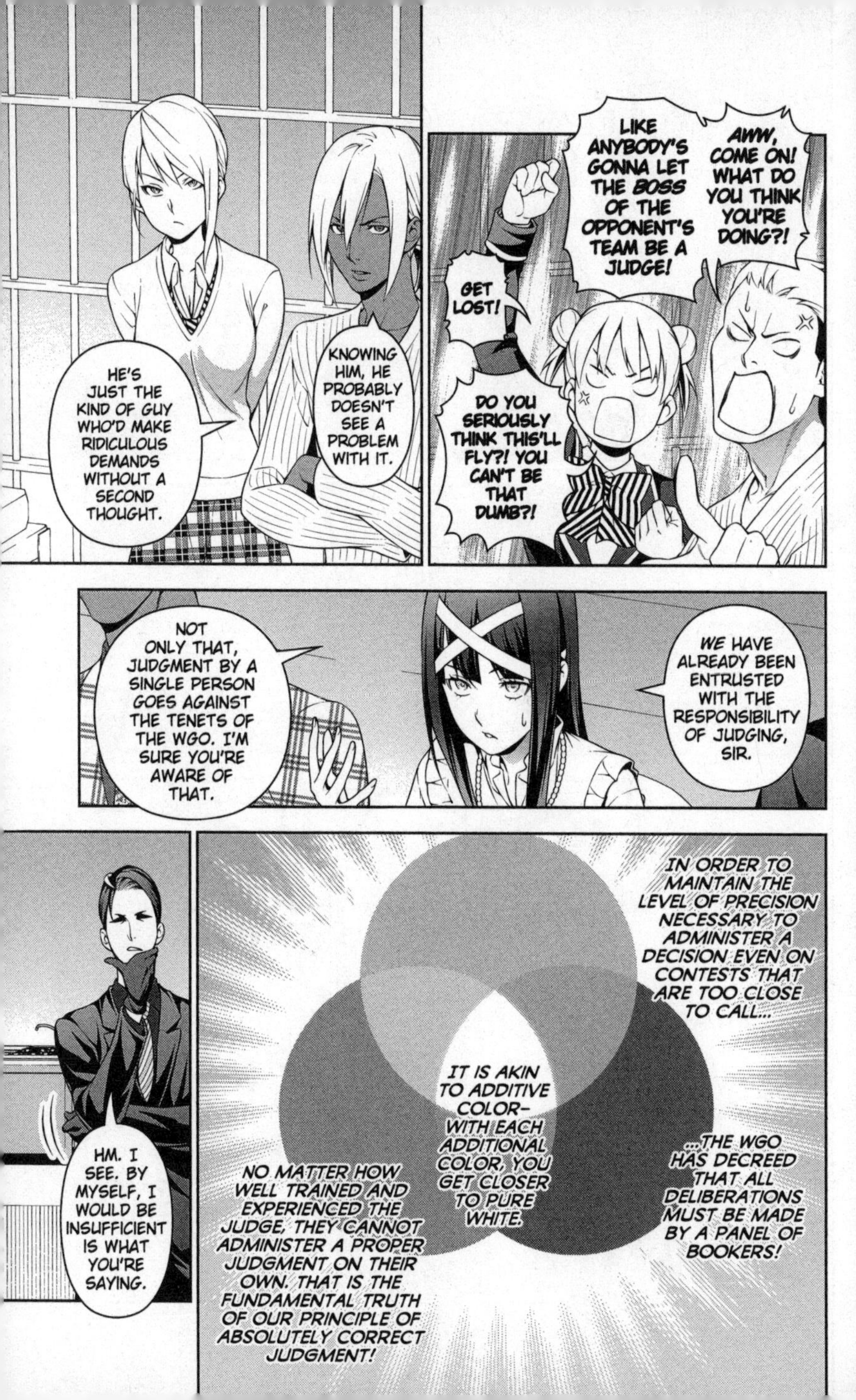
AWW, COME ON! WHAT DO YOU THINK YOU'RE DOING?!
LIKE ANYBODY'S GONNA LET THE BOSS OF THE OPPONENT'S TEAM BE A JUDGE!
GET LOST!
DO YOU SERIOUSLY THINK THIS'LL FLY?! YOU CAN'T BE THAT DUMB?!
KNOWING HIM, HE PROBABLY DOESN'T SEE A PROBLEM WITH IT.
HE'S JUST THE KIND OF GUY WHO'D MAKE RIDICULOUS DEMANDS WITHOUT A SECOND THOUGHT.
WE HAVE ALREADY BEEN ENTRUSTED WITH THE RESPONSIBILITY OF JUDGING, SIR.
NOT ONLY THAT, JUDGMENT BY A SINGLE PERSON GOES AGAINST THE TENETS OF THE WGO. I'M SURE YOU'RE AWARE OF THAT.
IN ORDER TO MAINTAIN THE LEVEL OF PRECISION NECESSARY TO ADMINISTER A DECISION EVEN ON CONTESTS THAT ARE TOO CLOSE TO CALL...
...THE WGO HAS DECREED THAT ALL DELIBERATIONS MUST BE MADE BY A PANEL OF BOOKERS!
IT IS AKIN TO ADDITIVE COLOR– WITH EACH ADDITIONAL COLOR, YOU GET CLOSER TO PURE WHITE.
NO MATTER HOW WELL TRAINED AND EXPERIENCED THE JUDGE, THEY CANNOT ADMINISTER A PROPER JUDGMENT ON THEIR OWN. THAT IS THE FUNDAMENTAL TRUTH OF OUR PRINCIPLE OF ABSOLUTELY CORRECT JUDGMENT!
HM. I SEE. BY MYSELF, I WOULD BE INSUFFICIENT IS WHAT YOU'RE SAYING.

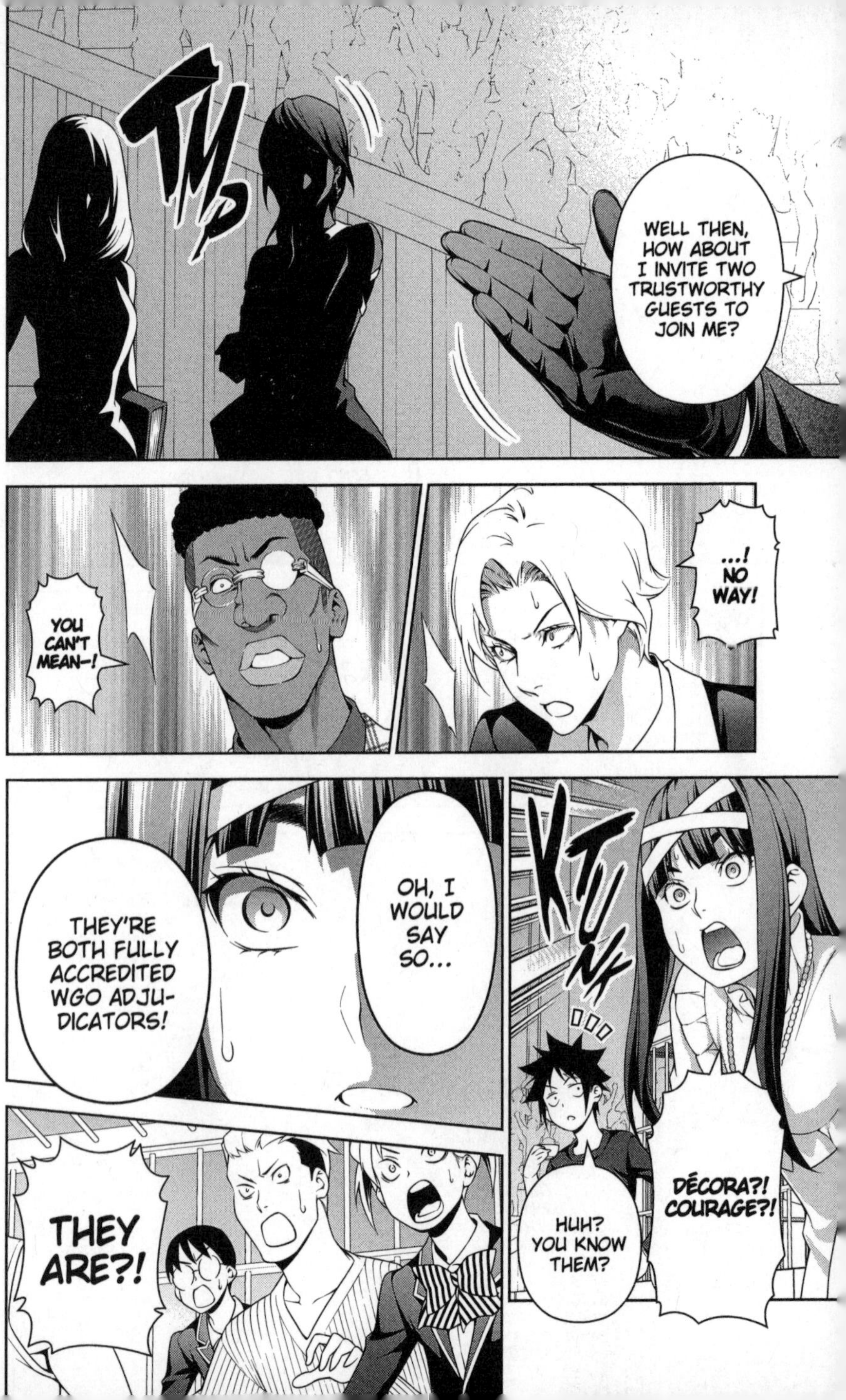
WELL THEN, HOW ABOUT I INVITE TWO TRUSTWORTHY GUESTS TO JOIN ME?
TMP
...! NO WAY!
YOU CAN'T MEAN—!
KTUNK
DÉCORA?! COURAGE?!
HUH? YOU KNOW THEM?
OH, I WOULD SAY SO...
THEY'RE BOTH FULLY ACCREDITED WGO ADJU-DICATORS!
THEY ARE?!

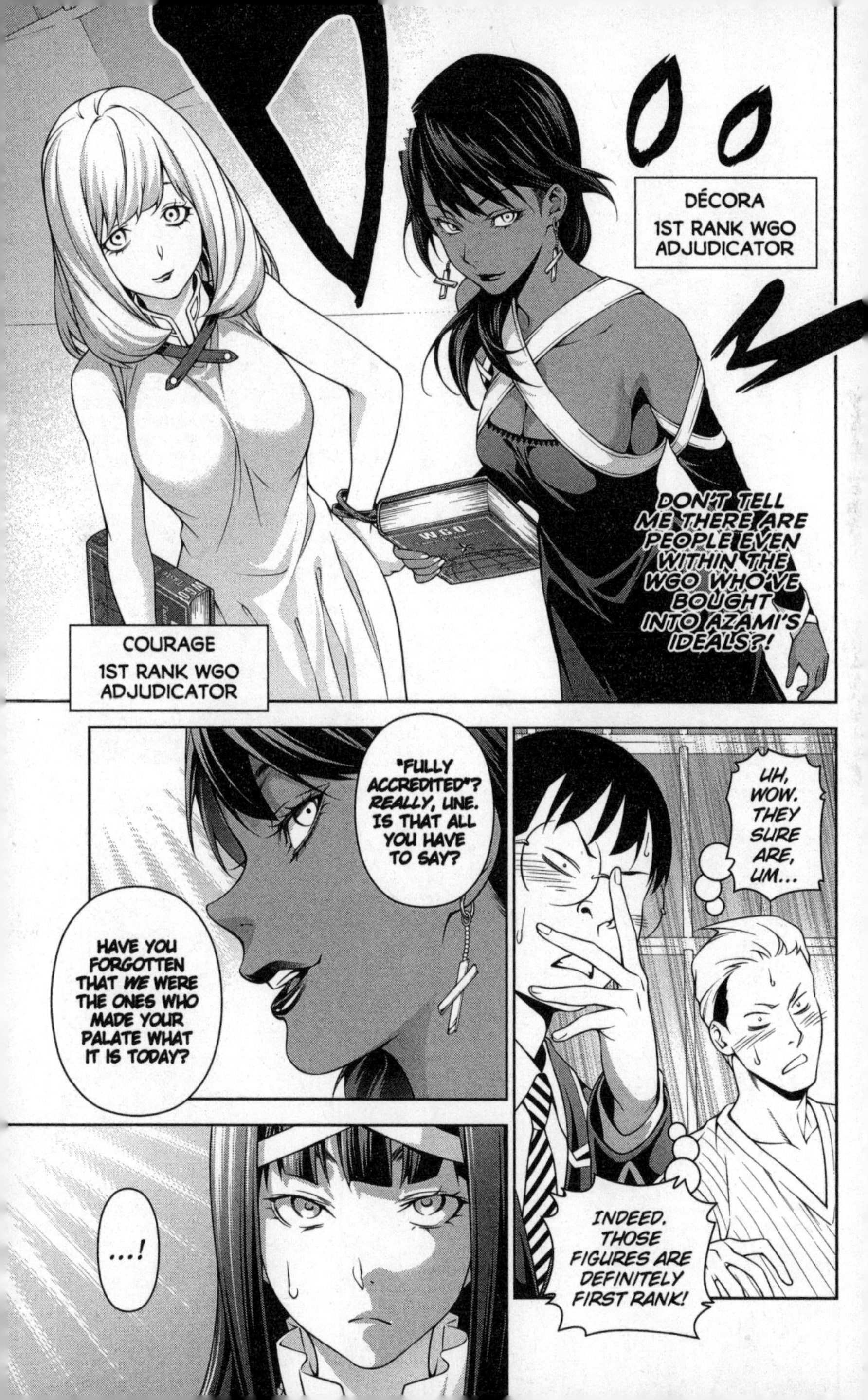
DOOM
DÉCORA 1ST RANK WGO ADJUDICATOR
DON'T TELL ME THERE ARE PEOPLE EVEN WITHIN THE WGO WHO'VE BOUGHT INTO AZAMI'S IDEALS?!
COURAGE 1ST RANK WGO ADJUDICATOR
UH, WOW. THEY SURE ARE, UM...
INDEED. THOSE FIGURES ARE DEFINITELY FIRST RANK!
"FULLY ACCREDITED"? *REALLY*, UNE. IS THAT ALL YOU HAVE TO SAY?
HAVE YOU FORGOTTEN THAT *WE* WERE THE ONES WHO MADE YOUR PALATE WHAT IT IS TODAY?
...!

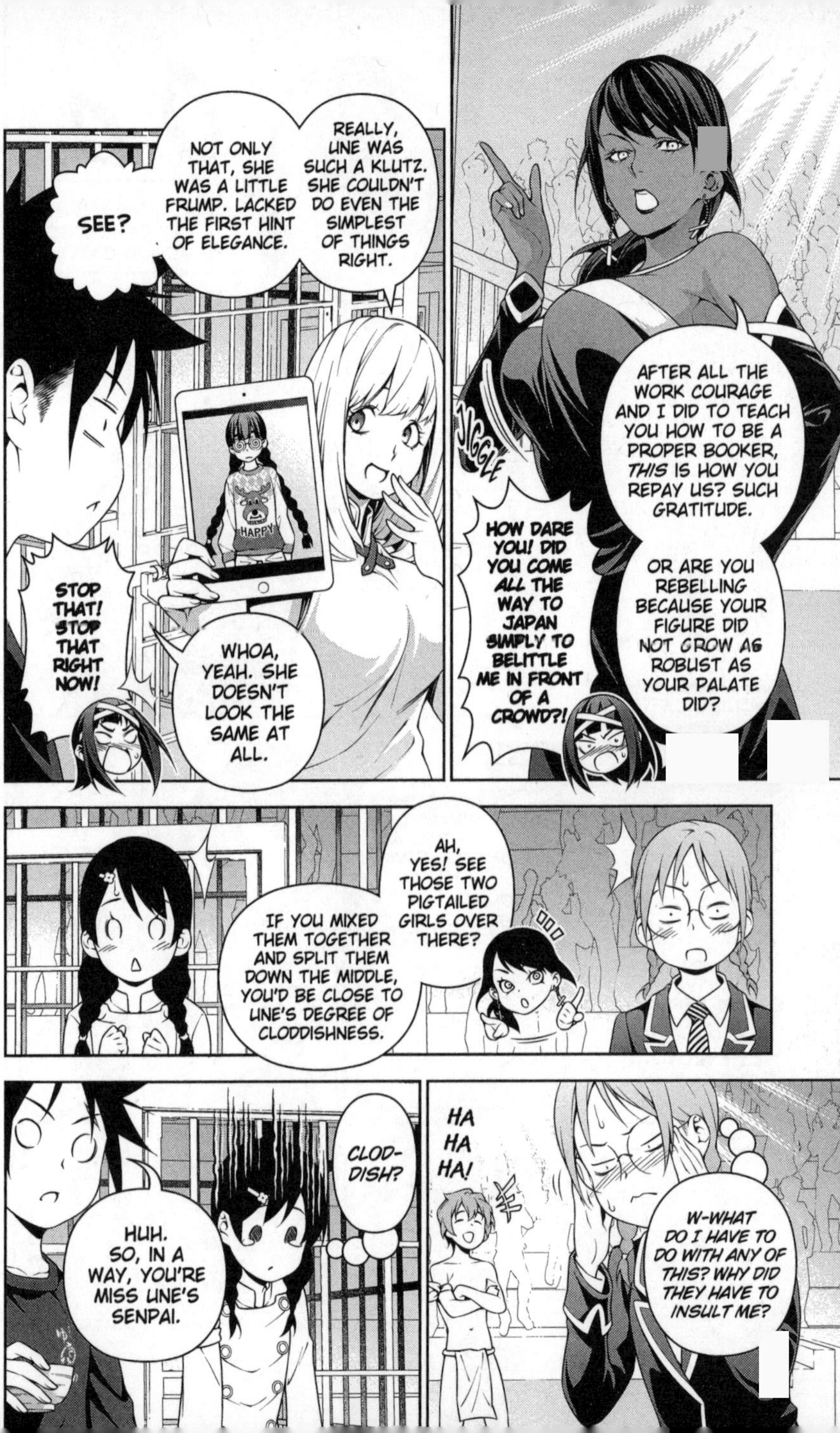
AFTER ALL THE WORK COURAGE AND I DID TO TEACH YOU HOW TO BE A PROPER BOOKER, *THIS* IS HOW YOU REPAY US? SUCH GRATITUDE.
OR ARE YOU REBELLING BECAUSE YOUR FIGURE DID NOT GROW AS ROBUST AS YOUR PALATE DID?
JIGGLE
HOW DARE YOU! DID YOU COME *ALL* THE WAY TO JAPAN SIMPLY TO BELITTLE ME IN FRONT OF A CROWD?!
REALLY, UNE WAS SUCH A KLUTZ. SHE COULDN'T DO EVEN THE SIMPLEST OF THINGS RIGHT.
NOT ONLY THAT, SHE WAS A LITTLE FRUMP. LACKED THE FIRST HINT OF ELEGANCE.
SEE?
HAPPY
WHOA, YEAH. SHE DOESN'T LOOK THE SAME AT ALL.
STOP THAT! STOP THAT RIGHT NOW!
AH, YES! SEE THOSE TWO PIGTAILED GIRLS OVER THERE?
IF YOU MIXED THEM TOGETHER AND SPLIT THEM DOWN THE MIDDLE, YOU'D BE CLOSE TO UNE'S DEGREE OF CLODDISHNESS.
HA HA HA!
W-WHAT DO I HAVE TO DO WITH ANY OF THIS? WHY DID THEY HAVE TO INSULT ME?
CLOD-DISH?
HUH. SO, IN A WAY, YOU'RE MISS UNE'S SENPAI.

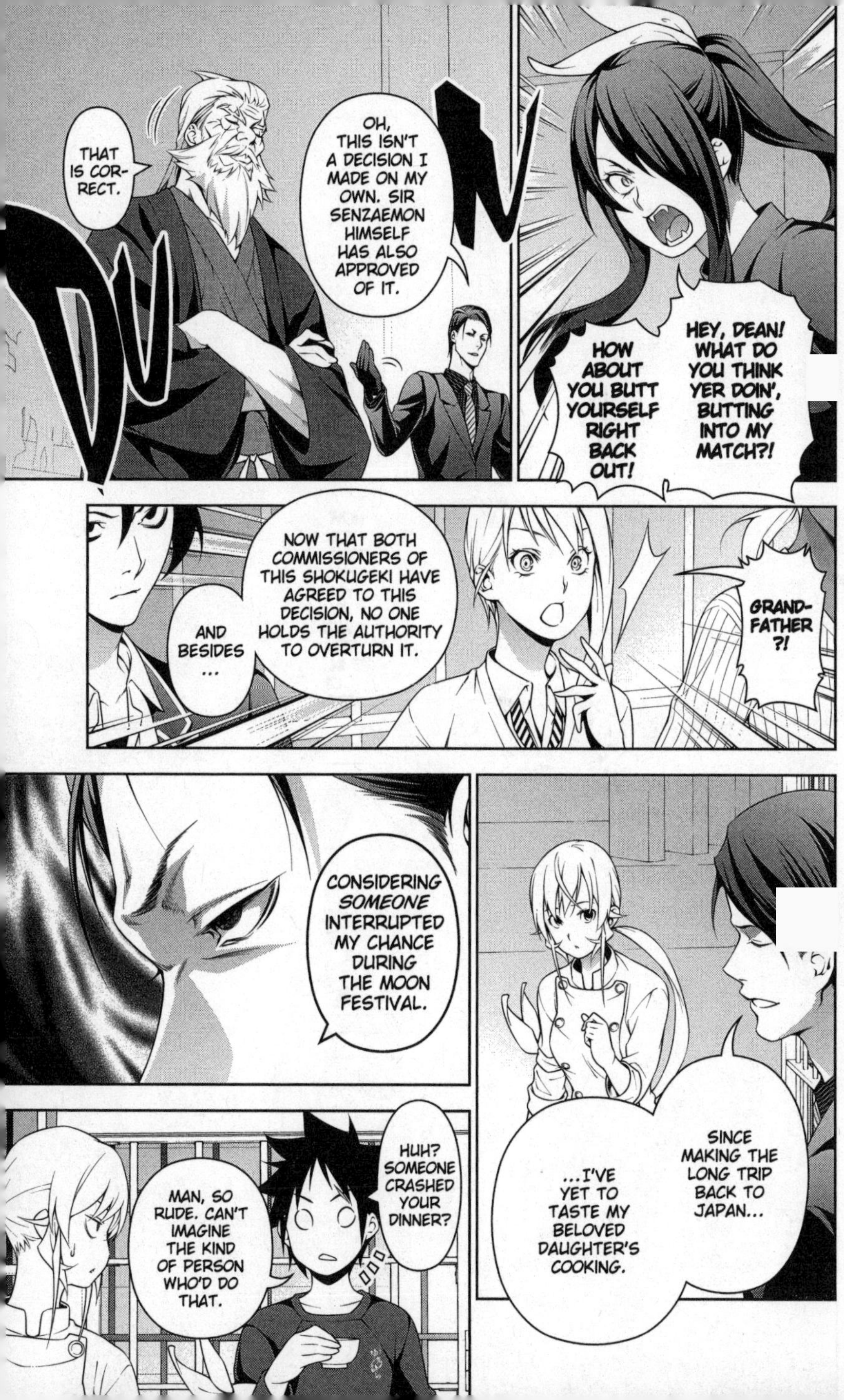
HEY, DEAN! WHAT DO YOU THINK YER DOIN', BUTTING INTO MY MATCH?!
HOW ABOUT YOU BUTT YOURSELF RIGHT BACK OUT!
OH, THIS ISN'T A DECISION I MADE ON MY OWN. SIR SENZAEMON HIMSELF HAS ALSO APPROVED OF IT.
THAT IS COR-RECT.
GRAND-FATHER?!
NOW THAT BOTH COMMISSIONERS OF THIS SHOKUGEKI HAVE AGREED TO THIS DECISION, NO ONE HOLDS THE AUTHORITY TO OVERTURN IT.
AND BESIDES...
SINCE MAKING THE LONG TRIP BACK TO JAPAN...
...I'VE YET TO TASTE MY BELOVED DAUGHTER'S COOKING.
CONSIDERING *SOMEONE* INTERRUPTED MY CHANCE DURING THE MOON FESTIVAL.
HUH? SOMEONE CRASHED YOUR DINNER?
MAN, SO RUDE. CAN'T IMAGINE THE KIND OF PERSON WHO'D DO THAT.

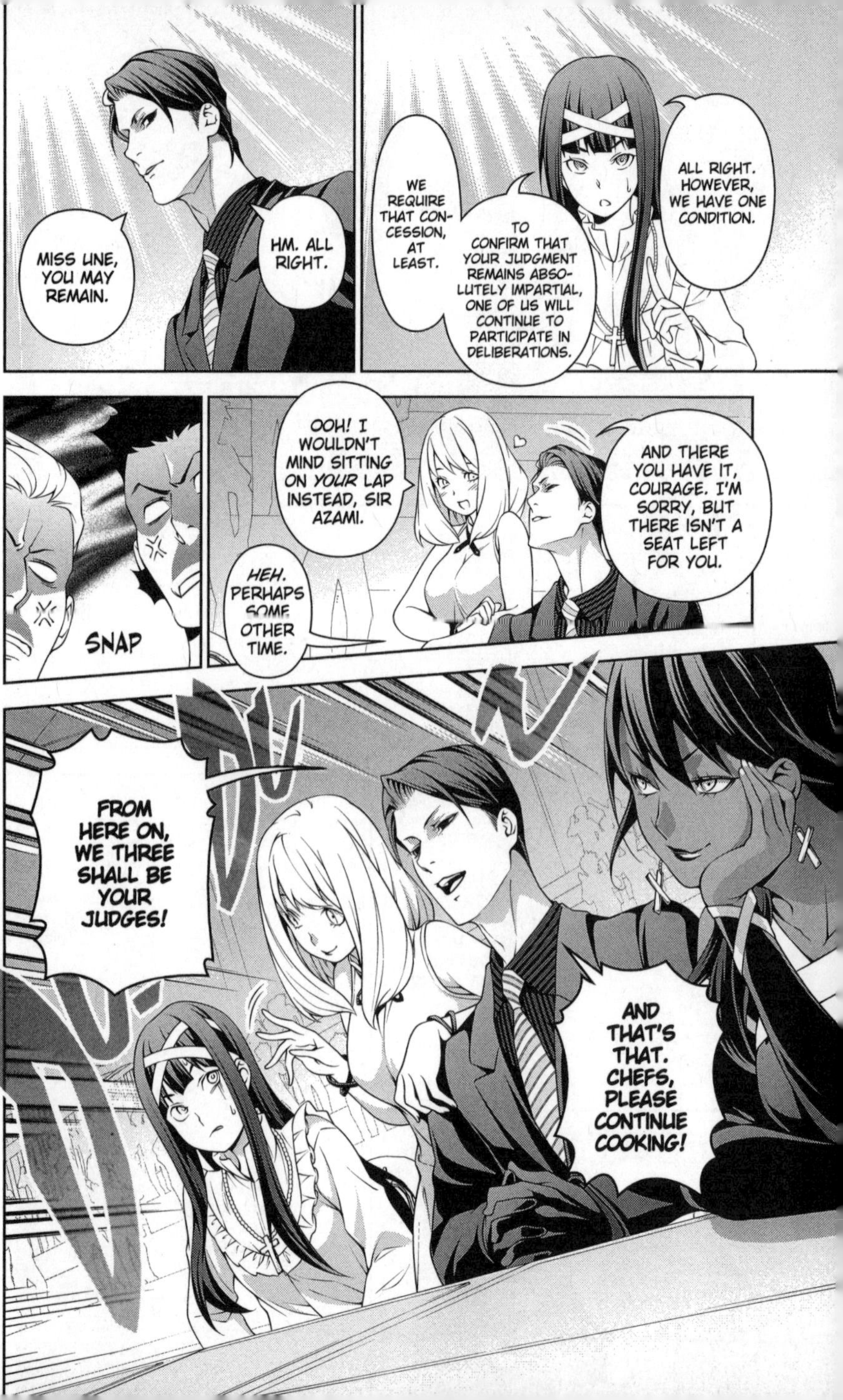
ALL RIGHT. HOWEVER, WE HAVE ONE CONDITION.
TO CONFIRM THAT YOUR JUDGMENT REMAINS ABSOLUTELY IMPARTIAL, ONE OF US WILL CONTINUE TO PARTICIPATE IN DELIBERATIONS.
WE REQUIRE THAT CONCESSION, AT LEAST.
HM. ALL RIGHT.
MISS UNE, YOU MAY REMAIN.
AND THERE YOU HAVE IT, COURAGE. I'M SORRY, BUT THERE ISN'T A SEAT LEFT FOR YOU.
OOH! I WOULDN'T MIND SITTING ON *YOUR* LAP INSTEAD, SIR AZAMI.
HEH. PERHAPS SOME OTHER TIME.
SNAP
FROM HERE ON, WE THREE SHALL BE YOUR JUDGES!
AND THAT'S THAT. CHEFS, PLEASE CONTINUE COOKING!

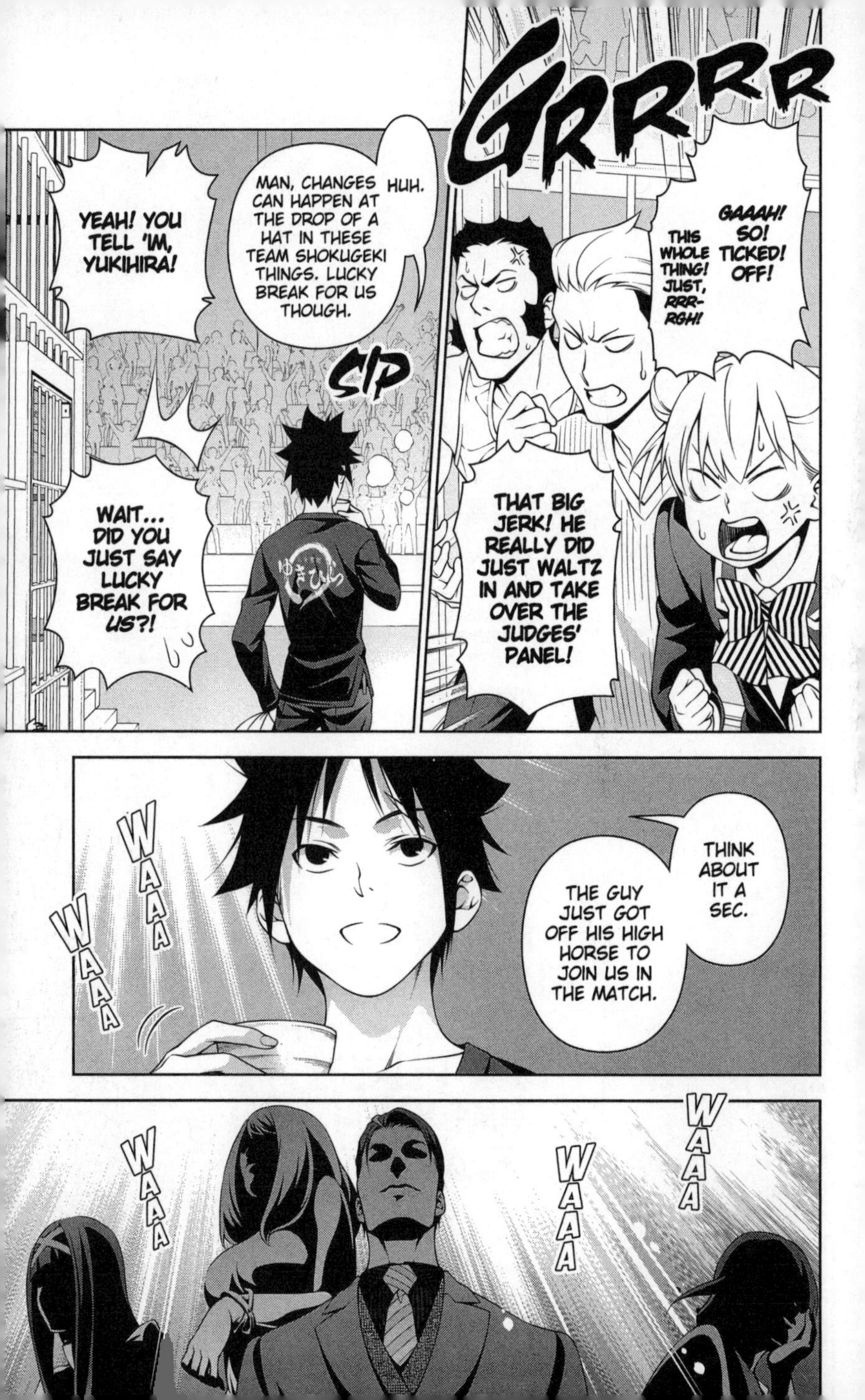
GRRRR
GAAAH! SO! TICKED! OFF!
THIS WHOLE THING! JUST, RRR-RGH!
THAT BIG JERK! HE REALLY DID JUST WALTZ IN AND TAKE OVER THE JUDGES' PANEL!
HUH.
MAN, CHANGES CAN HAPPEN AT THE DROP OF A HAT IN THESE TEAM SHOKUGEKI THINGS. LUCKY BREAK FOR US THOUGH.
YEAH! YOU TELL 'IM, YUKIHIRA!
SIP
WAIT... DID YOU JUST SAY LUCKY BREAK FOR US?!
THINK ABOUT IT A SEC.
THE GUY JUST GOT OFF HIS HIGH HORSE TO JOIN US IN THE MATCH.
WAAA
WAAA
WAAA
WAAA
WAAA

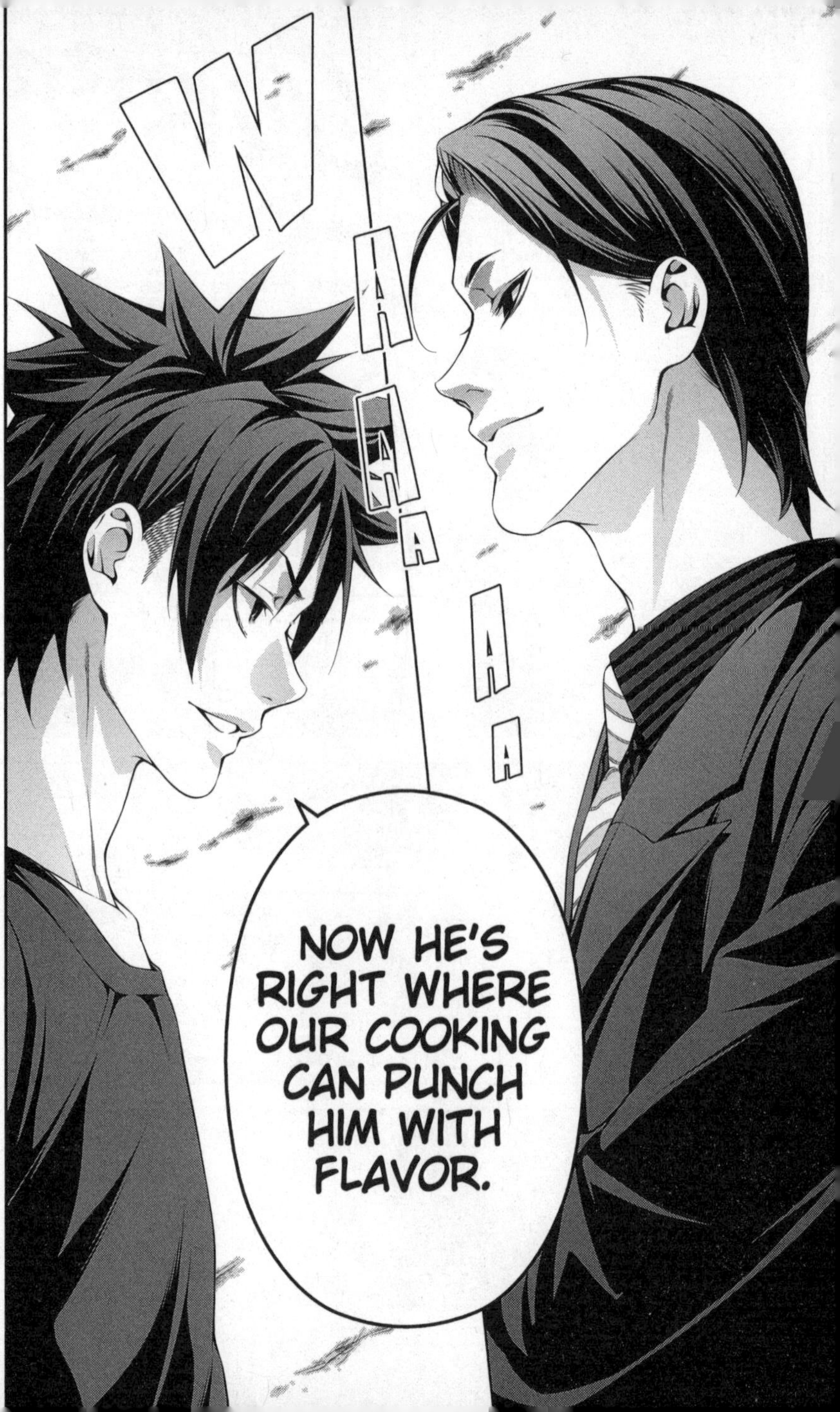
WAAAAAA
NOW HE'S RIGHT WHERE OUR COOKING CAN PUNCH HIM WITH FLAVOR.

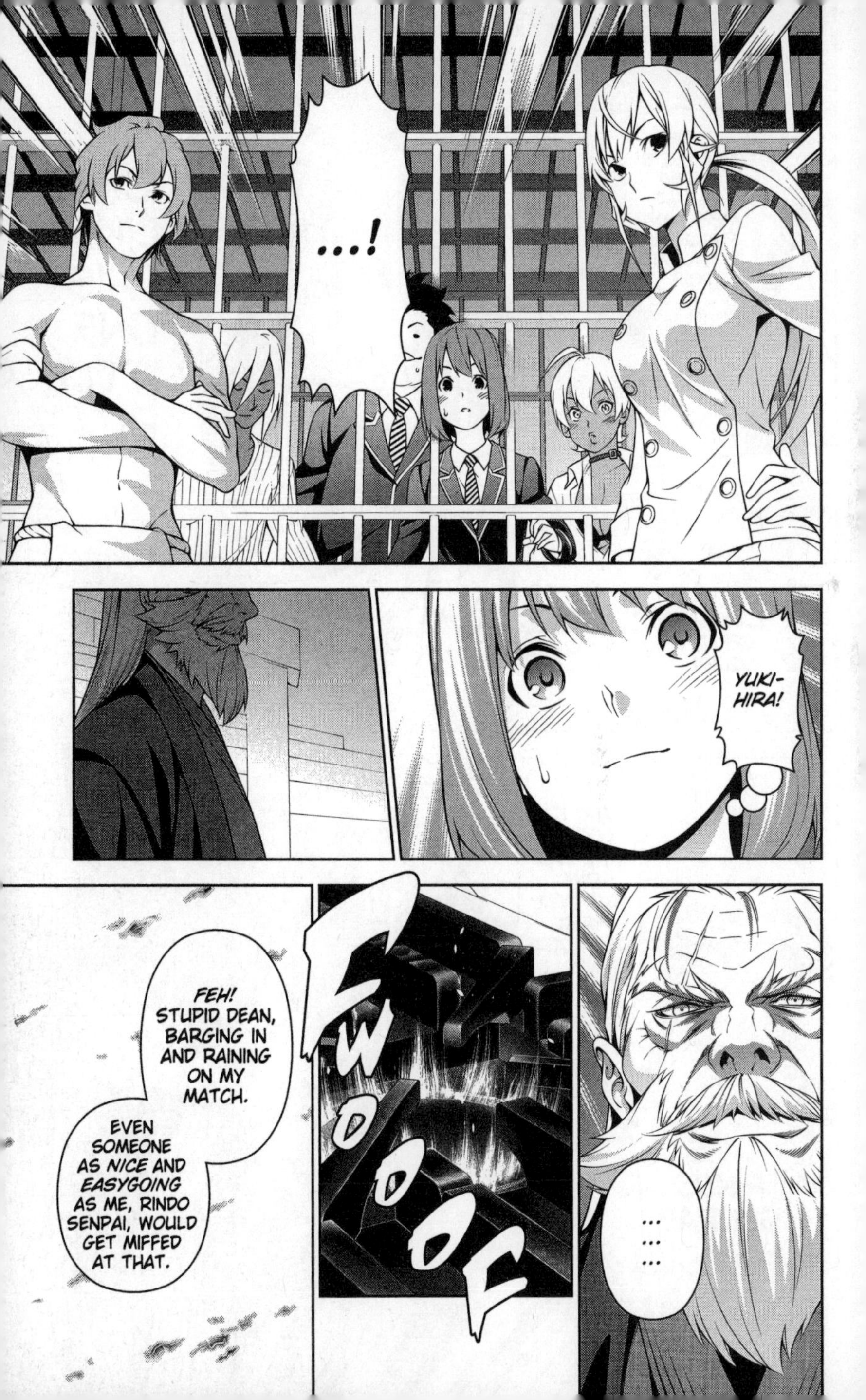
...!
YUKI-HIRA!
......
FWOOOC
FEH! STUPID DEAN, BARGING IN AND RAINING ON MY MATCH.
EVEN SOMEONE AS *NICE* AND *EASYGOING* AS ME, RINDO SENPAI, WOULD GET MIFFED AT THAT.

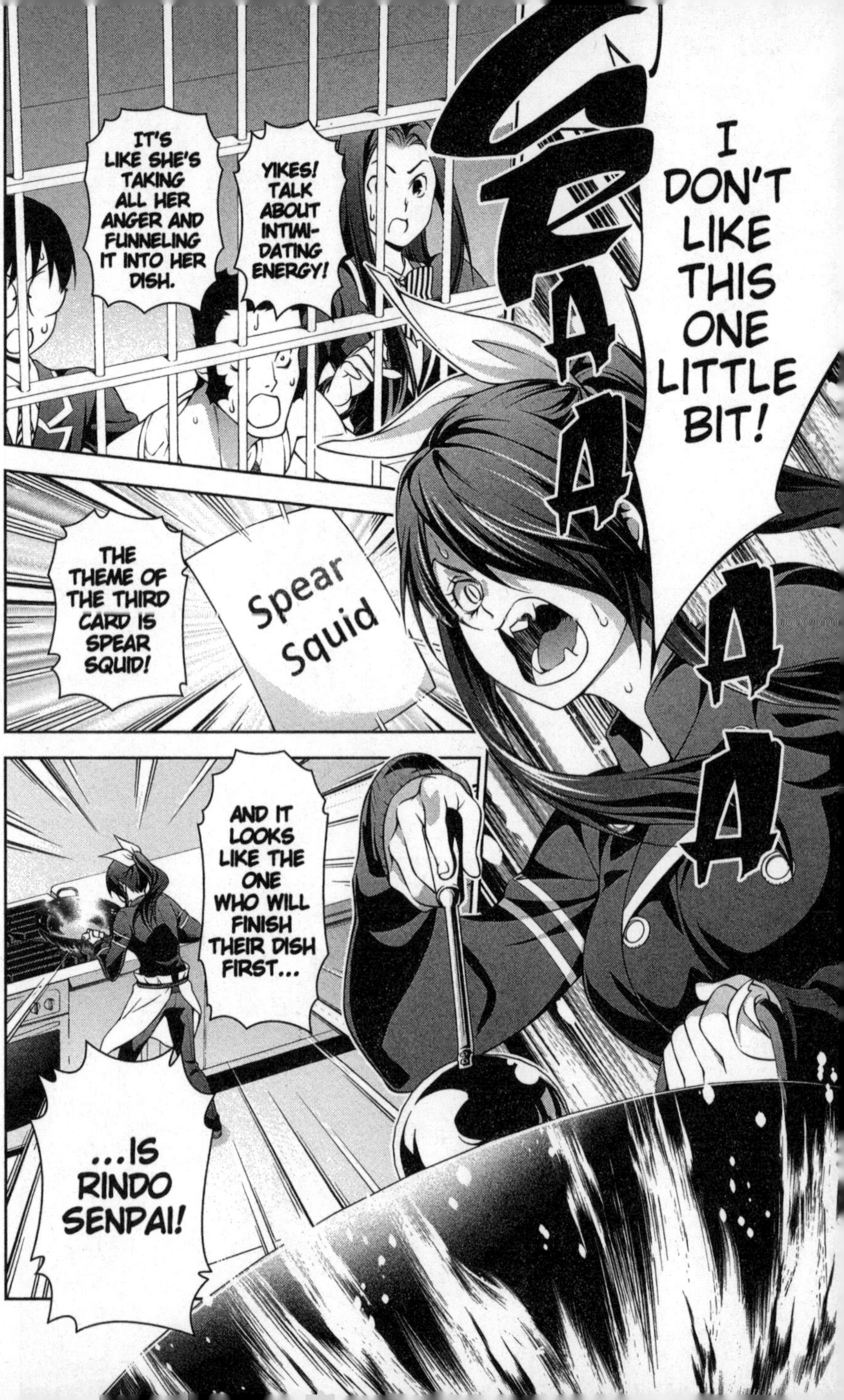
I DON'T LIKE THIS ONE LITTLE BIT!
YIKES! TALK ABOUT INTIMI-DATING ENERGY!
IT'S LIKE SHE'S TAKING ALL HER ANGER AND FUNNELING IT INTO HER DISH.
Spear Squid
THE THEME OF THE THIRD CARD IS SPEAR SQUID!
AND IT LOOKS LIKE THE ONE WHO WILL FINISH THEIR DISH FIRST...
...IS RINDO SENPAI!

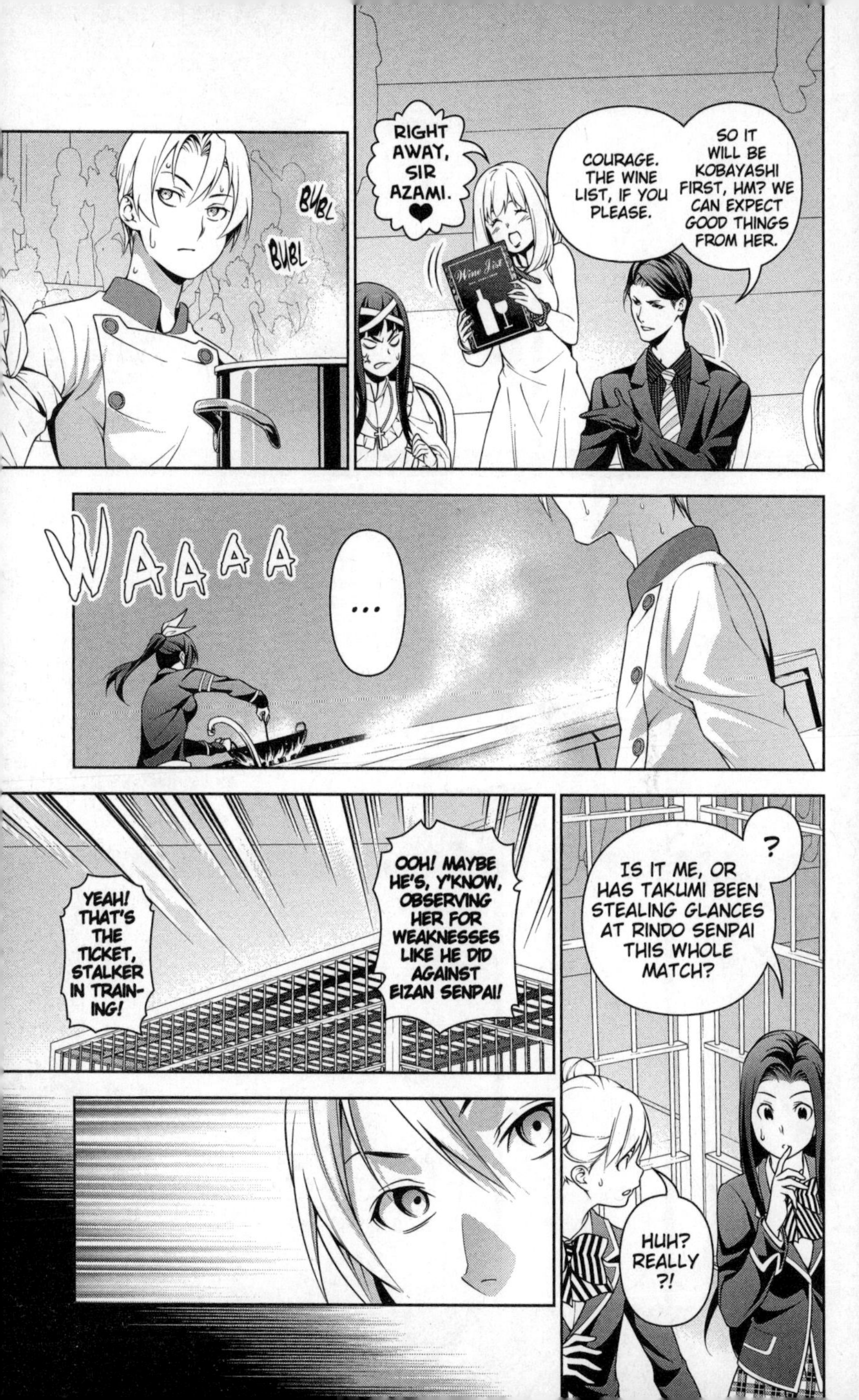
SO IT WILL BE KOBAYASHI FIRST, HM? WE CAN EXPECT GOOD THINGS FROM HER.
COURAGE. THE WINE LIST, IF YOU PLEASE.
RIGHT AWAY, SIR AZAMI. ♥
Wine List
BUBL
BUBL
...
WAAAA
?
IS IT ME, OR HAS TAKUMI BEEN STEALING GLANCES AT RINDO SENPAI THIS WHOLE MATCH?
HUH? REALLY ?!
OOH! MAYBE HE'S, Y'KNOW, OBSERVING HER FOR WEAKNESSES LIKE HE DID AGAINST EIZAN SENPAI!
YEAH! THAT'S THE TICKET, STALKER IN TRAINING!

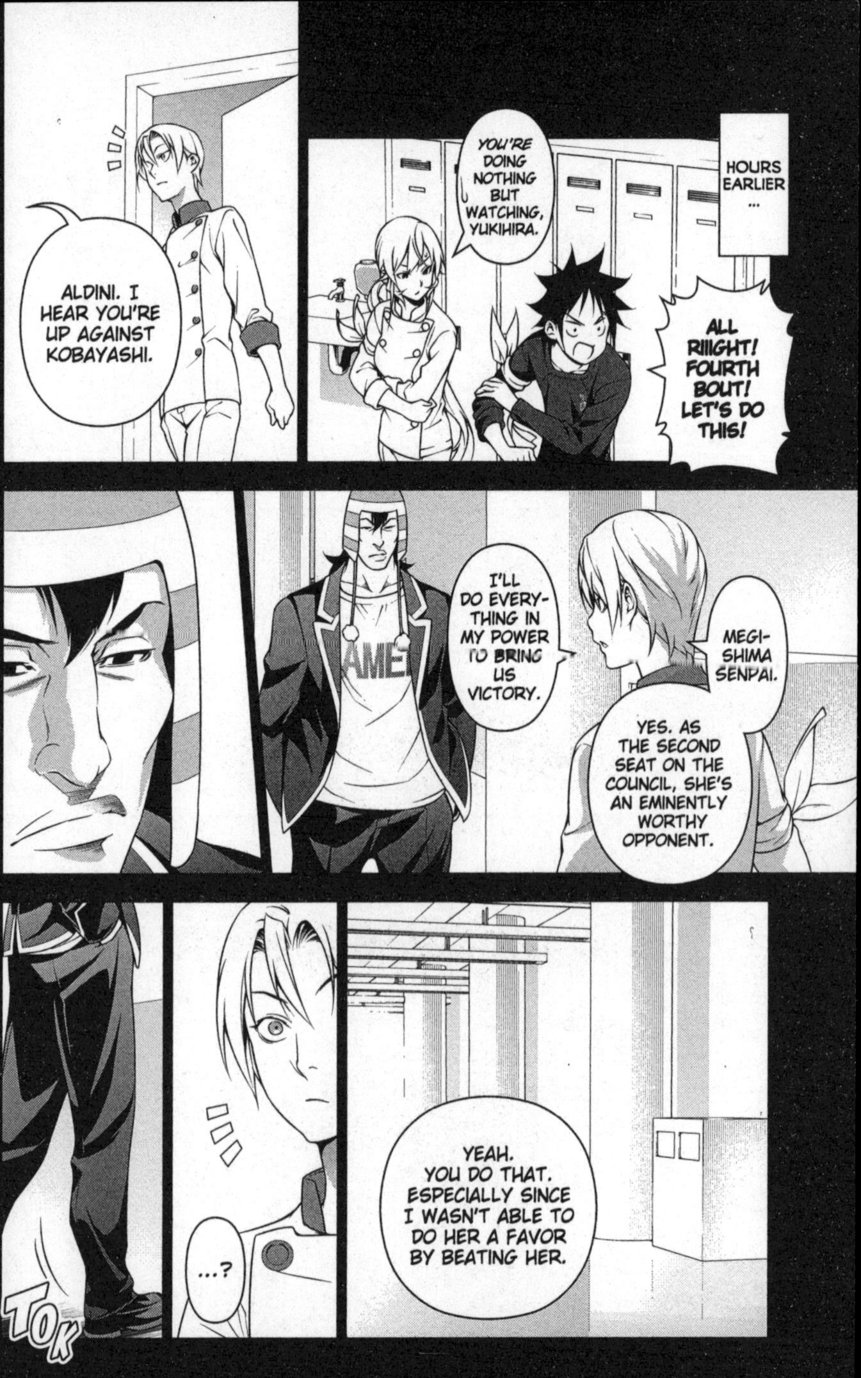

HOURS EARLIER ...
ALL RIIIGHT! FOURTH BOUT! LET'S DO THIS!
YOU'RE DOING NOTHING BUT WATCHING, YUKIHIRA.
ALDINI. I HEAR YOU'RE UP AGAINST KOBAYASHI.
MEGI-SHIMA SENPAI.
YES. AS THE SECOND SEAT ON THE COUNCIL, SHE'S AN EMINENTLY WORTHY OPPONENT.
I'LL DO EVERY-THING IN MY POWER TO BRING US VICTORY.
YEAH. YOU DO THAT. ESPECIALLY SINCE I WASN'T ABLE TO DO HER A FAVOR BY BEATING HER.
...?
TOK

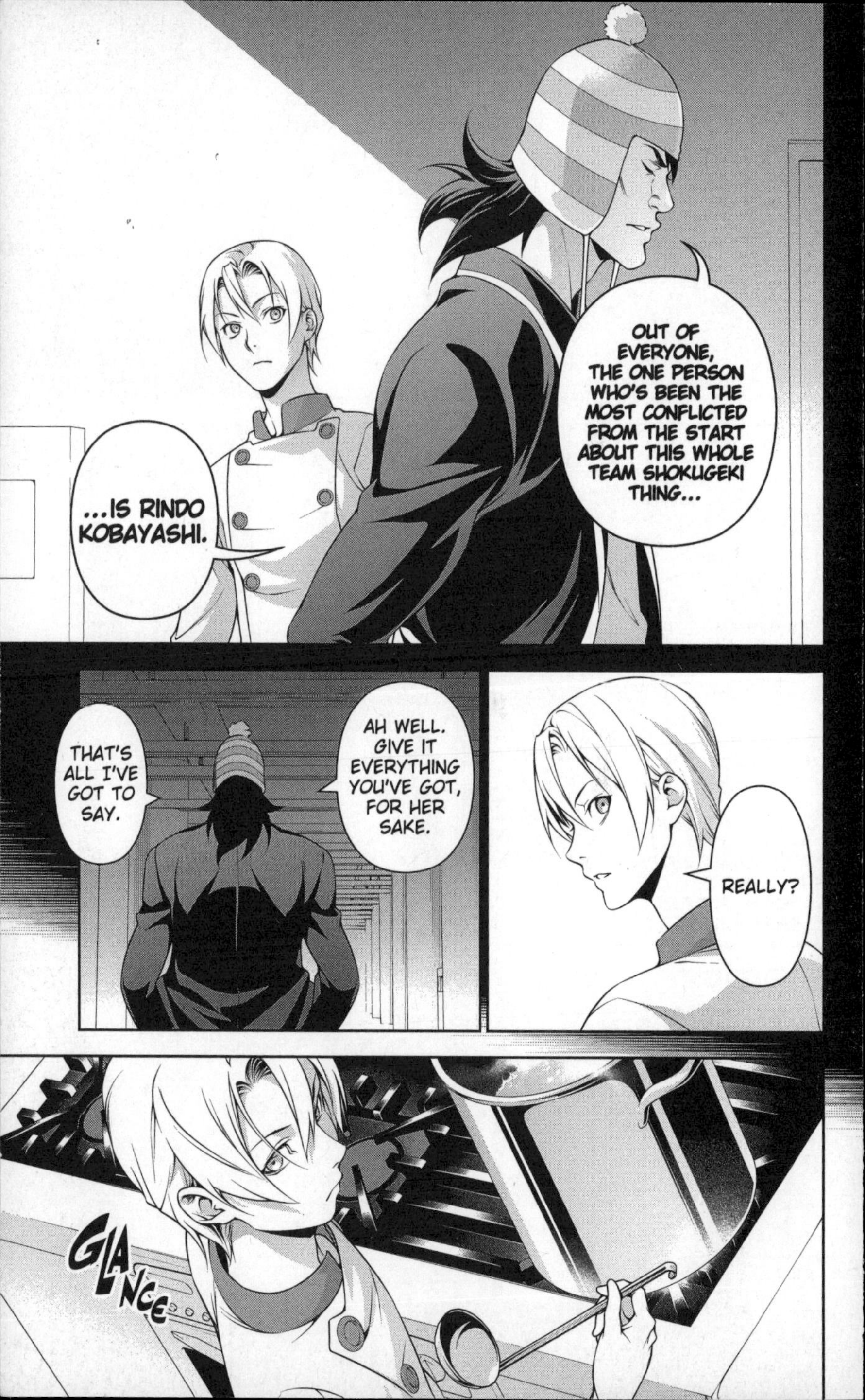
OUT OF EVERYONE, THE ONE PERSON WHO'S BEEN THE MOST CONFLICTED FROM THE START ABOUT THIS WHOLE TEAM SHOKUGEKI THING...
...IS RINDO KOBAYASHI.
REALLY?
AH WELL. GIVE IT EVERYTHING YOU'VE GOT, FOR HER SAKE.
THAT'S ALL I'VE GOT TO SAY.
GLANCE

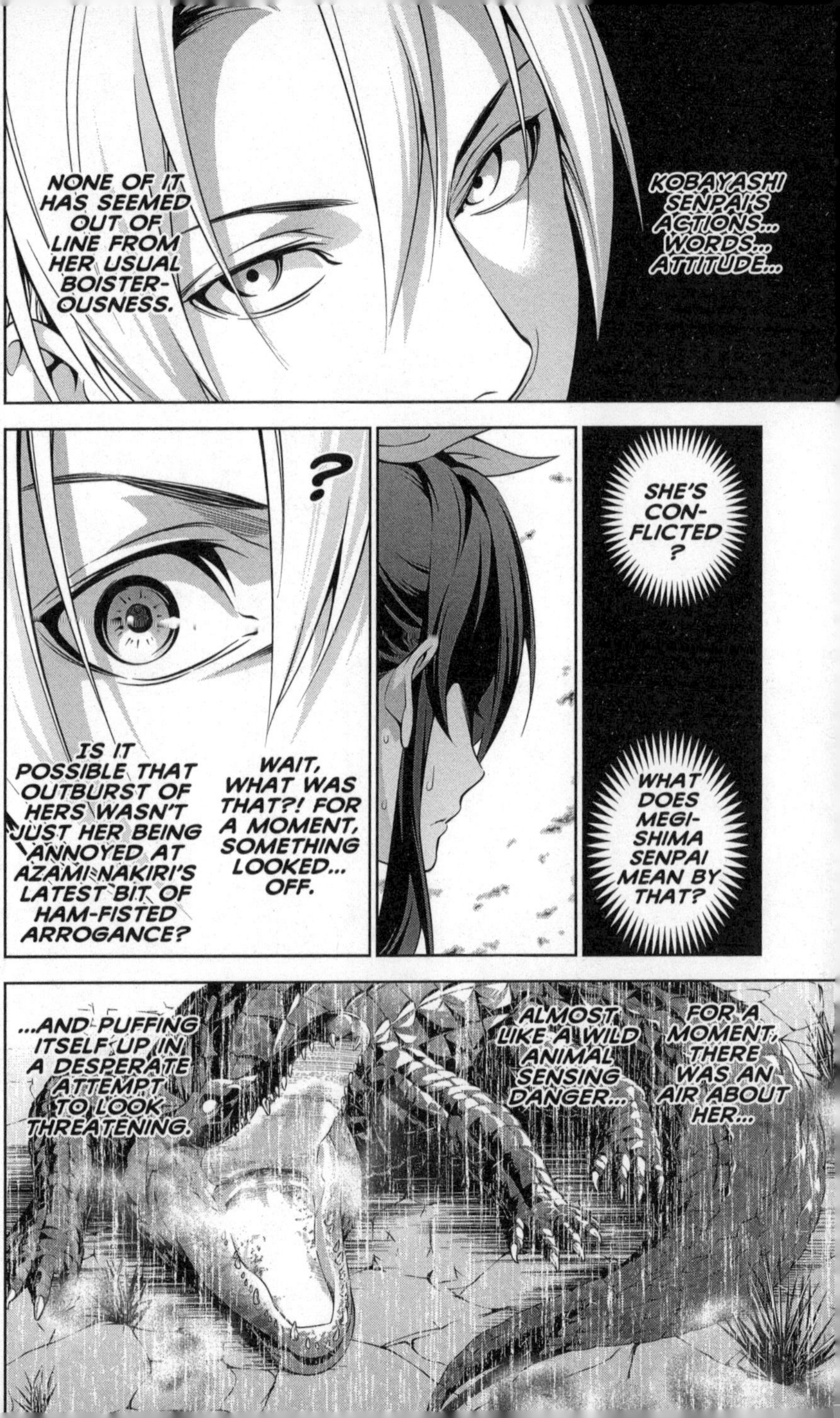
KOBAYASHI SENPAI'S ACTIONS... WORDS... ATTITUDE...
NONE OF IT HAS SEEMED OUT OF LINE FROM HER USUAL BOISTER-OUSNESS.
SHE'S CON-FLICTED?
WHAT DOES MEGI-SHIMA SENPAI MEAN BY THAT?
?
WAIT, WHAT WAS THAT?! FOR A MOMENT, SOMETHING LOOKED... OFF.
IS IT POSSIBLE THAT OUTBURST OF HERS WASN'T JUST HER BEING ANNOYED AT AZAMI NAKIRI'S LATEST BIT OF HAM-FISTED ARROGANCE?
FOR A MOMENT, THERE WAS AN AIR ABOUT HER...
ALMOST LIKE A WILD ANIMAL SENSING DANGER...
...AND PUFFING ITSELF UP IN A DESPERATE ATTEMPT TO LOOK THREATENING.

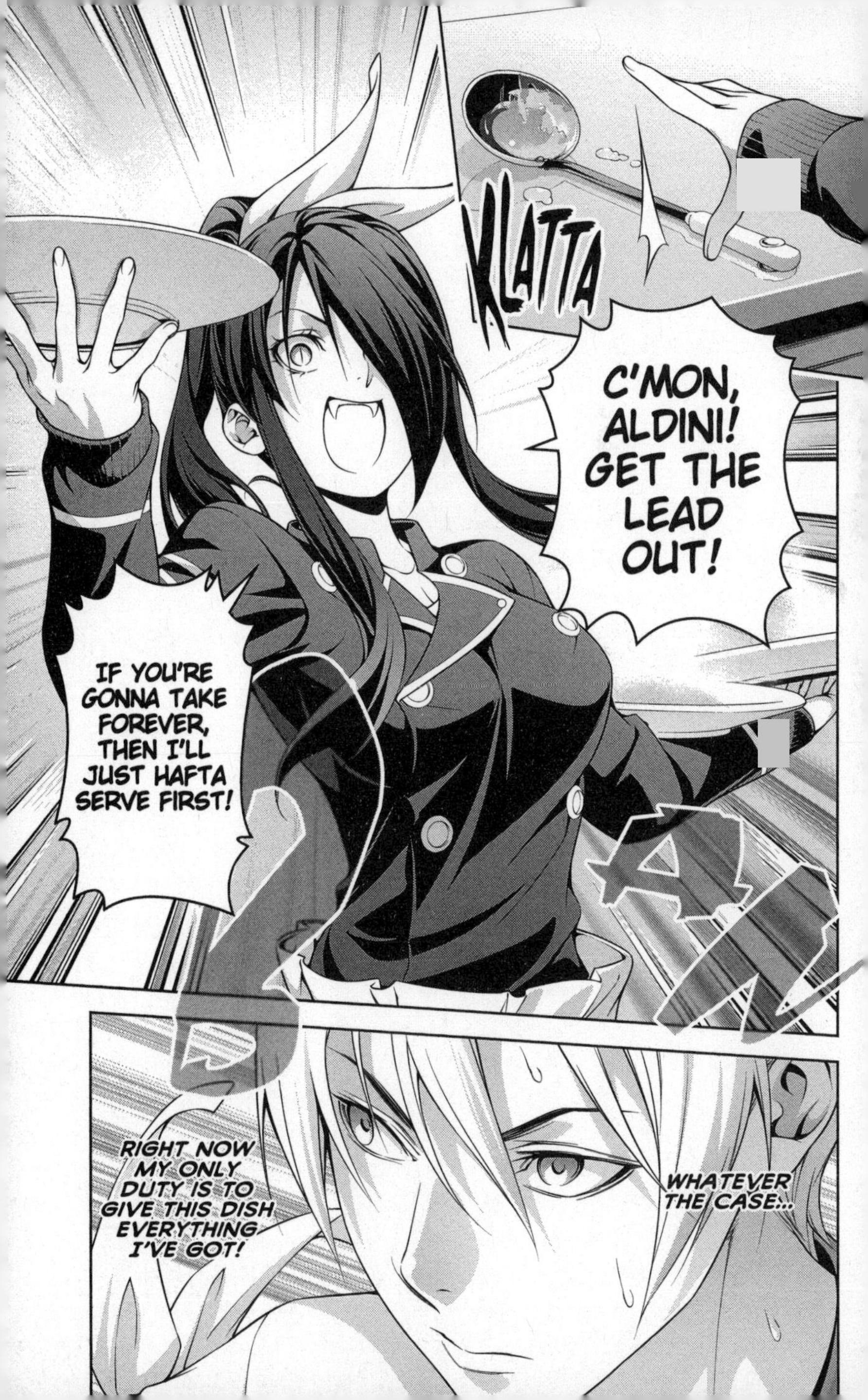
KLATTA
C'MON, ALDINI! GET THE LEAD OUT!
IF YOU'RE GONNA TAKE FOREVER, THEN I'LL JUST HAFTA SERVE FIRST!
WHATEVER THE CASE...
RIGHT NOW MY ONLY DUTY IS TO GIVE THIS DISH EVERYTHING I'VE GOT!

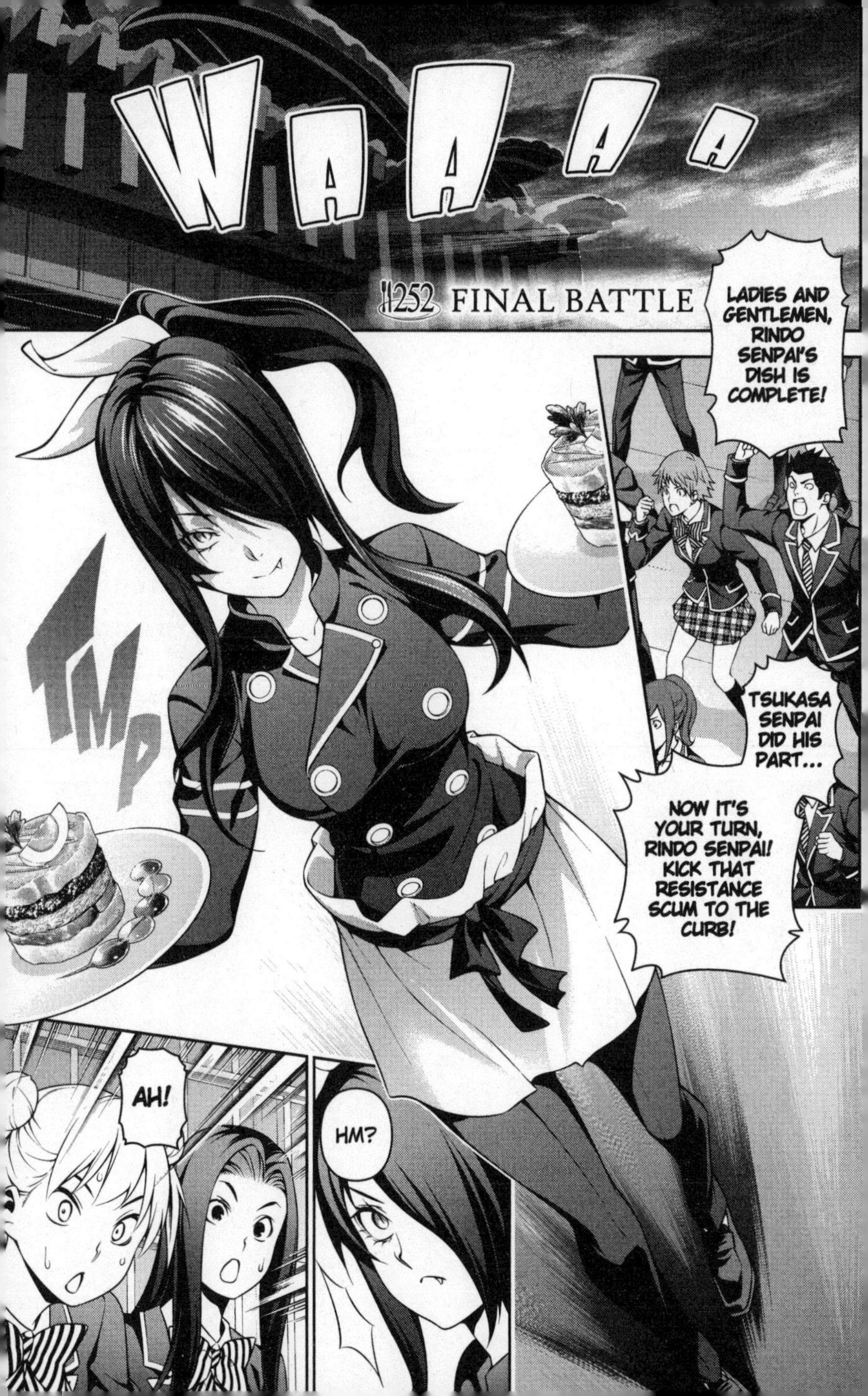
WAAAA
#252 FINAL BATTLE
LADIES AND GENTLEMEN, RINDO SENPAI'S DISH IS COMPLETE!
TSUKASA SENPAI DID HIS PART...
NOW IT'S YOUR TURN, RINDO SENPAI! KICK THAT RESISTANCE SCUM TO THE CURB!
TMP
HM?
AH!

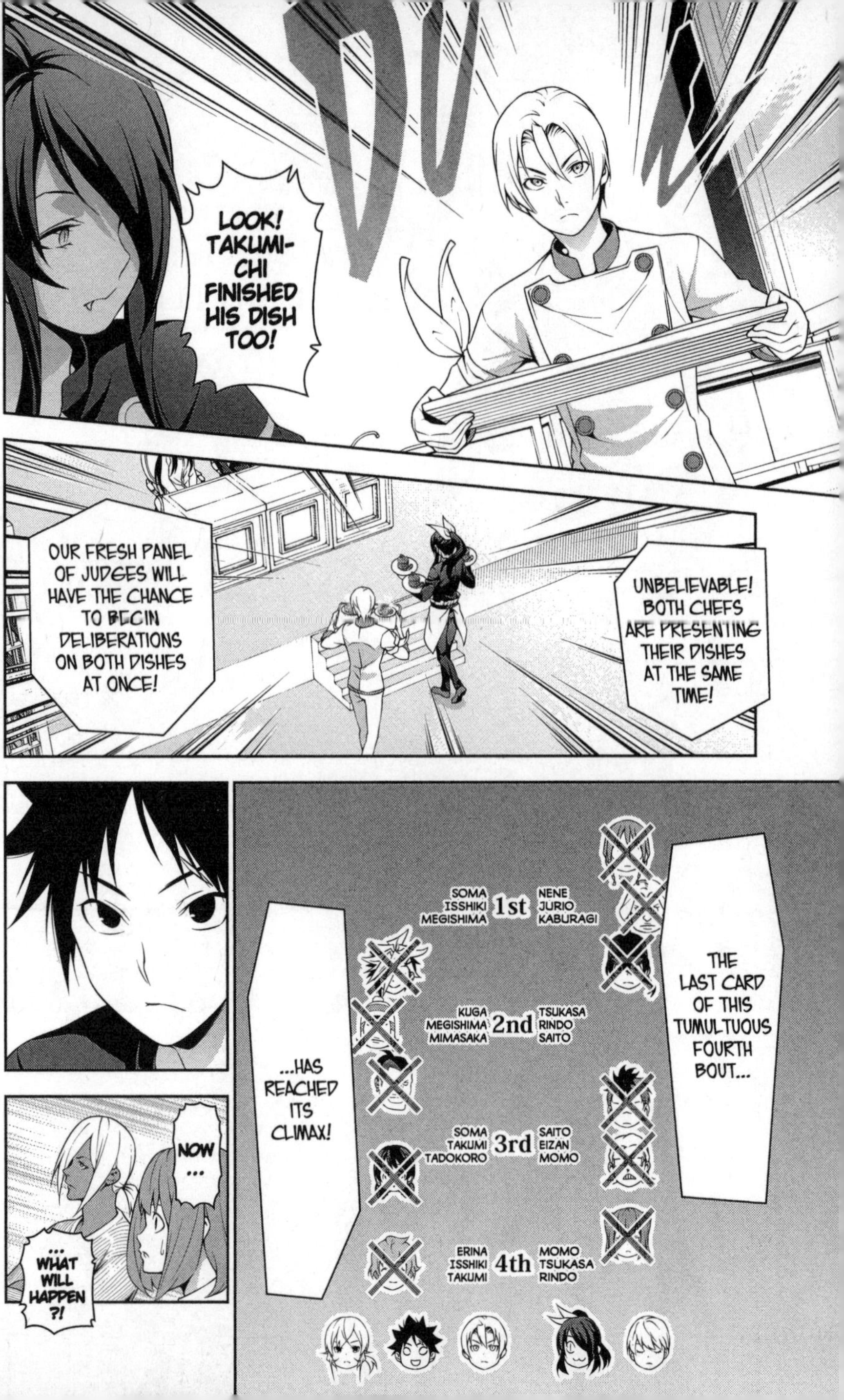
LOOK! TAKUMI-CHI FINISHED HIS DISH TOO!
UNBELIEVABLE! BOTH CHEFS ARE PRESENTING THEIR DISHES AT THE SAME TIME!
OUR FRESH PANEL OF JUDGES WILL HAVE THE CHANCE TO BEGIN DELIBERATIONS ON BOTH DISHES AT ONCE!
THE LAST CARD OF THIS TUMULTUOUS FOURTH BOUT...
SOMA ISSHIKI MEGISHIMA 1st NENE JURIO KABURAGI
KUGA MEGISHIMA MIMASAKA 2nd TSUKASA RINDO SAITO
SOMA TAKUMI TADOKORO 3rd SAITO EIZAN MOMO
ERINA ISSHIKI TAKUMI 4th MOMO TSUKASA RINDO
...HAS REACHED ITS CLIMAX!
NOW...
...WHAT WILL HAPPEN?!

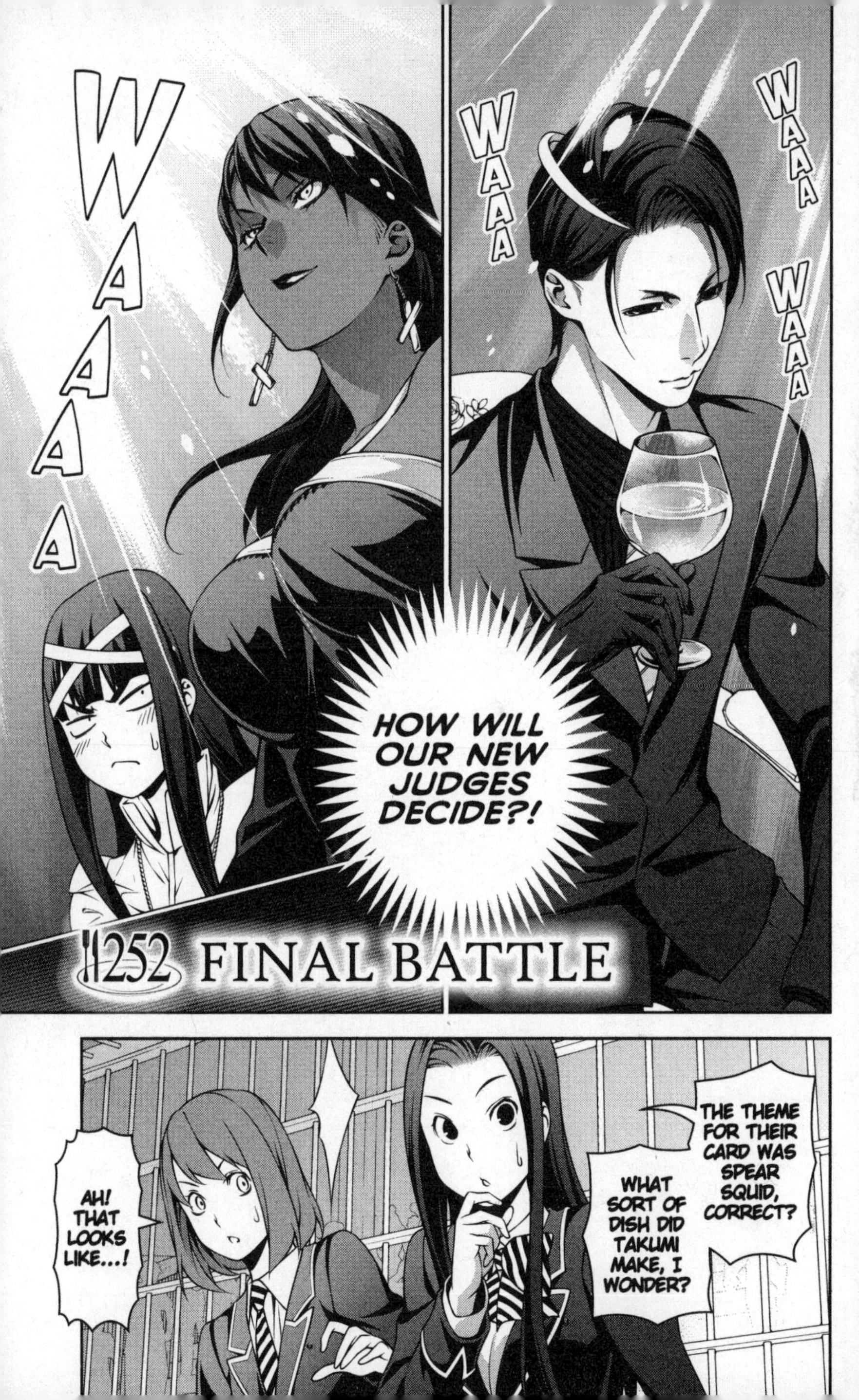
WAAA WAAA
WAAA WAAA
WAAAAAA
HOW WILL OUR NEW JUDGES DECIDE?!
252 FINAL BATTLE
THE THEME FOR THEIR CARD WAS SPEAR SQUID, CORRECT?
WHAT SORT OF DISH DID TAKUMI MAKE, I WONDER?
AH! THAT LOOKS LIKE...!

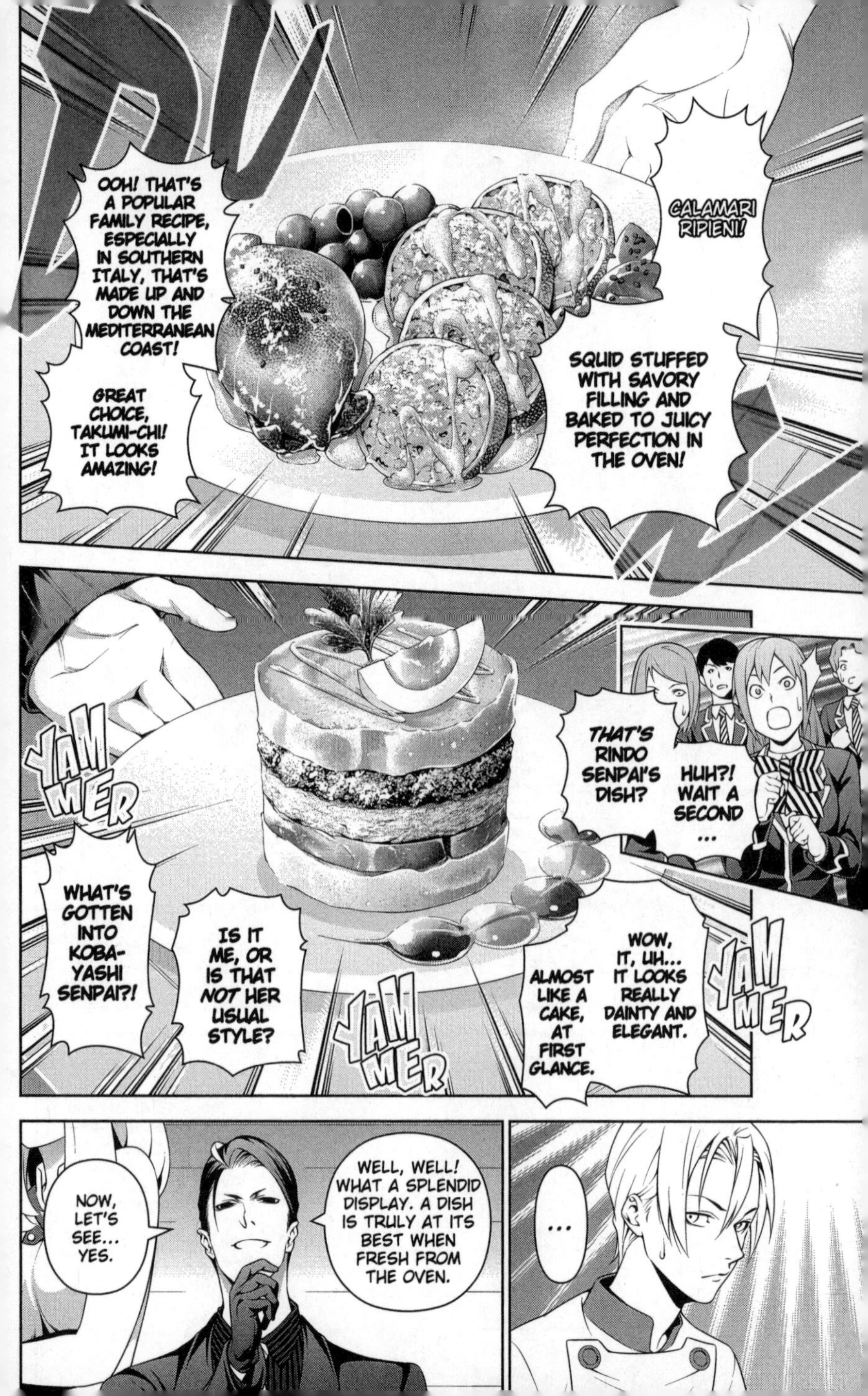
CALAMARI RIPIENI!
SQUID STUFFED WITH SAVORY FILLING AND BAKED TO JUICY PERFECTION IN THE OVEN!
OOH! THAT'S A POPULAR FAMILY RECIPE, ESPECIALLY IN SOUTHERN ITALY, THAT'S MADE UP AND DOWN THE MEDITERRANEAN COAST!
GREAT CHOICE, TAKUMI-CHI! IT LOOKS AMAZING!
HUH?! WAIT A SECOND ...
THAT'S RINDO SENPAI'S DISH?
YAMMER
WOW, IT, UH... IT LOOKS REALLY DAINTY AND ELEGANT.
ALMOST LIKE A CAKE, AT FIRST GLANCE.
YAMMER
IS IT ME, OR IS THAT *NOT* HER USUAL STYLE?
WHAT'S GOTTEN INTO KOBA-YASHI SENPAI?!
YAMMER
...
WELL, WELL! WHAT A SPLENDID DISPLAY. A DISH IS TRULY AT ITS BEST WHEN FRESH FROM THE OVEN.
NOW, LET'S SEE... YES.

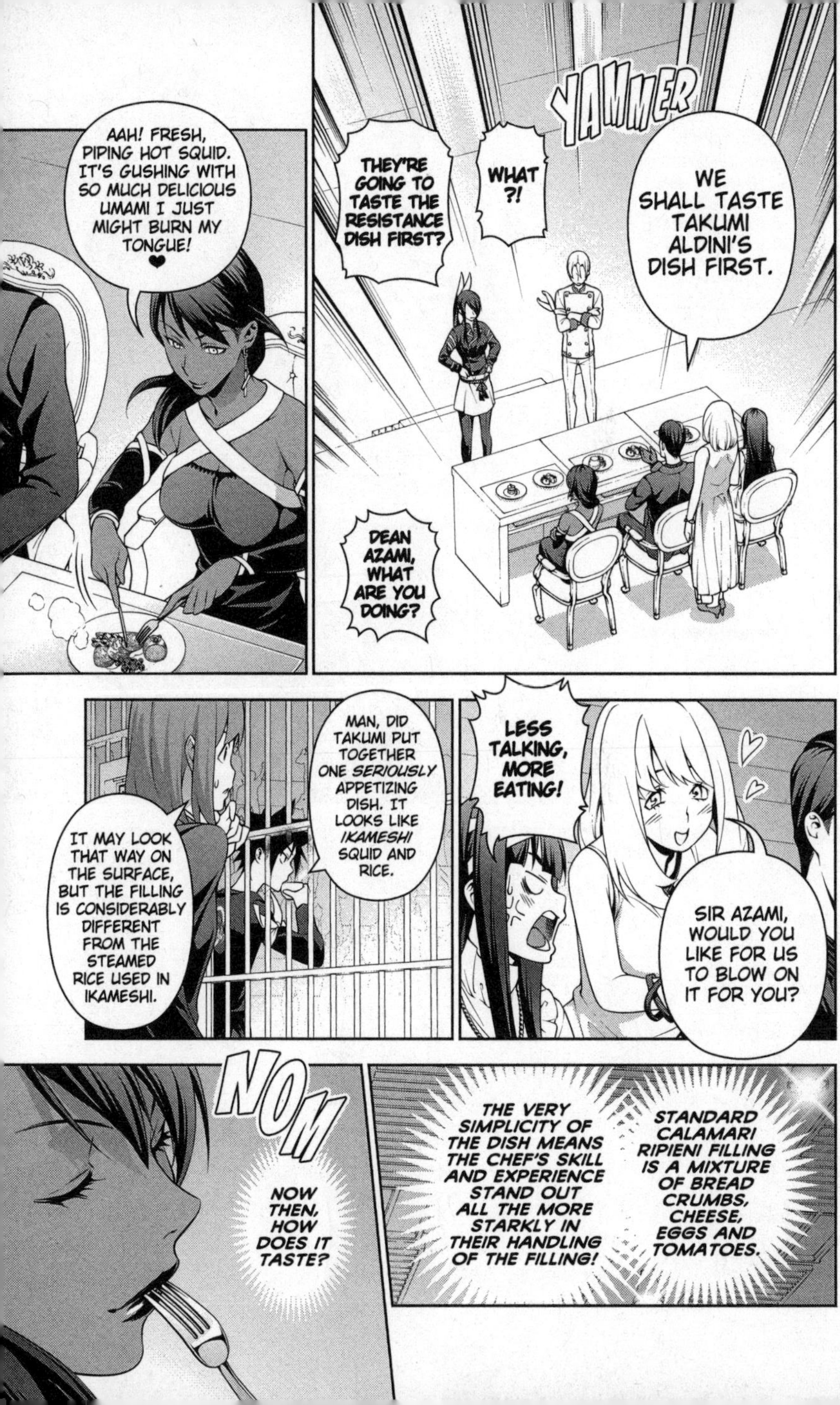
YAMMER
WE SHALL TASTE TAKUMI ALDINI'S DISH FIRST.
WHAT?!
THEY'RE GOING TO TASTE THE RESISTANCE DISH FIRST?
DEAN AZAMI, WHAT ARE YOU DOING?
AAH! FRESH, PIPING HOT SQUID. IT'S GUSHING WITH SO MUCH DELICIOUS UMAMI I JUST MIGHT BURN MY TONGUE! ❤
SIR AZAMI, WOULD YOU LIKE FOR US TO BLOW ON IT FOR YOU?
LESS TALKING, MORE EATING!
MAN, DID TAKUMI PUT TOGETHER ONE *SERIOUSLY* APPETIZING DISH. IT LOOKS LIKE *IKAMESHI* SQUID AND RICE.
IT MAY LOOK THAT WAY ON THE SURFACE, BUT THE FILLING IS CONSIDERABLY DIFFERENT FROM THE STEAMED RICE USED IN IKAMESHI.
STANDARD CALAMARI RIPIENI FILLING IS A MIXTURE OF BREAD CRUMBS, CHEESE, EGGS AND TOMATOES.
THE VERY SIMPLICITY OF THE DISH MEANS THE CHEF'S SKILL AND EXPERIENCE STAND OUT ALL THE MORE STARKLY IN THEIR HANDLING OF THE FILLING!
NOM
NOW THEN, HOW DOES IT TASTE?

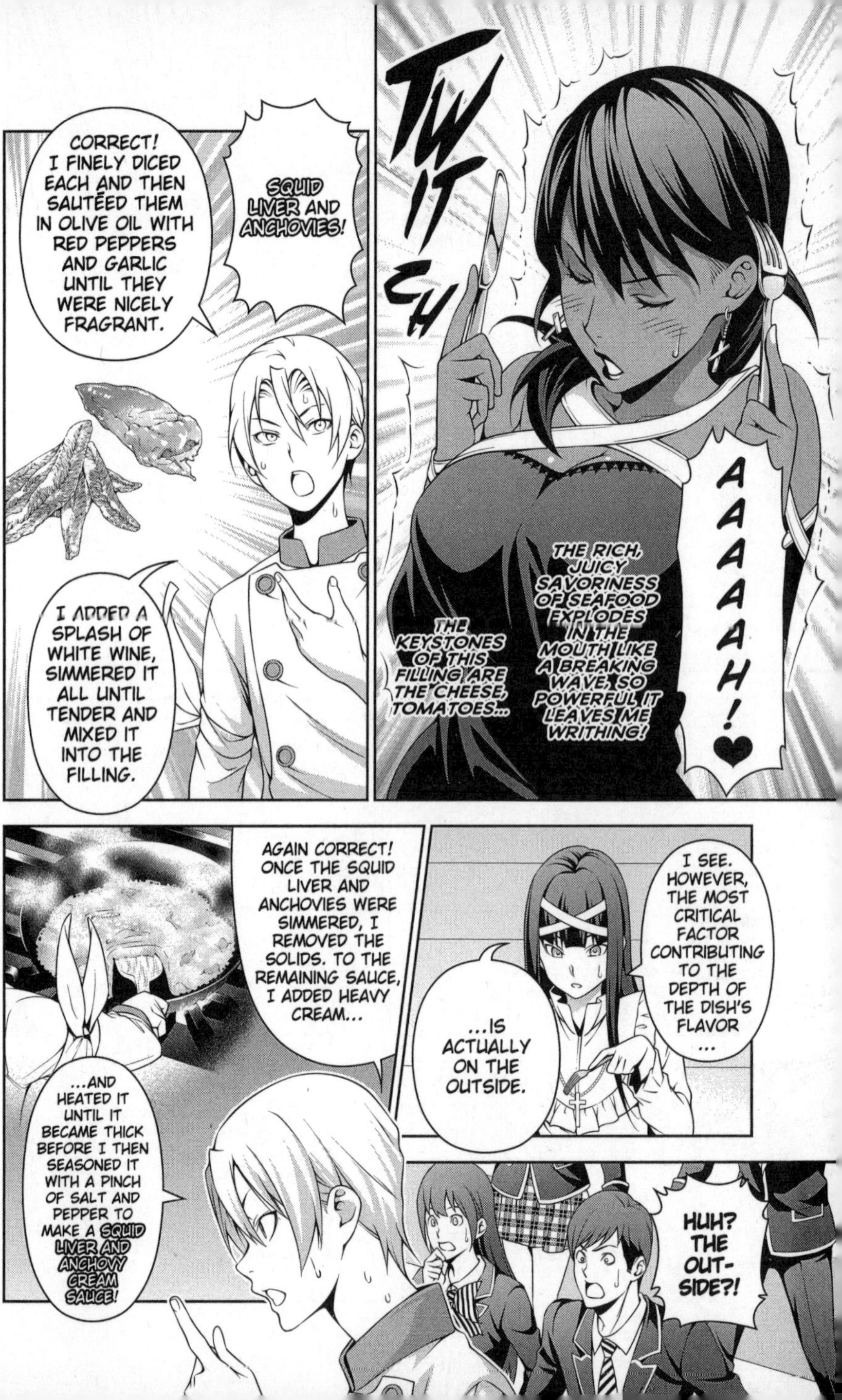
TWITCH
AAAAAAH!♥
THE RICH, JUICY SAVORINESS OF SEAFOOD EXPLODES IN THE MOUTH LIKE A BREAKING WAVE, SO POWERFUL IT LEAVES ME WRITHING!
THE KEYSTONES OF THIS FILLING ARE THE CHEESE, TOMATOES...
SQUID LIVER AND ANCHOVIES!
CORRECT! I FINELY DICED EACH AND THEN SAUTÉED THEM IN OLIVE OIL WITH RED PEPPERS AND GARLIC UNTIL THEY WERE NICELY FRAGRANT.
I ADDED A SPLASH OF WHITE WINE, SIMMERED IT ALL UNTIL TENDER AND MIXED IT INTO THE FILLING.
I SEE. HOWEVER, THE MOST CRITICAL FACTOR CONTRIBUTING TO THE DEPTH OF THE DISH'S FLAVOR...
...IS ACTUALLY ON THE OUTSIDE.
HUH? THE OUT-SIDE?!
AGAIN CORRECT! ONCE THE SQUID LIVER AND ANCHOVIES WERE SIMMERED, I REMOVED THE SOLIDS. TO THE REMAINING SAUCE, I ADDED HEAVY CREAM...
...AND HEATED IT UNTIL IT BECAME THICK BEFORE I THEN SEASONED IT WITH A PINCH OF SALT AND PEPPER TO MAKE A SQUID LIVER AND ANCHOVY CREAM SAUCE!

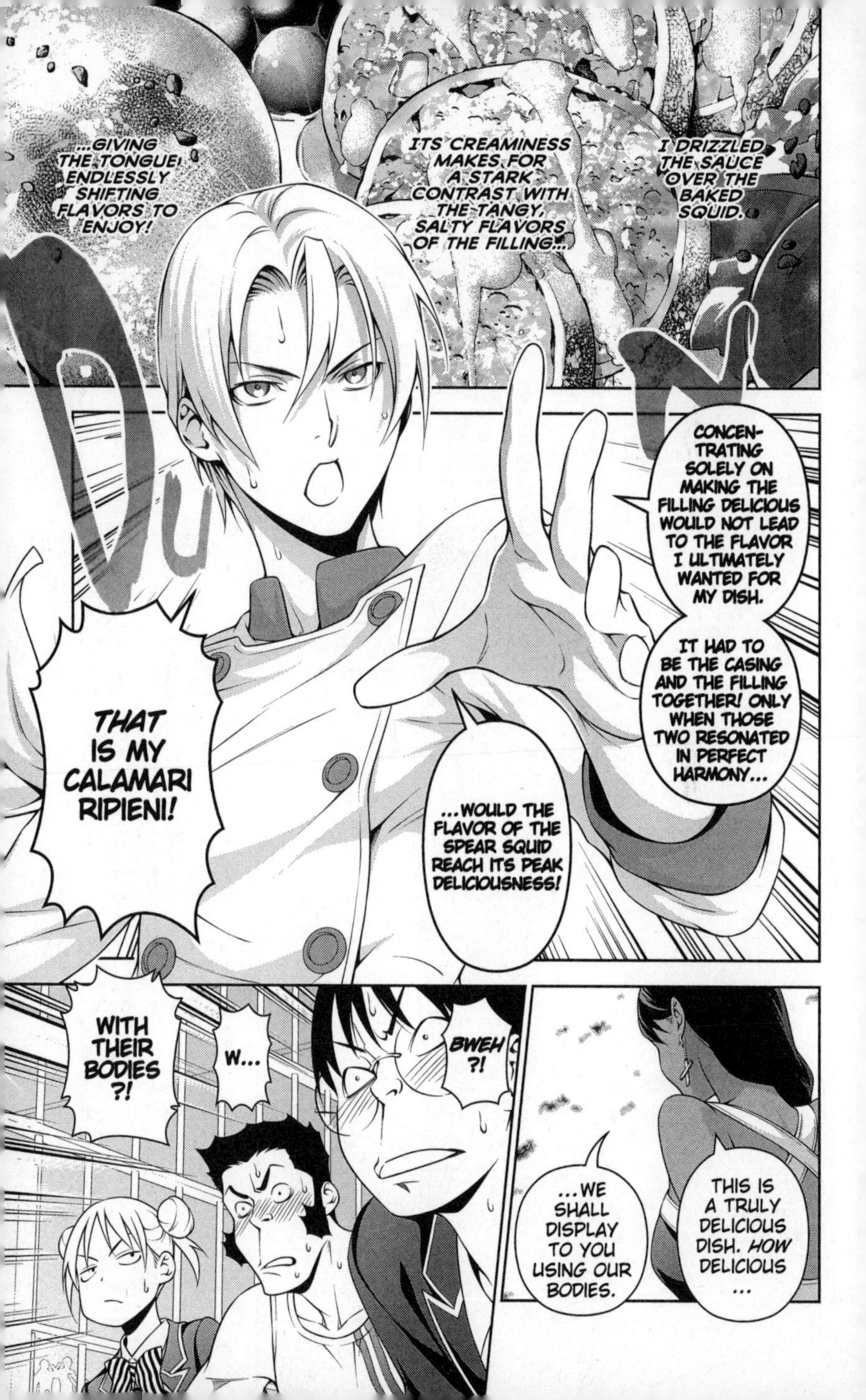
I DRIZZLED THE SAUCE OVER THE BAKED SQUID.
ITS CREAMINESS MAKES FOR A STARK CONTRAST WITH THE TANGY, SALTY FLAVORS OF THE FILLING...
...GIVING THE TONGUE ENDLESSLY SHIFTING FLAVORS TO ENJOY!
CONCENTRATING SOLELY ON MAKING THE FILLING DELICIOUS WOULD NOT LEAD TO THE FLAVOR I ULTIMATELY WANTED FOR MY DISH.
IT HAD TO BE THE CASING AND THE FILLING TOGETHER! ONLY WHEN THOSE TWO RESONATED IN PERFECT HARMONY...
...WOULD THE FLAVOR OF THE SPEAR SQUID REACH ITS PEAK DELICIOUSNESS!
THAT IS MY CALAMARI RIPIENI!
THIS IS A TRULY DELICIOUS DISH. HOW DELICIOUS ...
...WE SHALL DISPLAY TO YOU USING OUR BODIES.
BWEH ?!
W...
WITH THEIR BODIES ?!

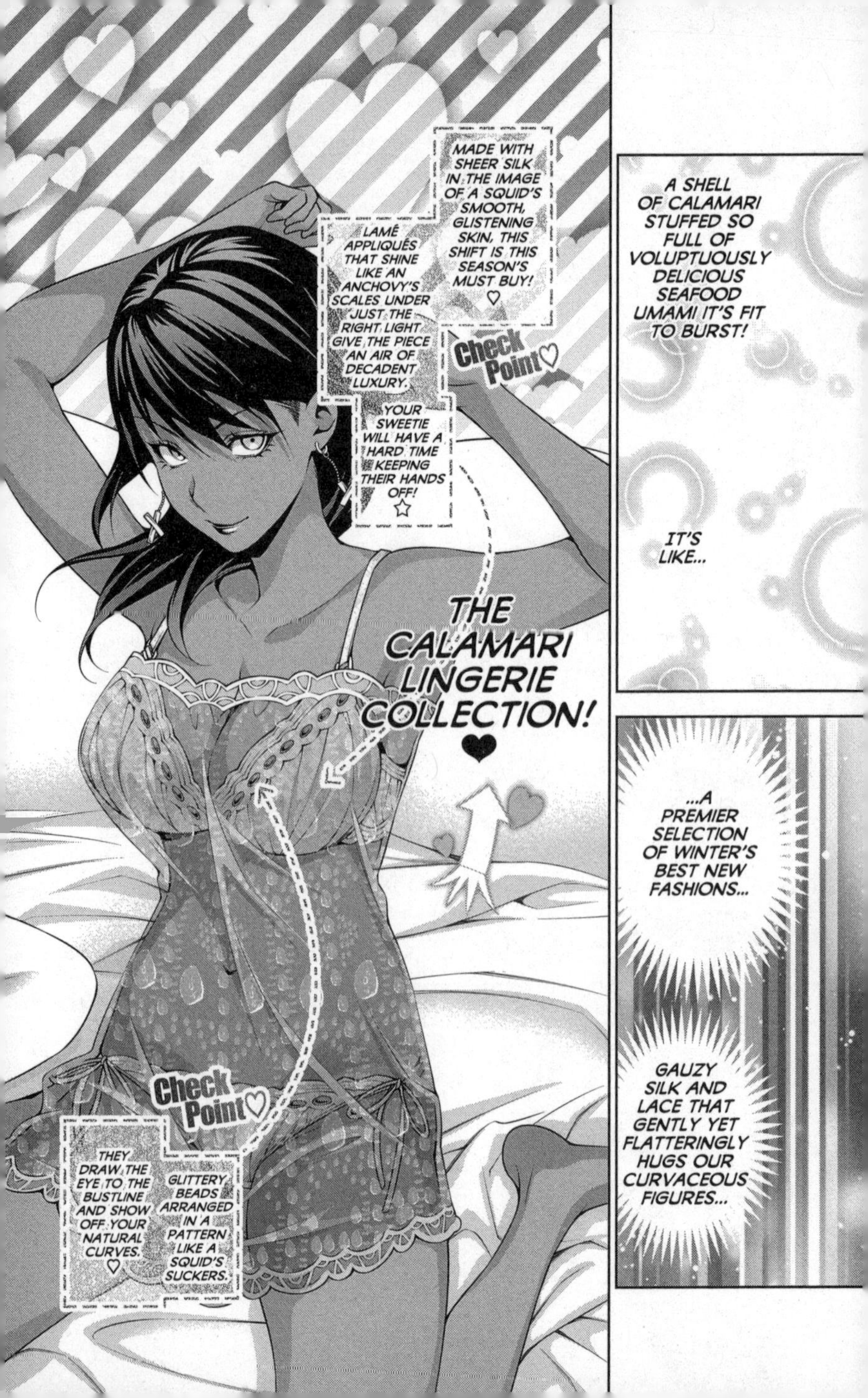
A SHELL OF CALAMARI STUFFED SO FULL OF VOLUPTUOUSLY DELICIOUS SEAFOOD UMAMI IT'S FIT TO BURST!
IT'S LIKE...
...A PREMIER SELECTION OF WINTER'S BEST NEW FASHIONS...
GAUZY SILK AND LACE THAT GENTLY YET FLATTERINGLY HUGS OUR CURVACEOUS FIGURES...
MADE WITH SHEER SILK IN THE IMAGE OF A SQUID'S SMOOTH, GLISTENING SKIN, THIS SHIFT IS THIS SEASON'S MUST BUY! ♡
LAMÉ APPLIQUÉS THAT SHINE LIKE AN ANCHOVY'S SCALES UNDER JUST THE RIGHT LIGHT GIVE THE PIECE AN AIR OF DECADENT LUXURY.
Check Point♡
YOUR SWEETIE WILL HAVE A HARD TIME KEEPING THEIR HANDS OFF! ☆
THE CALAMARI LINGERIE COLLECTION! ❤
Check Point♡
GLITTERY BEADS ARRANGED IN A PATTERN LIKE A SQUID'S SUCKERS.
THEY DRAW THE EYE TO THE BUSTLINE AND SHOW OFF YOUR NATURAL CURVES. ♡

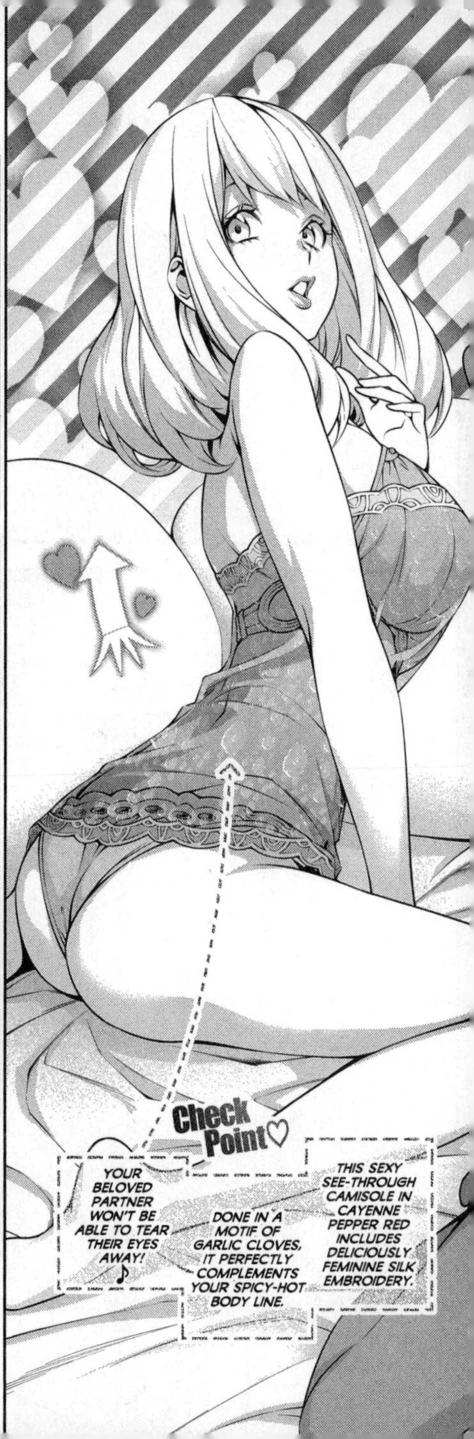
Check Point♡
THIS SEXY SEE-THROUGH CAMISOLE IN CAYENNE PEPPER RED INCLUDES DELICIOUSLY FEMININE SILK EMBROIDERY.
DONE IN A MOTIF OF GARLIC CLOVES, IT PERFECTLY COMPLEMENTS YOUR SPICY-HOT BODY LINE.
YOUR BELOVED PARTNER WON'T BE ABLE TO TEAR THEIR EYES AWAY! ♪

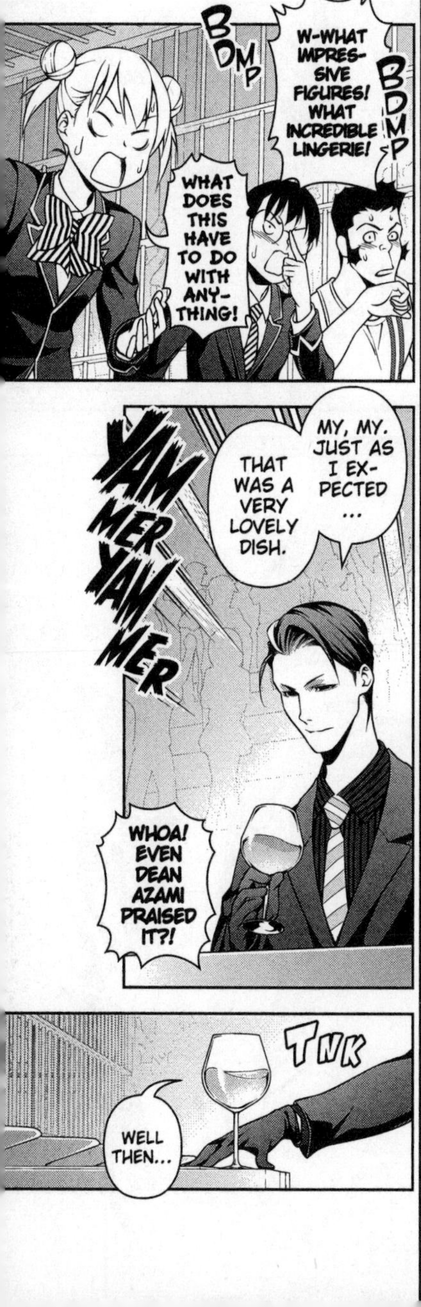
BDMP
W-WHAT IMPRESSIVE FIGURES! WHAT INCREDIBLE LINGERIE!
BDMP
WHAT DOES THIS HAVE TO DO WITH ANYTHING!
MY, MY. JUST AS I EXPECTED...
THAT WAS A VERY LOVELY DISH.
YAMMER YAMMER
WHOA! EVEN DEAN AZAMI PRAISED IT?!
TNK
WELL THEN...

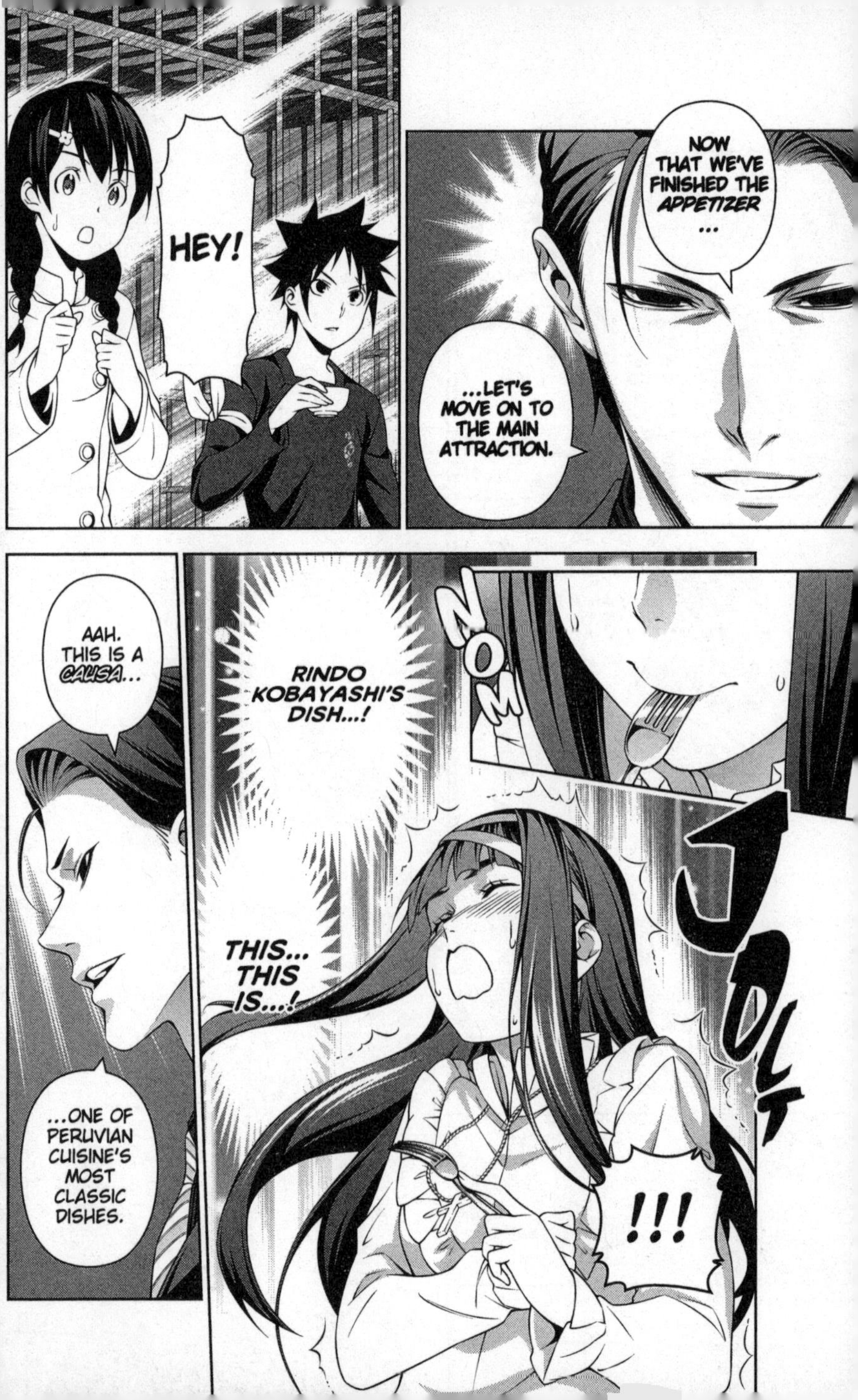
NOW THAT WE'VE FINISHED THE *APPETIZER*...
...LET'S MOVE ON TO THE MAIN ATTRACTION.
HEY!
NOM
RINDO KOBAYASHI'S DISH...!
THIS... THIS IS...!
!!!
AAH. THIS IS A *CAUSA*...
...ONE OF PERUVIAN CUISINE'S MOST CLASSIC DISHES.

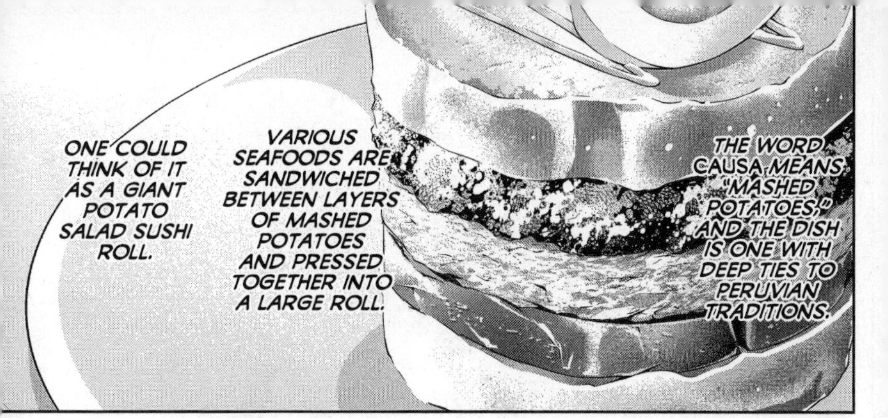
THE WORD CAUSA MEANS "MASHED POTATOES," AND THE DISH IS ONE WITH DEEP TIES TO PERUVIAN TRADITIONS.
VARIOUS SEAFOODS ARE SANDWICHED BETWEEN LAYERS OF MASHED POTATOES AND PRESSED TOGETHER INTO A LARGE ROLL.
ONE COULD THINK OF IT AS A GIANT POTATO SALAD SUSHI ROLL.

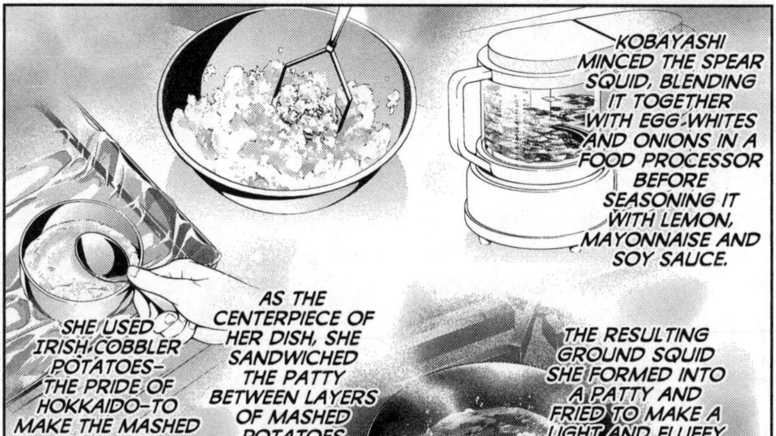
KOBAYASHI MINCED THE SPEAR SQUID, BLENDING IT TOGETHER WITH EGG WHITES AND ONIONS IN A FOOD PROCESSOR BEFORE SEASONING IT WITH LEMON, MAYONNAISE AND SOY SAUCE.
THE RESULTING GROUND SQUID SHE FORMED INTO A PATTY AND FRIED TO MAKE A LIGHT AND FLUFFY SQUID BURGER.
AS THE CENTERPIECE OF HER DISH, SHE SANDWICHED THE PATTY BETWEEN LAYERS OF MASHED POTATOES SEASONED WITH BRIGHT YELLOW AJÍ AMARILLO.
SHE USED IRISH COBBLER POTATOES—THE PRIDE OF HOKKAIDO—TO MAKE THE MASHED POTATOES. THEIR NATURAL SWEETNESS NICELY EMPHASIZES THE BODY OF THE SQUID'S FLAVOR.

AJÍ AMARILLO IS A TYPE OF YELLOW CHILI PEPPER. A TRADITIONAL SEASONING IN PERUVIAN CUISINE, IT HAS BOTH SPICINESS AND FRUITY SWEETNESS.

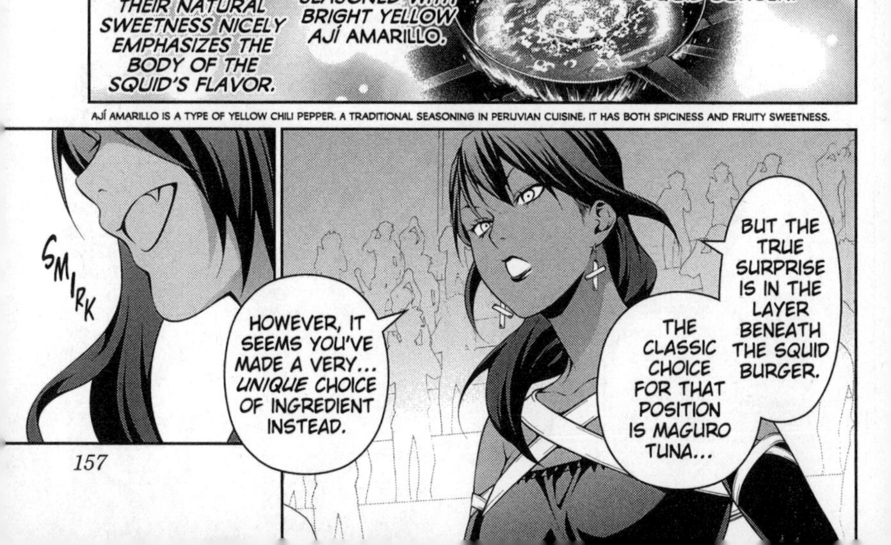
BUT THE TRUE SURPRISE IS IN THE LAYER BENEATH THE SQUID BURGER.
THE CLASSIC CHOICE FOR THAT POSITION IS MAGURO TUNA...
HOWEVER, IT SEEMS YOU'VE MADE A VERY... *UNIQUE* CHOICE OF INGREDIENT INSTEAD.
SMIRK

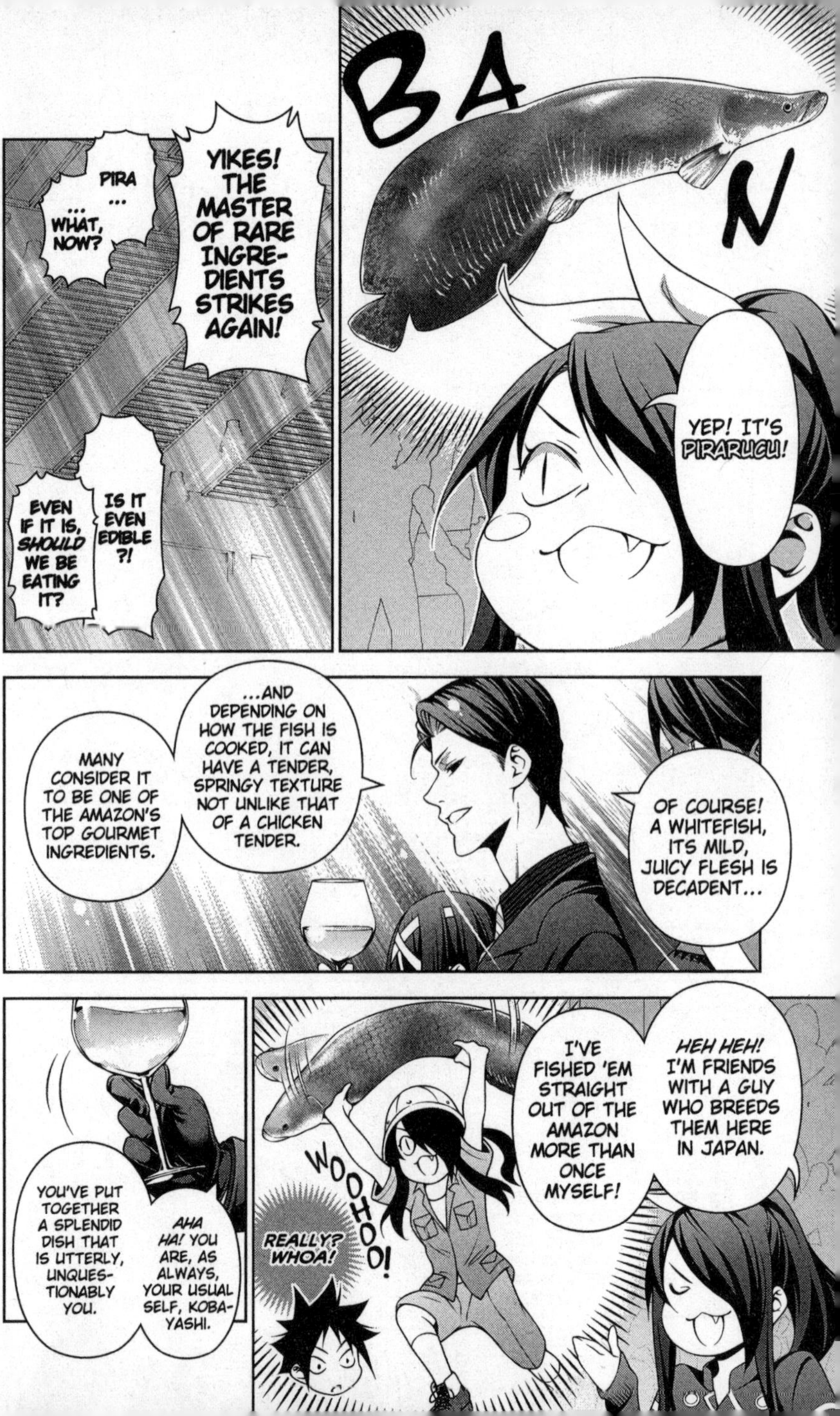
BAN
YEP! IT'S PIRARUCU!
YIKES! THE MASTER OF RARE INGREDIENTS STRIKES AGAIN!
PIRA... ...WHAT, NOW?
IS IT EVEN EDIBLE?!
EVEN IF IT IS, SHOULD WE BE EATING IT?
OF COURSE! A WHITEFISH, ITS MILD, JUICY FLESH IS DECADENT...
...AND DEPENDING ON HOW THE FISH IS COOKED, IT CAN HAVE A TENDER, SPRINGY TEXTURE NOT UNLIKE THAT OF A CHICKEN TENDER.
MANY CONSIDER IT TO BE ONE OF THE AMAZON'S TOP GOURMET INGREDIENTS.
HEH HEH! I'M FRIENDS WITH A GUY WHO BREEDS THEM HERE IN JAPAN.
I'VE FISHED 'EM STRAIGHT OUT OF THE AMAZON MORE THAN ONCE MYSELF!
WOOHOO!
REALLY? WHOA!
AHA HA! YOU ARE, AS ALWAYS, YOUR USUAL SELF, KOBAYASHI.
YOU'VE PUT TOGETHER A SPLENDID DISH THAT IS UTTERLY, UNQUESTIONABLY YOU.

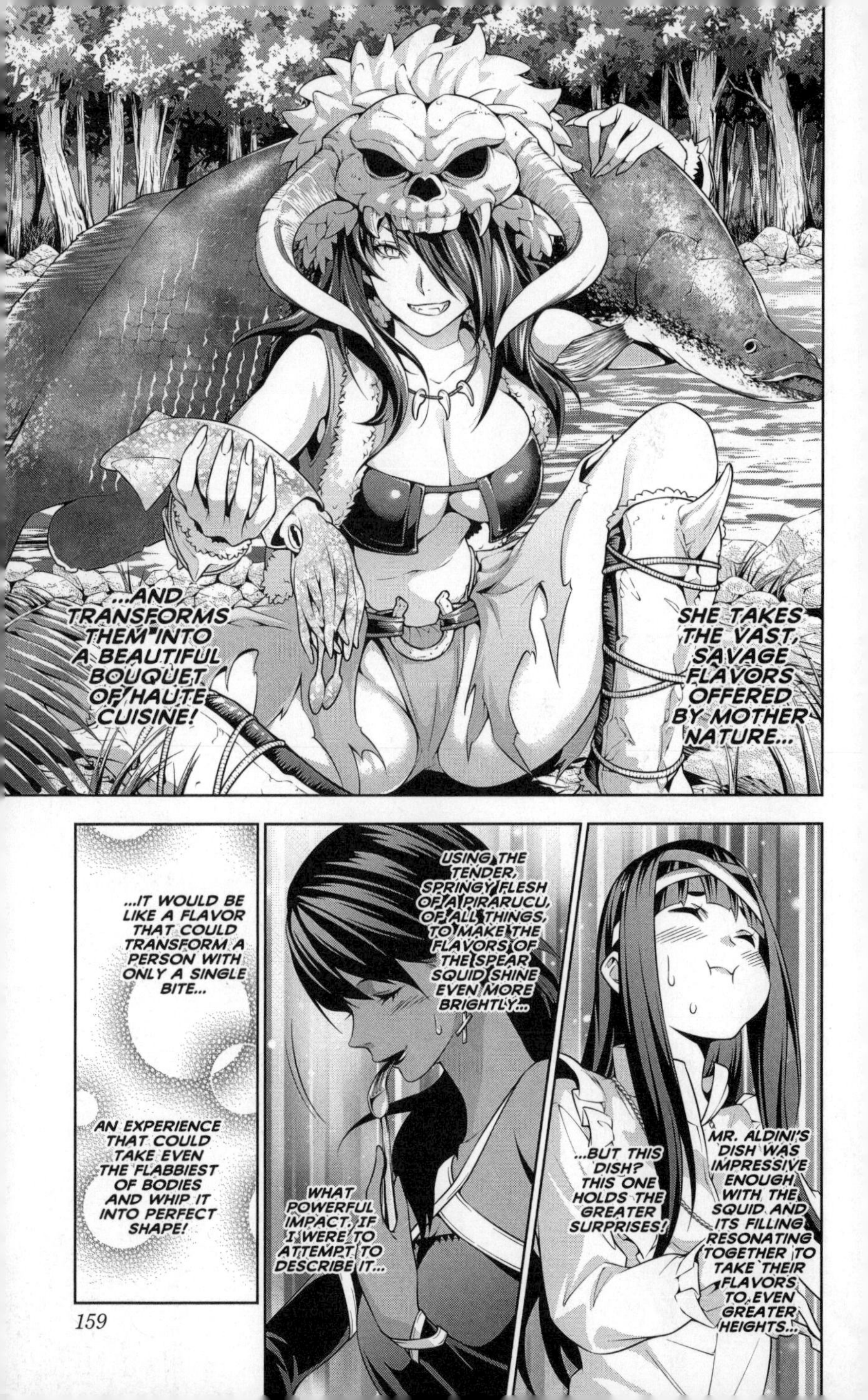
SHE TAKES THE VAST, SAVAGE FLAVORS OFFERED BY MOTHER NATURE...
...AND TRANSFORMS THEM INTO A BEAUTIFUL BOUQUET OF HAUTE CUISINE!
MR. ALDINI'S DISH WAS IMPRESSIVE ENOUGH, WITH THE SQUID AND ITS FILLING RESONATING TOGETHER TO TAKE THEIR FLAVORS TO EVEN GREATER HEIGHTS...
...BUT THIS DISH? THIS ONE HOLDS THE GREATER SURPRISES!
USING THE TENDER, SPRINGY FLESH OF A PIRARUCU, OF ALL THINGS, TO MAKE THE FLAVORS OF THE SPEAR SQUID SHINE EVEN MORE BRIGHTLY...
WHAT POWERFUL IMPACT. IF I WERE TO ATTEMPT TO DESCRIBE IT...
...IT WOULD BE LIKE A FLAVOR THAT COULD TRANSFORM A PERSON WITH ONLY A SINGLE BITE...
AN EXPERIENCE THAT COULD TAKE EVEN THE FLABBIEST OF BODIES AND WHIP IT INTO PERFECT SHAPE!

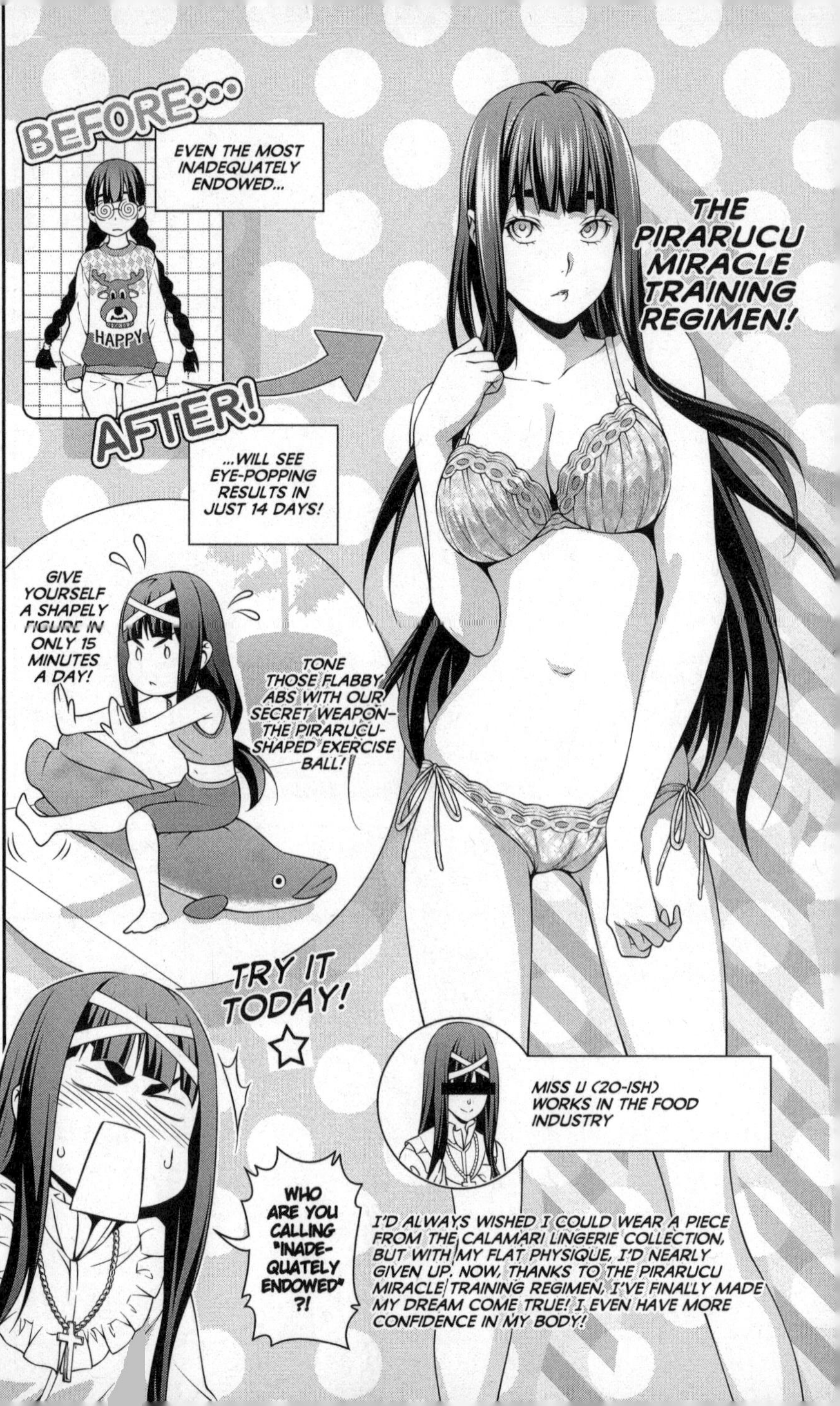
THE PIRARUCU MIRACLE TRAINING REGIMEN!
BEFORE...
EVEN THE MOST INADEQUATELY ENDOWED...
HAPPY
AFTER!
...WILL SEE EYE-POPPING RESULTS IN JUST 14 DAYS!
TONE THOSE FLABBY ABS WITH OUR SECRET WEAPON—THE PIRARUCU-SHAPED EXERCISE BALL!
GIVE YOURSELF A SHAPELY FIGURE IN ONLY 15 MINUTES A DAY!
TRY IT TODAY! ☆
MISS U (20-ISH) WORKS IN THE FOOD INDUSTRY
I'D ALWAYS WISHED I COULD WEAR A PIECE FROM THE CALAMARI LINGERIE COLLECTION, BUT WITH MY FLAT PHYSIQUE, I'D NEARLY GIVEN UP. NOW, THANKS TO THE PIRARUCU MIRACLE TRAINING REGIMEN, I'VE FINALLY MADE MY DREAM COME TRUE! I EVEN HAVE MORE CONFIDENCE IN MY BODY!
WHO ARE YOU CALLING "INADE-QUATELY ENDOWED"?!

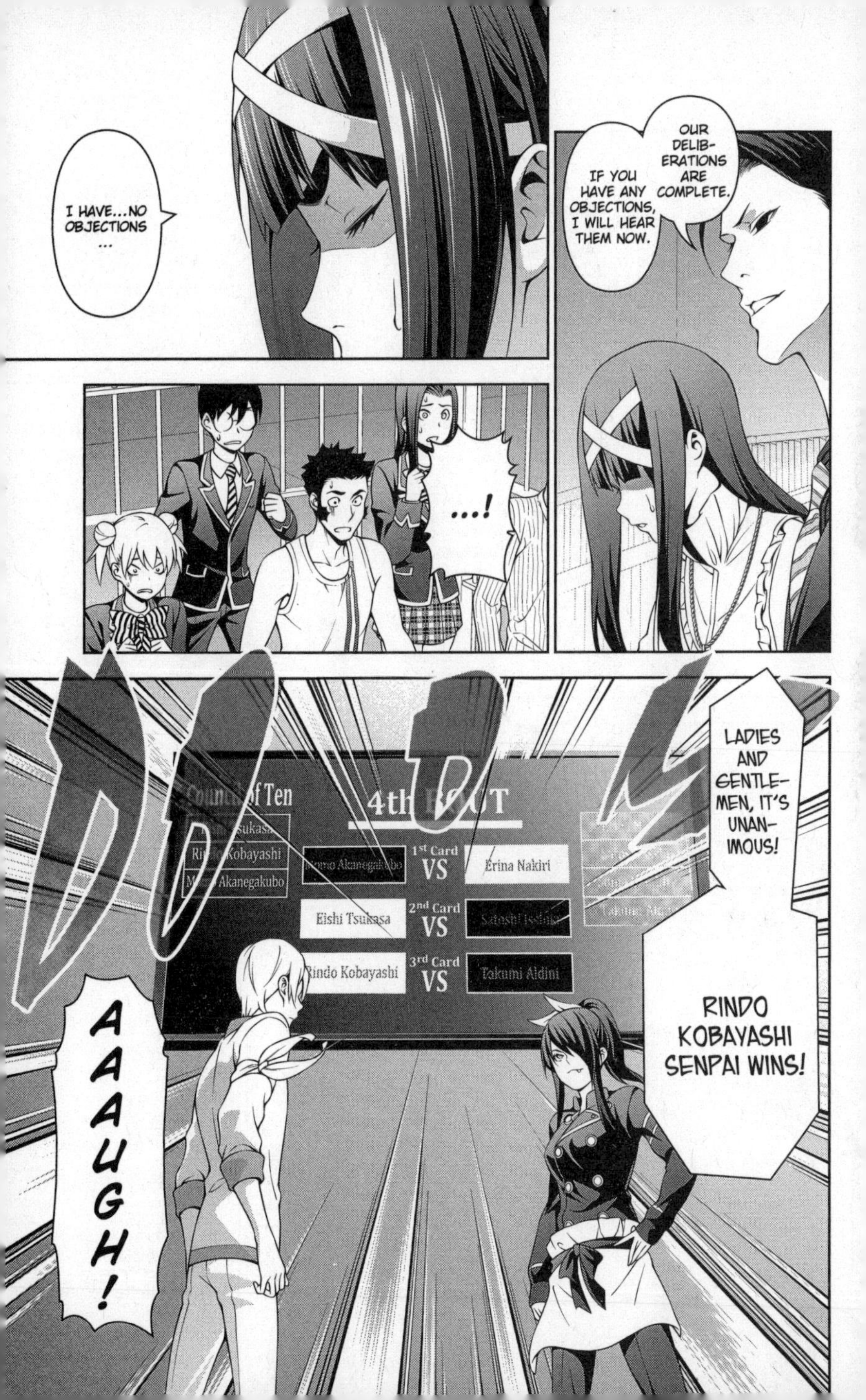
OUR DELIBERATIONS ARE COMPLETE.
IF YOU HAVE ANY OBJECTIONS, I WILL HEAR THEM NOW.
I HAVE...NO OBJECTIONS...
...!
LADIES AND GENTLEMEN, IT'S UNANIMOUS!
RINDO KOBAYASHI SENPAI WINS!
Council of Ten
4th
1st Card
VS
Erina Nakiri
Eishi Tsukasa
2nd Card
VS
Rindo Kobayashi
3rd Card
VS
Takumi Aldini
AAAAUGH!

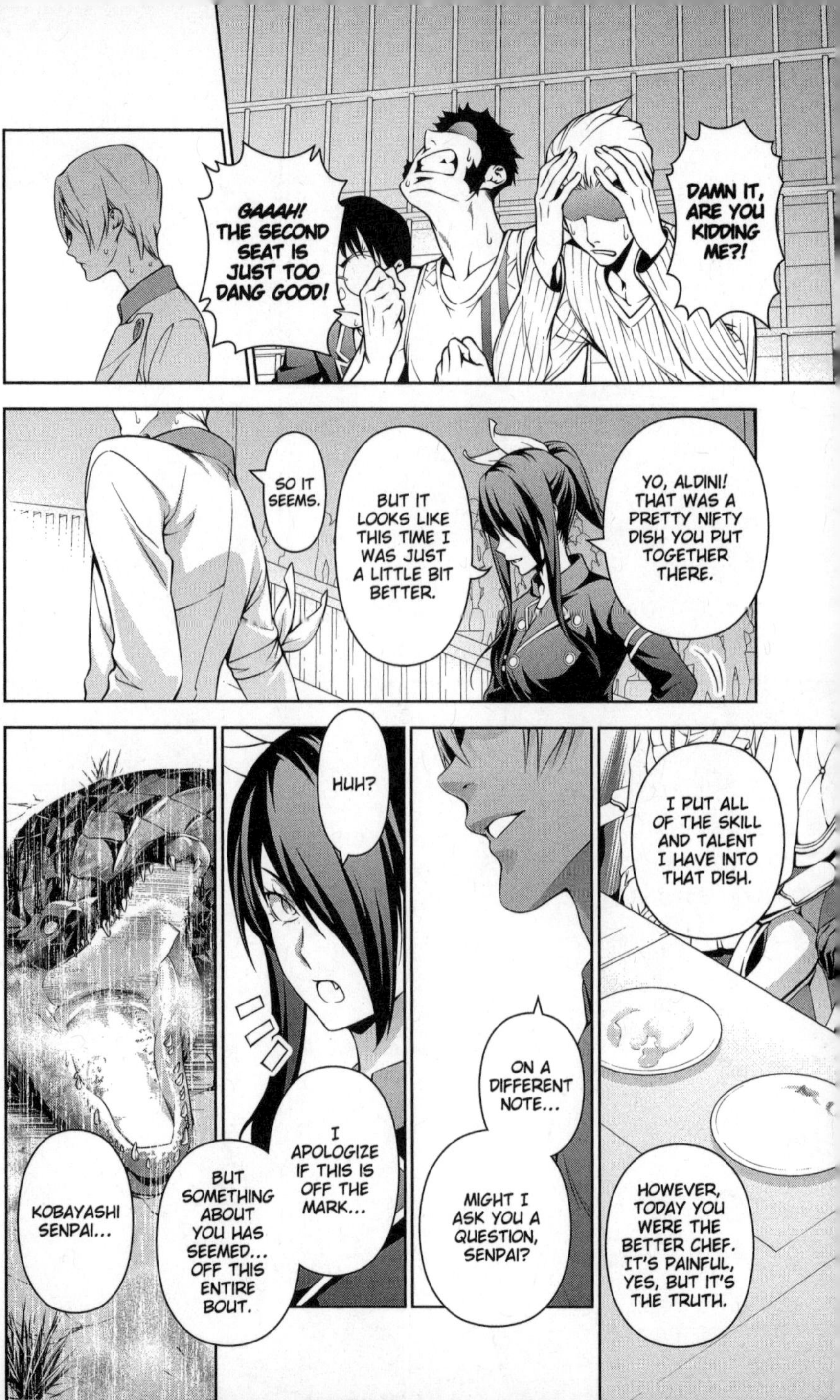
DAMN IT, ARE YOU KIDDING ME?!
GAAAH! THE SECOND SEAT IS JUST TOO DANG GOOD!
YO, ALDINI! THAT WAS A PRETTY NIFTY DISH YOU PUT TOGETHER THERE.
BUT IT LOOKS LIKE THIS TIME I WAS JUST A LITTLE BIT BETTER.
SO IT SEEMS.
I PUT ALL OF THE SKILL AND TALENT I HAVE INTO THAT DISH.
HOWEVER, TODAY YOU WERE THE BETTER CHEF. IT'S PAINFUL, YES, BUT IT'S THE TRUTH.
ON A DIFFERENT NOTE...
MIGHT I ASK YOU A QUESTION, SENPAI?
HUH?
I APOLOGIZE IF THIS IS OFF THE MARK...
BUT SOMETHING ABOUT YOU HAS SEEMED... OFF THIS ENTIRE BOUT.
KOBAYASHI SENPAI...

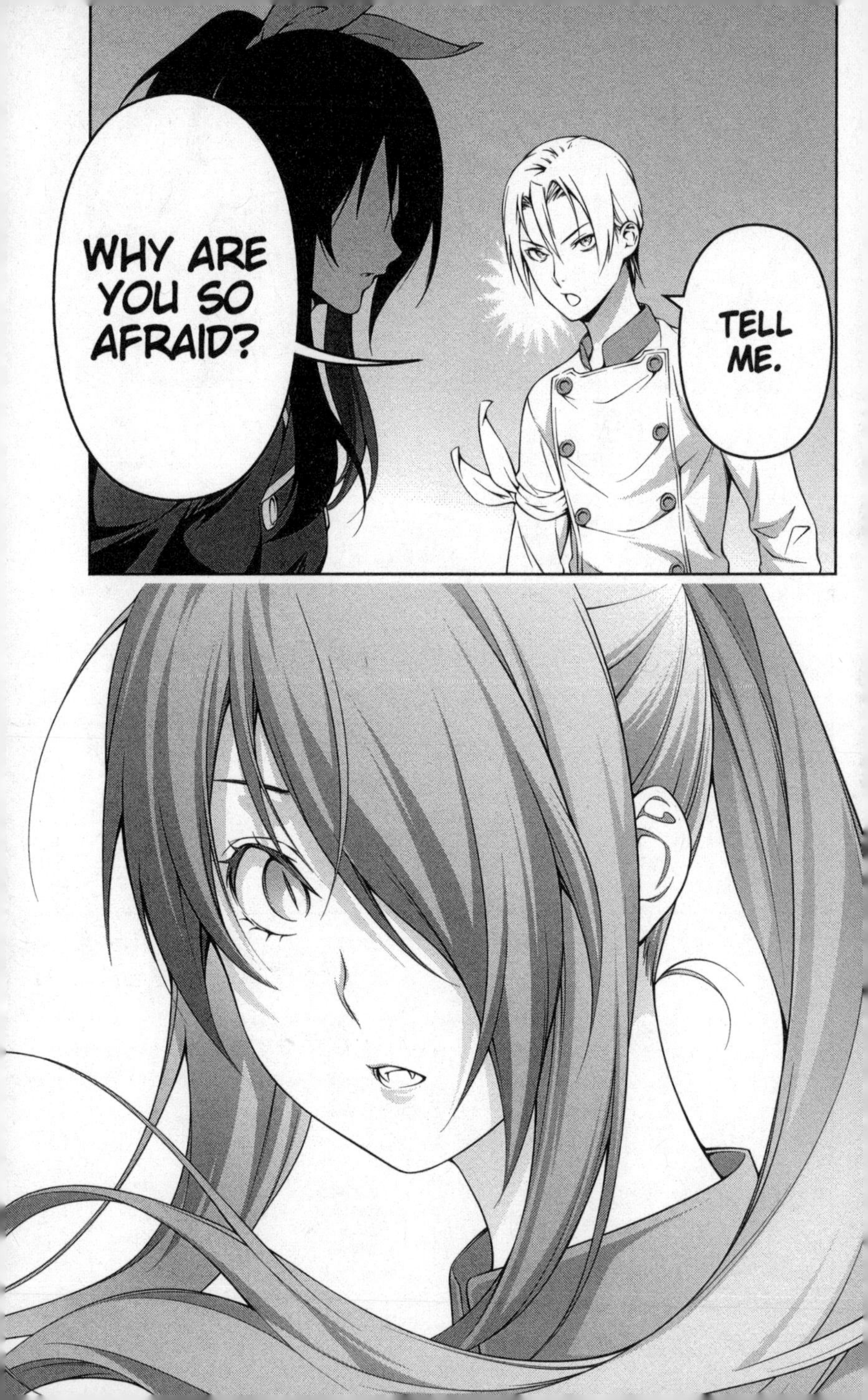
TELL ME.
WHY ARE YOU SO AFRAID?

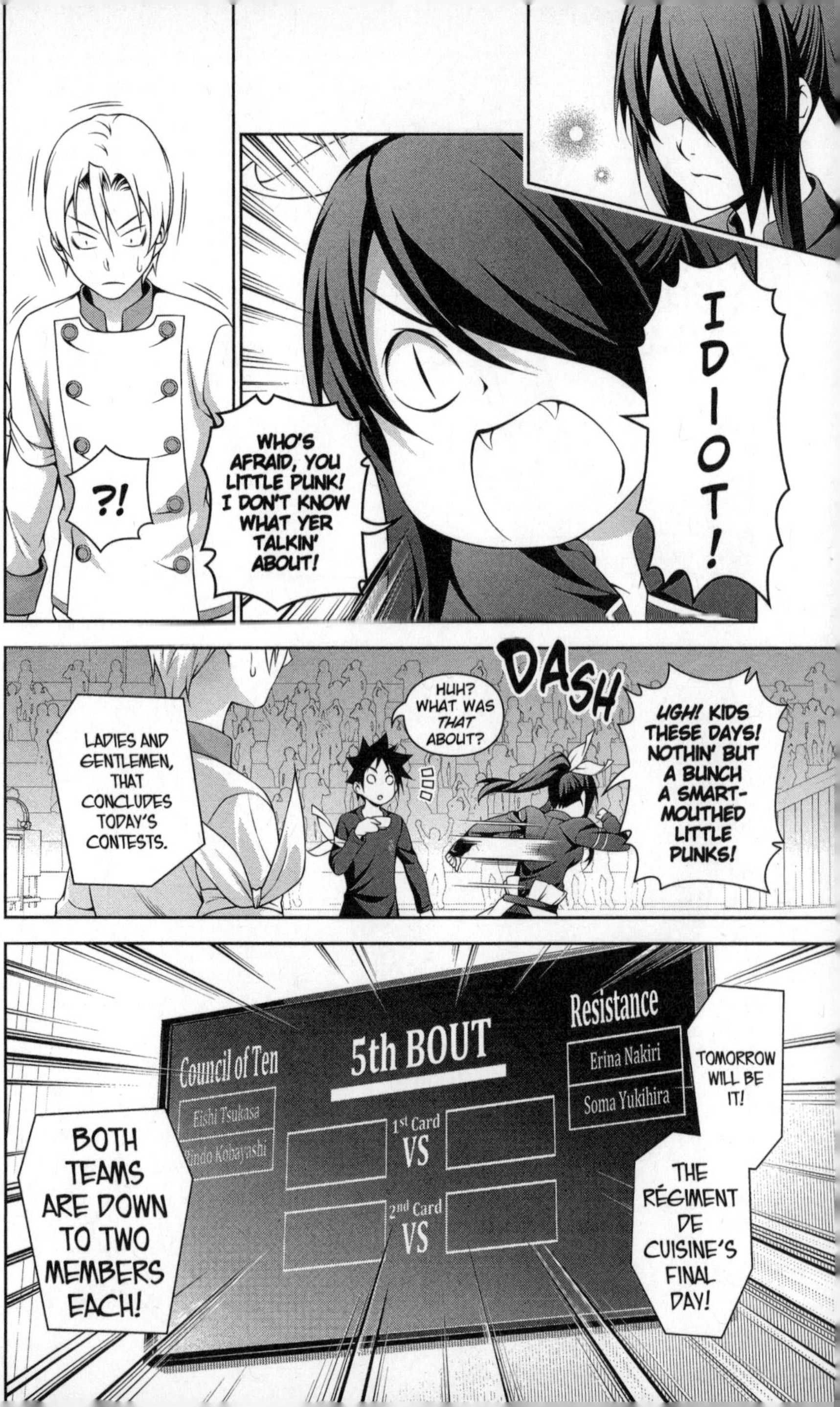
IDIOT!
WHO'S AFRAID, YOU LITTLE PUNK! I DON'T KNOW WHAT YER TALKIN' ABOUT!
?!
UGH! KIDS THESE DAYS! NOTHIN' BUT A BUNCH A SMART-MOUTHED LITTLE PUNKS!
DASH
HUH? WHAT WAS THAT ABOUT?
LADIES AND GENTLEMEN, THAT CONCLUDES TODAY'S CONTESTS.
TOMORROW WILL BE IT!
THE RÉGIMENT DE CUISINE'S FINAL DAY!
Resistance
Erina Nakiri
Soma Yukihira
5th BOUT
Council of Ten
Eishi Tsukasa
Rindo Kobayashi
1st Card VS
2nd Card VS
BOTH TEAMS ARE DOWN TO TWO MEMBERS EACH!

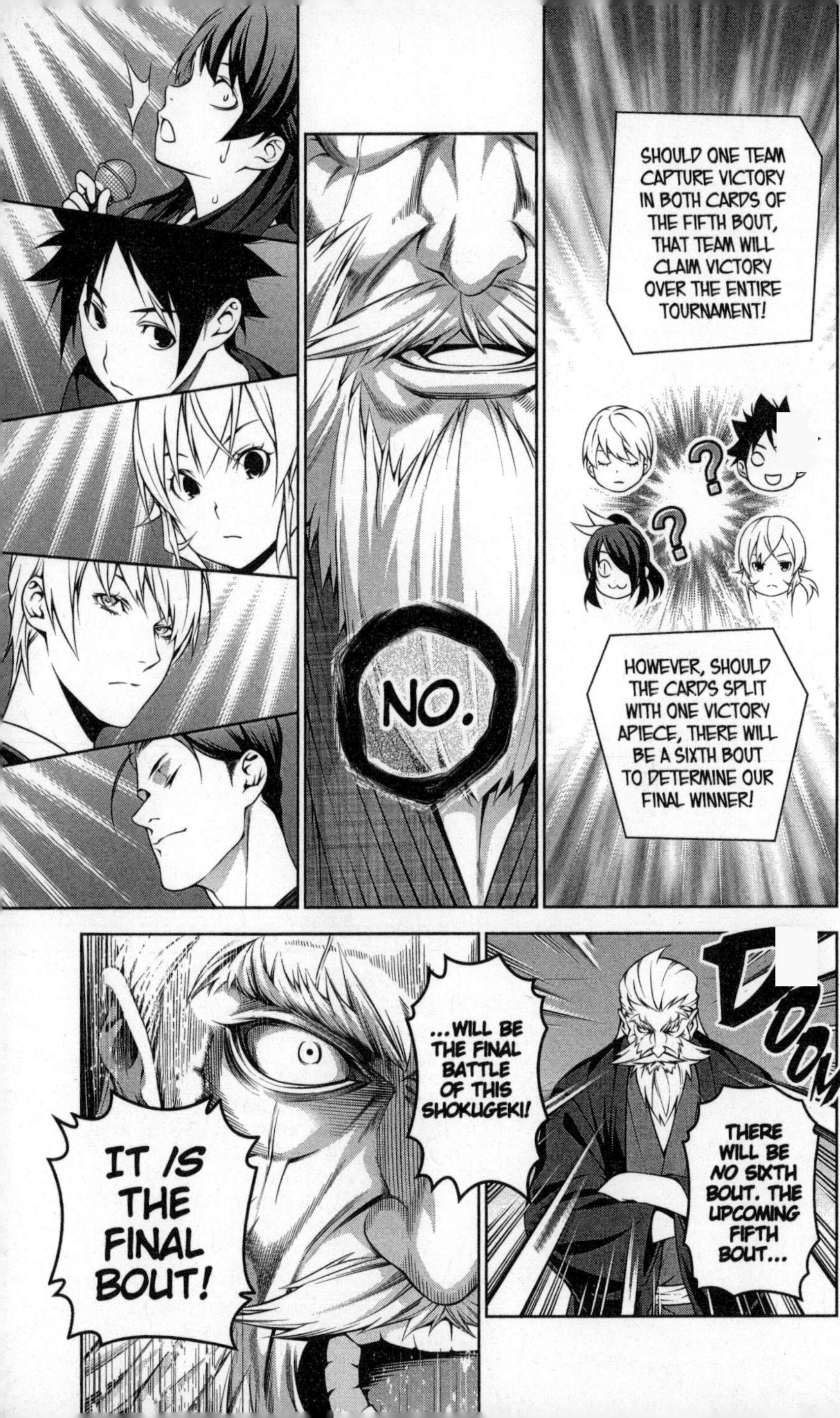
SHOULD ONE TEAM CAPTURE VICTORY IN BOTH CARDS OF THE FIFTH BOUT, THAT TEAM WILL CLAIM VICTORY OVER THE ENTIRE TOURNAMENT!
HOWEVER, SHOULD THE CARDS SPLIT WITH ONE VICTORY APIECE, THERE WILL BE A SIXTH BOUT TO DETERMINE OUR FINAL WINNER!
NO.
DOOM
THERE WILL BE *NO* SIXTH BOUT. THE UPCOMING FIFTH BOUT...
...WILL BE THE FINAL BATTLE OF THIS SHOKUGEKI!
IT *IS* THE FINAL BOUT!

SHOKUGEKI COLUMN

~A TOTALLY TRIVIAL TIDBIT~

During the storyboarding stage for chapter 252, the creative staff and editorial staff went back and forth for days in a passionate discussion over whether the calamari lingerie collection should be written in kata-kana or kanji, as the kanji characters would allow for a pun about clingy lingerie.

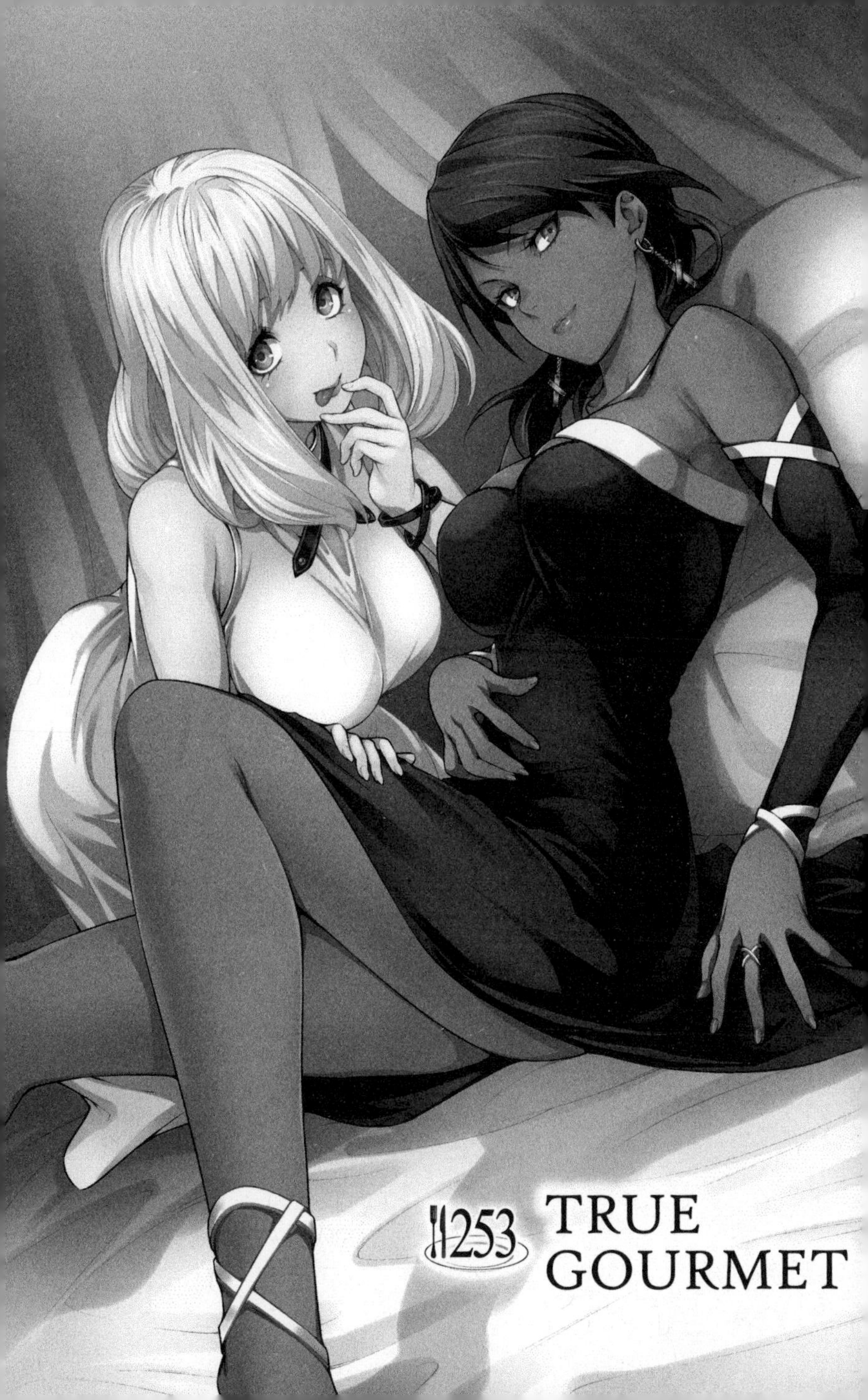
253
TRUE GOURMET

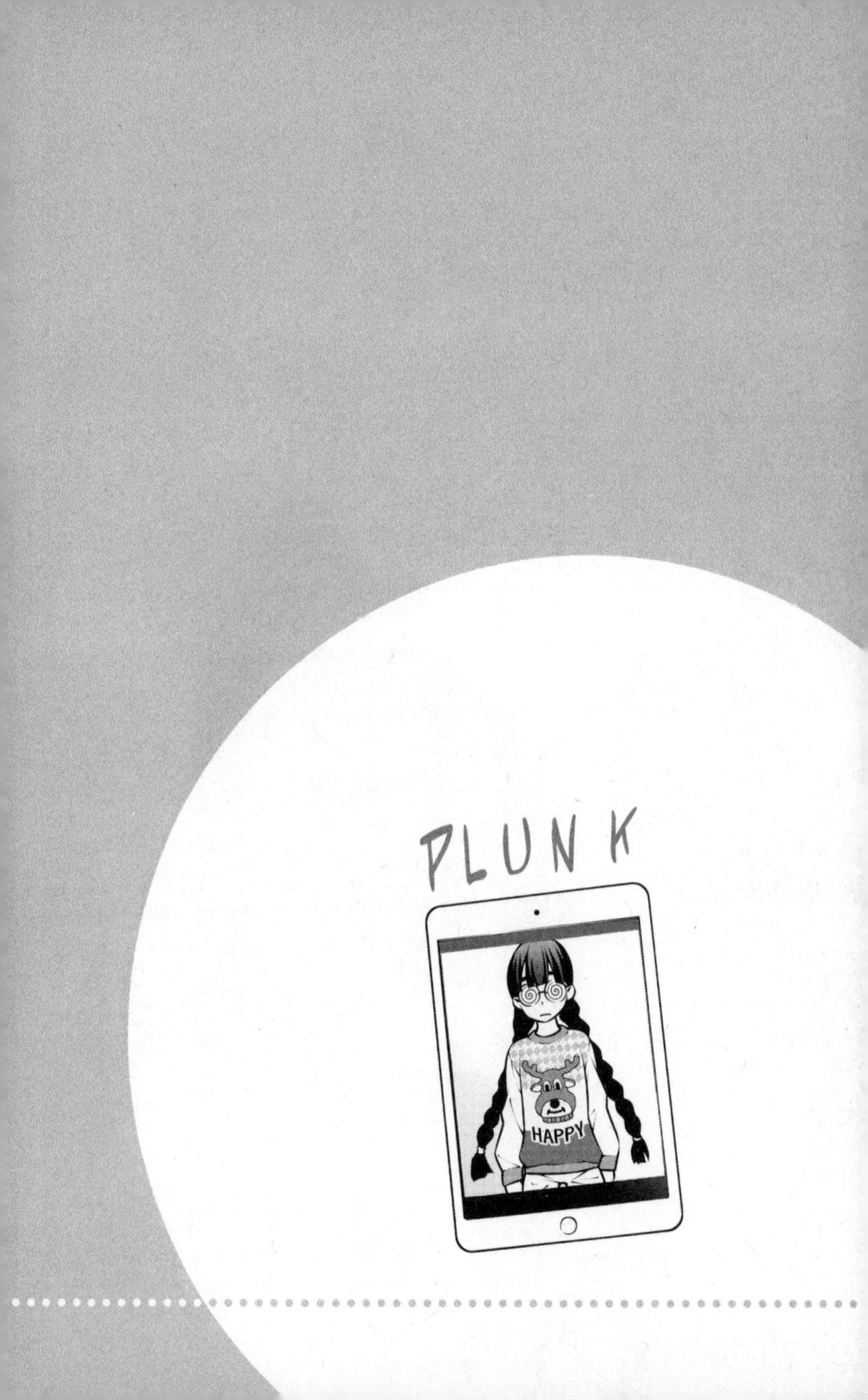
PLUNK
HAPPY

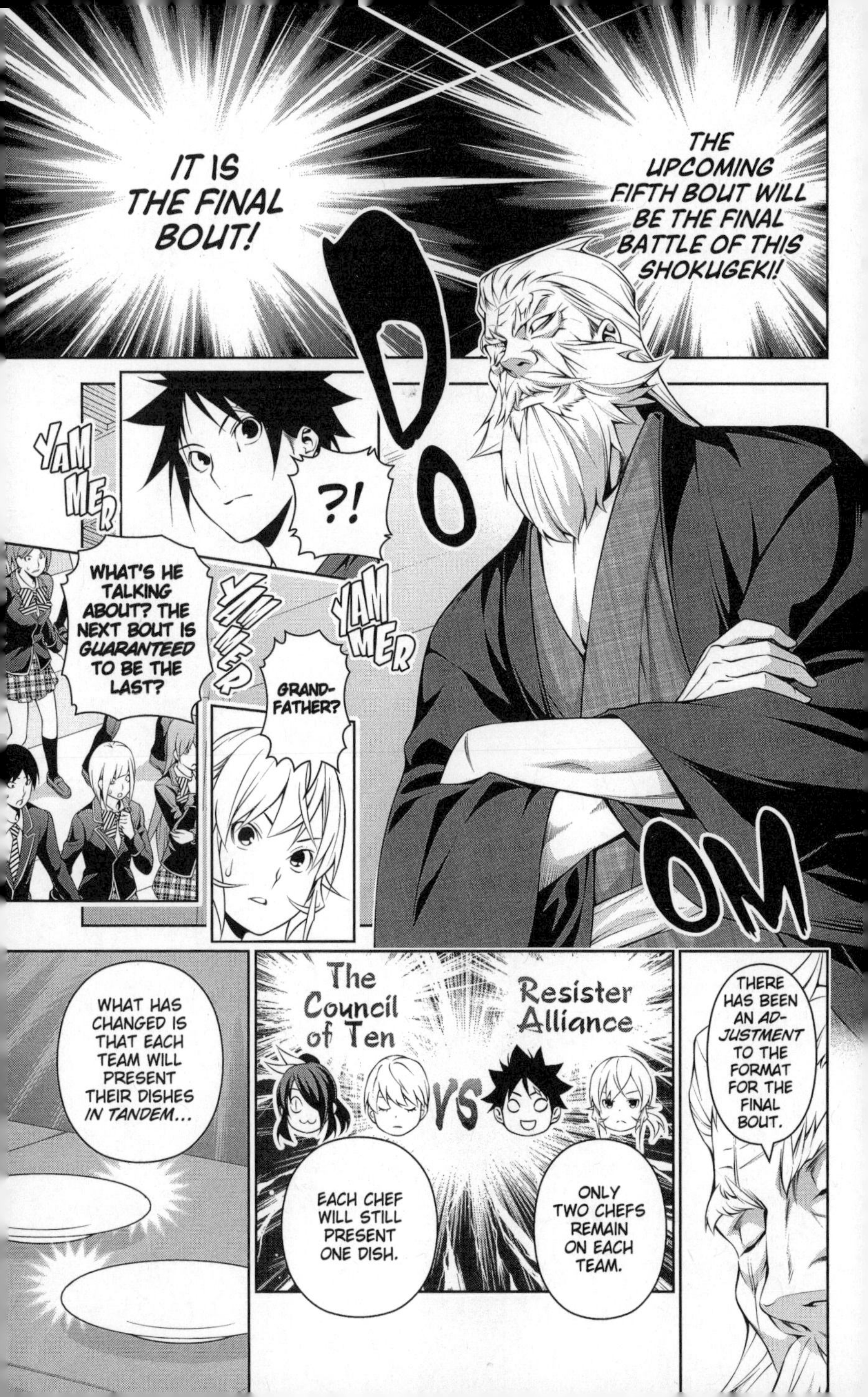
THE UPCOMING FIFTH BOUT WILL BE THE FINAL BATTLE OF THIS SHOKUGEKI!
IT IS THE FINAL BOUT!
DOOOM
?!
YAMMER
YAMMER
YAMMER
GRAND-FATHER?
WHAT'S HE TALKING ABOUT? THE NEXT BOUT IS *GUARANTEED* TO BE THE LAST?
THERE HAS BEEN AN *ADJUSTMENT* TO THE FORMAT FOR THE FINAL BOUT.
Resister Alliance
VS
The Council of Ten
ONLY TWO CHEFS REMAIN ON EACH TEAM.
EACH CHEF WILL STILL PRESENT ONE DISH.
WHAT HAS CHANGED IS THAT EACH TEAM WILL PRESENT THEIR DISHES *IN TANDEM*...

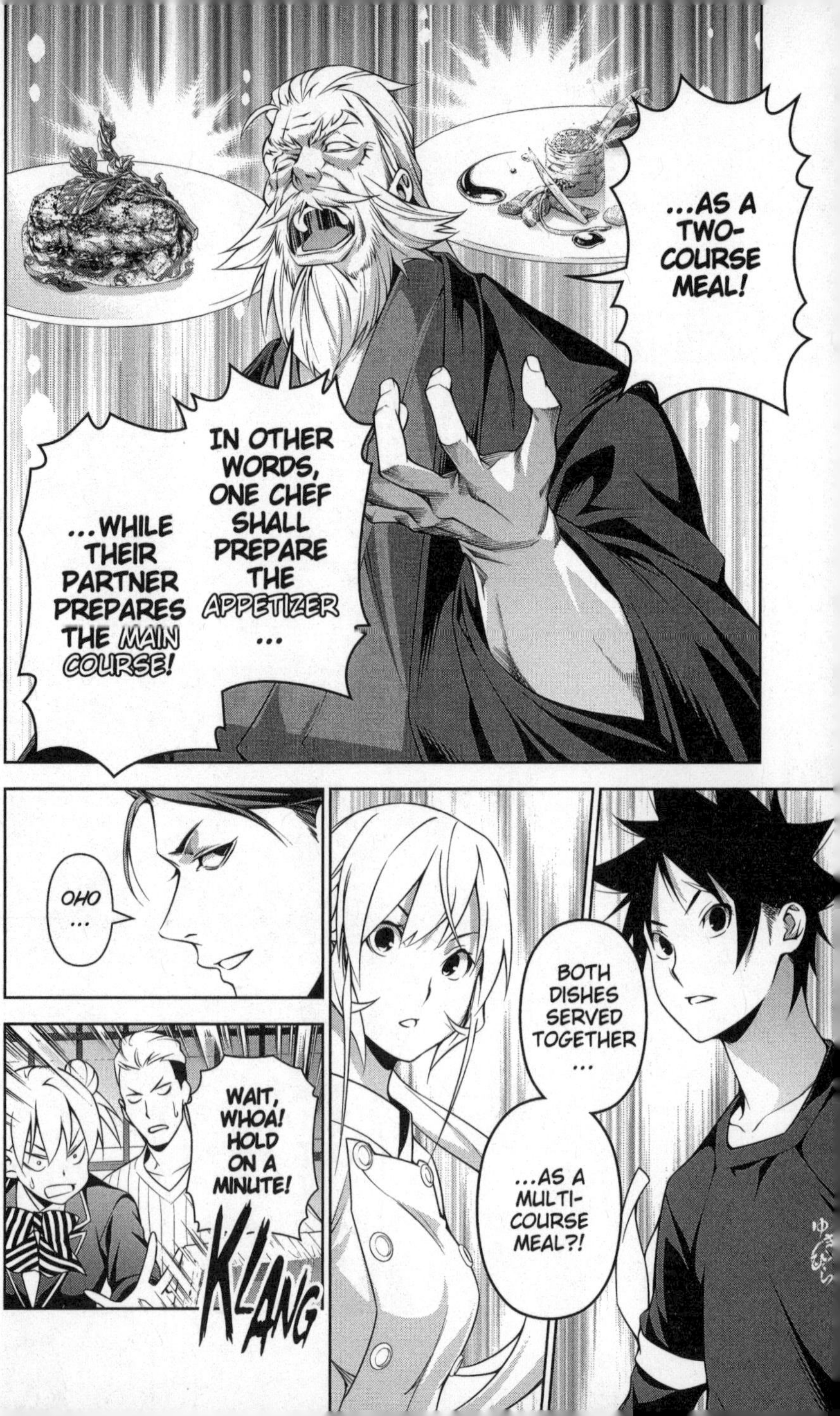
...AS A TWO-COURSE MEAL!
IN OTHER WORDS, ONE CHEF SHALL PREPARE THE APPETIZER...
...WHILE THEIR PARTNER PREPARES THE MAIN COURSE!
BOTH DISHES SERVED TOGETHER...
...AS A MULTI-COURSE MEAL?!
ゆきひら
OHO...
WAIT, WHOA! HOLD ON A MINUTE!
KLANG

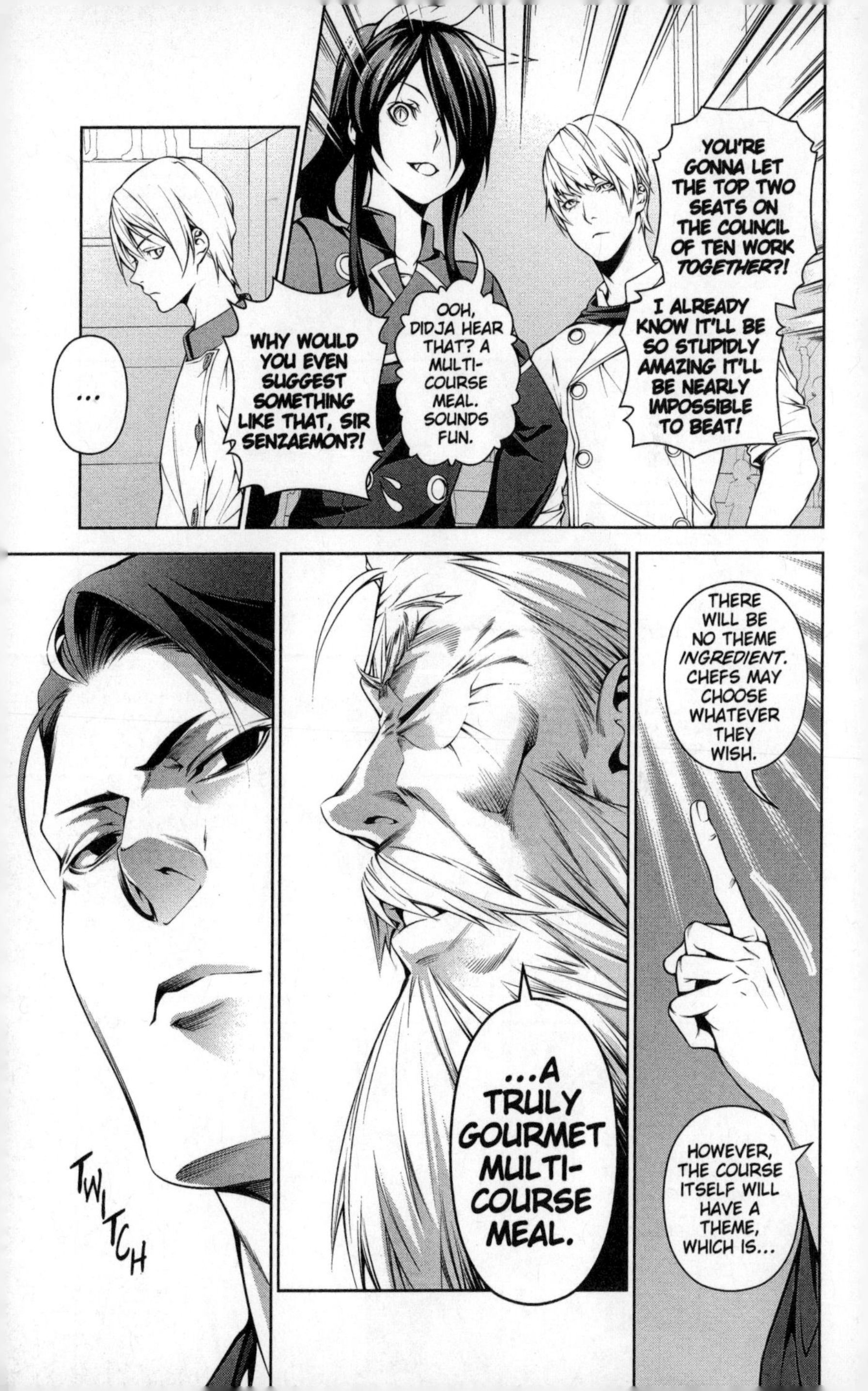
YOU'RE GONNA LET THE TOP TWO SEATS ON THE COUNCIL OF TEN WORK *TOGETHER*?!
I ALREADY KNOW IT'LL BE SO STUPIDLY AMAZING IT'LL BE NEARLY IMPOSSIBLE TO BEAT!
OOH, DIDJA HEAR THAT? A MULTI-COURSE MEAL. SOUNDS FUN.
WHY WOULD YOU EVEN SUGGEST SOMETHING LIKE THAT, SIR SENZAEMON?!
...
THERE WILL BE NO THEME *INGREDIENT*. CHEFS MAY CHOOSE WHATEVER THEY WISH.
HOWEVER, THE COURSE ITSELF WILL HAVE A THEME, WHICH IS...
...A TRULY GOURMET MULTI-COURSE MEAL.
TWITCH

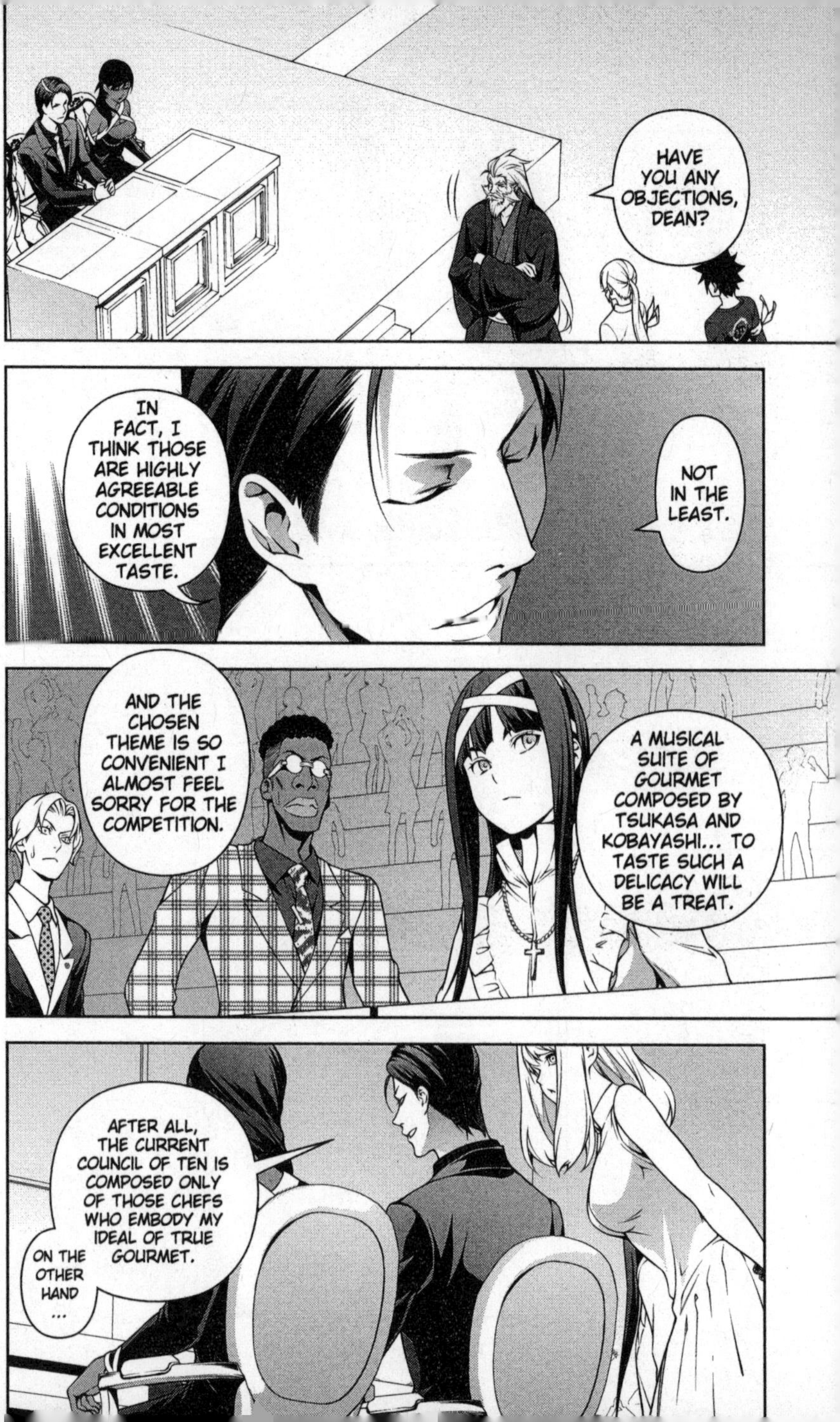
HAVE YOU ANY OBJECTIONS, DEAN?
NOT IN THE LEAST.
IN FACT, I THINK THOSE ARE HIGHLY AGREEABLE CONDITIONS IN MOST EXCELLENT TASTE.
A MUSICAL SUITE OF GOURMET COMPOSED BY TSUKASA AND KOBAYASHI... TO TASTE SUCH A DELICACY WILL BE A TREAT.
AND THE CHOSEN THEME IS SO CONVENIENT I ALMOST FEEL SORRY FOR THE COMPETITION.
AFTER ALL, THE CURRENT COUNCIL OF TEN IS COMPOSED ONLY OF THOSE CHEFS WHO EMBODY MY IDEAL OF TRUE GOURMET.
ON THE OTHER HAND ...

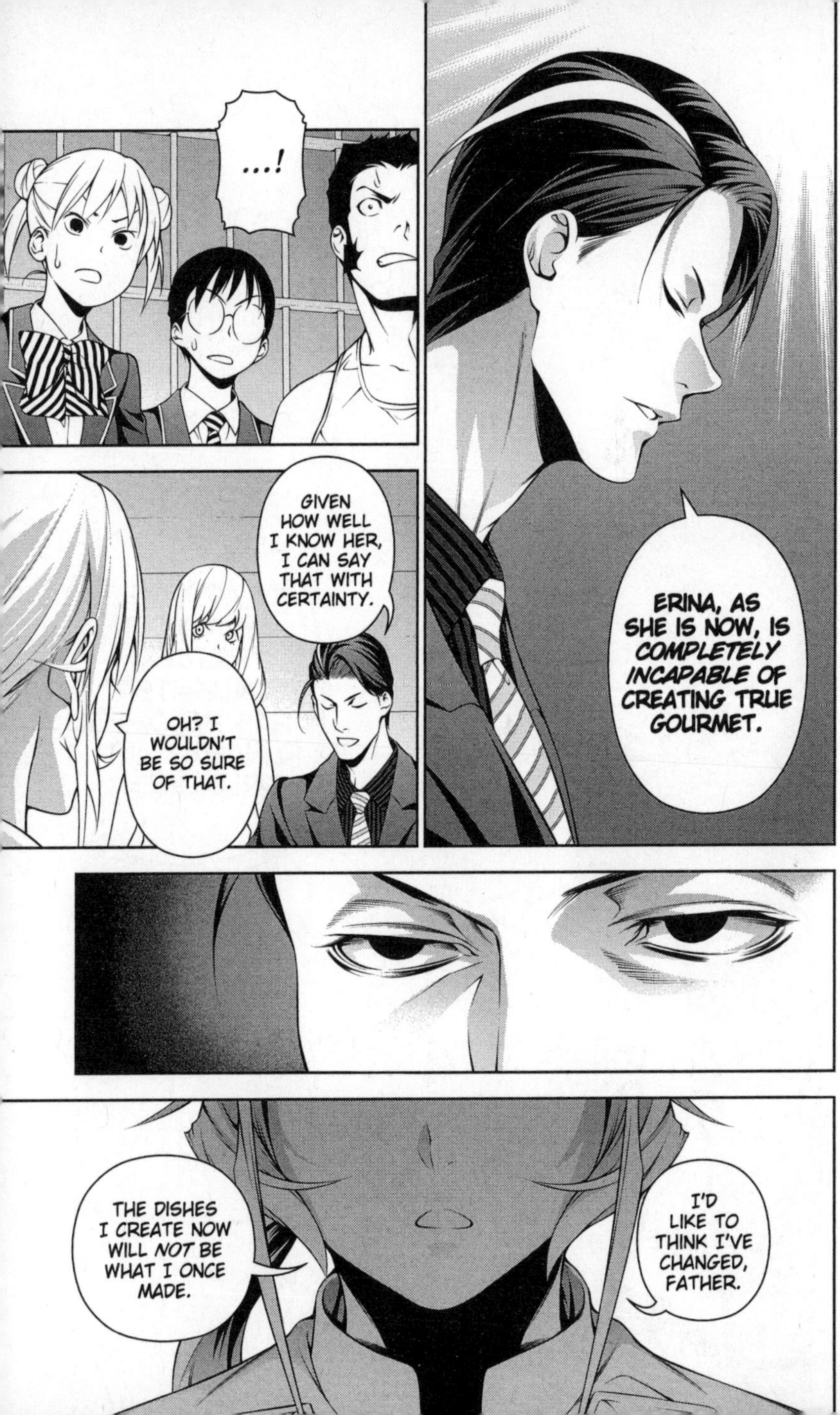
ERINA, AS SHE IS NOW, IS *COMPLETELY INCAPABLE* OF CREATING TRUE GOURMET.
...!
GIVEN HOW WELL I KNOW HER, I CAN SAY THAT WITH CERTAINTY.
OH? I WOULDN'T BE SO SURE OF THAT.
I'D LIKE TO THINK I'VE CHANGED, FATHER.
THE DISHES I CREATE NOW WILL *NOT* BE WHAT I ONCE MADE.

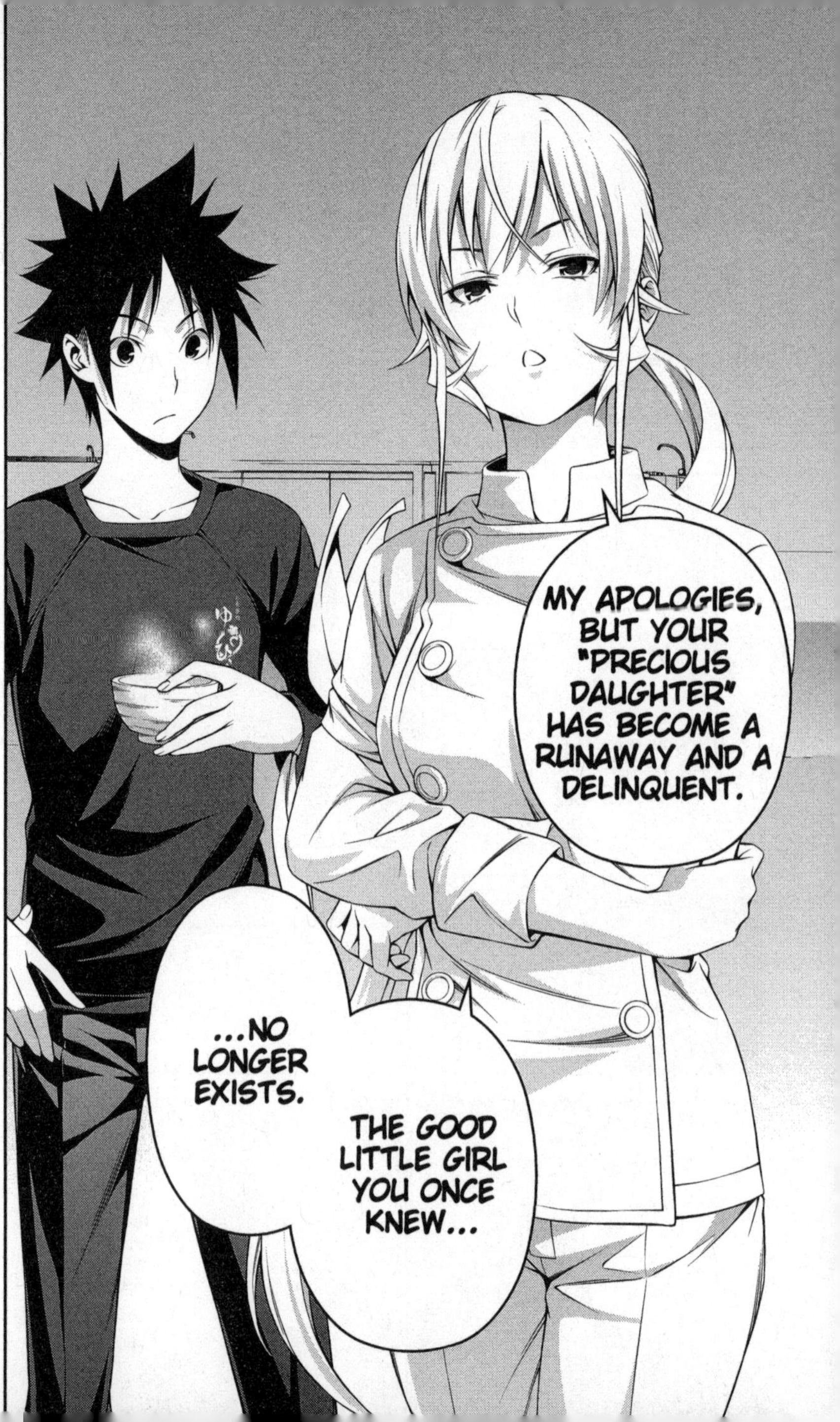
MY APOLOGIES, BUT YOUR "PRECIOUS DAUGHTER" HAS BECOME A RUNAWAY AND A DELINQUENT.
THE GOOD LITTLE GIRL YOU ONCE KNEW...
...NO LONGER EXISTS.

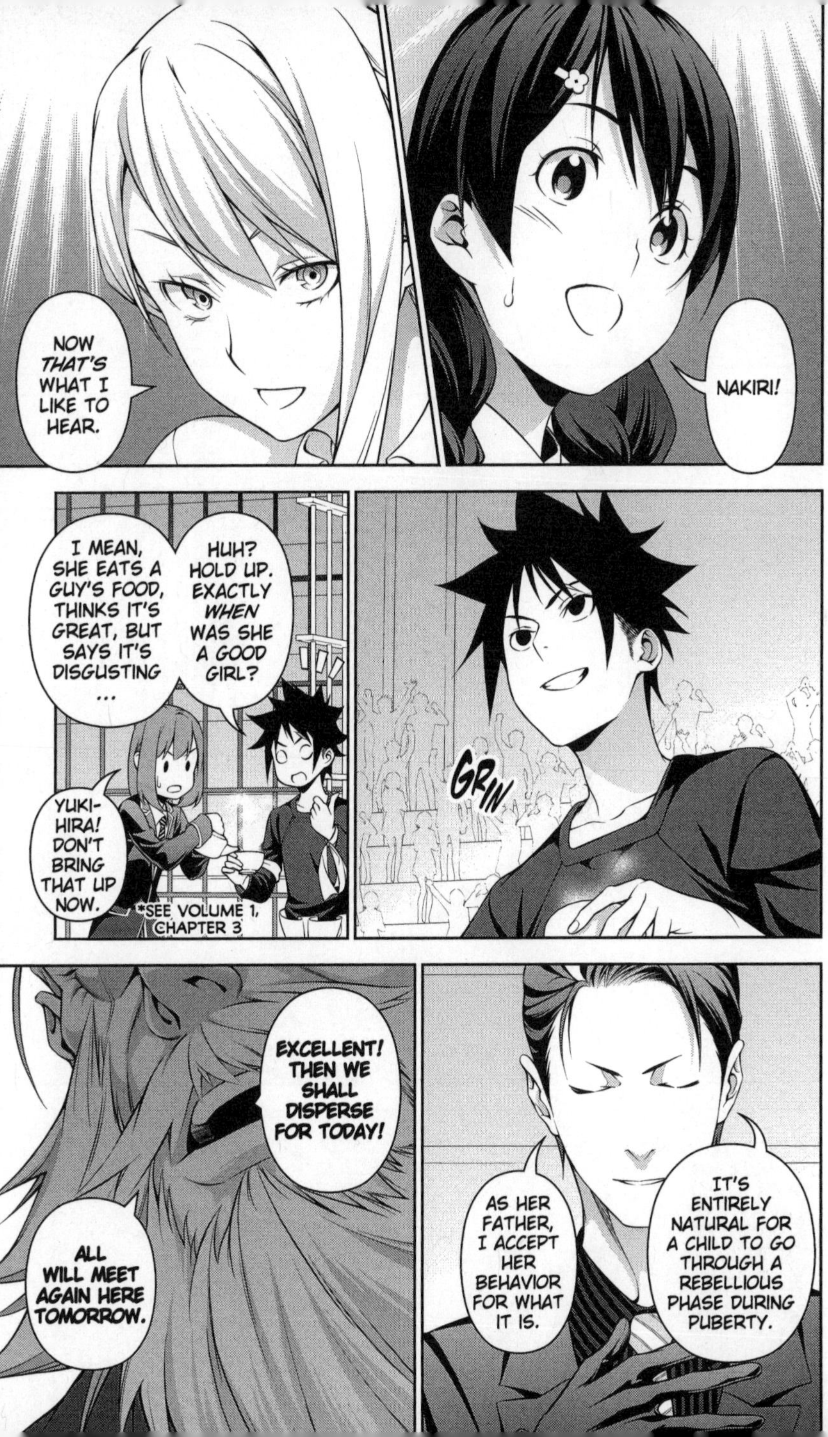
NAKIRI!
NOW *THAT'S* WHAT I LIKE TO HEAR.
GRIN
HUH? HOLD UP. EXACTLY *WHEN* WAS SHE A GOOD GIRL?
I MEAN, SHE EATS A GUY'S FOOD, THINKS IT'S GREAT, BUT SAYS IT'S DISGUSTING ...
YUKI-HIRA! DON'T BRING THAT UP NOW.
*SEE VOLUME 1, CHAPTER 3
IT'S ENTIRELY NATURAL FOR A CHILD TO GO THROUGH A REBELLIOUS PHASE DURING PUBERTY.
AS HER FATHER, I ACCEPT HER BEHAVIOR FOR WHAT IT IS.
EXCELLENT! THEN WE SHALL DISPERSE FOR TODAY!
ALL WILL MEET AGAIN HERE TOMORROW.

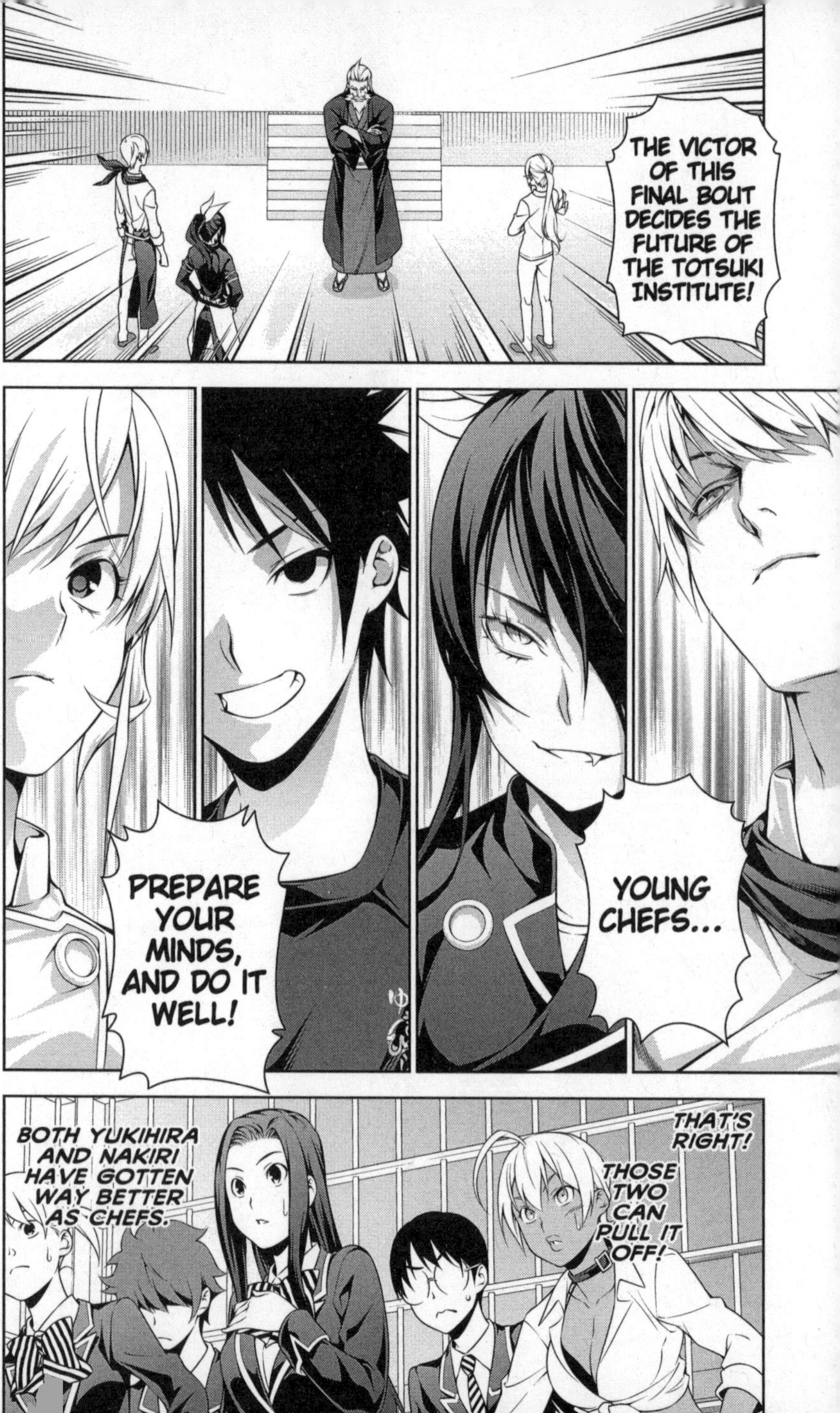
THE VICTOR OF THIS FINAL BOUT DECIDES THE FUTURE OF THE TOTSUKI INSTITUTE!
YOUNG CHEFS...
PREPARE YOUR MINDS, AND DO IT WELL!
THAT'S RIGHT!
THOSE TWO CAN PULL IT OFF!
BOTH YUKIHIRA AND NAKIRI HAVE GOTTEN WAY BETTER AS CHEFS.

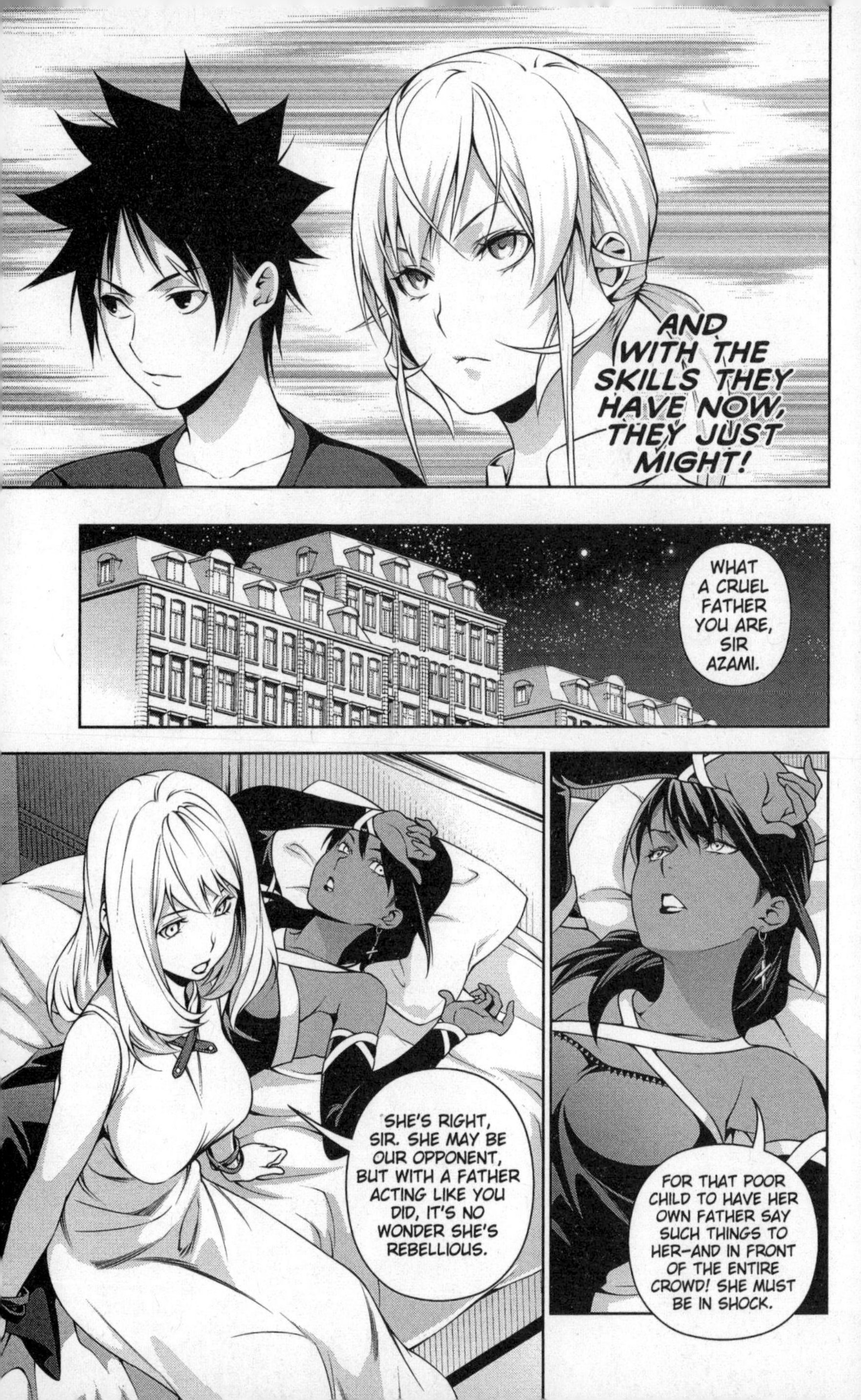
AND WITH THE SKILLS THEY HAVE NOW, THEY JUST MIGHT!
WHAT A CRUEL FATHER YOU ARE, SIR AZAMI.
FOR THAT POOR CHILD TO HAVE HER OWN FATHER SAY SUCH THINGS TO HER—AND IN FRONT OF THE ENTIRE CROWD! SHE MUST BE IN SHOCK.
SHE'S RIGHT, SIR. SHE MAY BE OUR OPPONENT, BUT WITH A FATHER ACTING LIKE YOU DID, IT'S NO WONDER SHE'S REBELLIOUS.

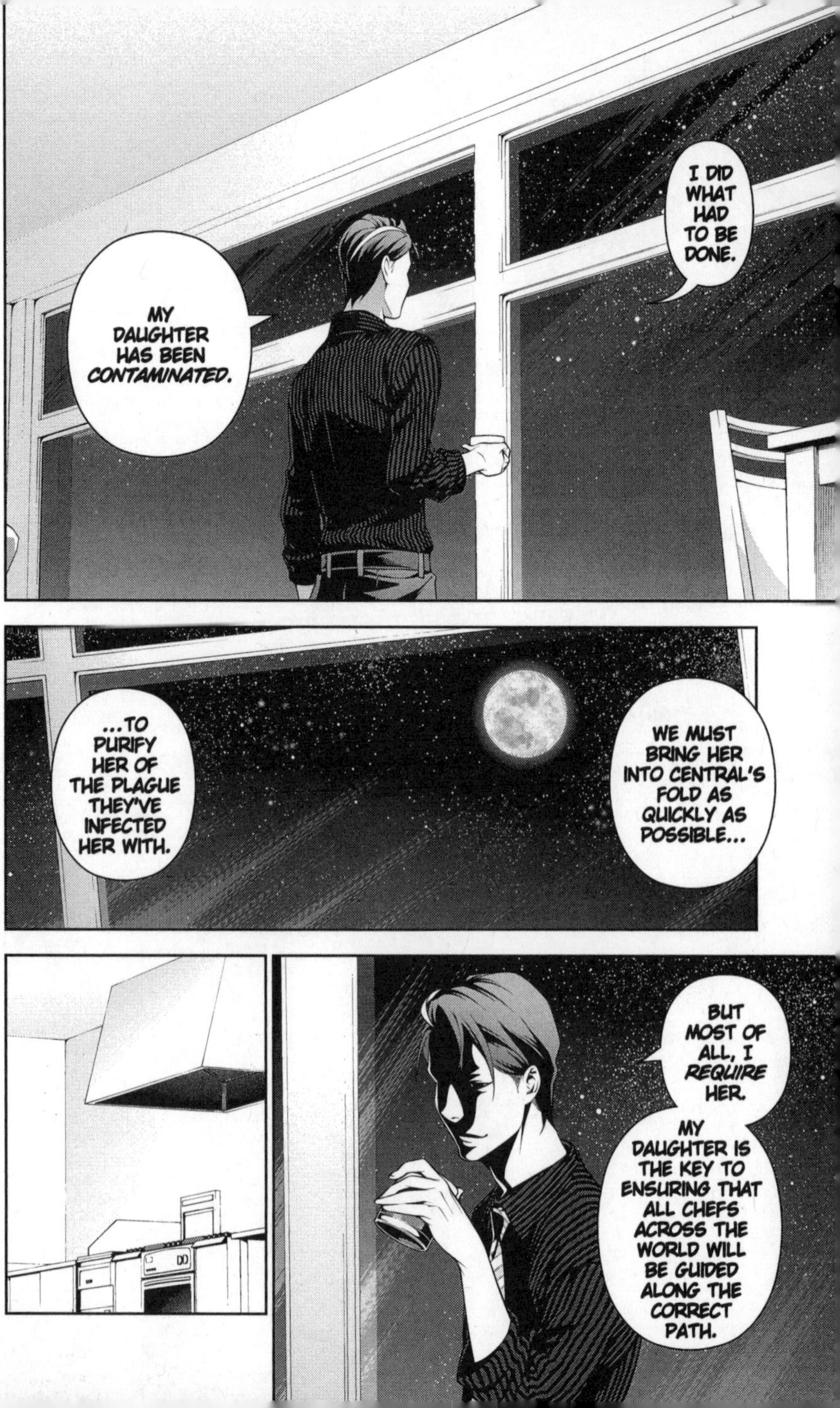
I DID WHAT HAD TO BE DONE.
MY DAUGHTER HAS BEEN CONTAMINATED.
WE MUST BRING HER INTO CENTRAL'S FOLD AS QUICKLY AS POSSIBLE...
...TO PURIFY HER OF THE PLAGUE THEY'VE INFECTED HER WITH.
BUT MOST OF ALL, I REQUIRE HER.
MY DAUGHTER IS THE KEY TO ENSURING THAT ALL CHEFS ACROSS THE WORLD WILL BE GUIDED ALONG THE CORRECT PATH.

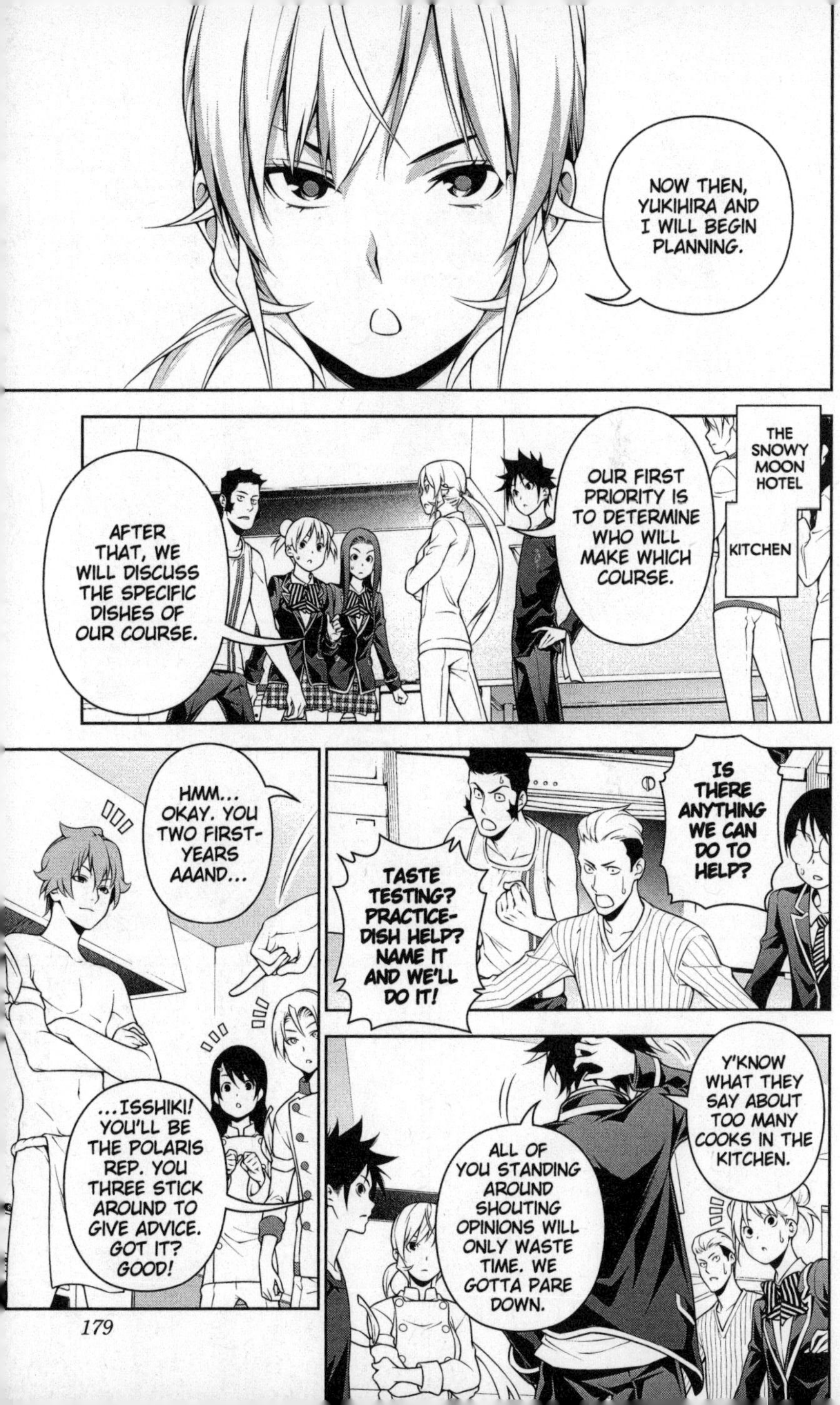
NOW THEN, YUKIHIRA AND I WILL BEGIN PLANNING.
THE SNOWY MOON HOTEL
KITCHEN
OUR FIRST PRIORITY IS TO DETERMINE WHO WILL MAKE WHICH COURSE.
AFTER THAT, WE WILL DISCUSS THE SPECIFIC DISHES OF OUR COURSE.
IS THERE ANYTHING WE CAN DO TO HELP?
TASTE TESTING? PRACTICE-DISH HELP? NAME IT AND WE'LL DO IT!
Y'KNOW WHAT THEY SAY ABOUT TOO MANY COOKS IN THE KITCHEN.
ALL OF YOU STANDING AROUND SHOUTING OPINIONS WILL ONLY WASTE TIME. WE GOTTA PARE DOWN.
HMM... OKAY. YOU TWO FIRST-YEARS AAAND...
...ISSHIKI! YOU'LL BE THE POLARIS REP. YOU THREE STICK AROUND TO GIVE ADVICE. GOT IT? GOOD!

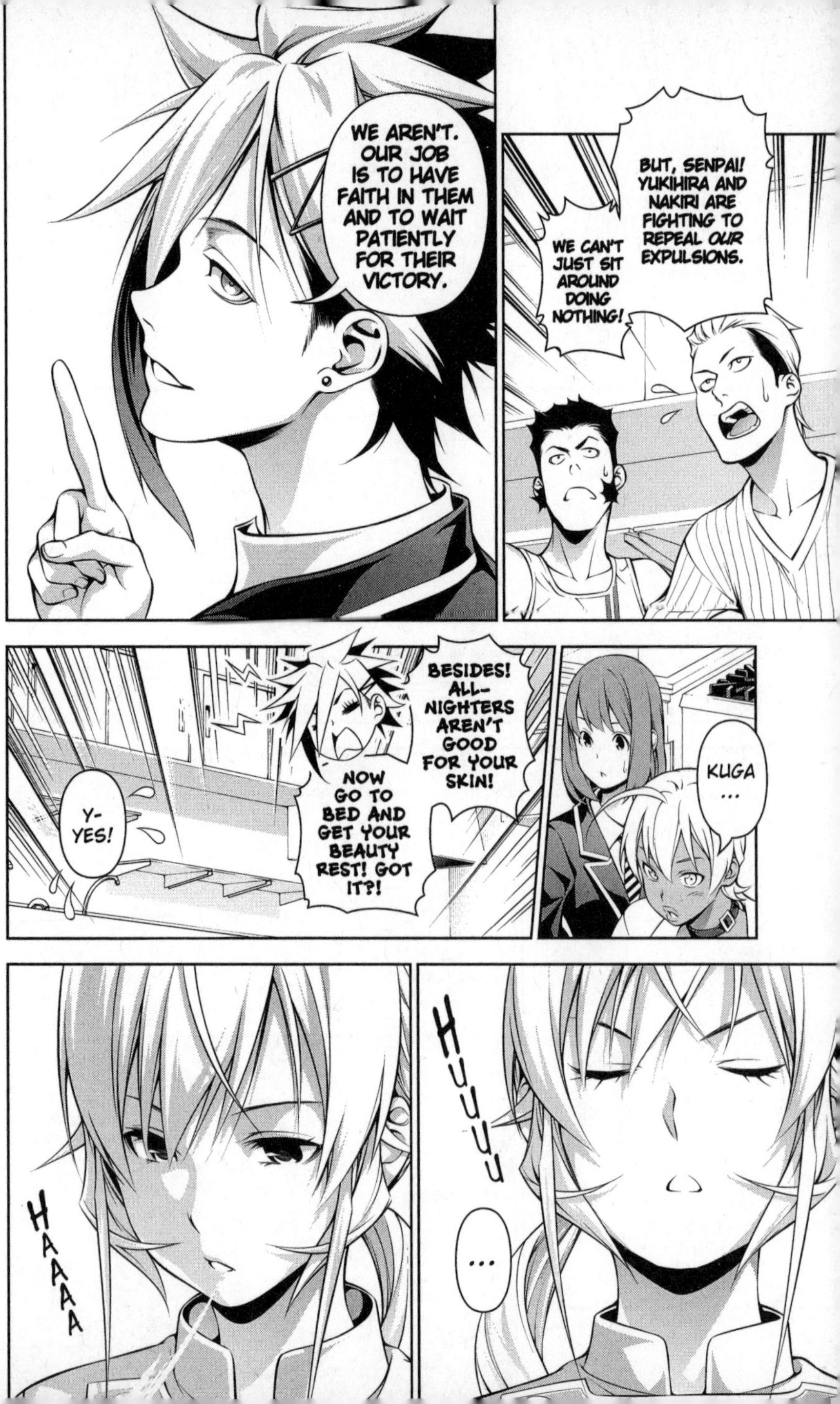
BUT, SENPAI! YUKIHIRA AND NAKIRI ARE FIGHTING TO REPEAL *OUR* EXPULSIONS.
WE CAN'T JUST SIT AROUND DOING NOTHING!
WE AREN'T. OUR JOB IS TO HAVE FAITH IN THEM AND TO WAIT PATIENTLY FOR THEIR VICTORY.
KUGA...
BESIDES! ALL-NIGHTERS AREN'T GOOD FOR YOUR SKIN!
NOW GO TO BED AND GET YOUR BEAUTY REST! GOT IT?!
Y-YES!
HUUUU
...
HAAAA

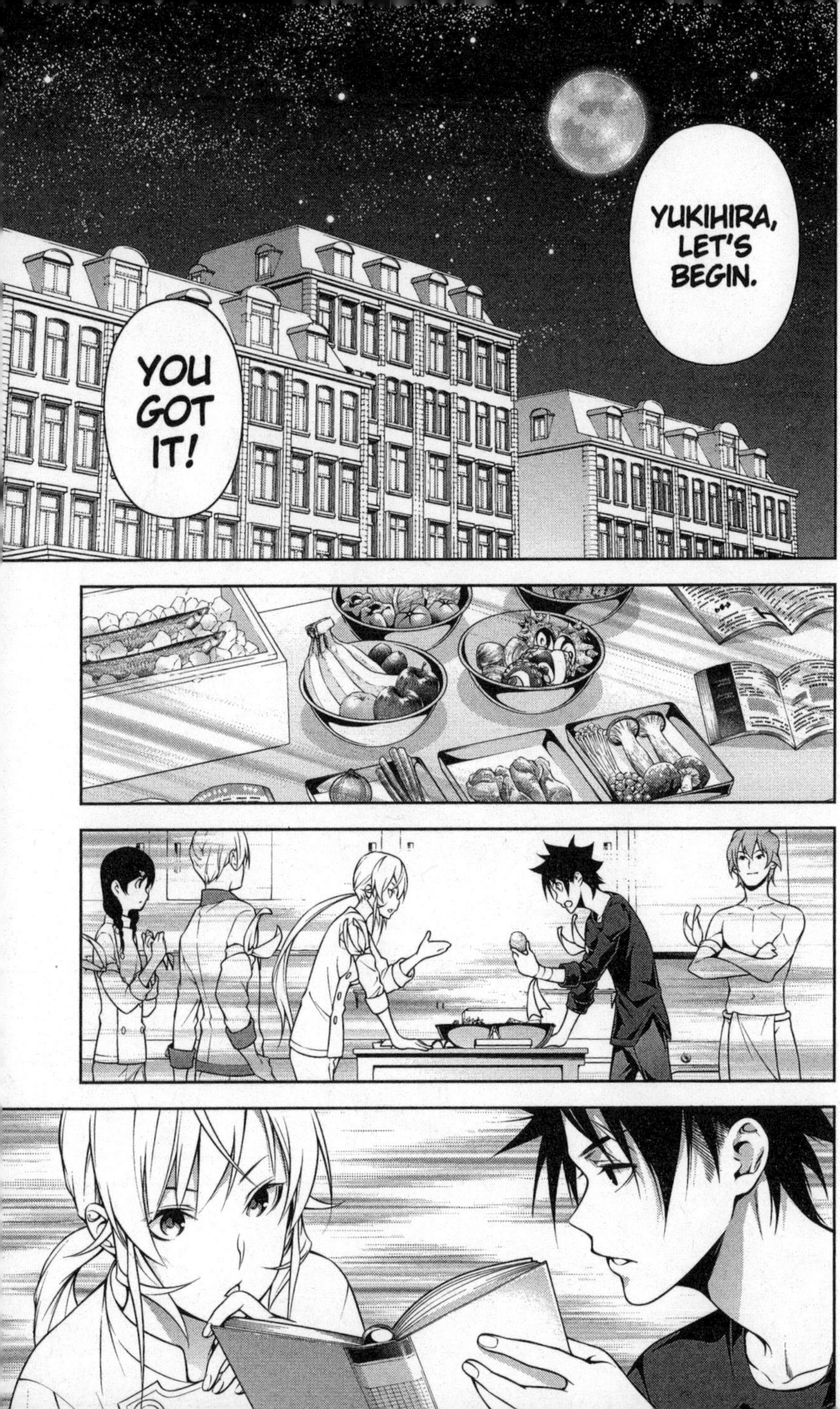
YUKIHIRA, LET'S BEGIN.
YOU GOT IT!

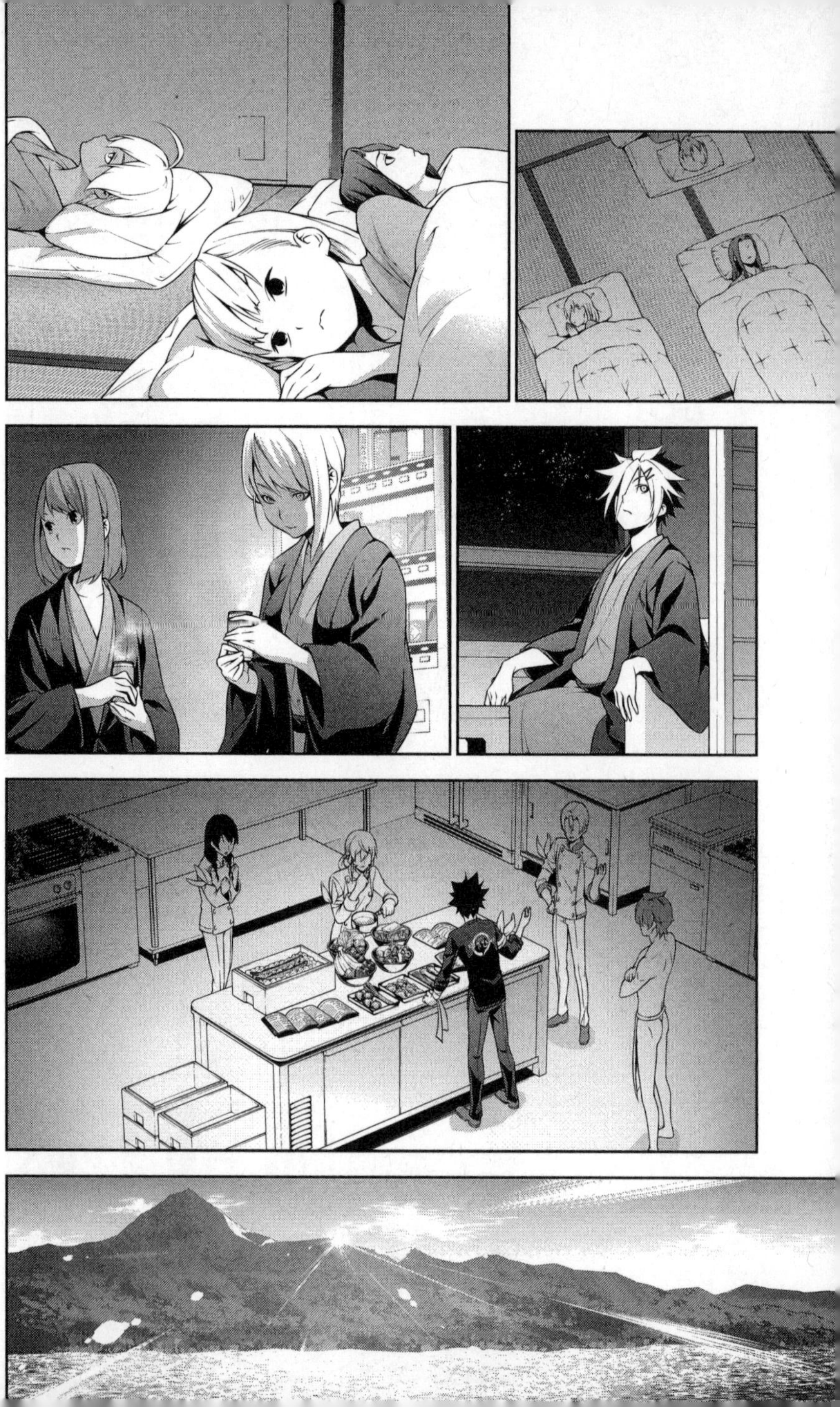

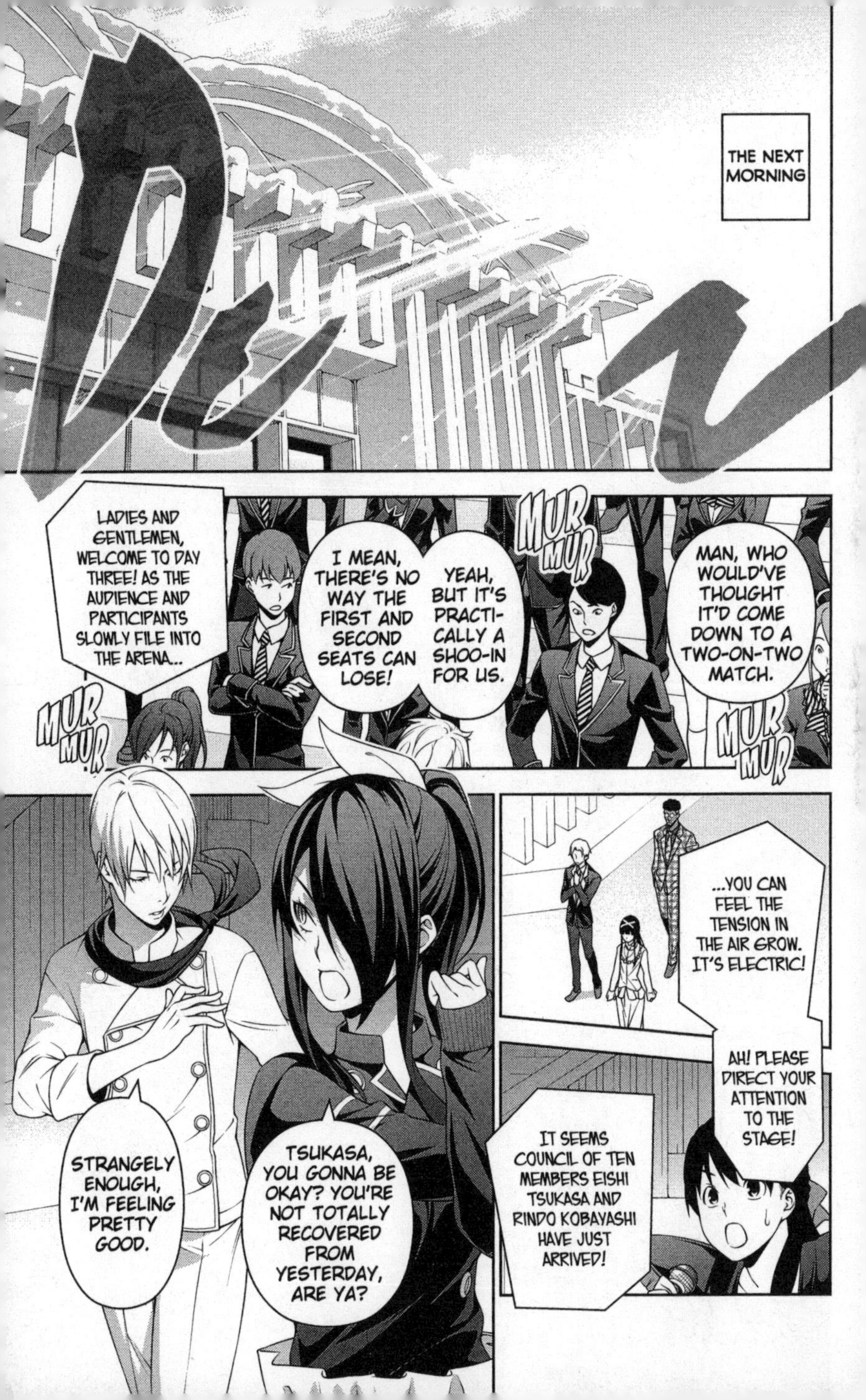
THE NEXT MORNING
MAN, WHO WOULD'VE THOUGHT IT'D COME DOWN TO A TWO-ON-TWO MATCH.
MUR MUR
MUR MUR
YEAH, BUT IT'S PRACTI-CALLY A SHOO-IN FOR US.
I MEAN, THERE'S NO WAY THE FIRST AND SECOND SEATS CAN LOSE!
LADIES AND GENTLEMEN, WELCOME TO DAY THREE! AS THE AUDIENCE AND PARTICIPANTS SLOWLY FILE INTO THE ARENA...
MUR MUR
...YOU CAN FEEL THE TENSION IN THE AIR GROW. IT'S ELECTRIC!
AH! PLEASE DIRECT YOUR ATTENTION TO THE STAGE!
IT SEEMS COUNCIL OF TEN MEMBERS EISHI TSUKASA AND RINDO KOBAYASHI HAVE JUST ARRIVED!
TSUKASA, YOU GONNA BE OKAY? YOU'RE NOT TOTALLY RECOVERED FROM YESTERDAY, ARE YA?
STRANGELY ENOUGH, I'M FEELING PRETTY GOOD.

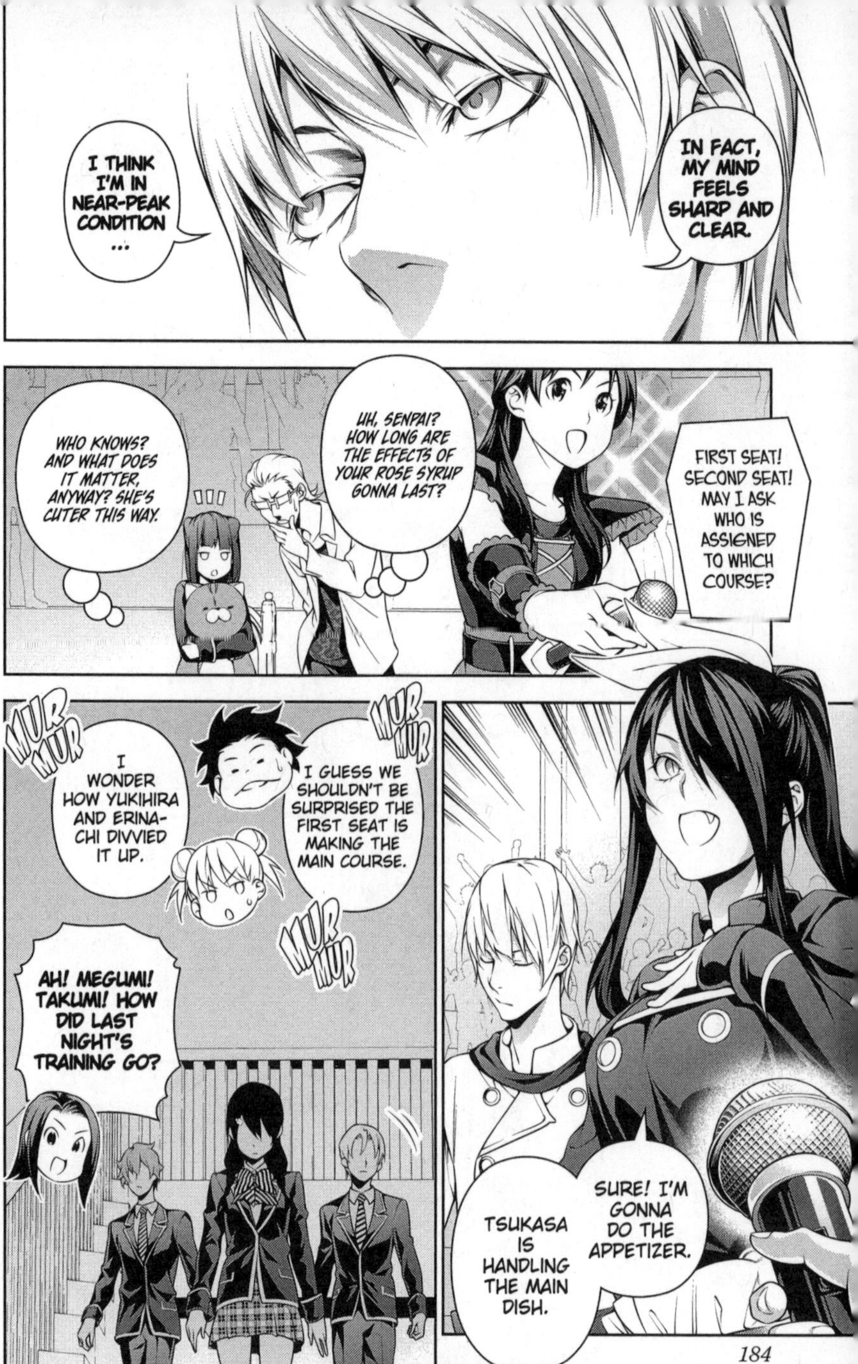
IN FACT, MY MIND FEELS SHARP AND CLEAR.
I THINK I'M IN NEAR-PEAK CONDITION ...
FIRST SEAT! SECOND SEAT! MAY I ASK WHO IS ASSIGNED TO WHICH COURSE?
UH, SENPAI? HOW LONG ARE THE EFFECTS OF YOUR ROSE SYRUP GONNA LAST?
WHO KNOWS? AND WHAT DOES IT MATTER, ANYWAY? SHE'S CUTER THIS WAY.
SURE! I'M GONNA DO THE APPETIZER.
TSUKASA IS HANDLING THE MAIN DISH.
MUR MUR
I GUESS WE SHOULDN'T BE SURPRISED THE FIRST SEAT IS MAKING THE MAIN COURSE.
I WONDER HOW YUKIHIRA AND ERINA-CHI DIVVIED IT UP.
MUR MUR
MUR MUR
AH! MEGUMI! TAKUMI! HOW DID LAST NIGHT'S TRAINING GO?

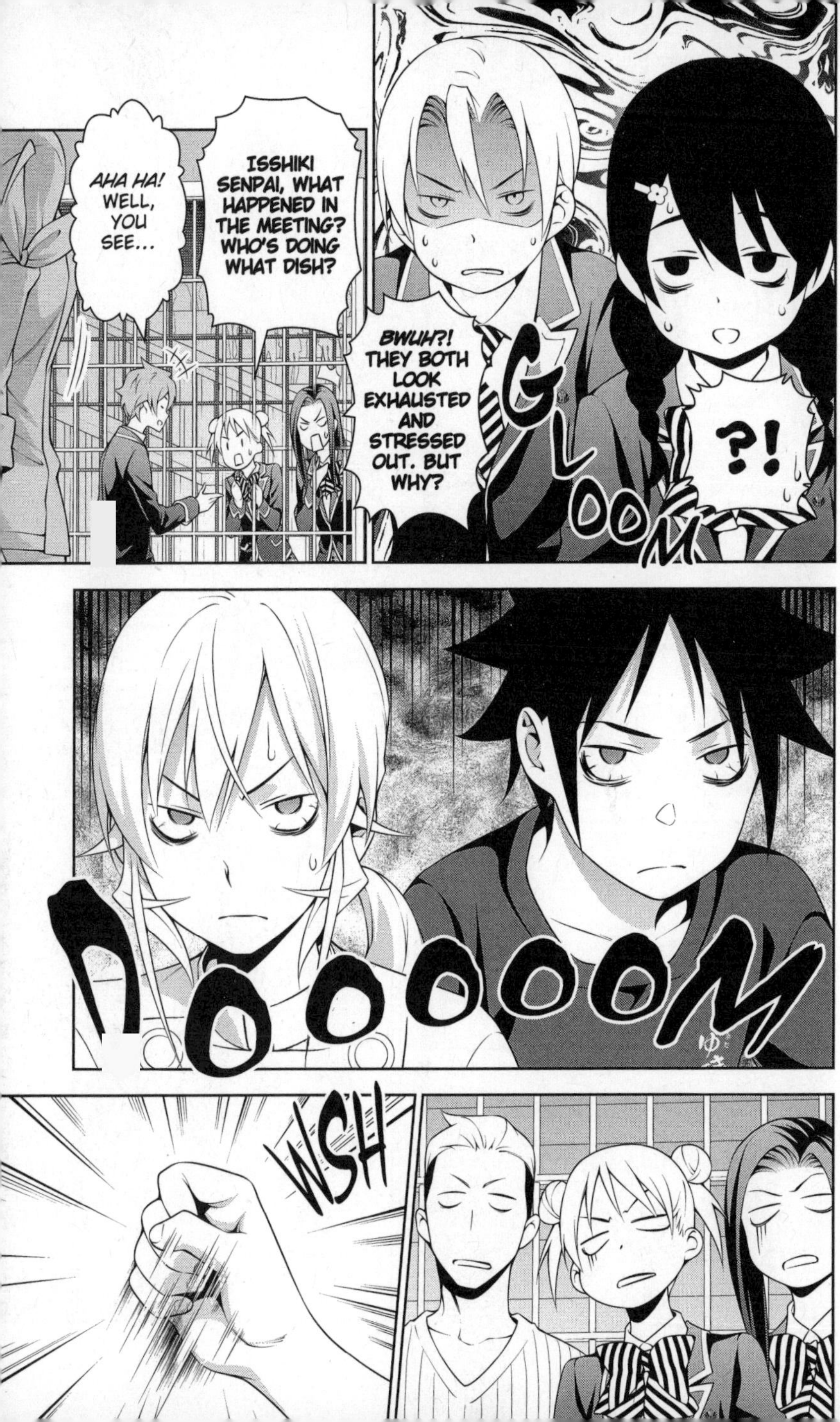
GLOOM
?!
BWUH?! THEY BOTH LOOK EXHAUSTED AND STRESSED OUT. BUT WHY?
ISSHIKI SENPAI, WHAT HAPPENED IN THE MEETING? WHO'S DOING WHAT DISH?
AHA HA! WELL, YOU SEE...
DOOOOOM
WSH

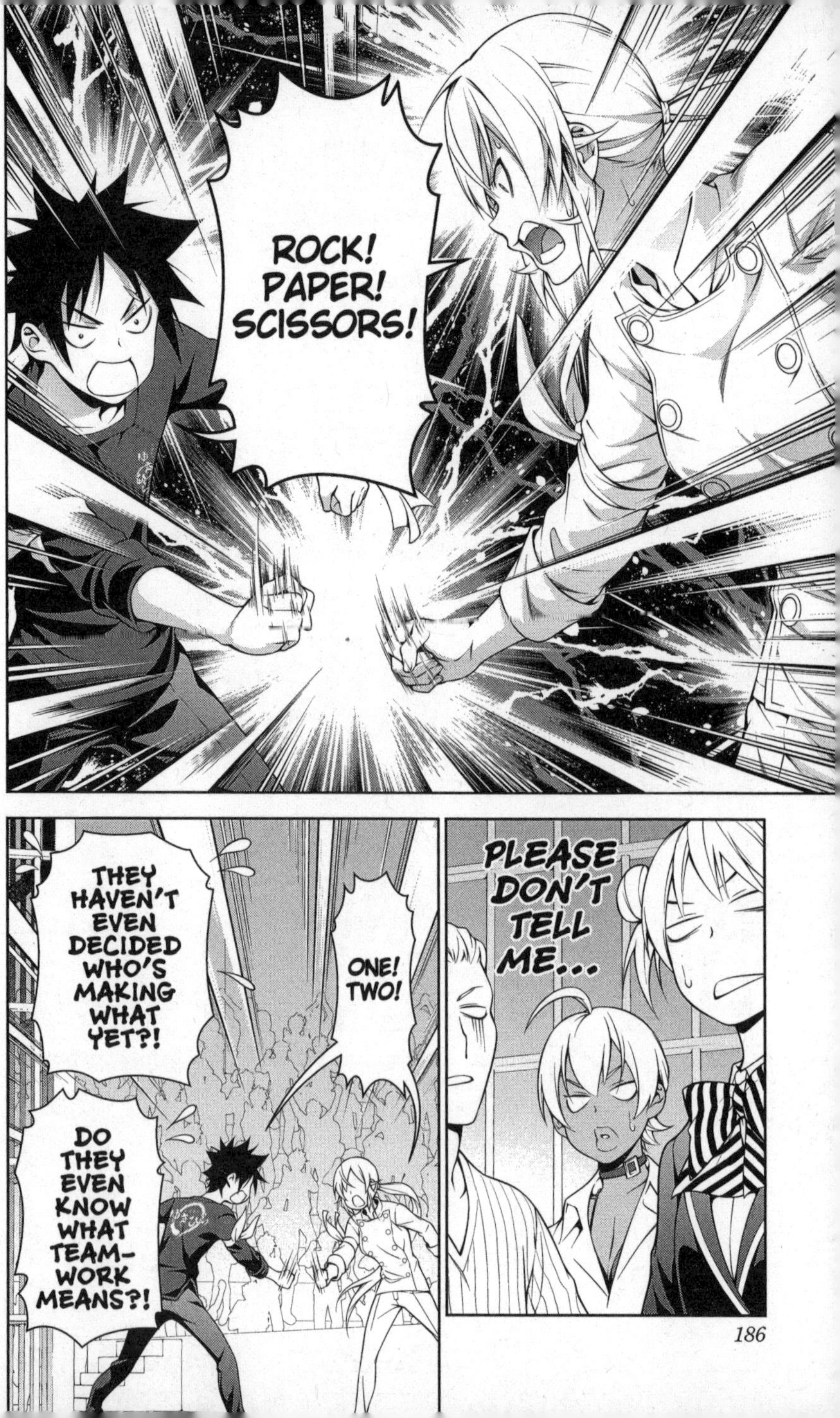
ROCK! PAPER! SCISSORS!
PLEASE DON'T TELL ME...
ONE! TWO!
THEY HAVEN'T EVEN DECIDED WHO'S MAKING WHAT YET?!
DO THEY EVEN KNOW WHAT TEAM-WORK MEANS?!

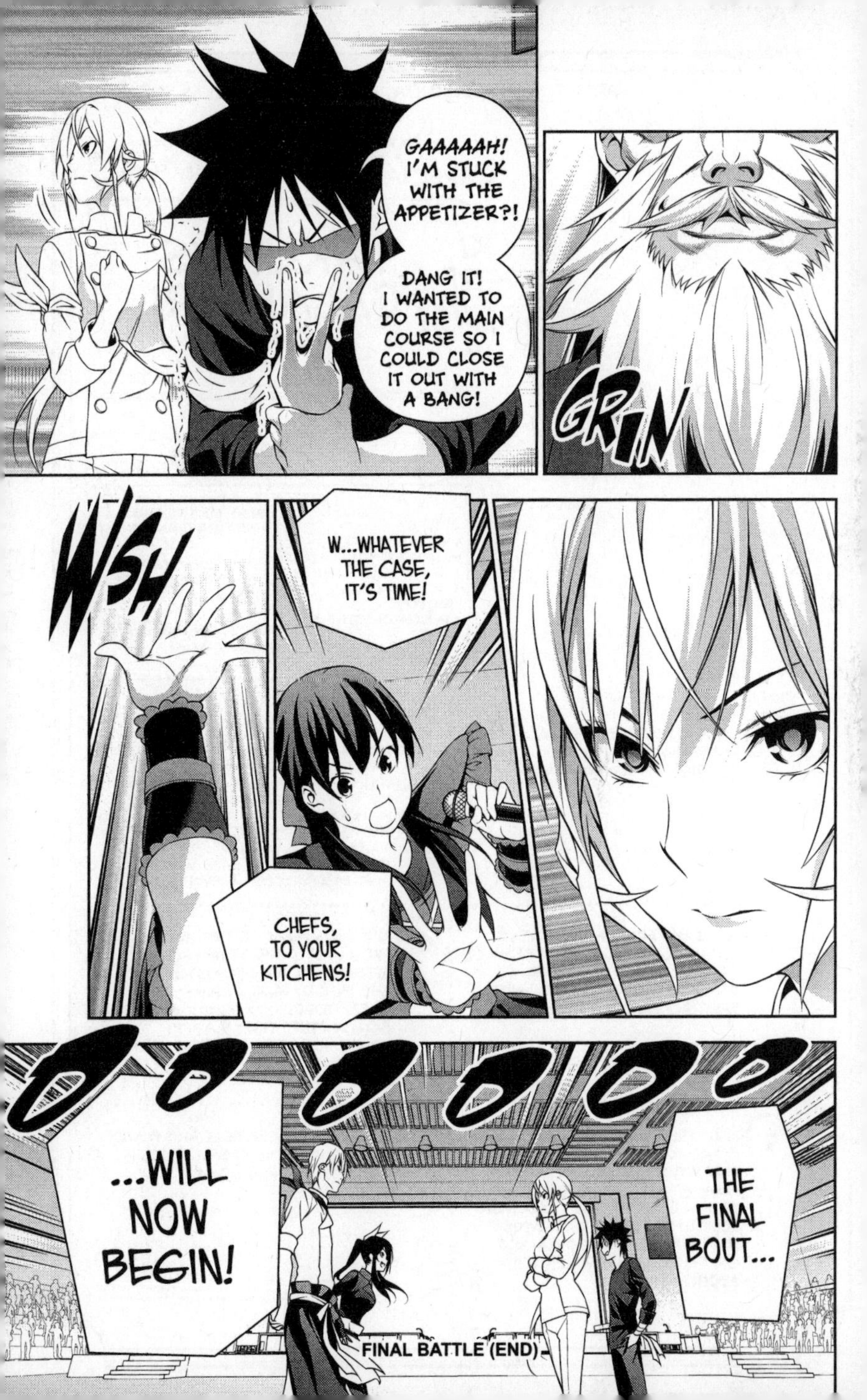
GRIN
GAAAAAH! I'M STUCK WITH THE APPETIZER?!
DANG IT! I WANTED TO DO THE MAIN COURSE SO I COULD CLOSE IT OUT WITH A BANG!
W...WHATEVER THE CASE, IT'S TIME!
CHEFS, TO YOUR KITCHENS!
WSH
OOOOOOOO
THE FINAL BOUT...
...WILL NOW BEGIN!
FINAL BATTLE (END)

ARTIST: YUTO TSUKUDA RECIPE BY: YUKI MORISAKI

VOLUME 29
SPECIAL SUPPLEMENT!

PRACTICAL RECIPE #4

STARE
SWSH

TAKUMI'S CALAMARI RIPIENI

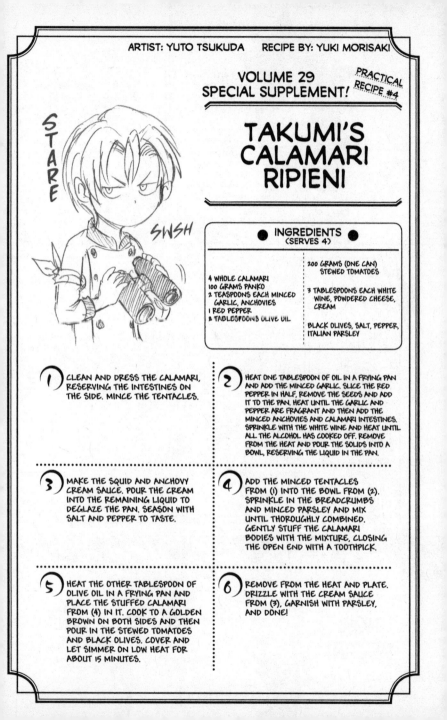

INGREDIENTS
(SERVES 4)

- 4 WHOLE CALAMARI
- 100 GRAMS PANKO
- 2 TEASPOONS EACH MINCED GARLIC, ANCHOVIES
- 1 RED PEPPER
- 2 TABLESPOONS OLIVE OIL

- 200 GRAMS (ONE CAN) STEWED TOMATOES
- 3 TABLESPOONS EACH WHITE WINE, POWDERED CHEESE, CREAM
- BLACK OLIVES, SALT, PEPPER, ITALIAN PARSLEY

1. CLEAN AND DRESS THE CALAMARI, RESERVING THE INTESTINES ON THE SIDE. MINCE THE TENTACLES.
2. HEAT ONE TABLESPOON OF OIL IN A FRYING PAN AND ADD THE MINCED GARLIC. SLICE THE RED PEPPER IN HALF, REMOVE THE SEEDS AND ADD IT TO THE PAN. HEAT UNTIL THE GARLIC AND PEPPER ARE FRAGRANT AND THEN ADD THE MINCED ANCHOVIES AND CALAMARI INTESTINES. SPRINKLE WITH THE WHITE WINE AND HEAT UNTIL ALL THE ALCOHOL HAS COOKED OFF. REMOVE FROM THE HEAT AND POUR THE SOLIDS INTO A BOWL, RESERVING THE LIQUID IN THE PAN.
3. MAKE THE SQUID AND ANCHOVY CREAM SAUCE. POUR THE CREAM INTO THE REMAINING LIQUID TO DEGLAZE THE PAN. SEASON WITH SALT AND PEPPER TO TASTE.
4. ADD THE MINCED TENTACLES FROM (1) INTO THE BOWL FROM (2). SPRINKLE IN THE BREADCRUMBS AND MINCED PARSLEY AND MIX UNTIL THOROUGHLY COMBINED. GENTLY STUFF THE CALAMARI BODIES WITH THE MIXTURE, CLOSING THE OPEN END WITH A TOOTHPICK.
5. HEAT THE OTHER TABLESPOON OF OLIVE OIL IN A FRYING PAN AND PLACE THE STUFFED CALAMARI FROM (4) IN IT. COOK TO A GOLDEN BROWN ON BOTH SIDES AND THEN POUR IN THE STEWED TOMATOES AND BLACK OLIVES. COVER AND LET SIMMER ON LOW HEAT FOR ABOUT 15 MINUTES.
6. REMOVE FROM THE HEAT AND PLATE. DRIZZLE WITH THE CREAM SAUCE FROM (3), GARNISH WITH PARSLEY, AND DONE!

VOLUME 29
SPECIAL SUPPLEMENT!

PRACTICAL RECIPE #5

RINDO SENPAI PRESENTS A WILD CAUSA

HUH?! WHAT'RE YOU STARIN' AT?!
RAAAH!

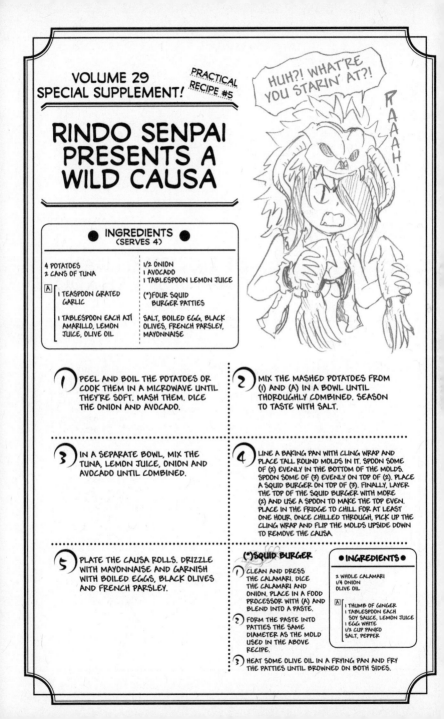

INGREDIENTS
(SERVES 4)

4 POTATOES
2 CANS OF TUNA

[A]
- 1 TEASPOON GRATED GARLIC
- 1 TABLESPOON EACH AJÍ AMARILLO, LEMON JUICE, OLIVE OIL

1/2 ONION
1 AVOCADO
1 TABLESPOON LEMON JUICE

(*)FOUR SQUID BURGER PATTIES

SALT, BOILED EGG, BLACK OLIVES, FRENCH PARSLEY, MAYONNAISE

1. PEEL AND BOIL THE POTATOES OR COOK THEM IN A MICROWAVE UNTIL THEY'RE SOFT. MASH THEM. DICE THE ONION AND AVOCADO.
2. MIX THE MASHED POTATOES FROM (1) AND (A) IN A BOWL UNTIL THOROUGHLY COMBINED. SEASON TO TASTE WITH SALT.
3. IN A SEPARATE BOWL, MIX THE TUNA, LEMON JUICE, ONION AND AVOCADO UNTIL COMBINED.
4. LINE A BAKING PAN WITH CLING WRAP AND PLACE TALL ROUND MOLDS IN IT. SPOON SOME OF (2) EVENLY IN THE BOTTOM OF THE MOLDS. SPOON SOME OF (3) EVENLY ON TOP OF (2). PLACE A SQUID BURGER ON TOP OF (3). FINALLY, LAYER THE TOP OF THE SQUID BURGER WITH MORE (2) AND USE A SPOON TO MAKE THE TOP EVEN. PLACE IN THE FRIDGE TO CHILL FOR AT LEAST ONE HOUR. ONCE CHILLED THROUGH, PICK UP THE CLING WRAP AND FLIP THE MOLDS UPSIDE DOWN TO REMOVE THE CAUSA.
5. PLATE THE CAUSA ROLLS. DRIZZLE WITH MAYONNAISE AND GARNISH WITH BOILED EGGS, BLACK OLIVES AND FRENCH PARSLEY.

(*)SQUID BURGER

INGREDIENTS

2 WHOLE CALAMARI
1/4 ONION
OLIVE OIL

[A]
- 1 THUMB OF GINGER
- 1 TABLESPOON EACH SOY SAUCE, LEMON JUICE
- 1 EGG WHITE
- 1/2 CUP PANKO
- SALT, PEPPER

1. CLEAN AND DRESS THE CALAMARI. DICE THE CALAMARI AND ONION. PLACE IN A FOOD PROCESSOR WITH (A) AND BLEND INTO A PASTE.
2. FORM THE PASTE INTO PATTIES THE SAME DIAMETER AS THE MOLD USED IN THE ABOVE RECIPE.
3. HEAT SOME OLIVE OIL IN A FRYING PAN AND FRY THE PATTIES UNTIL BROWNED ON BOTH SIDES.

BONUS STORY

OUR GOLDEN DAYS ON MOON'S SHADOW

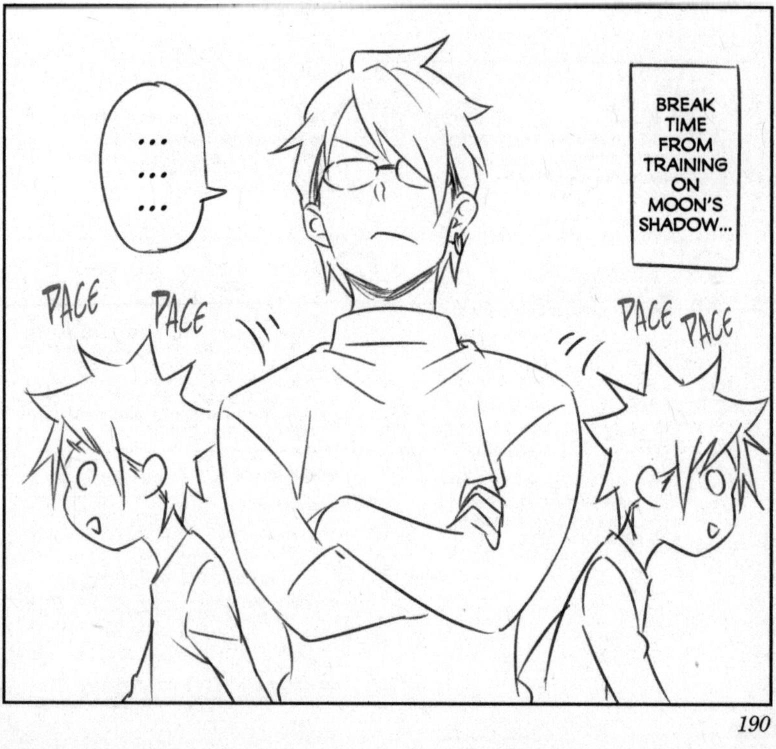
BREAK TIME FROM TRAINING ON MOON'S SHADOW...
...
...
...
PACE PACE
PACE PACE

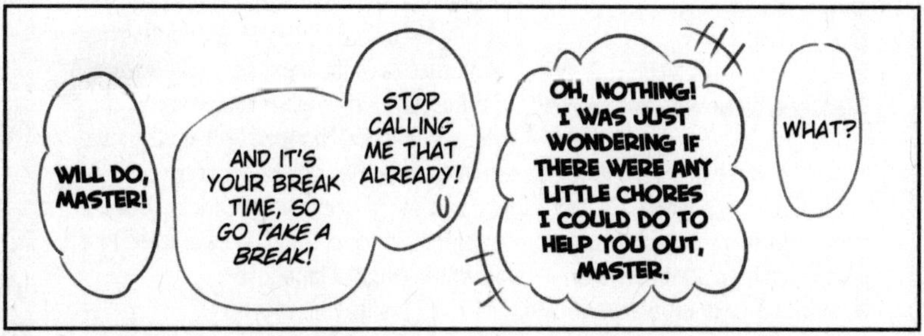
WHAT?
OH, NOTHING! I WAS JUST WONDERING IF THERE WERE ANY LITTLE CHORES I COULD DO TO HELP YOU OUT, MASTER.
STOP CALLING ME THAT ALREADY!
AND IT'S YOUR BREAK TIME, SO GO TAKE A BREAK!
WILL DO, MASTER!
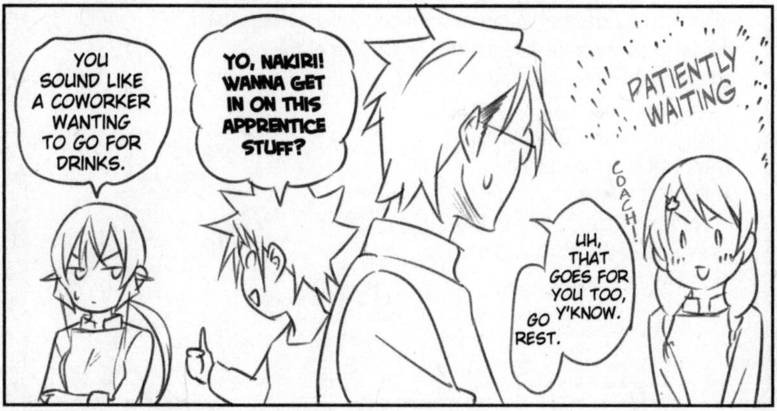
PATIENTLY WAITING
COACH!
UH, THAT GOES FOR YOU TOO, Y'KNOW.
GO REST.
YO, NAKIRI! WANNA GET IN ON THIS APPRENTICE STUFF?
YOU SOUND LIKE A COWORKER WANTING TO GO FOR DRINKS.

END

You're Reading in the Wrong Direction!!

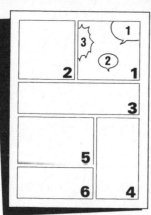

Whoops! Guess what? You're starting at the wrong end of the comic!

...It's true! In keeping with the original Japanese format, **Food Wars!** is meant to be read from right to left, starting in the upper-right corner.

Unlike English, which is read from left to right, Japanese is read from right to left, meaning that action, sound effects and word-balloon order are completely reversed... something which can make readers unfamiliar with Japanese feel pretty backwards themselves. For this reason, manga or Japanese comics published in the U.S. in English have sometimes been published "flopped"—that is, printed in exact reverse order, as though seen from the other side of a mirror.

By flopping pages, U.S. publishers can avoid confusing readers, but the compromise is not without its downside. For one thing, a character in a flopped manga series who once wore in the original Japanese version a T-shirt emblazoned with "M A Y" (as in "the merry month of") now wears one which reads "Y A M"! Additionally, many manga creators in Japan are themselves unhappy with the process, as some feel the mirror-imaging of their art skews their original intentions.

We are proud to bring you Yuto Tsukuda and Shun Saeki's **Food Wars!** in the original unflopped format.

For now, though, turn to the other side of the book and let the adventure begin...!

—Editor

RAWR